David Fincher's *Zodiac*

The Fairleigh Dickinson University Press
Series in Law, Culture, and the Humanities

Series Editor: Caroline Joan "Kay" S. Picart, MPhil (Cantab), PhD, JD, Esquire

Attorney at Law; Adjunct Professor, FAMU College of Law; former English & HUM professor, FSU

The Fairleigh Dickinson University Press Series in Law, Culture, and the Humanities publishes scholarly works in which the field of Law intersects with, among others, Film, Criminology, Sociology, Communication, Critical/Cultural Studies, Literature, History, Philosophy, and the Humanities.
On the Web at http://www.fdu.edu/fdupress

Publications

Matthew Sorrento and David Ryan, *David Fincher's* Zodiac*: Cinema of Investigation and (Mis)Interpretation* (2021)

T. Patrick Hill, *No Place for Ethics: Judicial Review, Legal Positivism, and the Supreme Court of the United States* (2021)

Caroline Joan "Kay" S. Picart, *Monsters, Law, Crime: Explorations in Gothic Criminology* (2020)

Elaine Wood, *Gender Justice and the Law: Theoretical Practices of Intersectional Identity* (2020)

Orit Kamir, *Betraying Dignity: The Toxic Seduction of Social Media, Shaming, and Radicalization* (2019)

Marouf A. Hasian Jr., *Lawfare and the Ovaherero and Nama Pursuit of Restorative Justice, 1918–2018* (2019)

George Pate, *Enter the Undead Author: Intellectual Property, the Ideology of Authorship, and Performance Practices since the 1960s* (2019)

Victor Li, *Nixon in New York: How Wall Street Helped Richard Nixon Win the White House* (2017)

Marouf A. Hasian Jr., *Kafkaesque Laws, Nisour Square, and the Trials of the Former Blackwater Guards* (2017)

Michaela Stockey-Bridge, *The Lure of Hope: On the Transnational Surrogacy Trail from Australia to India* (2017)

Ted Laros, *Literature and the Law in South Africa, 1910–2010: The Long Walk to Artistic Freedom* (2017)

Peter Robson and Johnny Rodger, *The Spaces of Justice: The Architecture of the Scottish Court* (2017)

Doran Larson, *Witness in the Era of Mass Incarceration: Discovering the Ethical Prison* (2017)

Raymond J. McKoski, *Judges in Street Clothes: Acting Ethically Off-the-Bench* (2017)

H. Lowell Brown, *The American Constitutional Tradition: Colonial Charters, Covenants, and Revolutionary State Constitutions 1578——1786* (2017)

Arua Oko Omaka, *The Biafran Humanitarian Crisis, 1967–1970: International Human Rights and Joint Church Aid* (2016)

Marouf A. Hasian Jr., *Representing Ebola: Culture, Law, and Public Discourse about the 2013–2015 West Africa Ebola Outbreak* (2016)

Jacqueline O'Connor, *Law and Sexuality in Tennessee Williams's America* (2016)

Caroline Joan "Kay" S. Picart, Michael Hviid Jacobsen, and Cecil E. Greek, *Framing Law and Crime: An Interdisciplinary Anthology* (2016)

Caroline Joan "Kay" S. Picart, *Law in and as Culture: Intellectual Property, Minority Rights, and the Rights of Indigenous Peoples* (2016)

David Fincher's *Zodiac*

Cinema of Investigation and (Mis)Interpretation

Edited by
Matthew Sorrento
David Ryan

FAIRLEIGH DICKINSON UNIVERSITY PRESS
Vancouver • Madison • Teaneck • Wroxton

Published by Fairleigh Dickinson University Press
Copublished by The Rowman & Littlefield Publishing Group, Inc.
4501 Forbes Boulevard, Suite 200, Lanham, Maryland 20706
www.rowman.com

86-90 Paul Street, London EC2A 4NE, United Kingdom

Copyright © 2022 by The Rowman & Littlefield Publishing Group, Inc. for edited collections

All rights reserved. No part of this book may be reproduced in any form or by any electronic or mechanical means, including information storage and retrieval systems, without written permission from the publisher, except by a reviewer who may quote passages in a review.

Fairleigh Dickinson University Press gratefully acknowledges the support received for scholarly publishing from the Friends of FDU Press.

British Library Cataloguing in Publication Information Available

Library of Congress Cataloging-in-Publication Data

Names: Sorrento, Matthew, 1976– editor. | Ryan, David, 1968– editor.
Title: David Fincher's Zodiac : cinema of investigation and (mis)interpretation / edited by Matthew Sorrento, David Ryan.
Description: Vancouver ; Madison : Fairleigh Dickinson University Press, [2022] | Series: The Fairleigh Dickinson University Press series in law, culture, and the humanities | Includes bibliographical references and index. | Summary: "David Fincher's Zodiac, the first book-length study of the critically acclaimed 2007 release, offers various critical approaches to the film ranging from early influences, studies in genre and narrative, and media analysis including cinema history, game theory, musicology, and extensions in television studies"—Provided by publisher.
Identifiers: LCCN 2021035731 (print) | LCCN 2021035732 (ebook) | ISBN 9781683933267 (cloth) | ISBN 9781683933274 (epub) | ISBN 9781683933281 (paperback)
Subjects: LCSH: Fincher, David—Criticism and interpretation. | Zodiac Killer—In motion pictures. | Zodiac (Motion picture : 2007) | Serial murderers in motion pictures. | Serial murderers—United States—History. | Serial murder investigation—United States—History. | Motion pictures—United States—History—21st century.
Classification: LCC PN1997.2.Z63 D38 2022 (print) | LCC PN1997.2.Z63 (ebook) | DDC 791.43/72—dc23
LC record available at https://lccn.loc.gov/2021035731
LC ebook record available at https://lccn.loc.gov/2021035732

Contents

Acknowledgments   ix

Foreword: *Zodiac*, the American Murderer, and the End of Reason   xi
Christopher Sharrett

Introduction: The Future of the "Last Serial Killer Movie"   1
Matthew Sorrento

SECTION ONE: BEFORE FINCHER   13

1. Framing the "Mass" Killer: Horror and Spatiality in Peter Bogdanovich's *Targets* (1968)   15
  Matthew Sorrento

2. Fear and Exploiting in the Age of Aquarius: Early Representations of the Zodiac Killer in 1970s Film and Television   31
  Christopher Weedman

3. Hacked to Pisces: An Interview with Tom Hanson on *The Zodiac Killer* (1971)   53
  Rod Lott

SECTION TWO: *ZODIAC* AND NARRATIVE   67

4. *Zodiac* and the Melding Criminal Minds of David Fincher   69
  Jeremy Carr

5. Subverting the Investigator as Hero: Masculinity and Failure in David Fincher's *Zodiac*   85
  Theresa Rodewald

6	Performing the Zodiac: Piffle, Paradox, and Self-Promotion *Daniel R. Fredrick*	101
7	Allegories of Obsession: David Fincher's *Zodiac* and Edgar G. Ulmer's *The Black Cat* (1934) *George Toles*	121

SECTION THREE: *ZODIAC* AND MEDIA — 149

8	The Dantesque Desires of David Fincher's *Zodiac* *Martin Kevorkian*	151
9	The Zodiac Strikes a Blue Chord: Evoking Art-Horror in Music *Andrew M. Winters*	169
10	Algorithmic Anxiety: Data Hegemony and Mediated Murder in David Fincher's *Zodiac* *Jake Rutkowski*	189
11	Gaming the Ripper Coast: Mapping the Radicalized Acts of the Zodiac Killer *David Ryan*	209
12	The Killers Speak: The Sound of Violence in David Fincher's *Zodiac* and *Mindhunter* (2017–2019) *Deborah L. Jaramillo*	229

Index	251
About the Contributors	257

Acknowledgments

The editors would like to thank Caroline Joan S. (Kay) Picart, series editor of Law, Culture, and Humanities; James Gifford, Director of Fairleigh Dickinson University Press; and Zachary Nycum, associate editor at Rowman & Littlefield for their continual support, along with the contributors to this collection. Thanks also to the American Genre Film Archive and Frank Henenlotter for assistance, and to Tom and Scott Hanson for their time and generosity.

Foreword

Zodiac, *the American Murderer, and the End of Reason*

Christopher Sharrett

I can by no means recall the source (I think it may have been the fanzine *Film Threat* in the 1980s), but someone wrote long ago that the serial killer is the "folk hero of the era." Such an idea should seem preposterous, but after the long U.S. attack on Southeast Asia, the political murders of the 1960s, the U.S. sponsorship of various rightist coups (Chile, Indonesia), the Watergate affair (which, as Robin Wood [2003] has noted, meant the end of the symbolic father—the president of the United States—but also the fathers we all have, and the internalized father, the superego [122]), and the reactionary retrenchment in the Reagan era and the neoliberal order that followed with each succeeding regime, such an idea is no longer outlandish. The idea may be especially reasonable given American adulation of the Wild West and its "gunfighters," many of whom were settling old grudges from the Civil War and Reconstruction. We can, however, find something of the psychopath in John Wesley Hardin, Wild Bill Hickok, and Billy the Kid, if the histories of these people can be treated as reliable (we always need to apply John Ford's caution from *The Man Who Shot Liberty Valance*, 1962).

That such men still capture the popular imagination helps explain where we are now, although the Wild West has fallen drastically in the popular mind since the days of the TV Western, which virtually dominated television of the postwar era. We might reflect now on the myth of the West as history finally sinks in, and we understand the West mostly as the Old South getting what it wanted: Western expansion, if not with slavery, then with the racist mentality that destroyed Reconstruction, and informed the genocide of the indigenous population. Today we call this land the Red States of the new reaction, the gathering place of what H. L. Mencken called the "booboisie" (Rodgers 2007, 194).

What exactly, then, is a "serial killer," or a "mass murderer?" A serial killer (statistically, almost always male) is a somewhat special category in human violence, but the Nazis, the most important mass murderers of recent history—easily vilified as unique in barbarism—help us understand what the category means; when we consider how much all of us have fetishized the Nazis, things get sticky (Sontag's "Fascinating Fascism" [1975] is a good introduction to the problem). The cinema is full of conscience-stricken Nazis (*Judgment at Nuremberg* [1961], *Cross of Iron* [1977]), but not a lot about the Soviets, or boring partisans, except in the European cinema. Gar Alperovitz's book *The Decision to Use the Atomic Bomb* (1995) informs us that the annihilation of two Japanese cities, on the excuse that more of "our boys" would be sacrificed in the invasion of the Japanese mainland, was an act of cynical pragmatists, if not cavalier mass murderers. So that war revealed a lot about America, although it is a knowledge of which we have little availed ourselves (except in books like Studs Terkel's *"The Good War": an Oral History of World War II* [1997/1984]—the quotation marks of his title are important).

But the comforts of suburbia were limited, as film noir informed us, with its perverse heroes, and less-than-heroic backstories of the war (*Act of Violence* [1949] are representative, although the utter savagery and stupidity of Robert Aldrich's Mike Hammer in *Kiss Me Deadly* [1955] is one of our most honest appraisals of the postwar male mind), along with fear of almost everything, not merely the Soviets and Chinese. Our children, these "juvenile delinquents," were a real danger, and comic book writers were suspects, along with the usual racial others. About the Bomb we were ambivalent—it supposedly had benefits in keeping the commies away, but it might arouse long-dead dinosaurs. In other words, the 1950s was an age less of anxiety than insanity.

Then along came people like Ed Gein and Charles Starkweather. Starkweather was given a romantic aura since he "looked just like James Dean" (he didn't), allowing teen angst to be combined with rage. Ed Gein was another case: he was the unhappy, isolated Midwest protestant who lived with his mother, the lonely but fairly congenial local handyman, the puritan ethic exploding. Like others to follow—Ted Bundy, John Wayne Gacy, Jeffrey Dahmer, and earlier demented killers—like the terrifying Carl Panzram, who frightened Karl Menninger—these men seemed sheer monsters, yet by the 1970s they spawned large cults and found their way onto comic books, trading cards, T-shirts, and rock band names. Bundy and others got by because their small talk and ideologies made them fit in perfectly. After all, we were told that Charles Manson, a total loon, was one of us, and signified the "end of the 60s," that is, the end of humane values and the return to militarism and savagery. This coincided with the rise of Reagan, austerity, neoliberal economics, and a new complacency about warfare and interventionism. The desire to "kick ass" was in vogue, as the film *Rambo: First Blood Part II* (1985) said on its poster "this time we win" (the Vietnam War). The age of unreason became entrenched, to this very writing, with a psychopathic real estate grifter now in charge of a huge nuclear arsenal.

In the movies, the changes to the villain were notable. Frankenstein, Dracula, and the Wolfman went through permutations and vanished, perhaps because of audience recognition that they were sympathetic Others after all. In their place came Freddy Krueger, a child rapist/killer; Jason, a huge, machete-wielding murderer in a dirty hockey mask; and Michael Myers, another hulking killer with a butcher knife and a William Shatner mask, unmotivated except for apparent unfulfilled incestuous longings focused on his sister. We can tack on Pinhead, the "Black Pope of Leviathan" with his Cenobite army in the *Hellraiser* franchise. The Cenobites, clad in long black cassocks adorned with medieval torture gadgets, seemed to appear, like Jason, Michael, and their spawn, when teenagers showed sexual curiosity. With a diligence that would amaze the Mathers, Pinhead and crew would appear when sex raised its ugly head, the Cenobites dragging them off to hell. Yet, in *Hellraiser III: Hell on Earth*, we learn that the Cenobites were born in the fires of world wars, with Pinhead taking his revenge on the Catholic Church for its hypocritical nonsense, Pinhead performing hilarious acts of blasphemy. In typically postmodern style, one could make of *Hellraiser* what one wanted. Was Pinhead a return of American puritanism in time for Reagan, or the kind of nihilistic *joie de vivre* of heavy metal, or Scandinavian church-burners?

The changing face of horror is notable in the rise of the serial killer per se in absolutely idealized form, particularly the Hannibal Lecter of *The Silence of the Lambs* (1991), another killer whose roots are in the Gein story, although Lecter is an all-seeing genius on the order of Dr. Mabuse. The skies of *The Silence of the Lambs* are permanently overcast, a visual conceit used in TV cop shows like the *Law and Order* franchise, suggesting the approach of doomsday. In David Fincher's *Se7en* (1995), the important predecessor to the focus of this book, we have a permanent nightworld, and one where rain won't end—until the sun comes out in the gory twist ending that underlines hopelessness. Here, the serial killer is an emblem of a deep crisis: the failure of the older man to teach, and of the younger man to learn. The sage and his acolyte have been basic to the American narrative for generations, certainly to the cinematic Western (see, e.g., *Shane* [1951] and *The Tin Star* [1957]). In *Se7en*, the older man goes back into classical culture, where he thinks he will find clues about the killer's motivations. His stupid young underling prefers to take shortcuts with Cliff Notes, which he throws away after a minute's frustration. The passing-on of knowledge from one male to another has fallen to pieces, guaranteeing the collapse not just of the male order but of civilization itself.

This brings us to Fincher's *Zodiac* (2007), where clues appear in maps of strange, semi-astrological hieroglyphs. The ratiocination and deductive reasoning of M. Dupin and Holmes to interpret them have become meaningless in a nation that is throwing away the humanities and enjoys something called "reality television," whose definition of reality seems as arcane as the academy that spawned semiotics. The Zodiac Killer is never caught in Fincher's telling; instead, the killer creates a massive and very obsessed fan base more chilling than murder.

Fincher's film is quite an achievement in capturing this phenomenon, as the contributors of this collection attest. In my reading, *Zodiac* is about where we live today, a nation that could care less about consciousness (even as this study becomes a growth area of the sciences—does human consciousness really exist? What is it?). Now, mentation is too often broken down into various hobbies, like Beatles and *Star Trek* clubs where aficionados know their minutia like evangelical ministers know their Bibles (but to what purpose?). The nullity of the cult of murder in America, as I suggested, was always manifest, from frontier gunfighters to valorizations of mass death in the age of the atom. In *Zodiac*, we end up where we started, a Euclidean dot in the middle of nothing, and no one to wonder, with Beckett's angst tempered with levity, what we're waiting for. *Zodiac* concludes with a chilling afterthought: we all go nowhere, each monad (in Fredric Jameson's [1991] postmodern rhetoric) isolated, alienation now a preferred way of being. The complexity of this idea and the film's unique representation offer various avenues to explore, as you'll see the chapters that follow.

REFERENCES

Alperovitz, Gar. 1995. *The Decision to Use the Atomic Bomb*. New York, NY: Vintage.

Jameson, Frederick. 1991. *Postmodernism, or, the Cultural Logic of Late Capitalism*. Durham, NC: Duke University Press.

Rodgers, Marion Elizabeth. 2007. *Mencken: The American Iconoclast*. Oxford, UK: Oxford University Press.

Sontag, Susan. 1975. "Fascinating Fascism." *The New York Review of Books*, February 6. Accessed, January 11, 2020, https://www.nybooks.com/articles/1975/02/06/fascinating-fascism/.

Terkel, Studs. 1997/1984. *"The Good War": and Oral History of World War II*. New York, NY: The New Press.

Wood, Robin. 2003. *Hollywood from Vietnam to Reagan...and Beyond*. New York, NY: Columbia UP.

Introduction

The Future of the "Last Serial Killer Movie"

Matthew Sorrento

Director David Fincher and writer-producer James Vanderbilt's 2007 film *Zodiac* is one of the most respected works of cinema of the early years of this century. Fincher had sizable ambitions to make "the last serial killer film" ("Zodiac Production Notes" 2007), which was a comeback for him (after a five-year hiatus, following 2002's *Panic Room*), and the reactions have been overwhelmingly positive.[1] Yet, as an adaptation of one of the most famous and discussed serial killers in history, the film has become, like its source material, a phenomenon often obscured by its source subject. Books continue to appear on the historical Zodiac Killer, with the title "This is the Zodiac Speaking" (from the killer's August 7, 1969, letter received by *The San Francisco Examiner* [Graysmith 1986, 55–57]) used for both a compelling criminological study of the figure, by Michael D. Kelleher and David Van Nuys (2001), and as a publication by popular culture journalist Chuck Klosterman (2010). While the latter uses the killer's phrase to present insights on the serial killing phenomenon, Kelleher and Van Nuys carefully analyze primary evidence of the subject, his writings (letters/cyphers) to the press, to bring us as close as, in one critic's words, "anyone has ever come to knowing the true identity of this elusive killer" (Kurtz 2004, 410). With publications revealing new developments (Fagan 2020) or pointing to a new suspect as a selling point (see Stewart 2014), Kelleher and Van Nuys analyze the Zodiac for greater importance, as an example of one suffering from dissociative identity disorder. Countless websites offer details of the killings along with updates, while promoting searches for killer (see https://zodiackiller.com/, boasting that it is "the only Zodiac Killer website recognized by law enforcement"), while some books on the Zodiac even entered the Young Adult market (see Haugen 2010).

Figure 0.1 Zodiac fan art by **Siwaquth.** Used with permission.

Much of Zodiac culture involves sensationalist fan involvement by focusing on the murders for classic "true crime" interest. The figure's original representations on screen in the early 1970s, in two films, was both distinct, with *Dirty Harry* (Don Siegel, 1971), and minor in the underground, with *The Zodiac Killer* (Tom Hanson, 1971; see chapter 3 for an interview with Hanson and chapter 2 for a discussion of early films on theme).

In spite of such as massive cultural following, Robert Graysmith, as an unofficial investigator directly involved in the case and later reporting on it in his 1986 book (and to an extent, his 2002 follow-up, *Zodiac Unmasked*), remains the definitive source of the Zodiac. Cartoonist Graysmith was not with the police or working as an investigative journalist (though with the press). Hence, he aligns to the unofficial avenger figure so prominent in crime movies (Leitch 2002, 14–17). The noir angle of his voice relating the events (as a private eye often narrates film noir in voiceover) offers a unique aspect to its vivid and detailed suspense. After lagging in development for some time (Vanderbilt 2008), the property finally became a film by David Fincher, with Graysmith adapted by Vanderbilt; it was released in the post-9/11 surge of "extremist" crime cinema.[2]

This new wave of crime cinema owed less to the fan-craze for Quentin Tarantino and more to a return to the paranoid style of the 1970s (Douthat 2008). With a post-9/11 tradition reflecting the previous new wave of thrillers (*All the President's Men, Marathon Man* [both 1976], *Night Moves* [1975], etc.) the more recent films present a unique style of revisionism, borrowing from extreme treatments of other genres. A standout film in the post-9/11 era, though regretfully not discussed in light of *Zodiac*, is *Michael Clayton* (2007), written and directed by Tony Gilroy, in which a fixer for a law firm turns into an avenger against the agricultural conglomerate employing his firm. If he finds an awakening, due to the influence of his colleague Arthur Edens (whose drive as a prosecutor leads to his breakdown and assassination), Clayton is doomed, in thrall by the firm who employs him (he breaks a nondisclosure agreement he had signed to get an $80,000 bonus for a new contract). *Inside Man* (2006), a heist film directed by Spike Lee and written by Russell Gewirtz, also directly invokes the paranoid thrillers of the 1970s (namely, *Marathon Man*, with a Nazi [Christopher Plummer] in hiding with wartime loot) to create a dialogue with its revision of *Dog Day Afternoon* (1975). Likely the most popular in the post-9/11 cycle, *No Country for Old Men* (Joel and Ethan Coen, 2007, which won the Academy Award for Best Picture in 2008), presents an uber-monstrous hitman whose actions and influence create a milieu nearly as disastrous as he is.

Even among these strong titles, the 1970s-set *Zodiac* stands out. As an auteurist work,[3] the film serves as a follow-up for Fincher, who had already made the allegorical serial killer film *Se7en* (1995), popular with audiences and fitting what James Naremore describes as arthouse crime (2008, 267). There's little need to note the dark visual style for which the filmmaker has become renown (with the assistance of various cinematographers), in his treatments of minimalistic suspense (*Panic Room*, 2002), pop-surrealism (*Fight Club*, 1999), and science fiction horror in his feature debut (*Alien³*, 1992). While using this trademark visual palette, Fincher's two serial killer films, however, are markedly distinct from one another (Sorrento 2012, 66), as the scripts of each allowed Fincher and his teams to modify the respective visual styles. With fluid realism meshing with a controlled, hyperreal stylization, and Fincher's familiarity with the area,[4] *Zodiac* invokes a flexible style—moving from realism, hyperrealism, to expressionism, at critical moments—while delivering a journalistic account accurate to Graysmith's books: the Zodiac Killer is shown only in scenes featuring victims who survived to bear witness.

As a fusion of the crime film genre and investigative newspaper movie, *Zodiac* features an ensemble of performers at the top of their abilities, making the film a standout of performance. This film shows a triumph in the casting stage alone (with the collaboration of Fincher's longtime casting director, Laray Mayfield), while the production made some less likely choices.

Jake Gyllenhaal, as Robert Graysmith, was an effective casting choice for the film and its promotion. Having become a cult figure from his lead role in *Donnie Darko* (2001), Gyllenhaal gave a standout performance in the 2005 modern classic *Brokeback Mountain*. The film is famous for its other lead, the late Heath Ledger, in a non-naturalistic, transformative role as Ennis Del Mar. Even if Ledger resounds, Gyllenhaal answers Ledger's power with a naturalistic, emotive take on Jack Twist.[5] In *Zodiac*, Robert Downey Jr., playing *San Francisco Chronicle* crime reporter Paul Avery, matches Gyllenhaal's strong central performance. With a long career as a standout in supporting roles (while on occasion fueling routine projects as a lead, as in the *Iron Man* films), since starring in *Chaplin* (1992) Downey has delivered effective non-naturalistic performances where he transforms his manner and diction for roles, while not losing his trademark intensity and focus.

To fill out two pivotal roles of police investigators, the production went for two standout naturalistic actors. Mark Ruffalo, as homicide inspector David Toschi, performs his famous role as an everyman, a style that has resounded in many films, like the late actor Philip Seymour Hoffman. Playing Inspector Dave Toschi of the San Francisco Police, a figure already famed for his appearance in media and representations in pop culture (as an inspiration for *Bullitt*, 1968), Ruffalo grounds the outsized figure to fuel his connections to Graysmith and Avery. Similar strong support comes from Anthony Edwards (as Inspector Bill Armstrong), who has advanced from his work on television, and far from his 1980s comedy roots, and Elias Koteas, as Sergeant Jack Mulanax. Even smaller roles were casted with care, to highlight their pivotal nature: Brian Cox plays star attorney Melvin Belli, and John Carroll Lynch resounds as prime suspect Arthur Leigh Allen, with very little screen time, along Chloë Sevigny as Melanie, Graysmith's bemused wife, witnessing their marriage fall apart.

The cast calls for an extended studies in film performance, which we hope will motivate future studies. Our intention here remains the film's unique treatment as crime cinema, in its rendition and portrayal of law/deviance, investigation, and (mis)interpretation; the film's influences regarding these areas; and *Zodiac*'s use of media along with related areas of intertextuality for all three. In a film with such a unique style, it appears accurate to call *Zodiac* a David Fincher film, one that sports all the director's trademarks—especially measured framing and controlled, close-framed composition—and a heightened, hyper-focused rendition of them. Thus, this collection treats the film as a trademark auteur text, one that has engaged fans of both popular and arthouse cinema.

Introduction 5

Figure 0.2 The "340 Cypher" received by the *San Francisco Chronicle* on November 8, 1969.

The performances and director's treatment notwithstanding, Graysmith's 1986 source book (and, to a lesser extent, his 2002 follow-up, *Zodiac Unmasked*) and writer-producer James Vanderbilt's crisp screenplay adaptation of the works fuel the production. These aspects allow this film to be analyzed beyond its auteurism, as a true collaborative effort involving cinematographer Harris Savides, editor Angus Wall, and several others behind the production. This text, while not a study in adaptation, focuses on how *Zodiac* delivers a unique cinematic experience in relation to a fact-based work of investigative journalism in dialogue with other investigative, and serial killer, cinema.

Though committed to the experience of an author surrogate, Gyllenhaal's Graysmith, *Zodiac* works as a story of investigation via numerous perspectives screened through a central figure. These include Downey Jr.'s Avery and Ruffalo's portrayal of homicide inspector Toschi, who also works against obstacles and is aided by his less celebrated but exacting partner, Edward's Armstrong. Bleak in its treatment of the killings, this crime film uses elements of the noir tradition (Leitch 2002, 130) (specifically in the unofficial investigator form) and the police thriller (215), while being measured into a paced study of investigation. In the latter sense, *Zodiac* is akin to the "private eye" film (194), though Graysmith's role of an unofficial investigator goes beyond the PI realm. Fincher's film thus stands out as an expression antithetical to and critical of popular crime television of the late twentieth and early twenty-first centuries,[6] which selects real-life cases, or fashioning neat ones, where the criminal/killer is always caught.

Gyllenhaal's Graysmith, while working for the *Chronicle* as a cartoonist, becomes taken by the visual patterns of the killer's ciphers mailed to the press. When the first letter arrives to the *San Francisco Chronicle* (with copies also received by the *San Francisco Examiner* and *Vallejo Times-Herald*) on August 1, 1969, Graysmith connects the letter to the 1932 film adaptation of Richard Connell's story (published in *Collier's* on January 19, 1924), "The Most Dangerous Game." As popular culture motivates the actions of the killer, it would soon reflect of the killings (most famously, with *Dirty Harry*). Working alone from reporters and investigators, but in contact with them, Graysmith explores several angles not apparent to traditional investigators. Thus, he works like a noir unofficial investigator, in that his work is often logical, where it can be, but at times emphatic, based on more emotional hunches and pushing interviewees for information (Krutnik 1991, 92). He begins the film as a professional family man, thus part of the conservative unit (regularly celebrated in popular culture), then slowly becomes a loner akin to the central roles of the noir tradition, isolating himself from his family and other close connections. As this transformation occurs, what has worked as an ensemble film narrows in on just Graysmith's perspective, thus intensifying an already suspenseful treatment of the source material. When all his evidence proves inadequate for an arrest of Allen, all Graysmith can do is publish his 1986 book.

While Graysmith does not situate himself at the center of the book, Vanderbilt's script places the cartoonist-author as the center to highlight unofficial investigation. Graysmith's skill at visual art and its analysis remain key, a convergence that reflects the power of the story's representation onscreen. Fincher has noted that *All the President's Men* worked as a template, and a reference point ("Zodiac Production Notes" 2007). *Zodiac* serves as a period piece, and one in dialogue with Pakula's film (and the paranoid thrillers of that film's era, the 1970s) while reworking its style like the others in the new paranoid style, as discussed by Douthat.

While as a sure-handed work of period investigation, *Zodiac* establishes a dialogue with the serial killer film tradition, hence situating itself in that cycle of films. The film invokes much of the traditions and unifying them in its unique portrayal of the killings, the realistic struggle of investigation, and the network of parties involved. Known for directing the allegorical *Se7en*, David Fincher was the top choice for the project. Vanderbilt and producer Bradley J. Fischer figured they would offer him the project, expecting a pass, and prepared to meet other directors (Vanderbilt 2008). To their surprise the project piqued Fincher's interest, for him to make what would be a distinct hybrid of the crime/horror genres, what makes the serial killer onscreen so compelling. As Toschi notes in the film, that they are "already making films about [the Zodiac]," *Zodiac* takes a hard look not only into a puzzling mystery but as to why we crave serials killing tales. Graysmith's investigation to seek the Zodiac is, on one hand, one of duty and public safety, but on another level, a means to probe our fascination with the truth behind enigmas, more than the glamorization. In portraying the search for the most elusive of serial killers, the film presents John Carroll Lynch's Arthur Leigh Allen as an arrival late in the narrative. He cleverly works as a new version of Harry Lime (of Carroll Reed's *The Third Man*, 1949), in the sense that he's a character long awaited and a payoff for viewers, though Allen's importance to the investigation is never proven by the law with evidence.

Graysmith's 1986 study appeared a little over ten years after the case cooled off,[7] and appropriately, it took twenty years after the release of Graysmith's *Zodiac* for the film to emerge. In portraying the killer's actions, victims' perspectives, and societal response, the film comes close to being an authoritative, realistic account. However, as noted above, the film's hyperreal moments, especially scenes depicting the murders, lead to questions of the film's realism and its boundaries; this aspect also underscores the presence of *Zodiac* as a landmark piece of digital cinema, one that employs a measured visual style and seamless CGI effects. Eddie Muller, who operates between the popular and the scholarly in his writing and appearances, has commended the film's controlled point of view and how it avoids the unhinged perspective of many horror films, where the camera randomly borrows the point of view of victims and killers (Muller 2010). Along with these considerations are *Zodiac*'s unique media representations and ties to other popular arts. While offering distinct critical approaches to the film along these lines, the chapters of this collection, which employs various approaches, encourage further conversations about such an innovative, complex film with a sizable viewership.

By setting out to develop *Zodiac* studies,[8] this book begins with chapters on early responses to the Zodiac Killer and predecessors to Fincher's film (Section One), followed by a section on *Zodiac* and Narrative, and finishing with chapters on the film's relation to, and use of, media (Section Three).

Section One, "Before Fincher," begins with my discussion of a cornerstone work in developing the cinema's treatment of the serial killer, Peter Bogdanovich's *Targets* (1968). While the film mainly uses the spree killer Charles Whitman as its reference, I discuss how Bogdanovich, along with cowriters Polly Platt and Samuel Fuller (the latter uncredited), use three steps of "spatial reference" to depict a cinematic framework for the serial killer's action and interpretation. In chapter 2, Christopher Weedman discusses the mainstream and lesser-known onscreen responses to the Zodiac Killer. Siegel's *Dirty Harry* (1971) served as the most famous mainstream response, and with its use of an extreme threat as the faux-hippy, drug-addled Scorpio Killer (based on the Zodiac) fueling the famous rogue cop's action. Weedman's survey also considers perspectives outside feature films, such as the porn film *Sam Dobbs Meets the Zodiac* (1971) and "Samaritan" (1979), an episode of *Lou Grant* (CBS, 1977–1982), a dramatic series that was a spin-off of the sitcom *The Mary Tyler Moore Show* (1970–77).

Chapter 3 returns to the most direct (if campy) early response to the Zodiac, Tom Hanson's *The Zodiac Killer* (1971), a cheapo (and less than faithfully adapted) exploitation project that has grown into a cult curio. In Rod Lott's extensive interview with Hanson, the filmmaker discusses his approach to exploitation filmmaking (reflecting the attention to the crimes and killer), the influence of sensationalism on budget film practice, and his use of stunt programming (i.e., a project conceived to catch the killer at the theatrical screening) (Poggiali). The details of this production, its limited theatrical distribution, and reemergence as a cult item reflect early media interest and processing of the Zodiac, on which Fincher and Vanderbilt would later reflect.

Section 2, "Narrative and Investigation in *Zodiac*," begins with Jeremy Carr's reading of the film (chapter 4) as cinema that critiques investigation (similarly with the other works of Fincher), in which the hero/investigator eventually proves to be a "an ominous, potentially hazardous counterpart" to the hunted criminal. In chapter 5, Theresa Rodewald analyzes the strained investigation as a study of gender, in "how failing to convict the killer reflects back on (the narrative) Graysmith's strained masculinity." Daniel R. Fredrick, in chapter 6, uses rhetorical theory to inspect the Zodiac Killer's letters and their representation in the film, through which the figure aimed to persuade the public and police of his status. By unpacking this methodology, and analyzing the letter's "piffle and paradox," Frederick explains how this shapes the investigation in the film. In the closing chapter of the section (7), George Toles analyzes the intertextuality between *Zodiac* (with its relation to "The Most Dangerous Game") and Universal Studio's enigmatic horror film *The Black Cat* (1932). Toles connects the two films to underscore the "steady proliferation of odd, forking paths and circuitous routes to discovery" in *Zodiac*, with special attention to the film's famous "basement scene."

Section 3, "*Zodiac* and Media," begins with Martin Kevorkian's study of mimesis in the film (chapter 8). Kevorkian sees *Zodiac*'s use of existing media texts as constructing an "ambiguous popular culture competition between originals and copies." The chapter connects Fincher to the mimetic practice in Dante's *Inferno*, in which "desire is fundamentally mimetic, a mimesis that readily leads to conflict." In chapter 9, Andrew Winters discusses the use of the Zodiac Killer and horror themes in music to reflect on the media power of the figure and its representation in Fincher's film, especially how musicians use the "capacity to evoke the feeling of being, what Nöel Carroll has labeled, *art-horrified*." In chapter 10, Jake Rutkowski analyzes *Zodiac* for its representation of data management and data dumping. In addressing the film's depiction of data collection and proliferation, Rutkowski discusses the media's place in "creating" narrative, and thus leading to its hegemony in culture. This collection's coeditor, David Ryan, analyzes the representation of game theory in *Zodiac* (chapter 11). Ryan discusses the film's "intermedial analysis" while using "content analysis of Fincher and screenwriter James Vanderbilt's narrative to illustrate organizational behavior and individual character choices." Finally, in chapter 12, Deborah L. Jaramillo focuses on the use of sound in both *Zodiac* and the first season of the Fincher-produced series, *Mindhunter*. Jaramillo reads sound design in both works "not only to explore their contrasting expressions of violence, but to draw greater attention to dialogue as a vehicle for horrific detail."

By closing this volume with discussions of media, and in showing the intertextuality related to *Zodiac* overall, we hope to encourage further conversations on the film. With a work so revealing by the study of film genre, auteurism, narrative, and media analysis, we look forward to further conversations in these avenues and others on a figure so uniquely represented on screen, and one inducing such a fascinating network of dialogues.

NOTES

1. The film ranked 12th on the BBC's "The 100 Greatest Films of the 21st Century" poll, based on the votes of 177 critics.
2. See Sorrento 2012, 5–14 for an introduction of this new wave of crime cinema.
3. Though Fincher dislikes when the term is applied to him (Knapp 2014, ix).
4. Fincher grew up in the San Francisco bay area (Levy 2007, 118) and once had his school bus escorted by the state police after the Zodiac threatened to attack a school bus (Pierce 2007, 119).
5. While Gyllenhaal's earlier roles, including *Zodiac*, show him working in a naturalistic style, the actor has since moved into non-naturalistic approaches, especially in Dan Gilroy's 2014 film, *Nightcrawler*.
6. Though Fincher has been involved in a crime series that challenges convention, *Mindhunter* (Netflix, 2017–2019, created by Joe Penhall and executive produced by Fincher), discussed in chapters 4 and 12.
7. The final "official" letters by the Zodiac sent to the *Chronicle* were postmarked July 8, 1974 (Graysmith 2007, 156–157).

8. For a film as celebrated as *Zodiac* is in the press, there have been few scholarly responses, aside from Sutton 2011, Schreiber 2016, Browning 2010, Miley 2010, and Dickson 2016, and informed discussions of the film in visual effects studies by Marcks 2007 and Prince 2010.

REFERENCES

BBC Culture. 2016. "The 100 Greatest Films of the 21st Century." August 23. Accessed December 12, 2020, https://www.bbc.com/culture/article/20160819-the-21st-centurys-100-greatest-films.

Browning, Mark. 2010. *David Fincher: Films that Scar.* Santa Barbara, CA: Praeger.

Dickson, Sam. 2016. "*Zodiac* and the Ends of Cinema." *Senses of Cinema* 78 (March). Accessed February 18, 2019, https://www.sensesofcinema.com/2016/feature-articles/zodiac/.

Douthat, Russ. 2008. "The Return of the Paranoid Style." *The Atlantic*, April. Accessed February 20, 2020, https://www.theatlantic.com/magazine/archive/2008/04/the-return-of-the-paranoid-style/306733/.

Fagan, Kevin. 2020. "Zodiac '340 Cipher' Cracked by Code Experts 51 Years After It was Sent to the *S.F. Chronicle*." *San Francisco Chronicle*, December 11. Accessed September 25, 2020, https://www.sfchronicle.com/crime/article/Zodiac-340-cypher-cracked-by-code-expert-51-years-15794943.php.

Graysmith, Robert. 1986. *Zodiac.* New York, NY: St. Martin's.

—. 2007/2002. *Zodiac Unmasked.* New York, NY: Berkley.

Haugen, Brenda. 2010. *The Zodiac Killer: Terror and Mystery.* Mankato, MN: Compass Point.

Kelleher, Michael D., and David Van Nuys. 2001. *"This is the Zodiac Speaking": Into the Mind of a Serial Killer.* 2nd ed. New York, NY: Greenwood.

Klosterman, Chuck. 2003. "This Is Zodiac Speaking." In *Sex, Drugs, and Cocoa Puffs: A Low Culture Manifesto.* New York, NY: Scribner, 187–202.

Knapp, Laurence F. 2014. "Introduction." In *David Fincher: Interviews.* Jackson, MS: University of Mississippi Press.

Krutnik, Frank. 1993. *In a Lonely Street: Film Noir, Genre, Masculinity.* London, UK: Routledge.

Kurtz, Christopher J. 2004. "Review of *This Is the Zodiac Speaking: Into the Mind of a Serial Killer* by Michael D. Kelleher and David Van Nuys." *Criminal Justice Review* 29 (2): 410–411.

Leitch, Thomas. 2002. *Crime Films.* Cambridge, UK: Cambridge University Press.

Levy, Shawn. 2007. "David Fincher of *Zodiac.*" In *David Fincher: Interviews*, edited by Laurence F. Knapp. Jackson, MS: University of Mississippi Press: 116–118.

Marcks, Greg. 2007. "The Future of Image Capture." *Film Quarterly* 61 (1): 8–9.

Miley, Mike. 2010. "Deciphering the Indecipherable: Procedure as Art in Fincher's *Zodiac.*" *Bright Lights Film Journal.* Accessed January 18, 2019, https://brightlightsfilm.com/wp-content/cache/all/deciphering-the-indecipherable-procedure-as-art-in-finchers-zodiac/#.W51D26ZKiUk.

Muller, Eddie. 2010. "A Writer's Evolution." Interviewed by Matthew Sorrento. *Bright Lights Film Journal*, April 30. Accessed February 10, 2020, https://brightlightsfilm.com/a-writers-evolution-an-interview-with-eddie-muller/.

Naremore, James. 2008. *More Than Night: Film Noir in Its Contexts*. Berkeley, CA: University of California Press.

Pierce, Nev. 2007. "The Devil is in the Detail." In *David Fincher: Interviews*, edited by Laurence F. Knapp. Jackson, MS: University of Mississippi Press: 119–126.

Poggiali, Chris. 2012. "Zodiac Hunter: An Interview with Tom Hanson." *Temple of Schlock*, December 31. Accessed August 19, 2020, http://templeofschlock.blogspot.com/2012/12/zodiac-hunter-interview-with-tom-hanson.html.

Prince, Stephen. 2010. "Through the Looking Glass: Philosophical Toys and Digital Visual Effects." *Projections* 4 (2): 19–40.

Schreiber, Michele. 2016. "Tiny life: Technology and Masculinity in the Films of David Fincher." *Journal of Film and Video* 68 (1): 3–18.

Sorrento, Matthew. 2012. *The New American Crime Film*. Jefferson, NC: McFarland.

Sutton, Damian. 2011. "Time-Lapse, Time Map: the Photographic Body of San Francisco in David Fincher's *Zodiac*." *L'Atalante: Revista de Estudios Cinematográficos* 12. Accessed Decmeber 18, 2020, https://eprints.mdx.ac.uk/7849/.

Stewart. Gary L. 2014. *The Most Dangerous Animal of All: Searching for My Father...and Finding the Zodiac Killer*. New York, NY: Harper.

Vanderbilt, James. 2008. "Interview with James Vanderbilt." Special Feature on *Zodiac: the Director's Cut DVD*. Burbank, CA: Paramount Home Video.

"*Zodiac* Production Notes." 2007. Paramount Pictures. *MovieWeb*, February 14. Accessed January 25, 2019, http://media.movieweb.com/galleries/3158/notes.pdf.

SECTION ONE

BEFORE FINCHER

Chapter 1

Framing the "Mass" Killer

Horror and Spatiality in Peter Bogdanovich's Targets *(1968)*

Matthew Sorrento

Of all the societal menaces in the latter half of the twentieth century, the serial killer has been a challenge to adapt on-screen. While filmmakers have taken bold strides in developing the theme, audiences have struggled with how to receive it: are they watching a crime film, featuring the psychology of the most severe of criminals, or are they watching a horror film, with humanity as the new monster? Advertising of the releases often abandon the clear crime film associations by selling the films as horror pieces.[1] And yet, the serial killer's connections to the crime film styles—with an extreme form of criminal and dogged law enforcement after them—are absolute.

The generic blending of the serial killer film reflects the complicated history of horror styles: supernatural versus realistic. While recent studies of the early horror film have asserted the prevalence of realistic terror,[2] the presence of the nonhuman monster as a mainstream conceit is undeniable. With the runaway success of Universal Studios' *Dracula* (Tod Browning) and *Frankenstein* (James Whale, both 1931), studio production became committed to supernatural conceits of horror (or the products of mad science), with occasional exceptions, like Tod Browning's *Freaks* (Browning 2014, 233). The push to adapt literary works with horror associations led to Paramount Studios filming H.G. Wells's *The Island of Dr. Moreau* (1896) as *The Island of Lost Souls* (Erle C. Kenton, 1932), with the actions of the eponymous mad scientist (Charles Laughton) echoing the supernatural creations of Dr. Frankenstein, though a very human product of technology. Universal Studios followed their two hits with a series of Edgar Allan Poe adaptations (in name only), featuring such strange terrors of Bela Lugosi's Dr. Mirakle in *Murders in the Rue Morgue* (Robert Florey, 1932) and Boris Karloff's Dr. Poelzig in

The Black Cat (Edgar G. Ulmer, 1934), a Satanist who preserves bodies of women to present their beauty (see George Toles's chapter on pp. 121–147). The strange manipulations of these power-hungry human monsters present a terror that is more "superhuman" than that of the night-stalking killer. In these early horror films, strange human powers came in place of supernatural ones, in adaptations of literary works with a taste of prestige. While the supernatural/superhuman tendency continued (though challenged by producers like Val Lewton in his suggestive horrors of the 1940s) in the wake of *Dracula* and *Frankenstein*, the 1950s atomic-age culture transformed the monstrous into alien forms coming from beyond the skies or bestial products of atomic energy (a new form of mad science, now threatening the entire world, as Vivian Sobchack [2004] has noted [30]).

With these powers beyond humankind's potential for the monstrous, the killers of Alfred Hitchcock's *Psycho* and Michael Powell's *Peeping Tom* (both 1960) were everymen. As gothic criminology urges us to see the serial killer as a monster (like a vampire, according to Caroline Joan "Kay" S. Picart and Cecil Greek[3]), his common existence and proximity to potential victims aligns the style to the crime film: as in film noir, he's a loner straying toward deviance. In this volume, Christopher Weedman addresses several early responses to the Zodiac Killer in chapter 2 (pp. 31–51); this chapter, however, telescopes on the use of spatiality in Peter Bogdanovich's *Targets* (1968), what can be described as a "spree killer" film that informed the serial killer's hybrid genre development in the 1970s. After detailing the containment in visualizing serial killers in earlier US cinema and spatial film theory related to *Targets*, I discuss how visual space in *Targets* portrays the threats and effects of the "mass killer"[4] and how these elements are received by audiences (the film achieves this in three stages). This approach forges a unique genre cinema form for viewers to interpret a new type of human monster as an element of realism, even if the figure is regularly otherized.

SHAPING THE SERIAL KILLER, CENSORING THE MONSTROUS

With the gradual move away from gothic/atomic-age horror to the human monster (from the late 1950s into the 1960s), we see horror moving from the *symbolic* to the *actual*. *Psycho* and other influential films in Europe—*Diabolique* (Henri-Georges Clouzot, 1955), *Eyes Without a Face* (Georges Franju, 1960), and *Peeping Tom*, which all accentuated violence and sexuality—signaled the need for more adult-oriented cinematic entertainment. Hence, the 1960s called for a new form of monster. Hitchcock and Joseph Stefano's take on a "normal" monster (named "Norman" to underscore this) represents "a collective

American disposition towards violence" (Grant 2018, 5) especially for audiences witnessing civil rights violations and growing distress in response to anticommunist tensions in Asia, specifically Vietnam. The "threat next door" was haunting to moviegoers now, a substantive human-borne terror in contrast to the creatures of 1930s horror. With the continued challenge to the Production Code in the late 1950s and 1960s, the relaxing of film censorship in 1968 (with the establishment of the rating system of the Motion Picture Association of American [MPAA]) opened room for portraying human monstrosity.

And with the new human monster (post-*Psycho*), the gothic monsters of yesteryear took on an especially symbolic quality. It was in the 1970s that Robin Wood developed his theory of the horror film, stating that the creatures of 1930s horror, though supernatural and very removed from the human experience, embodied associations to societal outsiders (2003, 63–69). This theory accounts for the horror film's whiteness, noting that 1930s horror had embraced an Anglo-Saxon status quo while "othering" racial and societal outsiders (Wood 2018, 78). The strong contrast between text and subtext of 1930s horror—the textual supernatural monster, which implicates a subtextual human outsider—offers a reference for later horror to develop its treatment of the monstrous in sundry forms.

The introduction of a popularized human monster, one made actual and realistic, led to a kind of crime-horror hybrid film. Stanley Kramer (distributing through Columbia) packaged one notable 1950s "mass killer" film, Edward Dymytrk's *The Sniper* (1952, described as a sex crime story at the time[5]), as a crime-themed social problem film (produced by a specialist in such material, Stanley Kramer). The project resulted in a challenge in contrasting labels, with its prestige and exploitation identities opposing each other. The repeated killings by Eddie Miller (Arthur Franz), fueled by a psychological ailment he recognizes, offer a noir criminal perspective (Hirsch 1981, 168), with the analysis of psychiatrist (Richard Kiley as Dr. James G. Kent), working alongside police as moralistic commentary.[6] As the criminal murders several women, Dr. Kent analyzes the killer for some pop-psychology. Earlier serial killer films, like Fritz Lang's *M* (1931, starring Peter Lorre as a child rapist/killer), benefited from an art cinema approach, one employing crime film conventions to dramatize sensational subject matter. Hitchcock's 1934 version of *The Man Who Knew Too Much* also uses Lorre for his haunting presence, here with less psychological development, mainly fueling a suspense thriller. Similar in theme to *The Sniper*, the earlier 59-minute programmer *Follow Me Quietly* (Anthony Mann, 1949) avoids generic complications by featuring investigation instead of the killer and his pathology or psychology (Alvarez 2013, 156).

Such negotiations of criminal versus monstrous on-screen led to the serial killer film. The mature entries of the 1990s (*Henry: Portrait of a Serial Killer*

[1986, released 1990] and *Se7en* [1995]) position themselves as crime thrillers (the former film, a criminal-centered one, and the latter a grisly investigative piece, with both focusing on procedure of crime and investigation) while using motifs of human-monster horror to underscore the extremity of the threat. With *Henry*, the downtime of the title killer (Michael Rooker) builds his character, but when he begins killing on-screen (with an accomplice, Otis, played by Tom Towles), he takes on qualities of an especially consumptive monster, once he films and views his crimes with a home movie camera (Picart and Greek 2007b, 234). In *Se7en*, an anti-realistic neo-noir visual style makes the American city into a stylized, gothic dreamscape, where volatile avenger figures (here the investigators are a pair) search out a serial killer with mythical associations (acting out the Seven Deadly Sins in his killings).

Prior to these films, the negotiations between crime/horror were especially important to how the Zodiac Killer, one of the most notorious on the loose, was presented on-screen. The goal-oriented style of crime cinema in the United States, in which victims regularly avenge the wrongs against them (Leitch 2002, 84), led to the creation of the rogue cop thriller: in *Dirty Harry* (1971), Harry Callahan's drive shapes his denial of due process to capture a Zodiac-inspired serial killer (see pp. 41–45). While mainly a police thriller, *Dirty Harry* (like *Follow Me Quietly*) minimizes the killer's activities on-screen (like *The Boston Strangler*, 1968 and other films cited in chapter 2). It would take a portrayal of a "spree killer" (different than a serial killer in criminology, but offering several connections, which I discuss below) to create the on-screen killer in *Targets*.

Mass Killing: Serial Versus Spree Killer

Though *serial killer* and *spree killer* have specific associations in criminology and on-screen, James Alan Fox and Jack Levin (2015) stress the need to focus on "motivation more than timing" in the definition and, hence, prefer "to eliminate the need for the 'spree killer' designation" (25). The authors argue that focus on the cooling off period—that is, the time in between killings that the serial killer allots for himself—has led to more of a distraction in media coverage (24). This declassification defuses any resistance to reading the spree-like killings in *Targets* as part of the serial killer tradition on-screen. Further, the condensed series of killings by Bobby Thompson (Tim O'Kelly) reveal how the crime motifs can hybridize with horror to portray the modern psychopath/human monster on-screen (Douglass 1981, 35). The condensed terror of the killings in *Targets* reflects the "mass effect" (in Fox and Levin's concept) of the human monstrous and the viewer's access to him. To highlight the connections between serial and spree killing, I will use the term "mass killing" to discuss *Targets* and its new direction in portraying such events.

The more liberated cinema of the late 1960s struggled in portraying the prolonged actions of the serial killer on-screen. Both *Dirty Harry* and *The Boston Strangler* focus sizable screentime on the investigation into the respective killings. Such a portrayal would require extensive character development of the human monster (the kind we see in the anti-melodramatic *Henry*, while *The Boston Strangler* focuses only on the investigation in the first half, to smooth out the dread of facing the killer in his apprehension and analysis in the second half). Bogdanovich along with cowriter Polly Platt, and their uncredited cowriter, famed genre film artist Samuel Fuller, depict the mass killer at three locations (his home, an oil tank by a highway, and a drive-in movie theater—each discussed in detail later). They use three steps to show the degrees of the killer's violence: (1) against the family, (2) against the population, in transit, and (3) against a "sitting" population at a public entertainment gathering, centered on spectatorship (drive-in movie patrons, thus tied to auto-transportation). The first two threaten established lifeways of citizens (the nuclear family then highway transportation). Robin Wood (2018) notes that the 1975 film *Race with the Devil* introduces the concept that everyone is potentially monstrous (71). As a film predating *Race*, *Targets* in its "third step" asserts that everyone watching (the diegetic drive-in feature, and *Targets*) is a potential victim of a human monster.

To achieve this breakthrough commentary on fear, *Targets* hybridizes the crime film genre with horror. It does so by visualizing the former genre with a spatial progression that achieves the effects of the latter, a sensation-based genre (Kawin 2012, 5).[7] In other words, the "mass killings" are depicted to achieve mass dread, in increments.

SPATIALITY IN EARLIER CRIME CINEMA

To assess *Targets*' use of space to hybridize genres, I want to introduce spatial theory related to film, specifically as it concerns the crime film and, specifically, its subgenre of film noir (the most analyzed of the crime film styles). Edward Branigan (1981) notes theories of cinematic space to address issues of subjectivity, among character, camera, object, and narrator/viewer working as a "quadratic predicate . . . . [I]n order to describe a changing point of view . . . one must consider how these terms change through time (onscreen)" (59). While laying out a broad framework, Branigan addresses the variety of application in diverse cinemas, in that reading this mediation depends on cultural convention (60). This open framework reflects *Targets*' subjective point of view (to the killer Thompson, in his portion of the film[8]), and how his visual experience reflects the terror spread over several Los Angeles scenes, shot on location.

In discussing film as spatial practice, Les Roberts and Julia Hallam (2013) question the need for critics to assess whether films adhere to regular concepts of built environment and landscape, or if films challenge these notions (6). Their concern is much like those of genre critics (the late Robin Wood, and Christopher Sharrett) committed to assessing if a work aligns to or challenges the dominant political ideology.

To develop Branigan's commentary, Hallam (2014, 174) defines three modes of "cinespatial" practice (though this framework focuses on cinema's ability to represent visual space, with less attention to how it informs narrative or character): (1) "topophilia"—a love of space that leads to mapping as self-discovery in politics and poetics of space on-screen; (2) basic mapping of an area; and (3) surveying by walking—that is, reflecting visual experience. The first two modes address cinematic mapping (not really *Targets'* concern, since the film exploits the randomness of a few Los Angeles locations).[9] The third mode, however—survey by walking—informs the depiction, and ramifications of, Thompson's travel from his three murder locations: home, to transit space, to entertainment destination, as I will discuss further.

Edward Dimendberg's *Film Noir and Spaces of Modernity* (2004), in focusing of the crime film style that inspired *Targets*, is especially helpful. Dimendberg focuses on how the noir tradition gains subjective views of expanding urban spaces of the mid-twentieth-century, postwar boom. In working off the spatial concepts of French philosopher/sociologist Henri Lefebvre, Dimendberg (2004) notes how postwar urban locations have transformed from what had been abstract spaces into commodified built environments (106). Thus, in a Marxist lens, this transition of development creates spatial anxiety upon the individual (Dimendberg 2004, 109). In fact, this concept reflects on how Bogdanovich's film lines up free-moving citizens as human targets. While one response to Dimendberg assumes that "spatial and subversive impulses have got lost in more recent incarnation of the so-called neo-noir" (Frey 2006, 64), this reading skips ahead to neo-noirs of the 1990s, beyond Bogdanovich's New Hollywood treatment. Though not citing Bogdanovich's film, Dimendberg underscores the treatment of (1) the suburban home, like Bobby Thompson's featured in *Targets*, along with the film's use of (2) the urban arterial highway, and (3) the transportation-reliant entertainment center—that is, the drive-in theater—as Thompson's three-step spree.

In discussing the trend for noir protagonists to move from the "urban center to periphery," Dimendberg (2004) notes that

Nostalgia and longing for older urban forms combined with a fear of new alienating urban realities pervade film noir. The loss of public space, the homogenization of everyday life, the intensification of surveillance, and the eradication of old neighborhoods by urban renewal and redevelopment projects are seldom absent from these films . . . the protagonists in film noir appear cursed by an inability to move anywhere. (7)

Dimendberg organizes his analysis of film space in film noir through two categories: centripetal space and centrifugal space. The former reflects "how attitudes, behaviors, and shared interpretations" are the result of "developments in architecture, urbanism, and technology" (99) and are often depicted through surveillance and detection. Analysis of this category reflects the fear of feeling overwhelmed by space (and) fears of restriction (171–2).

Dimendberg notes that centripetal space on-screen reflects the common practice of "a walk through the metropolis" and the visual and emotional experiences attached to this movement.[10] The 1950s film noir *Kiss Me Deadly* (Robert Aldrich, 1955) offers an example of cinematic text lacking coherent pedestrian space (161). While Mike Hammer (Ralph Meeker) has high vantage point in his apartment, the film overall offers "less a sense of visual mastery than a recognition of spatial homogeneity" (162).[11] In this film, Hammer's vantage point reflects his approach to detection, which is more emphatic in trailing (and often roughing up!) leads and suspects. High vantage points in *The Sniper* have the same disorienting effect.

Centrifugal space depicts the "temporality and uncertainty produced by a spatial environment increasingly devoid of landmarks and centers and often likely seen to be in *permanent motion*" (italics mine, 171), while both forms—centripetal and centrifugal—are compatible with one another (177). While *Targets* captures the feeling of Dimendberg's "walk," the actions of Thompson exploit the centrifugal, disorienting experience of urbanites in transit, who often suddenly come to rest.

CINE-SPACE FOR THE MASS KILLER: *TARGETS*

As set in Los Angeles, *Targets* demythologizes the "western mirage" of the city's location sensed by urbanites in the East (Olivier and Trigo 2002, 229). A more popular 1969 release, the film version of Horace McCoy's Depression-era novel *They Shoot Horses, Don't They?* (1935), similarly undercuts notions of paradise at the end of the "frontier." The spatial considerations, in conjunction with genre hybridity and revision, make *Targets* a bold act of genre even if scholars have regretfully ignored the film. This fact is likely due to the enormous success, critically and financially, of Bogdanovich's follow-up film, *The Last Picture Show* (1971). A 2003 Paramount DVD release, and thoughtful comments in Jason Zinoman's popular horror study, *Shock Value*, have helped bring attention back to the film (2011, 43–48). In the DVD commentary, Bogdanovich describes how Fuller, a journalist-turned-filmmaker, helped the young writer-director work through several narrative problems. With such a strong revisionist approach to the horror genre (one Fuller didn't work in), it's clear that Fuller is largely responsible for the new treatment of the human monster. Famous for his work in 1950s noir (*Pickup on South Street*, 1953), Fuller created exceptional generic revisions of the Western with *I Shot Jesse James* (1949), an early entry in the psychological Westerns of the 1950s (the work of Anthony Mann and Budd Boetticher), and the war film with *The Steel Helmet* (1951). Fuller's psychological treatment of the Western, an environment and action-based genre, is evident in his frequent use of close-ups, to investigate the motivation behind the act of Robert Ford and his regret and torment over it. With *The Steel Helmet*, Fuller reworks the World War II-style combat film into a tale of despairing defeat set in the Korean conflict (based on notes for a planned World War II script he took while serving in World War II Europe, where he filmed the liberation of the Falkenau Nazi concentration camp in Czechoslovakia [Orgeron 2006, 39]). It was the first war film to note that "There Is No End to This Story" (as a closing title), that real combat feels like a continued state of confusion, whereas the World War II combat films prior presented a clear goal and victory for the enlisted.

While Fuller worked in a studio environment in his early filmmaker career (and controlled his more experimental entries, like the newspaper epic *Park Row* [1952]), *Targets* was conceived under constraints of the exploitation market. Producer Roger Corman ordered Bogdanovich to film 20 minutes of footage of Boris Karloff (who had two days left over in his contract for Corman), incorporate 20 minutes of the Corman film *The Terror* (1963), and film 40 new minutes (Bogdanovich, 2003). With the piecemeal plan set, it would seem that Bodganovich would write another historical gothic horror to fit in the footage from *The Terror* seamlessly. Bogdanovich and his cowriter, Polly Platt, instead decided to use the Karloff footage in a script about an aging horror star meeting another kind of monster: a spree killer based loosely on Charles Whitman. This torn-from-the-headlines approach to horror was a bold move by the writing team, much to the credit of Fuller. Producer Roger Corman added an unintentional incentive: he agreed to release the film through Paramount if it came together well (Bogdanovich 2003), thus offering to present the film as a prestige production, like a genre feature by Hitchcock, in spite of the project's exploitation roots. It indeed ended up with Paramount, instead of American International Pictures, which Corman would use as a distributor if the film finished as a lesser effort.

With just 60 minutes of new footage available to film, it was a time-sensitive project and, thus, the screenwriters went for suspense. As a filmmaker aiming for drama (the approach to his follow-up film), Bogdanovich also aimed for all the humanity possible.[12] In an article written post-New Hollywood (1981), Wayne J. Douglass contextualizes *Targets* in the rise of the criminal psychopath as hero, stemming from a post-1930s gangster tradition featuring small-time gangsters who couldn't take lead of the gang, with impulsive actions that lead to the gang's downfall (*Kiss of Death*, Henry Hathaway, 1947; *White Heat*, Raoul Walsh, 1947) (Douglass 1981, 32–33). These films led to more tortured gangster figures in late 1950s budget cycle of the genre, who, in turn, preceded the psychopaths emerging as serial murders in *Targets* and soon after, more popularly, *Dirty Harry* (35–6). The New Hollywood loner psychopaths grew out of anti-communalism in the gangster film, and these misfit hoods emerged from the hectic urban crowd as monstrous threats.

In an "economy" film assignment from Corman, Bogdanovich exploits the growing trend of the cinema psychopath by invoking Whitman, the University of Texas mass shooter (August 1, 1966). Like Whitman, Thompson first kills his family,[13] before turning to a random population. Thompson's shooting of his family, and then a delivery boy, indicates his rage emerging but also, in the greater sequence of killings, embodies the attack on the repressive traditional family unit. Thompson, a veteran (portrayed briefly in a mantle photo in fatigues), has a quiet rage toward the middle-class complacency of his family. Living with his parents and wife, Thompson hears their superficial conversation the night before, dry and pointless, like their bland home entertainment (mass produced art, a radio playing synthetic rock 'n' roll [Dixon 2013]).[14] His actions the next morning are hardly sensible, and yet Thompson annihilates the institution that "represses and oppresses" (Wood 2016, 79). His first killing, of his wife, is filmed in clever montage—with both Thompson and his wife filmed in separate shots. Bogdanovich has noted his desire to reflect Alfred Hitchcock's action-reaction editing in *Rear Window* (1954) (Bogdanovich, 2003). The approach of proximity in framing, along with the disconnect in editing, shows the two in isolation, the wife offering routine physical comfort while not even really seeing what her spouse is experiencing. By connecting proximity to isolation, Bogdanovich reflects the cultural isolation in interaction that represses anger and boils into rage. Beginning with the murder scene at home, *Targets* creates a series of spaces subjective to Thompson, as a looker/shooter who scopes the population, as the film further employs Hitchcock's action-reaction approach. In light of Branigan's theory, the viewer—by gaining Thompson's perspective—receives a construct for presenting mass killing genre(s). As the killer progresses to stage two and three, we see how the genre frames killings on grander scales.

We should also note that Thompson's annihilation of his family, through the murder of his wife, his mother, and a visitor (grocery delivery boy) portrays a young white Anglo-Saxon suburban male aggressively reclaiming his position as oppressor.[15] The murders immediately following his wife's, the killing of his mother-in-law and a grocery delivery boy in quick succession (in the kitchen), appear in a boarder visual space to remove outsiders to the white male experience. Killing the woman first, Thompson's gun then sweeps to the right—invoking a military maneuver, and hence, his time in Vietnam—to aim and fire at a grocery delivery boy. The one-two maneuvering also echoes Thompson's visit to a rifle practice range, a day earlier in the narrative. It's a scene in which, we recall with shock during the spree, that Thompson aimed his sights on his father (who merely scolds him for careless firearm practice). Here, Thompson merely threatens oppressive patriarchy, via a representative, though he will soon murder the women close to him, and a service-class worker. Once he has killed the women family members in his home, Thompson quickly progresses to murder to the societal representative who visits, a store representative. This final murder here indicates that Thompson will continue to attack not just his social institutions of his association, but society outside, through random killings. In the parallel narrative, concerning fading horror actor Byron Orlok (Boris Karloff) and Sammy Michaels (Bogdanovich), the latter wakes from a nightmare just after Thompson's spree has begun. To underscore the development of the human monster, a scene of Thompson cleaning up after his killings recalls Norman Bates cleaning up Marion Crane's murder in *Psycho*, though now the murders will continue in rapid succession in lieu of reactions to cover-up. Thompson progresses to a transit location and commuter entertainment location (the drive-in) to express his rage through suburban spheres, his rage amplifying out into urban space. He manages to manipulate urban space and its routines (via surveillance, through his riflescope) that have been homogenized through urban development (Dimendberg 2004, 171–2), in linking the middle-class routine of home life (first murders), then transit (shootings of motorists) to large-scale entertainment (killings at the drive-in).

The second stage of his spree, atop an oil tank aside a highway, recalls Whitman directly (in the vantage point), though the roaming sea or cars accentuates the randomness of the threat and violence. The streams of automotive combustion engines transporting citizens indicate Thompson's inner rage hidden in his calm demeanor, along with the rattling clangs of the oil tank.[16] Carrying out an activity beyond a target range (at a seaside booth, or a skeet shot), the highway embodies an evolution away from the small communal establishments of early twentieth century (Schlosser 1998, 7–8). The vantage point shows the criminal's exploitation of overproduction, in that urban spaces have become ones of "spectacle and consumption" (Hallam and

Roberts 2014, 9), and our vulnerability in such locales. The actual highway traffic replaces the memory of Dimendburg's (2004) walks to a town center (7), where citizens would find their shopping and entertainment (and downtown theaters), along with a train station, which connected small communities before they sprawled together though mass automotive ownership. (In the film, the movie theaters have been replaced by the auto-age one, the drive-in, which we will see in stage three of the spree.) The random gunshots reach the cars (filmed without a permit, which I'll discuss later) which have removed society from small communities. Unlike the "high angle overhead shots of the [city] street" in Fritz Lang's proto-noir *M* (1931) and film noir *Scarlet Street* (1945) (Dimendberg 2003, 118), Thompson uses his highway position to exploit homogeneity as a mass target—the plurality of the title underscoring the numerous potential victims the highway offers.

The fact that Bogdanovich, coached by producer Corman, shot the footage guerilla-style without a permit (since all filming on the highway was illegal [Bogdanovich 2003]) adds rough style of *verite* to the highway footage, from Thompson's scope vision, in contrast to the cooler formalism in which Bogdanovich shoots Kelly as Thompson atop the tower. Even as a budget production, *Targets* revises the social problem approach in *The Sniper* and, to an extent, *The Boston Strangler* to address not a call for analysis, but the effects of overproduction on the American self (Dixon 2013).

From afar, Thompson expands his reach to society at random by shooting out drivers and passengers on the highway. Though he kills less in this stage than Whitman did during his comparable incident, Thompson has accessed a greater range than in the real event, which concerned a small section of society (those on a college campus) and not true arterial cross-section. The killer's final stage of the spree will concern another type of societal cross-section, this time directly reflecting his practice of viewing and scrutinizing through a riflescope.

The third step is shrewd in connecting to the previous one's relevance to automobiles and car culture: while the second phase targets passersby on the highway, in Thompson's final one, he situates himself behind the object of their gaze: a drive-in movie screen. No longer "moving targets," the victims are now "sitting ducks," in lockdown, for this late twentieth-century hunter, now shooting at the masses virtually face-to-face (though different in design, the killer has an eerie resemblance to the 2012 Aurora, Colorado shooter [PBS News Hour 2015]). Essentially, the *mise-en-scene* lines up free-moving citizens as "human targets" (an earlier title for the film [Bogdanovich 2003]). At the start of the final narrative movement, patrons slowly arrive to the drive-in, in contrast to the rushing entrance of Thompson. In slowing the overall pace, Bogdanovich underscores the final showdown approaching, as we note the appointed arrival to the theater of Orlok, former horror star, as guest of the screening of his film (comprising the requisite footage from Corman's *The Terror*).

The "drive-in" stage works as a synthesis of the first two: the close attack of the home killings emphasizes the impact of random gun violence (stage one), while stage two emphasizes the scope (and wide effect of the violence) of such violence. The synthesis of the first two resolves in a "communal" attack against a social microcosm at the drive-in theater, a metafilmic space (stable, and one targeting even more children, families, and the elderly).[17] While Thompson, behind the screen, reaches the autos farthest away in a large sea of cars, he also hits those nearby and at clearer range, including a patron in a phone booth, even reaching the theater's projectionist.[18]

The narrative trajectory has Thompson, a new kind of horror film monster, meeting this one of old. But as Karloff's Frankenstein monster never really died, viewers worry little of bullets taking Orlok down: Orlok triumphing over Thompson, in their strategic showdown, is a guarantee. Approaching Thompson, Orlok becomes as a dual presence—one on-screen, and the actual actor-character walking in front of it. The projected image reflects a grand tradition: Karloff on-screen, looming over Thompson, asserts that the new monster is hardly terrifying. Here Orlok approaches the sterile, child-like killer and downs him, shrugging, "Is this what we were afraid of?"—a feat possible only once Thompson has run out of bullets.

In a celebration of gothic horror (the drive-in, echoing traditional movie-going), the film downplays the real threat for a conservative ending, thus working against its social commentary on social ills and cinematic space for the subgenre. The pat finale offers little of the kind of psychological treatment that we see in *The Boston Strangler* and even *Psycho*.[19] In dealing with an aged Karloff out of gothic make-up (he'd die the year after the film's release), we see the figure behind Wood's various stages of political horror. And yet, in recalling the Frankenstein monster's killing of a child in the first film of the series (1931), the misunderstood outsiders—the monsters of gothic horror—resound, underscoring the need for treating the psychopath. Karloff, as a bemused horror star, speaks eloquently throughout the film, even getting a poetic monologue, a far cry from the grunting, wordless monster of *Frankenstein*. Meanwhile, the young killer is nearly wordless, reflecting the film's silence on society's lack of understanding about him. With the "new monster" defeated, cowering, *Targets* pushes for a Hollywood ending, in spite of its call for understanding the "new" monstrous outsider. The earlier part of the narrative, in its three-part framework, offers visual language, in the film's spatiality that reflects the film taking up from localized fear of the gothic monster to widespread terror of the mass murderer. The ending processes the fear without turning the mirror for analysis. Yet, in reflecting viewer response, *Targets* previews the systematic effects of the mass murderer, which Fincher's *Zodiac* would process as systematic investigation forty years later.

NOTES

1. For example, the poster art for David Fincher's *Se7en* (1995), featuring the stars Brad Pitt and Morgan Freeman, uses violent slash marks to reflect the quantity of the murders, along with distorted imagery reflecting modern gothic settings (like a basement) and fire.
2. See Rhodes 2018, Phillips 2018, and Grant 2018.
3. For a discussion from various perspectives, see Picart and Greek 2007a.
4. As I discuss later, while the serial killer has dominated as a hybrid of the crime-horror film, I prefer to use the term "mass killer" to relate to real-life figures responsible for multiple killings.
5. See Muller 2009. It's also important to note that the term "serial killer" was introduced in the United States at the time. FBI investigator Robert Ressler takes credit for coining the term sometime in the 1970s, though German investigator Ernst Gennat introduced the "Serienmörder," a literal translation of the term, in 1930 (Gavin and Porter 2015, 145).
6. The initial screenwriters for *The Sniper*, Edna and Edward Anhalt, undertook considerable research into the "sex killer" for the project (Muller 2009).
7. See also Williams 2012.
8. The alternate narrative, featuring Boris Karloff as fading film star Byron Orlok, gets sizable screen time.
9. Other films set in LA use the Los Angeles River as a connector—for example, see *Repo Man* (1984) and *Return of the Living Dead III* (1993).
10. See Dimendberg (2004), chapter 3: "Walking Cures," 119–165.
11. *The Sniper*, while focusing mainly on claustrophobic interiors, uses a city view atop a building when, notably, the killer gets spotted.
12. Interestingly, the film's inspiration wasn't the first spree killer, as widely thought. Before Whitman, Howard Unruh went on a killing spree through his Camden, New Jersey, neighborhood on September 6, 1949, killing thirteen (including three children). See Berger 1949.
13. Unlike Thompson, Whitman attacked his family with knives.
14. Robin Wood's concept of the "terrible house" (2018, 97) in modern horror applies to Thompson home's complacency in bland pop culture and style.
15. Robin Wood (2018) has noted how possession of a rifle, even in a progressive genre film like *Dawn of the Dead*, invokes the male's act to reclaim power (168).
16. Thompson's shooting from the top of a large oil tank recalls the apocalyptic terror of *White Heat*'s (1949) climax, Jarrett raging over the loss of his mother and his psychosomatic effects of his relationship to her. In *Targets*, ironically, Thompson's sheer disconnect leaves him removed from his family, a modernized take on the film noir tradition of the loner moved to crime (see *Double Indemnity*), and mundanely consuming sandwiches as he takes lives.

17. Though drive-ins are nostalgic for many movie lovers, *Targets* presents the type of theater as pop-cultural junk, with Bogdanovich himself noting that he was never a fan of the theater type (see Bogdanovich 2003).

18. His earlier threading of the film through the projection, carefully filmed by László Kovács, reflects the swift passage of this killer through three locations, and indicates the camera, itself showing and commenting on this horror, as—in the tradition of Sam Fuller—a kind of weapon.

19. In David Fincher's *Zodiac*, such treatment is cause for a small but standout dramatic appearance, in John Carroll Lynch's portrayal of Arthur Leigh Allen, the prime Zodiac suspect. Though still thought to be guilty, police officially ruled him out, and Fincher asked Lynch to play the role as if he was innocent.

REFERENCES

Alvarez, Max. 2013. *The Crime Films of Anthony Mann*. Oxford: University of Mississippi Press.

Berger, Meyer. 1949. "Veteran Kills 12 in Mad Rampage on Camden Street." *The New York Times*, September 7. Accessed June 7, 2019, https://www.nytimes.com/1949/09/07/archives/veteran-kills-12-in-mad-rampage-on-camden-street-shoots-4-others-in.html.

Bogdanovich, Peter. 2003. "Interview with Peter Bogdanovich." *Targets* DVD. Burbank, CA: Paramount Home Entertainment.

Branigan, Edward. 1981. "The Spectator and Film Space: Two Theories." *Screen* 22 (1): 55–78.

Browning, John Edgar. 2014. "Classical Hollywood Horror." In *A Companion to the Horror Film*, edited by Harry M. Benshoff, 225–236. Hoboken, NJ: Wiley-Blackwell.

Dimendberg, Edward. 2003. "Down These Seen Streets a Man Must Go: Siegfried Kracauer, 'Hollywood's Terror Films,' and the Spatiality of Film Noir." *New German Critique: Film and Exile* 89 (Spring/Summer): 113–143.

Dimendberg, Edward. 2004. *Film Noir and the Spaces of Modernity*. Cambridge, MA: Harvard University Press.

Dixon, Wheeler Winston. 2013. "The Future Catches Up with the Past: Peter Bogdanovich's *Targets*." *Film International,* January 17. Accessed May 12, 2019, https://filmint.nu/the-future-catches-up-with-the-past-peter-bogdanovichs-targets/.

Douglass, Wayne J. 1981. "Criminal Psychopath as Hollywood Hero." *Journal of Popular Film and Television* 8 (4) (Winter): 30–39.

Frey, Mattias. 2006. "No(ir) Place to Go: Spatial Anxiety and Sartorial Intertextuality in *Die Unberührbare*." *Cinema Journal* 45 (4): 64–80.

Gavin, Helen, and Theresa Porter. 2015. *Female Aggression*. Hoboken, NJ: Wiley-Blackwell.

Grant, Barry Keith. 2018. *Monster Cinema*. New Brunswick, NJ: Rutgers University Press.

Hallam, Julia. 2013. "Mapping the City Film: 1930–1980." In *Locating the Moving Image: New Approaches to Film and Place*, edited by Les Roberts and Julia Hallam. Bloomington: Indiana University Press, 173–196.

Hirsch, Foster. 1981. *The Dark Side of the Screen: Film Noir*. New York: Da Capo Press.

Kawin, Bruce. 2012. *Horror and the Horror Film*. London, UK: Anthem Press.

Leitch, Thomas. 2002. *Crime Films*. Oxford, UK: Oxford University Press.

Lynch, John Carroll. 2017. "John Carroll Lynch on Whether *Zodiac*'s Arthur Leigh Allen Was Guilty." Interviewed by Hillary Luehring-Jones. *Uinterview*, October 18. Accessed February 25, 2020, https://uinterview.com/news/john-carroll-lynch-whether-zodiacs-arthur-leigh-allen-guilty-video-exclusive/.

Muller, Eddie. 2009. Commentary on *The Sniper* (1952). Burbank, CA: Sony Picture Home Entertainment.

Oliver, Kelly and Benigno Trigo. 2002. *Noir Anxiety*. Minneapolis, MN: University of Minnesota Press.

Orgeron, Marsha. 2006. "Liberating Images?: Samuel Fuller's Film of Falkenau Concentration Camp." *Film Quarterly* 60 (2 Winter): 38–47.

PBS News Hour. 2015. "Colorado Shooting DA Says Two Evaluations Found Holmes Sane." April 27. Accessed June 2, 2019, https://www.pbs.org/newshour/show/colo-shooting-da-says-two-evaluations-found-holmes-sane.

Phillips, Kendall R. 2018. *A Place of Darkness: A Rhetoric of Horror in Early American Cinema*. Austin, TX: University of Texas Press.

Picart, Caroline Joan (Kay), and Cecil Greek, ed. 2007a. *Monsters in and Among Us: Toward a Gothic Criminology*. Madison, NJ: Fairleigh Dickinson University Press.

Picart, Caroline Joan (Kay), and Cecil Greek. 2007b. "The Compulsions of Real/Reel Serial Killers and Vampires: Toward a Gothic Criminology." In *Monsters in and Among Us: Toward a Gothic Criminology*, edited by Caroline Joan (Kay) Picart and Cecil Greek, 227–255. Madison, NJ: Fairleigh Dickinson University Press.

Rhodes, Gary D. 2018. *The Birth of the America Horror Film*. Edinburgh, UK: Edinburgh University Press.

Roberts, Les, and Julia Hallam. 2013. "Film and Spatiality: Outline of a New Empiricism." In *Locating the Moving Image: New Approaches to Film and Place*, edited by Les Roberts and Julia Hallam, 1–30. Bloomington, IN: Indiana University Press.

Schlosser Eric. 1998. *Fast Food Nation: the Dark Side of the All-American Meal*. New York, NY: Houghton-Mifflin.

Sobchack, Vivian. 2004. *Screening Space: The American Science Fiction Film*. New Brunswick, NJ: Rutgers University Press.

Williams, Linda. 2012 (1991). "Film Bodies: Gender, Genre, Excess." In *Film Genre Reader IV*, edited by Barry Keith Grant, 159–177. Austin, TX: University of Texas Press.

Wood, Robin, 2003. *Hollywood from Vietnam to Reagan...and Beyond*. New York, NY: Columbia University Press.

Wood, Robin. 2018. *Robin Wood on the Horror Film*. Detroit, MI: Wayne State University Press.

Zinoman, Jason. 2011. *Shock Value: How a Few Eccentric Outsiders Gave Us Nightmares, Conquered Hollywood, and Invented Modern Horror*. New York: Penguin.

Chapter 2

Fear and Exploiting in the Age of Aquarius

Early Representations of the Zodiac Killer in 1970s Film and Television

Christopher Weedman

Midway through director David Fincher's critically acclaimed film *Zodiac* (2007), Inspector David Toschi (Mark Ruffalo), a homicide detective with the San Francisco Police Department, finds himself at a pivotal crossroads in his pursuit of the elusive "Zodiac Killer." After being thwarted in his effort to build a circumstantial case against prime suspect Arthur Leigh Allen (John Carroll Lynch), Toschi heeds the advice of his superior, Captain Marty Lee (Dermot Mulroney), to take time off and watch a movie with his family. The beleaguered detective would have been wise to select something farther removed from reality than *Dirty Harry* (Don Siegel, 1971). Not surprisingly, the police thriller hits Toschi too close to home with its violent tale of rogue cop Inspector Harry Callahan hunting a serial murderer, dubbed "Scorpio," stalking the streets of San Francisco. Albeit only loosely based on the still-at-large Zodiac, Toschi is worried about how *Dirty Harry* could undermine the murder investigation. When *San Francisco Chronicle* cartoonist Robert Graysmith (Jake Gyllenhaal) approaches Toschi in the lobby of the cinema, he unsuccessfully tries to reassure the detective that he will eventually solve the case. Filled with growing doubt and despair, Toschi cynically retorts, "Pal, they're already making films about it!"

This moment of growing pessimism in Fincher's docu-thriller underscores how swiftly (not to mention how unabashedly) 1970s American film and television began harvesting the gruesome headlines surrounding the Zodiac murders for new plots and characters. *Dirty Harry* was the most financially successful of these Zodiac-inspired narratives (labeled as "Zodiacsploitation" by film historian Nathaniel Thompson), but 1971 also

Figure 2.1 Zodiac "Wanted" poster, created by the San Francisco Police Department, October 18, 1969.

saw the release of two exploitation films, the horror film *The Zodiac Killer* (Tom Hanson, 1971) and the "porn noir" *Sam Dobbs Meets the Zodiac* (John Lamb, 1971) (Thompson). These lesser-known features demonstrated that the cinematic fascination with the Zodiac extended far beyond *Dirty Harry* to the more disreputable margins of the filmmaking industry. Eight years later, these three films were followed by a compelling episode of the Emmy-winning television drama *Lou Grant* entitled "Samaritan" (Paul Leaf, 1979), which capitalized on renewed interest in the murders amidst swirling, yet subsequently disproven, allegations that the real-life Toschi (the chief investigator in the San Francisco Police Department's branch of the case) forged a new Zodiac letter in late April 1978 to seek publicity. This chapter examines how these 1970s film and television narratives through their reconfiguration of elements from the Zodiac investigation exploited, and arguably exacerbated, the era's growing lack of faith in the legal system and fear of random acts of murder, which dominated press headlines during the encroaching pessimism of 1970s America. This alarming "state of the union" was subsequently encapsulated in the documentary *The Killing of America* (Sheldon Renan, 1981), but the dark and pessimistic tone of this controversial film permeates these four Zodiac-inspired narratives as well. All of them employ the cultural boogeyman of the Zodiac to present a dystopian nightmare where their madmen are merely symptomatic of larger social and political uncertainty.

THE ZODIAC AND THE CINEMA: A RECIPROCAL RELATIONSHIP

American film and television share an intriguing reciprocal relationship with the Zodiac, since the *outré* violence produced by both (fictional and actual, respectively) were significantly influenced by one another. As outlined by the real-life Robert Graysmith in his books *Zodiac* and *Zodiac Unmasked*, the Zodiac is suspected to have been a cinephile, who may have frequented the Avenue Theatre in San Francisco's Portola district.[1] This element of the Zodiac's character profile is supported by the fact that the August 1, 1969, letter that he simultaneously sent to *The San Francisco Chronicle*, *The San Francisco Examiner*, and *The Vallejo Times-Herald* contained a three-part cipher with an allusion to *The Most Dangerous Game* (Irving Pichel and Ernest B. Schoedsack, 1932). As Graysmith explains, this precode Hollywood thriller was screened multiple times at the Avenue during the late 1960s (Graysmith 1996, 47–55, 230). It is also believed that the murderer partially patterned the sinister black costume and knife that he used in the stabbings at Lake Berryessa in Napa County, California, on September 27, 1969, after those of big-game hunter Count Zaroff (Leslie Banks), who relishes hunting man for sport in this unnerving film.

Furthermore, Graysmith briefly posits that the Zodiac found additional inspiration from the *Alfred Hitchcock Presents* (CBS and NBC, 1962-65) television episode "Museum Piece" (Paul Henreid, 1961) (Graysmith 2007, 250). Loosely inspired by the same 1924 short story by Richard Connell that served as the literary basis for *The Most Dangerous Game*, this teleplay includes a chilling remark from a revengeful museum owner (Larry Gates) about how the manhunt of a man is "the most dangerous game" (Connell 2011/1924, 130). More importantly, the episode features a pivotal scene with a hunter (played by actor and future game show host Bert Convy), who approaches a couple (Tom Gilleran and Darlene Tompkins) necking in a barn. After a hostile altercation, the hunter shoots one of them accidentally with a rifle mounted with a flashlight for greater accuracy. This murder in "Museum Piece" may lack the cold-blooded premeditation of the one committed by the Zodiac at Blue Rock Springs Park in Vallejo, California, on July 4, 1969, but, nevertheless, the type of victims, rural setting, and a firearm paired with a flashlight remain disturbingly similar.

Likewise, the macabre panache of the Zodiac's modus operandi proved too tantalizing for 1970s Hollywood to ignore. The influx of Zodiac-influenced narratives reached its apex in 1971, which saw three cinematic reworkings of the murders that were of varying artistic merit. *Dirty Harry* garnered, by far, the largest amount of attention. Not only did the film gross almost $60 million at the worldwide box office, but it also cemented Clint Eastwood's reputation as one of the decade's most prominent Hollywood stars (Eliot 2009, 138–9). Conversely, less fanfare greeted *The Zodiac Killer* and *Sam Dobbs Meets the Zodiac*. Whereas the former was a low-budget exploitation horror film that was designed as a publicity stunt to catch the real-life murderer, the latter was an early adult film vehicle for John Holmes as a serial rapist also dubbed "The Zodiac." While lacking any pronounced artistic pretensions and instead designed to exploit the media attention surrounding the Zodiac investigation, both films, like *Dirty Harry*, remain intriguing cultural documents that demonstrate the degree to which the Zodiac was lingering in the collective imagination of early 1970s America.

THE ZODIAC KILLER (TOM HANSON, 1971)

The Zodiac Killer is a once largely forgotten exploitation film, which was unearthed and digitally remastered for Blu-ray and DVD by the American Genre Film Archive and Something Weird Video in 2017. Initially given a four-wall screening at the RKO Golden Gate Theatre in San Francisco on April 7, 1971, the film was subsequently picked up in mid-August for domestic distribution by Radley Metzger's Audubon Films (in association with producer Billy Fine of Prudential Pictures) and played drive-in double bills throughout the United States with, quite inexplicably, the stylish Italian erotic thriller *Femina ridens* (Piero Schivazappa, 1969, released stateside as *The Frightened Woman*) (*Variety* 1971a, 3; *Boxoffice* 1971, W-3; *Variety* 1971b, 20). The notice brought to *The Zodiac Killer* by this Blu-ray/DVD release, as well as in-depth articles by Chris Poggiali (2012) and Clark Collis (2017, 73–8), has garnered the film an unexpected cult following with exploitation film enthusiasts. This newfound attention has only increased after airings on Turner Classic Movies as part of the cable network's late night "TCM Underground" series.

Admittedly, *The Zodiac Killer* is not so much a great film and more aptly, to quote Collis, a fascinating "pop culture artifact" (Collis 2017, 74). It possesses the unique distinction of being the first film to dramatize the Zodiac murders. More interestingly, however, the film was purportedly made in a failed attempt to identify the murderer and bring him to justice. In this respect, *The Zodiac Killer* might be considered one of, if not the only,

Fear and Exploiting in the Age of Aquarius 35

Figure 2.2 Poster for *The Zodiac Killer* (Tom Hanson, 1971). Courtesy of Scott Hanson.

genuine "vigilante film," an oft-condemned cycle of action thrillers (epitomized by British director Michael Winner's controversial 1974 film *Death Wish*) that gained momentum during the 1970s amidst the social unrest over rising crime rates and the protests surrounding Civil Rights, Women's Liberation, Vietnam, and Watergate. Yet the reasons that motivated the film's director Tom Hanson to attempt to catch the still-at-large murderer was neither fueled by a desire for justice nor, as in the case of Charles Bronson's architect-turned-vigilante Paul Kersey in *Death Wish*, personal revenge. Instead, *The Zodiac Killer* was designed as an unorthodox plan to galvanize his own filmmaking career.

In 1964, seven years before embarking on this bold venture, Hanson was proclaimed by entertainment columnist Mike Connolly as "the most industrious actor in Hollywood today" (Connolly 1964, 10). This bit of hyperbole was not entirely ill-deserved. After managing a series of A&W and Chicken Delight restaurants, Hanson owned the successful Pizza Man pizzeria chain in Los Angeles in the mid-1960s, while simultaneously working as a part-time actor. He appeared in a pair of micro-budget genre features for producer Anthony Cardoza: Bailey Chastain in the Cold War crime film *Night Train to Mundo Fine* (Coleman Francis, 1966, aka *Red Zone Cuba*) and Moongoose in the outlaw biker film *The Hellcats* (Robert F. Slatzer, 1968).[2] Undoubtedly, Hanson's entrepreneurial background spurred him to take his film career into his own hands and become a director. Fully understanding the limitations of low-budget filmmaking from his work with Cardoza, Hanson developed an elaborate plan to make a feature with the type of built-in publicity that would enable him to subsequently make more expensive pictures. Not content to simply make a routine exploitation film, he was audacious enough to try and produce a film that would succeed where the police had failed—apprehend the Zodiac. "I shot it with the intention of bringing it up to San Francisco and four-walling a theater, which I did, with six guys to set a trap and catch that son of a bitch," the director admitted. "I was gonna catch him and use that for the end of the film, and I thought that would then launch me into making other films with a few more bucks and doing it right" (Poggiali 2012).

The ambition to catch the Zodiac was certainly unique, but the concept of producing a film about a serial murderer during the ongoing manhunt for the real-life subject echoed the recent production history of the Albert DeSalvo-inspired film *The Strangler* (Burt Topper, 1964). This Allied Artists release was originally announced in May 1963 as *The Boston Strangler*, before producers Samuel Bischoff and David Diamond later changed the title in an apparent attempt to distance the narrative from the murders (*Variety* 1963, 16; *Boxoffice* 1963, W-5). In this fascinating antecedent to *The Zodiac Killer*, Victor Buono followed up his Oscar-nominated performance in the thriller *What Ever Happened to Baby Jane?* (Robert Aldrich, 1962) by giving a chilling turn as Leo Kroll, a medical technician who, in the words of the film's gregarious heavy-set star, "indulges a hearty case of paranoiac schizophrenia by following ladies home at night and garroting them with their stockings" (*Austin Statesman* 1964, 18). The film was released in April 1964, six months before the arrest of the 33-year-old handyman DeSalvo, who confessed to murdering thirteen women between June 1962 and January 1964.[3]

Hanson scraped up a paltry $13,000 and shot *The Zodiac Killer* on 16mm (subsequently blown up to 35mm for release) through his company, Adventure Productions, over the course of three weeks in 1971. The gorilla nature of the production is exemplified by the fact that the cast and crew were composed of mostly inexperienced friends and family, all of whom reportedly worked without pay. In the role of the Zodiac, Hanson cast actor Hal Reed, who, according to the director, "I ran into and I thought, shit, you could play this guy . . . I thought he might be going somewhere" (Poggiali 2012). Despite its no-name stars (minus veteran comedian Doodles Weaver, who appears in a minor role) and minimal production values, the film remains unnerving due its nihilistic depiction of an early 1970s San Francisco brewing with family dysfunction, illicit sex, and misogyny.

After the film's opening sequence featuring the random murders of both a police officer (shot in the head while ironically reading Sinclair Lewis's 1935 novel *It Can't Happen Here*) and a teenage girl walking home from school in a suburban neighborhood, Hanson and his co-screenwriters Ray Cantrell and Manny Cardoza present the audience with two potential suspects: a young mailman, Jerry (Reed), and a middle-aged truck driver, Grover McDerry (Bob Jones). Each are depicted as emotionally isolated with a seething hatred of women. While the cynical Jerry is reluctantly delivering Christmas cards (muttering "A waste of money. Who gives a damn, anyway?"), he gets into an abrasive argument with a landlady, Mrs. Crocker (Bertha Dahl), who is upset with him for not putting the advertising circulars in the mailboxes of her residents. Jerry's hostile behavior directed toward women is equaled by Grover, who is shown being belligerent with his ex-wife Helen (Dion Marinkovich) over alimony payments and her refusal to let him have visitations with his daughter Julie (Stacy Videen). His violent capabilities are further foregrounded when he gets into a fight with a female patron, Barbara (Barbara Schillaci), at Annette's Bar when she laughs at him after removing his toupee.

Although Jerry is shortly thereafter revealed to be the Zodiac, both men's misogynistic tendencies, uncontrollable anger, and quick trigger for violence demonstrate that both were equally capable of being the murderer. Among the more disquieting aspects of the film is that these traits are not only exhibited by Jerry and Grover, but also, to greater and lesser degrees, in several of the other male characters. These men include Jerry's elderly neighbor Doc (Weaver), who crassly utters, "Once they get over twenty, they're all no damn good." This negative attitude is further demonstrated by Paul (played by Hanson in a cameo), who tells Gloria (Norma Michaels) that he possesses no interest in marrying his pregnant girlfriend, Marlene, who he thinks may have been unfaithful toward him. These multiple examples serve to underscore Jerry's point—stated to his dead rabbit Leo—that people are "no good." These dark depictions suggest that the Zodiac is symptomatic of cultural tensions over changing attitudes about gender dynamics and sexual practices during the period.

Although he would only have a handful of roles after making the film (notably the lead in Hanson's second and final feature, the 1972 drug-smuggling action film *A Ton of Grass Goes to Pot*, aka *The Big Score*), Reed provides a convincing performance as the Zodiac. In this part docudrama, part fictionalization of the murders, the murderer is an unassuming everyman, who is depicted as an alienated male unable to make meaningful social connections, echoing the characterizations of Mark Lewis (Carl Boehm) in *Peeping Tom* (Michael Powell, 1960), Norman Bates (Anthony Perkins) in *Psycho* (Alfred Hitchcock, 1960), and Leo Kroll in *The Strangler*. Jerry demonstrates a softer side in his interactions with his pet rabbits (recalling Marlon Brando's brutish yet sensitive Terry Malloy with his pigeons in director Elia Kazan's 1954 film *On the Waterfront*), particularly when he sobs as he buries one of them that he unexpectedly finds dead in its cage. When asked about these scenes of vulnerability, Hanson admitted that they were "just made-up shit," but, at the same time, they reflect the childlike depictions of serial murderers that followed in the aftermath of both *Peeping Tom* and *Psycho* at the beginning of the previous decade (Poggiali 2012).

These fictitious elements are offset by realistic recreations of the murders, which were informed by inside knowledge of the case from journalist Paul Avery of *The San Francisco Chronicle* (portrayed by Robert Downey Jr. in Fincher's *Zodiac*) who served as a consultant and contributed a testimonial at the beginning of the film that stressed that "if some of the scenes, dialogue, and letters seem strange and unreal, remember—they happened." While not entirely based on fact, the film's scenes of the Zodiac shooting two young couples—Marilyn (Gloria Gunn) and Judd (Richard Styles), and Sandy (Jo Porrine) and Bill (Arthur Porrine)—and later a homophobic cab driver are eerily similar to the attacks on Michael Renault Mageau and Darlene Elizabeth Ferrin in Blue Rock Springs Park, Bryan Calvin Hartnell and Cecelia Ann Shepard at Lake Berryessa, and Paul Stine in the San Francisco neighborhood of Presidio Heights on October 11, 1969, respectively. These disturbing recreations are interspersed with a series of additional fictionalized murders, notably a pair of outrageous ones where the Zodiac kills two stranded female motorists with a spare tire and the hood of a car. Although possessing more than a generous dose of artistic license, these fictionalized murders strangely foreground, even if unintentionally, the fact that the Zodiac was known to take credit for additional crimes that he did not commit.

However, the theatrical premiere of *The Zodiac Killer* is more sensational than anything that was seen on the screen. After completing postproduction on the film, Hanson arranged to have it screened in the balcony "Penthouse Theatre" of the twin-screen RKO Golden Gate Theatre on Taylor Street in San Francisco. The film's modest promotional campaign included a raffle giveaway for a Kawasaki 350cc motorcycle and a poster tagline asking, "Who is he . . . What is he . . . When is he going to strike again?" Hanson orchestrated an elaborate plan to answer these pressing questions at the film's premiere on April 7, 1971. Believing the egotism of the Zodiac would compel him to attend, the director had all of those in attendance fill out a raffle card for the motorcycle, which asked them to answer the question, "I think the Zodiac kills because . . ." As each cinemagoer deposited their card in the box, a man hiding inside would check the handwriting against one of the Zodiac's published letters. If there was a match, a signaling system would be used to alert another man hiding in a nearby refrigerator, who would identify the suspect and signal others in the lobby to apprehend him (Poggiali 2012; Collis 2017, 76, 78).

During one of the screenings, a handwriting match was made, but, according to Hanson, they were unable to make a positive identification due to a series of unfortunate mistakes. The director also claimed that he and his associates briefly interrogated one suspicious man, who resembled the suspect in the well-circulated composite sketch released by the San Francisco Police Department. However, they were forced to let him go due to the fact that they did not have any evidence to give to the police. Hanson spent the next several years trying to help the police build a case against the suspect, but, given a lack of financial resources, was compelled to step aside (Poggiali 2012). The film subsequently disappeared as well. By the time *Dirty Harry* was released, *The Zodiac Killer* was reviewed unfavorably to its larger-budgeted successor. "If you saw *Dirty Harry* you have already seen this plot done much better and with less exploitation," asserted film critic Douglas Wayne of *The Daily Chronicle* when the double-bill reached the De-Val Drive-In in DeKalb, Illinois, in late February 1972 (Wayne 1972, 4). Yet, even if *The Zodiac Killer* failed in its objective to catch the Zodiac, it remains an unnerving film due, in large part, to the narrative's intermittent accuracy to the real-life horror that it depicts.

SAM DOBBS MEETS THE ZODIAC (JOHN LAMB, 1971)

Undoubtedly, the most shameless film to capitalize on the hysteria over the Zodiac investigation was *Sam Dobbs Meets the Zodiac* (John Lamb, 1971), a hardcore adult film released directly on the heels of *The Zodiac Killer*. The film was a quickly made sequel to *Sam Dobbs, Private Dick* (1971, also released under the even more tactless title *Sam Dobbs and the Guru Gangbang*) and, according to newspaper ads from the period, played such adult theaters as the Sho-Mor in Tucson, Arizona, in May 1971 and the Amusu in Corpus Christi, Texas, later that June—as well as, reportedly, other venues in Chicago and Los Angeles early the next year.[4] Mirroring the first entry of the series, *Sam Dobbs Meets the Zodiac* is a pornographic by-product of the renewed popularity of the hard-boiled private detective film with audiences in late 1960s and early 1970s. This interest was galvanized by a sub-cycle of detective-centered neo noirs that were released following the Hollywood box-office success of *Harper* (Jack Smight, 1966), but did not reach their creative apex until the height of Watergate with the more cynical New Hollywood films *The Long Goodbye* (Robert Altman, 1973) and *Chinatown* (Roman Polanski, 1974).

Both entries of the *Sam Dobbs* series featured the title anti-hero (Buddy Boone), a clean-cut private detective with a moniker apparently derived from the Humphrey Bogart characters Sam Spade in *The Maltese Falcon* (John Huston, 1941) and Fred C. Dobbs in *The Treasure of the Sierra Madre* (Huston, 1948). This peculiar blend of "porn noir" was riding the success of the *Johnny Wadd* series (1970–87) starring John Holmes, whose self-purported 16-inch "endowment" made him a 1970s adult film icon and, reportedly, the inspiration for Mark Wahlberg's character Dirk Diggler in the critically acclaimed drama *Boogie Nights* (Paul Thomas Anderson, 1997) (Erickson 2017, 220).[5] Both the *Johnny Wadd* and *Sam Dobbs* films shed the sexual innuendo that was indicative of classical Hollywood film noir and replaced it with an unabashedly hardcore explicitness, which soon became increasingly mainstream given the surprising box-office returns of the controversial adult films *Deep Throat* (Gerard Damiano, 1972), *Behind the Green Door* (Artie and Jim Mitchell, 1972), and *The Devil in Miss Jones* (Damiano, 1973).

Holmes was cast alongside Boone in *Sam Dobbs Meets the Zodiac* as "The Zodiac," the subject of Dobbs's latest investigation. As opposed to the mailman antagonist in *The Zodiac Killer*, the proclivities of this Zodiac bear little resemblance to his real-life counterpart and, in fact, he does not kill anyone throughout the film's scant 63-minute running time. The psychopath is instead a serial rapist and "Peeping Tom," who taunts Dobbs with cryptic phone calls (typically containing sexually suggestive clues) as he prays on a series of young women. Well aware of the Zodiac's crimes, the women are crassly portrayed as sex starved and eager to become his next victim.

If the onscreen Toschi from Fincher's *Zodiac* left a screening of *Dirty Harry* demoralized, one can only imagine how he would have felt about his alter-ego in *Sam Dobbs Meets the Zodiac*. Not only is Dobbs suffering from similar feelings of frustration about not being able to apprehend the rapist, but he also resents the fact that his failures have been plastered on the front page of the newspaper with the headline, "Zodiac Rapist Baffles Dobbs Detective." Not surprisingly, in a narrative of this type, Dobbs's secretary is called upon to restore the emasculated detective's lack of self-confidence. "The Zodiac couldn't possibly be as good as you, Dobbs," she assures him as the two make love on the top of his office desk. Nevertheless, Dobbs's renewed feeling of potency is undermined by the Zodiac, who, unbeknownst to the detective, is masturbating while gazing at them voyeuristically behind a cracked door.

Experienced in underwater filming from his low-budget film *Mermaids of Tiburon* (1962) and work as an underwater photographer on the popular television programs *Sea Hunt* (syndicated, 1958–61) and *Voyage to the Bottom of the Sea* (ABC, 1964–68), the film's uncredited director John Lamb included an elaborate sex sequence in *Sam Dobbs Meets the Zodiac* featuring the Zodiac ravishing a blonde woman (Linda Vroom) in a swimming pool. Lamb crosscuts between the underwater sexual imagery (boasting low-angle and spinning shots that have a low-rent Busby Berkeley quality) with shots of Dobbs receiving fellatio from one of his secretaries as he drives his sedan in hot pursuit of the Zodiac. The film's absurd sex scenes also possess a mocking, anti-establishment undercurrent. Not only is traditional detective work depicted as inept to catch this breed of criminal, but also the plaid-suited Dobbs is frequently laughed at or chastised by the Zodiac's female victims for interrupting the rapist's crimes. In the film's final moments, it is instead the Zodiac's egotism that is his undoing. After boldly barging into Dobbs's office to attack one of his secretaries, he is sexually subdued by an undercover policewoman (Andy Bellamy), who finally brings his crime spree to an end.

Certainly, one of the oddest examples of "Zodiacsploitation," *Sam Dobbs Meets the Zodiac* employs only a minimal number of Zodiac tropes (namely an obsessive detective hunting a serial criminal, who receives attention from the press by leaving bizarre clues) and uses them solely as a means to exploit the sensationalism surrounding the Zodiac investigation. More disturbingly, the film's fetishization of male rape fantasies both trivializes the act of rape and makes the narrative a thoroughly unpleasant affair (even by the already low standards of 1970s adult cinema) and likely limited its appeal to only the most perverse of the trench-coated crowd.

DIRTY HARRY (DON SIEGEL, 1971)

In stark contrast to the ineffectual Sam Dobbs, Inspector Harry Callahan emerged as the quintessential "super cop" of the New Hollywood cinema when *Dirty Harry* was released in late December 1971. The rogue nature of the character (later reprised by Eastwood in four successful sequels from 1973–88) was encapsulated in the tagline created by Warner Brothers for the studio's domestic publicity campaign: "You don't assign him to murder cases. You just turn him loose." Eastwood's Callahan followed in the footsteps of Steve McQueen's Lieutenant Frank Bullitt in *Bullitt* (Peter Yates, 1968) and Gene Hackman's Detective Jimmy "Popeye" Doyle in *The French Connection* (William Friedkin, 1971) as a tough and disillusioned anti-hero, who, despite carrying a badge (a symbol of the legal establishment that he renounces in the film's memorable final shot), bucked the "system" due to his adamant belief that violence and unorthodox police methods were, at times, necessary to fight an emerging breed of criminal that was beyond the pale. Rejecting due process and Miranda rights, Callahan would prefer his superiors to permit him to simply, in his own words, "meet up with the son of a bitch."

Each of these rogue cops were, in part, inspired by the exploits of real-life metropolitan detectives. Doyle was based on Eddie Egan of the New

York Police Department, who, in 1962, was instrumental in taking down an organized crime ring trying to move 112 pounds of heroin (Rotella 2002, 111). On the other hand, the bravado and style of both Bullitt and Callahan were instead loosely influenced by the real-life Inspector David Toschi of the San Francisco Police Department. Due to his high-profile status as the chief investigator in the Zodiac case, Toschi was cited as "one of the best-known big city cops in the world" (Reiterman and Glover 1978, 1). His demeanor and flamboyant appearance gave him the aura of a Hollywood star. "From his shoulder holster, to his broad bow tie, to the dark, curly hair that caused some to call him the Eddie Fisher of the Hall of Justice, he fit central casting's ideal of a dedicated detective unravelling knots and tangles of words and evidence," journalists Tim Reiterman and Malcolm Glover mused in *The San Francisco Examiner* (Reiterman and Glover 1978, 18). Even Hollywood stood up and took notice of Toschi. Not only did his "upside-down holster" inspire the one worn by McQueen in *Bullitt* (Graysmith 1996, 96), but also actor Karl Malden once admitted how much of an impression this trademark sidearm made on both him and Michael Douglas when they met Toschi during production of their hit television crime drama *The Streets of San Francisco* (ABC, 1972–77) (Alexander 1976, 35). If Toschi had succeeded in his quest to bring the Zodiac to justice, perhaps the detective would have been able to use his celebrity as an entryway into Hollywood—similar to Egan, who capitalized on his notoriety as the "real-life Popeye Doyle" to work steadily as a character actor and technical advisor in film and television throughout the 1970s and 1980s.[6]

Callahan, like his predecessors Bullitt and Doyle, channeled the social outrage that was surging in the United States during the late 1960s and early 1970s. The cultural climate was ripe for an anti-hero, in part due to the "post-Vietnam rejection of liberal policies toward crime" as Matthew Sorrento (2012, 61) has noted.[7] Yet, despite the immense popularity of these film characters, each of them are, as Christopher Barry aptly observes, "right-wing vigilantes" demonstrating "borderline psychotic behaviour." He explains:

> these cops are remarkably close in spirit to Paul Schrader/Robert De Niro's Travis Bickle in *Taxi Driver* (Martin Scorsese, 1976). Each of them—the cops, Bickle—"God's lonely man" unhappily embroiled within the "system," personifying a "real rain" ready, and more than willing to "wash the scum off the streets." However, cops can pop a bullet in a brain in the name of the law, while Bickle remains on the periphery of edict. (Barry 2004, 78)

Despite the parallels between the rogue cops of *Dirty Harry*, *Bullitt*, and *The French Connection*, part of what makes director Don Siegel's film particularly seductive is the fact that Callahan's extreme measures can be read, at least dramatically, as being more justified. This stems from the fact that his onscreen nemesis, unlike the antagonists of these other two crime thrillers, is characterized one-dimensionally as the embodiment of evil.

The object of Callahan's manhunt is Scorpio (Andrew Robinson), a deranged rooftop sniper whose astrological moniker leaves little doubt about the filmmakers' source of inspiration. Mirroring the Zodiac, Scorpio puts the city of San Francisco in a state of dread and panic with a series of random shootings. This killing spree commences with the shooting of a young woman in a yellow bathing suit (Diana Davidson) swimming atop the rooftop pool of the Holiday Inn Select Downtown and Spa on Kearny Street. The interrelationship between the real-life and fictional murderers is implied through Siegel and cinematographer Bruce Surtee's employment of a point-of-view shot from the perspective of Scorpio, who gazes at the woman from the roof of a nearby office building through the scope of his .30-06 rifle. The voyeuristic image of the soon-to-be-killed woman seen through Scorpio's cross-hairs recalls the symbol of the Zodiac (speculated to have been co-opted from the one emblazoned on Zodiac "Sea Wolf" wristwatches), which he used as his signature in his letters to the press (Graysmith 1996, 320; Graysmith 2007, ix). After the woman's body is discovered, Callahan arrives at the crime scene and locates a letter from Scorpio—further linking the onscreen murderer with his offscreen counterpart.

In this first in a series of foreboding letters, Scorpio expresses his delight in taunting the city's legal establishment, epitomized by the mayor (John Vernon) and the chief of police (John Larch). The murderer warns that he will continue his shooting spree unless the city pays his hefty ransom demand of $100,000. The letter is devoid of the ciphers that typified those penned by the Zodiac. However, it contains his trademark poor grammar and scratched out portions. More interestingly, while both the Zodiac and Scorpio derived pleasure from killing, the latter, to some degree, lacks the former's predisposition to primarily target white women. The opening scene and the subsequent kidnapping and murder of 14-year-old Ann Mary Deacon (played by an uncredited Debralee Scott) show that he has no objection to killing white women, yet he also directs his wrath at African Americans, homosexuals, and children. Not only is Scorpio depicted as someone who believes in equally affording death to everyone, but he is also portrayed in a manner that is devoid of any significant degree of humanization. Just as the character's description in the film's ending credits suggest, he is "The Killer" plain and simple.

Considering the intense media scrutiny attached to the Zodiac investigation, the fact that Siegel and his collaborators appropriated the Zodiac as one of their sources of inspiration is not surprising. In a draft of the script dated April 1, 1971, the film's screenwriters Harry Julian Fink, Rita M. Fink, and

Dean Riesner (the latter was brought in by Siegel and Eastwood to tighten the husband-and-wife team's script) more overtly outlined the character's physical image as a mundane, middle-aged everyman. This aligns with the composite sketch of a bespectacled Zodiac with an undistinguished face and a crewcut, which was produced by the San Francisco Police Department and circulated on wanted posters in mid-October 1969.[8] Scorpio was described in the film script as:

> middle-sized, nondescript, in his mid-thirties, hair [sic?] colored hair, going thin. You've seen him a hundred times and never really noticed him; he's Mr. Nobody, a million pale strangers rolled into one.

This depiction coincides with the version that actor Andrew Robinson (who played Scorpio) was first presented with, after the more prominent stars Keir Dullea and Rip Torn turned down the role. "Siegel and I created that character," Robinson has stated. "The screenwriters had some balding guy with a paunch in a white t-shirt hanging around Greyhound bus terminals. He was something altogether different" (Petkovich 1996, 51).

Despite the strong parallels between Scorpio and the Zodiac, the previously discussed scene in Fincher's film *Zodiac* has helped obscure the fact that Scorpio is a composite of a wide range of true crime antecedent figures from late 1960s and early 1970s American culture. The depiction of Scorpio as a baby-faced sniper recalls the "Texas Tower Sniper" Charles Whitman, whose notorious shooting rampage from atop the tower observation deck of the University of Texas campus on August 1, 1966, resulted in the deaths of seventeen victims and later served as inspiration for the drive-in shooter Bobby Thompson (Tim O'Kelly) in director Peter Bogdanovich's thriller *Targets* (1968).[9] Not only were Whitman and Scorpio both portrayed as young baby-faced snipers, but also, given that each served time in the military, they resonated with Vietnam-era audiences convinced that American males were coming back from the war traumatized with PTSD and having difficulty reintegrating themselves back into civilian life.

Additionally, the tense sequence featuring Scorpio forcing Callahan to run a bag of ransom money across San Francisco in order to save the life of Ann Mary Deacon, who he has kidnapped and buried alive bears striking similarities with the true case of Barbara Jane Mackle. In December 1968, convicted thief Gary Stephen Krist kidnapped the 20-year-old Emory University student from her motel room and entombed her in a coffin for three and a half days in order to extort money from her father, Robert F. Mackle, a millionaire real-estate developer from Miami.[10] Furthermore, Scorpio embodied early 1970s anxieties from both sides of the political aisle about crazed hippies (suggested by the peace symbol on Scorpio's belt buckle), homosexuals (alluded in the killer's sexually suggestive remark, "My, that's a big one," when Callahan removes his .44 Magnum from his holster), and other transgressive figures that were outside the parameters of the cultural mainstream. Robinson recognizes how "the character really encapsulated the tension of the time." Nevertheless, he admits that "the details were all in the subtext. The movie never spelled out this history" (Latchem 2008, 18).

LOU GRANT: "SAMARITAN" (PAUL LEAF, CBS, 1979)

The last and, in terms of its relationship to the Zodiac investigation, among the more interesting of these 1970s narratives is "Samaritan." This well-written and engrossing gem was aired on CBS on February 12, 1979 (later repeated on July 9), during the second season of *Lou Grant*. During its five-season run from 1977 to 1982, this dramatic series starring Edward Asner garnered thirteen Emmy Awards for its dramatic reworking of the actor's portrayal of the gruff but likable newsman from the hit sitcom *The Mary Tyler Moore Show* (CBS, 1970–77). This spin-off followed in the footsteps of the film *All the President's Men* (Alan J. Pakula, 1976) by creating an hour-long drama set at a fictional newspaper, which probed provocative and timely news stories of the period with a greater semblance of docudrama realism. In this installment, *Los Angeles Tribune* city editor Lou Grant and his dedicated team of journalists are faced with a dilemma about how to cover the reemergence of a serial murderer dubbed "Samaritan."

Five years earlier, from April to October 1973, Los Angeles was terrorized by this psychotic madman, who slayed six stranded motorists and hitchhikers while posing as a good Samaritan. The unpredictable nature of the murderer was the fact that, as he admitted in a series of ominous letters that he sent to the newspaper, he did not always kill his intended victims. On rare occasions, he would instead help them before disappearing into the night. At the height of the hysteria, over thirty detectives (led by the now-retired Lieutenant Bill Bergin, played by John Larch) were assigned to track down the murderer, before, in the vein of the Zodiac after his January 29, 1974, letter to *The San Francisco Chronicle*, he suddenly ceased communication and stopped killing without reason. "It is like a nightmare that all of a sudden stopped," managing editor Charles Hume (Mason Adams) recalls of the unsolved murders. "Samaritan back! I hate to think this city is going to have to go through that trauma again."

Hume urges Grant to assign the story to veteran reporter Jim McCrea (Ben Piazza), since he is an authority on Samaritan. McCrea built his reputation as a journalist on his prior coverage of the Samaritan murders. After initially deciding to withhold publication of the letter to keep from inciting the publicity-seeking madman to kill again, Grant and Hume are forced to later run it when the newspaper's colorful, alcoholic columnist Jack Towne (Richard B. Shull) leaks the news of Samaritan's return in his column. Mirroring the public reaction from five years earlier, the city of Los Angeles goes into a state of panic, which results in an actual good Samaritan being shot by a panicked motorist changing his tire. Further complicating matters, a psychologically disturbed man (James Gammon) turns himself in to the police after confessing to not only the Samaritan murders, but also, as McCrea states, "the Black Dahlia killing, the Lindbergh kidnapping, and the murder of Dr. Richard Kimble's wife." While the police grow increasingly bewildered at why Samaritan has yet to kill anyone, reporter Joe Rossi (Robert Walden) learns from the murderer's former police adversary Bergin that the new letters are forgeries. This startling revelation leads Grant to suspect that McCrea penned the letters himself to reinvigorate his sagging career and generate interest in his unpublished book manuscript about the Samaritan murders.

The script by novelist and screenwriter Elliot West is fascinating for its numerous allusions to both the Zodiac investigation and its cinematic intertexts, particularly *Dirty Harry* from eight years before. Not only does the episode draw upon the then-recent memory of the Zodiac with its depiction of Samaritan as a nondescript madman seeking the limelight of the press, but also the murderer, like his real-life counterpart, fuels city-wide terror by writing letters to the press that are characterized by a faux semi-literacy with "no punctuation, no capitals, words left out, printing like a child." Moreover, Samaritan possesses an ominous calling card by subverting the character archetype of the "Good Samaritan" (a biblical variation of the astrological names of the Zodiac and Scorpio in *Dirty Harry*) and signing each of his letters with a verse from Luke 10. Echoing *Dirty Harry* and anticipating Fincher's *Zodiac*, traditional police detection is largely portrayed as being inhibited by bureaucracy and egotism. Instead, outsiders of the system (the rogue cop Callahan in *Dirty Harry*, and the newspapermen Grant and Rossi in "Samaritan" and Graysmith in *Zodiac*) are compelled to seek justice on their own. Among the subtler nods to the legacy of the Zodiac in popular culture is the casting of Larch as Lieutenant Bergin, since the character actor was, at the time, best known to 1970s American audiences for having played the bureaucratic chief of police in *Dirty Harry*. The presence of the always reliable Larch suggests that the creative team behind *Lou Grant* did their homework and were well aware of the films connected to the Zodiac investigation.

Despite being cited as "the least fulfilling [episode of the second season] in terms of its journalistic content" by Douglass K. Daniel in his 1996 study *Lou Grant: The Making of TV's Top Newspaper Drama*, "Samaritan" was actually quite attentive to then-recent press reports surrounding the Zodiac investigation, particularly the Zodiac forgery accusations leveled against David Toschi the year before (Daniel 1996, 98). On April 24, 1978, an apparent Zodiac letter was sent to *The San Francisco Chronicle*, which declared his return and stated, "That city pig Toschi is good. but I am smarter and better he will get tired then leave me alone" (Graysmith 1996, 207). At the time, the letter was suspected to be the first correspondence from the Zodiac in four years and put the city of San Francisco again on high alert. Yet, after first being deemed authentic by police experts, the letter was shortly thereafter discredited as a forgery. In the weeks following, Toschi was accused of having penned the letter to draw increased attention to both him and his pet case. These accusations were compounded by the fact that the detective admitted to having sent anonymous fan letters praising his exploits to author Armistead Maupin of the *Tales of the City* series of novels (Graysmith 2007, 189). Although Toschi denied forging the Zodiac letter and was subsequently cleared, the detective's reputation was irrevocably damaged and, consequently, found himself reassigned by the San Francisco Police Department to "pawn shop detail" (Graysmith 2007, 189).[11]

Always known for ripping many of its storylines directly from contemporary headlines, *Lou Grant* apparently based its characterization of McCrea on Toschi. In a tearful eleventh-hour confession to Grant that is as swift as a witness box admission at the end of a typical *Perry Mason* episode (CBS, 1957–66), McCrea insists that a strange force within him compelled him to pen the new Samaritan letters. "It was someone else. Someone I didn't know, who wrote those letters . . . at my desk with my hands," the reporter admits. "I couldn't stop him. I wanted it so much. I miss Samaritan, Lou. I hated him, but I missed him. When he was around, the world was so much more alive." It is almost impossible to not retroactively observe parallels between McCrea and Jake Gyllenhaal's depiction of Graysmith in *Zodiac*—two newspaper men whose obsession with a serial murderer compels them to both solve the case and write a book. In the process, both destroy their marriages (McCrea's wife, like Graysmith's wife Melanie in Fincher's film, is said to have divorced him) and are left emotionally isolated. In a bizarre example of life mirroring art, the real-life Graysmith's account of the forged Zodiac letter eerily echoes the words of McCrea in "Samaritan," specifically the phrase, "I wanted it so much." In *Zodiac Unmasked*, Graysmith wrote, "I wanted it to be authentic, but as time went by, my doubts about the letter increased. The cunning forgery would cause agony for everyone" (Graysmith 2007, 184). Both of these sets of phrases highlight the degree to which an unsolved crime can forever haunt not just the victims and police investigators, but also those journalists committed to telling the story.

Except for a brief mention in Graysmith's *Zodiac Unmasked* that erroneously cited "Samaritan" as being about a serial murderer named "The Judge," the parallels with the Zodiac investigation appear to have gone mostly unnoticed (Graysmith 2007, 457). Interestingly, in a 1979 newspaper profile of the *Lou Grant* series, Bill Hayden of Gannett News Service read the episode as a composite of both "the Los Angeles Strangler [aka 'The Hillside Strangler'] and New York City's Son of Sam cases" (Hayden 1979, 18). There is irony in this misinterpretation, especially considering the fact that the forged Zodiac letter contained a line expressing the serial murderer's supposed desire to see "a good movie" about him and the case. "Samaritan" provided a solid attempt at a television reimagination of both the Zodiac investigation and the forged letter controversy. Nevertheless, as suggested by both Hayden's article and the lack of any mention of the case in Daniel's book, few detected the striking similarities.

The fact that the Zodiac has been subsequently depicted or, in some cases, reimagined in such diverse films as *The Exorcist III* (William Peter Blatty, 1990), *The Zodiac Killer* (Ulli Lommel, 2005), *The Zodiac* (Alexander Bulkley, 2005), *Curse of the Zodiac* (Lommel, 2007), *Awakening the Zodiac* (Jonathan Wright, 2017), and, of course, Fincher's *Zodiac* demonstrates an enduring cinematic fascination with the serial murderer's macabre exploits. However, despite the strong merits of Blatty and Fincher's films in particular, they lack the disquieting immediacy that *The Zodiac Killer*, *Sam Dobbs Meets the Zodiac*, *Dirty Harry*, and "Samaritan" possess to the Zodiac's reign of terror. Each of these films tap into the zeitgeist of this dark and contentions period, which, in the words of Paul Avery in his testimonial at the beginning of *The Zodiac Killer*, brought about "awareness of a present danger."

NOTES

1. Interestingly, the Avenue Theatre's domed ceiling featured "all the symbols of the Zodiac" painted along the chandelier in the auditorium (Graysmith 2007, 194).

2. Both Cardoza productions were relegated mostly to the American drive-in circuit, before later garnering a new cult audience in the 1990s from being lampooned on the comedic television series *Mystery Science Theater 3000* (KTMA, The Comedy Channel/Comedy Central, The Sci-Fi Channel, Netflix, 1988—present). For more information on the films of Cardoza, see Lacy 1962, 30A; Weaver n.d., "Anthony"; and Weaver n.d., "Return."

3. In another curious parallel between *The Zodiac Killer* and *The Strangler*, both films were soon afterward followed by big-budget Hollywood features, which featured similar villains in narratives with slicker production values: *The Boston Strangler* (Richard Flesicher, 1968, starring Tony Curtis in one of his finest performances as DeSalvo) and *Dirty Harry*, respectively.

4. See newspaper ads for *Sam Dobbs Meets the Zodiac* 1971a, 25 and 1971b, 11D. According to the liner notes for After Hours Cinema's DVD release of the

film (retitled *The Zodiac Rapist*), the film played in Chicago and Los Angeles in early 1972.

5. For more information on the life and work of John Holmes, see Sugar and Nelson 2010.

6. According to screenwriter Pete Hamill, Eddie Egan craved celebrity and was instrumental in creating his own legend, as he found out when working with him on the crime thriller *Badge 373* (Howard W. Koch, 1973). "He had left the police force and was living in Fort Lauderdale, trying to get into the movies," Hamill recounted. "I couldn't tell how much was Egan and how much was a performance for me. Eddie was his own fictional creation" (Rotella 2002, 165).

7. For further analysis of *Dirty Harry* in relationship to the film's sociopolitical context, see Cagin and Dray 1984, 212 and Street 2016.

8. Dean Riesner was brought in by Don Siegel to rewrite the original draft of the script by the husband-and-wife team of Harry Julian Fink and Rita M. Fink on the strength of his previous work on the films *Coogan's Bluff* (Don Siegel, 1968) and *Play Misty for Me* (Clint Eastwood, 1971). A close examination of two drafts of the script (one dated November 17, 1970, credited to Terrence Malick, John Milius, and Harry Julian Fink, and one dated April 1, 1971, credited to Harry Julian Fink and Dean Riesner) allows one to safely speculate that the majority of the characterization was conceived by the Finks and Riesner. Even though the Malick and Milius rewrite of the Fink script also revolves around the hunt for a sniper, the characterization bares only the slightest resemblance to Scorpio in the finished film.

9. See chapter 1, pp. 21–24. For more information on Charles Whitman and the UT shootings, see Lavergne 1997.

10. The Barbara Jane Mackle kidnapping was also dramatized for the small screen in two different made-for-television films: *The Longest Night* (Jack Smight, 1972) with David Janssen, James Farentino, and Phyllis Thaxter; and *83 Hours 'Til Dawn* (Donald Wrye, 1990) with Peter Strauss, Robert Urich, and Paul Winfield. For additional information on the case, see Krist 1972 and Miller 1971.

11. For more information on the forgery allegations against Toschi, see *San Francisco Examiner* 1978, 1, 12; Day 1978, 3; and *Los Angeles Times* 1978, 1.

REFERENCES

After Hours Collector. 2014. "*Zodiac Rapist*: 2-DVD Grindhouse Collection." Liner notes for *Zodiac Rapist* (*Sam Dobbs Meets the Zodiac*, John Lamb, 1971). After Hours Cinema AH-4244, 2014, DVD.

Alexander, Dick. 1976. "People: Color." *San Francisco Examiner*, November 5.

Austin Statesman. 1964. "To Regulate Roles, Buono Cuts Down on the Eating." (Austin, TX), March 31.

Barry, Christopher. 2004. "Violent Justice: Italian Crime/Cop Films of the 1970s." In *Alternative Europe: Eurotrash and Exploitation Cinema Since 1945*, edited by Ernest Mathijs, and Xavier Mendik, 77–89. London, UK: Wallflower Press.

Boxoffice. 1963. "*Boston Strangler* Now *Strangler*." September 2.

———. 1971. "Los Angeles." June 14.

Cagin, Seth, and Philip Dray. 1984. *Hollywood Films of the Seventies: Sex, Drugs, Violence, Rock 'n' Roll and Politics*. New York, NY: Harper & Row.

Collis, Clark. 2017. "To Catch the Zodiac Killer." *Entertainment Weekly*, June 2.

Connell, Richard. 2011/1924. "The Most Dangerous Game." In *The Big Book of Adventure Stories*, edited by Otto Penzler, 126–35. New York, NY: Vintage Crime/ Black Lizard.

Connolly, Mike. 1964. "Notes from Hollywood." *Independent* (Pasadena, CA), August 18.

Day, Nancy. 1978. "Maupin on the Spot: A Real-Life Tale of the City." *San Francisco Examiner*, July 12.

Daniel, Douglass K. 1996. *Lou Grant: The Making of TV's Top Newspaper Drama*. Syracuse, NY: Syracuse University Press.

Eliot, Marc. 2009. *American Rebel: The Life of Clint Eastwood*. New York, NY: Three Rivers Books.

Erickson, Hal. 2017. *Any Resemblance to Actual Persons: The Real People Behind 400+ Fictional Movie Characters*. Jefferson, NC: McFarland.

Fink, Harry Julian, and Dean Riesner. 1971. *Dirty Harry*. Screenplay, April 1 draft.

Graysmith, Robert. 1996. *Zodiac*. New York, NY: St. Martin's.

———. 2007. *Zodiac Unmasked*. New York, NY: Berkley Books.

Hayden, Bill. 1979. "*Grant* Show Concerns Itself with People." *Ithaca Journal* (Ithaca, NY), February 12.

Krist, Gary. 1972. *Life: The Man Who Kidnapped Barbara Mackle*. New York, NY: Olympia Press.

Lacy, John. 1962. "Doing Well in Dallas: *Beast of Yucca Flats* Seeks Entry to City." *Hartford Courant* (Hartford, CT), January 7.

Latchem, John. 2008. "Scorpio Speaks." *Home Media Retailing* 30 (18): 18.

Lavergne, Gary M. 1997. *A Sniper in the Tower: The Charles Whitman Murders*. Denton, TX: University of North Texas Press.

Malick, Terrence, John Milius, and Harry Julian Fink. 1970. *Dirty Harry*. Screenplay, November 17 draft.

Miller, Gene, and Barbara Jane Mackle. 1971. *83 Hours Till Dawn*. Garden City, NY: Doubleday.

Los Angeles Times. 1978. "Paper Gets Note Believed Written by 'Zodiac Killer.'" April 26.

Petkovich, Andrew. 1996. "Wrestling Scorpio: An Interview with Andrew Robinson." *Psychotronic* 23: 51.

Poggiali, Chris. 2012. "Zodiac Hunter: An Interview with Tom Hanson." *Temple of Schlock*. Last modified December 31, http://templeofschlock.blogspot.com/2012/12/zodiac hunter-interview-with-tom-hanson.html.

Reiterman, Tim, and Malcolm Glover. 1978. "Who is Dave Toschi and Why All the Intrigue?" *San Francisco Examiner*, July 12.

Rotella, Carlo. 2002. *Good with Their Hands: Boxers, Bluesmen, and Other Characters from the Rust Belt*. Berkeley: University of California Press.

Sam Dobbs Meets the Zodiac. 1971a. (John Lamb, 1971). Advertisement. *Tucson Daily Citizen* (Tucson, AZ), May 21.

Sam Dobbs Meets the Zodiac. 1971b. (John Lamb, 1971). Advertisement. *Corpus Christi Times* (Corpus Christi, TX), June 18.

San Francisco Examiner. 1978. "Inspector Toschi Removed—Zodiac Mystery Deepens." July 11.

Sorrento, Matthew. 2012. *The New American Crime Film.* Jefferson, NC: McFarland.

Street, Joe. 2016. *Dirty Harry's America: Clint Eastwood, Harry Callahan, and the Conservative Backlash.* Gainesville: University Press of Florida.

Sugar, Jennifer, and Jill C. Nelson. 2010. *John Holmes: A Life Measured in Inches.* Duncan, OK: BearManor Media.

Thompson, Nathaniel. n.d. "*The Zodiac Killer* (1971)." *TCM.com.* Accessed November 15, 2018, http://www.tcm.com/tcmdb/title/559485/The-Zodiac-Killer/articles.html.

Variety. 1963. "New York Sound Track." May 29.

Variety. 1971a. "Audubon's Pick-up of *Zodiac Killer*." August 18.

Variety. 1971b. "New York Sound Track." August 25.

Wayne, Douglas. 1972. "On the Beat." *Daily Chronicle* (DeKalb, IL), February 26.

Weaver, Tom. n.d. "Anthony Cardoza Recalls the Fallout from *Yucca Flats*." *The Astounding B Monster.* Accessed November 15, 2018, http://www.bmonster.com/scifi37.html.

———. n.d. "Return to *Yucca Flats*: Anthony Cardoza's Tor of the Desert." *The Astounding B Monster.* Accessed November 15, 2018, http://www.bmonster.com/profile37.html.

Chapter 3

Hacked to Pisces

An Interview with Tom Hanson on The Zodiac Killer *(1971)*

Rod Lott

If the world were just, the characters played by Jake Gyllenhaal and Mark Ruffalo in *Zodiac* would not have gone to see *Dirty Harry*. But they do, watching Clint Eastwood and his now-iconic .44 Magnum blow away the psychopathic Scorpio, a thinly fictionalized version of the Zodiac Killer. Afterward, in the theater lobby, Robert Graysmith (Gyllenhaal) expresses confidence that San Francisco police detective Dave Toschi (Ruffalo) will catch his prey. "Pal," responds Toschi, "they're already making movies about it."

Indeed. Released in the Christmas season of 1971, *Dirty Harry* may enjoy household-name status befitting a major studio release, but, as Toschi alluded, Tom Hanson beat Don Siegel to the screen, if not to the pop culture punch. Nearly nine months earlier and made for a low five figures, Hanson's *The Zodiac Killer* (1971) had been unleashed to an unsuspecting, unprepared public. As is the case with many a cult film, it took decades for the public to catch up.

"I'M GONNA HAVE TO STAB YOU PEOPLE!"

Originally titled *Zodiac*, Hanson's movie has one thing Fincher's does not: the onscreen endorsement of Paul Avery, the *San Francisco Chronicle* reporter (eventually played by Robert Downey Jr. for Fincher). Avery lends Hanson's work instant credibility through a statement on the opening titles that reads in part, "If some of the scenes, dialogue, and letters seem strange and unreal, remember—they happened."

The remaining 85 or so minutes squander that credibility, filling in the blanks of the true crime mystery with broad, messy strokes. To say the screenplay colors outside the lines of fact is an understatement. In Hanson's picture, the mass murderer gains an identity: a cocky mailman named Jerry (played by an unknown, Hal Reed) whose living room doubles as a rabbit hutch and his basement, a satanic lair. Considerable time is devoted to the crabapple Jerry making his rounds and interacting with people he obviously despises; even more time is dedicated to him hanging out with his best friend, Grover (Bob Jones), an overweight, balding divorcée who nonetheless considers himself quite the catch, so long as the ladies keep their mitts off his feather duster of a toupée: "Bitch, I told you a thousand times: Don't touch my hair!"

Grover overshadows the first half hour, what with repeated glimpses at his miserable existence, to a point where some viewers mistakenly assume he fills the title role. Just when viewers may start to think *The Zodiac Killer* lacks, well, *killing*, Act 2 sees Jerry embark on a homicidal spree following his pal's impulsive suicide by cop. The "strange and unreal" scenes kick in at a quick clip, including Jerry:

Figure 3.1 Photo of Tom Hanson. Courtesy of Scott Hanson.

- stalking women at the playground, in broad daylight;
- smashing an elderly woman's noggin with her own spare tire, in broad daylight;
- stabbing swimsuit-clad lovers (after a courteous heads-up of "I'm gonna have to stab you people!") in broad daylight;
- pushing a rolling bed-ridden retirement-home resident down one of Frisco's trademark super-steep streets, in broad daylight;
- and laughing as he phones the police to report his own murders, in broad daylight.

That list is merely partial. At least *The Zodiac Killer* concludes with one touch of reality, as Jerry remains on the loose, arrogantly evading authorities and ominously prowling the streets for his next victim—perhaps even *you*. Its dialogue is laughable. Its situations, preposterous. Its performances, amateurish. Its overall existence, hysterical. Despite its faults, but largely because of them, the movie is never boring. Not for nothing did it find life decades later through Something Weird Video (SWV).

"CATCH THAT SON OF A BITCH!"

What makes Hanson's film more than a curiosity, however, is the story *behind* it. In short, in a move that out-*Argo*s the faux sci-fi feature that drives the plot of *Argo*, Hanson claims to have gone through the trouble of helming his first feature not to grasp Tinseltown dreams, but to catch the real-life Zodiac Killer. There is no reason to doubt him.

"I shot it with the intention of bringing it up to San Francisco and four-walling a theater, which I did, with six guys to set a trap and catch that son of a bitch," Hanson is quoted in the liner notes of his movie's 2017 Blu-ray release from American Genre Film Archive (AGFA).

During the Zodiac's northern California reign of terror, Hanson had made his name in the fast-food business, having owned a chain of Pizza Man pizzerias and some Kentucky Fried Chicken franchise locations. By 1970, when fortune flip-flopped, opportunity knocked in the form of a unique idea: to make a movie to catch a crook. He reasoned the killer's arrogance, expressed through widely publicized communications with the police, would draw the elusive felon to the cinema.

Hanson was not a filmmaker, but he had a couple of credits under his belt as an actor in the biker pic *The Hellcats* (1967) and Coleman Francis's *Night Train to Mundo Fine* (1971). Credits beget connections, enabling him to begin filming immediately in the early weeks of 1971. Without permits (and it shows), Hanson shot in San Francisco, arguably the city most on edge about the serial killings.

On April 7, 1971, Hanson's *The Zodiac Killer* premiered with a weeklong engagement San Francisco's RKO Golden Gate Theatre, where it would sell less than 1,000 tickets. In the lobby stood the *coup de grâce*: a trap disguised as a sweepstakes, with a Kawasaki-donated motorcycle as a dangling bait.

To become eligible for the prize, audience members were asked to complete the sentence "I Believe the Zodiac Killed Because" in twenty-five words or fewer. Unbeknown to them, upon depositing their entry forms into a podium slot, someone hiding on the other side compared the handwriting to the Zodiac's letters, which had taunted police and terrorized readers from the front pages of several Bay Area newspapers. If a match were found, a switch would be flipped to alert others (including Hanson, leading man Reed and co-screenwriter/*Hellcats* co-star Ray Cantrell) staked out in the lobby, in the projection booth and elsewhere on the premises—even inside a freezer.

The plan sounds outlandish, yet was not without merit. In his first of two books on the Zodiac, Graysmith recalls seeing Hanson's film on opening day: "The film ends by hinting that Zodiac may be the man behind you in the theater. Since Zodiac was a movie fan and an egotist and since the movie played only to a limited audience in San Francisco, the chances he was in the seat behind you *were* pretty good" (179–180).

As we know, Hanson failed to collar the criminal, but he believes he came face-to-face with Zodiac in the theater restroom, when a fellow urinator remarked, "You know, real blood doesn't come out like that." The stranger's mug mirrored the wanted poster, but because Hanson and his crew weren't exactly badge-carrying authorities, the guy got away.

"I'M SO VERY THRILLED YOU LIKE THEM"

At the time of this writing, a documentary about Hanson and his plan, *Zodiac Man*, remains in production by director Jeff Broadstreet (dubiously known for his needless 2006 remake of *Night of the Living Dead* in 3-D). Serving as a companion to the doc is a book written by Hanson's grandson, Scott.

In other words, the story behind the story is still being told, with more iterations to come. To borrow a quote from Jerry, discussing roasted hot dogs with a pair of soon-to-be victims on the beach, "I'm so very thrilled you like them. Stick around, it'll get greater."

If not for SWV, it's likely *The Zodiac Killer* would have fallen out of memory. While the Seattle-based company had released the movie on VHS, Hanson's picture found a wider audience in the heyday of DVD, headlining a "Sharpshooter Triple Feature" disc (with Barry Mahon's *The Sex Killer* and Lee Frost's *Zero in and Scream* filling out the bill) from SWV in 2003.

More recently, its debut on Blu-ray marked the first high-definition partnership between SWV and the Austin, Texas-based AGFA. The decision to utilize *Killer* as a series kick-off just "felt right," according to AGFA's director, Joseph A. Ziemba:

> *The Zodiac Killer* is one of my all-time favorite Something Weird horror movies . . . The too-good-to-be-true backstory, the otherworldly feel, the gritty aesthetic—there's nothing else like it. In addition to our love for the movie, it never had the exposure of some of the bigger Something Weird horror titles like *Blood Feast, Night of the Bloody Apes*, or *Basket Case*. So we felt that it could be a happy discovery for people who were unaware of it.

Ziemba considers the film to be "more of a cultural artifact than a movie. It's like a fan-fiction take on the Zodiac's story while it was actually happening, using real locations and people. So I think that's a big part of the appeal. Who wouldn't want to watch that?"

"THE BEST WE COULD FOR WHAT WE HAD"

Hanson may have retired from filmmaking, but he's hardly retired. Now in his early eighties, he's back in the food-service business with Hanson Heat Lamps in Sun Valley, California.

The following interview was conducted in November 2018.

Tom, did you ever think you would still be talking about this film almost fifty years later?
No. I thought we'd catch him and then get it over with.

Why do you think we are still talking about it? What is it about the Zodiac Killer that has helped it survive?
I don't honestly know! It's been so long . . . As you know, it was an effort to make a film, especially when we didn't have the money to do it right. But we did the best we could for what we had.

Is it true you made the movie solely as an opportunity to try to catch the Zodiac Killer? Or was that simply secondary?
Yes. I thought he would *have* to come and see his story. So I thought, "If he comes, well, we gotta be able to figure out who the hell he is," which is why we set that trap. I thought he'd have to go see his story by [having read] the little notes and letters he wrote.

Figure 3.2 Ad for *The Zodiac Killer* **(Tom Hanson, 1971).** Courtesy of Scott Hanson. Note the motorcycle raffle notice on the bottom-right, a ploy to receive handwriting samples to compare to the Zodiac letters.

Are you from San Francisco, and did you live there when you made the film?
No, I'm from Minneapolis originally, and I didn't live in San Francisco at the time. I had been there years before [making the film], trying to get something going. That was about fifteen years before the production.

I've seen your movie three times so far, and something that struck me from the very beginning is San Francisco Chronicle *reporter Paul Avery's statement in the opening titles, suggesting the events are accurately depicted. How did you get Paul Avery involved in the project?*
Well, I just called him up and met him for a couple of drinks. He would wait across the street from the restaurant and bar, and I could see him waiting in an alley, I guess checking it out to make sure it was safe to come. He was *scared* all the time and he was packing, and I said, "Well, so am I." He said, "Are you kidding?" and I said, "No!" Because I didn't know who this guy was—he might be dangerous; he might not be.

How accurate do you think Robert Downey Jr.'s portrayal of Paul Avery was in David Fincher's Zodiac?
The movie is kind of vague in my memory right now, but no, I didn't think it was too accurate. But, I *knew* the guy, you know?

Obviously, your film plays very loosely with the facts. Why did you use the true story simply as a jumping-off point? How much research did you do?
Not much. Really, I had to do it in a hurry because I didn't know when the hell he would leave that San Francisco area. If you read his letters—and I probably had a little more than what was in the papers, because I think Paul got a hold of several there—to me, he was an egomaniac. And I can't believe an egomaniac wouldn't go see a story about himself.

How quick was the process to get it from shooting to being released in theaters?
Oh, hell, I think we did that one in about fourteen days or something like that. I actually made two films because I know when you've got a low-budget film, in case we had problems with catching him, we'd better have another one so we can run the goddamned thing. So I actually had to shoot another one: *A Ton of Grass Goes to Pot*, I think they later called it, or *The Big Score* or something. It's just a chapter in various things I've done in my life.

Did you say you saw the actual letters from the Zodiac Killer through your association with Paul?
I recall Paul Avery having some that were not in the newspaper. When reading [the killer's] dialogue, I can't believe he wouldn't want to see how he was depicted in my film. I just think he would've *had* to see it.

By that, do you mean you had purposely exaggerated some of the events to try to provoke a reaction out of him?
You know, I don't remember anything that was really thought of so much in that area. It was just get the damn thing done, get it together and get it up there while he's still there.

Most of the murders that occur in your movie take place in broad daylight, such as Jerry pushing the retirement home patient in the wheeled bed down the hill. I assume you shot these sequences at daytime because of budgetary issues?
It's difficult when you're shooting with cheap material, like film ends. It can be pretty bad. So I was more concerned just to get the damned thing completed, to catch him. To me, it didn't make a hell of a lot of difference what we shot—just get it done and get it out there while he's still in 'Frisco.

How quickly did you spring into action from when you had the idea in 1970? In other words, how soon did you begin making the movie after conceiving it?
Well, we did it pretty quickly. [We began] as soon as I was able to find guys to help get it done and up onscreen.

The scene I mentioned at the end, when Jerry pushes the patient from the retirement home down the hill: I know in some of the shots, it's clear there is a dummy in the bed, but in others, it's the actor, and it looks really dangerous.
It wasn't quite as dangerous as you thought, because we were prepared and he could steer that thing. I don't remember if it was with his feet or what, but I thought were okay. I didn't think he was going to go out onto the freeway or something.

No, but when he started hitting the stairs, I thought, "Wow, how did he not fall off and get hurt?"
Yeah, well, you know, when you do these things with a low budget, you're looking to get through without something bad happening. But we seemed to survive!

Did anything bad happen, other than your typical problems for shooting a low-budget movie?
Not really, no. I mean, the guys, for not getting paid, I think they did a hell of a job hustling to *get it done.*

Tom, if this was all about rushing it into theaters, and I know you did it for about $13,000, did you end up making money or did you lose your shirt?
I never got a dime out of either film. Billy Fine, who was distributing it, basically did the same thing he did to those brothers he did a film with: He just took whatever money there was. I never saw a dime on either movie.

Is that part of why you left the film business after A Ton of Grass Goes to Pot*?*
Well, you know, I had a family with three sons, so I had better start making some money somehow. And one of the guys at the place who did the all film work to get the thing ready, I think we owed him, oh, about $45,000 or so, and I met with him and I told him, "I just don't have it." And he wanted for me to stay in the business and I said, "I can't! I've got to earn a living somehow." So I had to go back to whatever I usually do or some damn thing—you know, get going again.

Other than that, what did you think of the finished product? Were you pleased with what you had done?

Figure 3.3 A still from *The Zodiac Killer* (Tom Hanson, 1971). Courtesy of Scott Hanson.

I knew it was kind of shabby, but for what you're doing with what we had, he would *have* to go see it and we'd catch him. I just thought we could.

How disappointed were you that you weren't able to get him? I know you think you had met him in the theater bathroom at the premiere, but ultimately, he's still out there . . . assuming he's still alive.
All I know is when you've been held up, like, six times—and twice with a shotgun—there are things that you study on a person's face: you know, nose, ears, eyes, chest, hairline. And that, to me, was on the wanted poster (see figure 2.1). If I had the poster in my hand and had looked at him, I'd say, "When did they take this picture of you?"

Removing that aspect, what was the reception to the film like?
It played all over the goddamn place, in LA and all across the country. One of the Smothers Brothers told me he thought [Fine] had picked up $150,000 or more from [me] than he did from [the Smothers Brothers], but I don't know. They had made a film—*Another Nice Mess*, I think it was called—and he

screwed them, too. So the one brother—I forget which one it was—thought maybe we should kill the son of a bitch. I said, "Well, we could invite him up to the Magic Castle and just beat the hell out of him and throw him in that [tank] where they got the live fish."

What did audiences and critics think of the film at the time?
You know, it seems like I remember a couple of so-so or lousy reviews or something, but I think those guys also knew it was low budget or shot with *no* budget. After a while, I just had to give up and get back to making money, you know?

How did you get Doodles Weaver in the film as Jerry's next-door neighbor?
I knew Doodles. I knew him and Bob Hope and a few other people that lived in Toluca Lake. He wanted to do it, so we put him in there. But he could never remember three lines. You'd give him his three lines and he'd have one of them and give you something else. He just couldn't concentrate on it. But we just shot it the best we could.

Did he do it free, as a favor to you?
You know, I honestly don't remember. We hardly paid anybody anything, so my guess would be we probably didn't pay him.

Among this cast of people you've never seen or heard of before, it's fun to see him pop up, even if his name is misspelled as "Doddles" in the credits.
Yeah, and I was trying to get Johnny Carson's brother (Dick Carson) to direct it. He agreed to it and then before we went up to shoot film, he called me to meet him. It was around 11 o'clock at night at a coffee shop in Hollywood and he just said he panicked. He got to talking with his wife and he thought [the Zodiac] might kill him! So he backed out. That was going to be my director. I thought he might help the film.

So that was the only reason you directed it: because Johnny Carson's brother, Dick, backed out.
Yes, I didn't have much choice! We had to get rolling on this thing.

And this was your first time to direct, correct?
Yeah, the only experience I had in film was little bits and stuff like that, maybe a half a dozen films and a half of dozen TV shows—just little things.

Is it true that Robert Towne, the screenwriter of Chinatown, The Last Detail, Shampoo, *is in the bar scene? He's credited on the Internet Movie Database as being "Man in Bar #3," under the name Robert Tubin.*

Wow, I don't remember. Some days, I'm lucky to remember my name!

Were you the first Zodiac Killer movie to be released? I ask because apparently there was an X-rated movie around the same time, too (Zodiac Rapist, starring John Holmes in the title role), but I wasn't sure who came first, if you'll pardon the unintentional pun.
Yes, we were the first. Clint Eastwood made a film. They didn't use the name "Zodiac," but . . .

What did you think of Dirty Harry? *Andrew Robinson played the Scorpio Killer in that.*
I kept thinking of how it's so hard to figure [the real killer]. Some of the latest developments, when they thought the Zodiac might be that guy who was living out in that shack in Montana or whatever

Ted Kaczynski, the Unabomber?
Yes! The reason [they] thought that was I guess when the two were killed at that beachfront [of Lake Berryessa], he mentioned that little town of [Deer Lodge, Montana, within an hour from Kaczynski's cabin]. And when you think of all the millions of little towns, that's pretty . . . peculiar, really. I don't know, it's hard to say. My guy, you know, he could be a copycat, but if he's a copycat, you think he would have turned on me early. I really don't know, maybe he's got a twin brother. I had somebody try to check and see if he did have a twin brother. I don't know if they found another or not.

Dirty Harry *was probably the most mainstream portrayal of the Zodiac Killer in popular culture until David Fincher's film, but they are not the only ones. Have you seen any of the other many Zodiac Killer movies that have come out since yours?*
No, not really. I don't think I've seen much. I know it's all over the internet, but it's strange how it could go like that. I talked to Peter Hurkos once—you know, that psychic? I tried to get him to go up there with me. And he said he didn't want to touch it, and I asked him why and he said, "Because the cities are fighting each other." He didn't want to get involved, but I thought he could have helped.

You have a scene in the film with a psychic. Is that based on Hurkos?
Might be. [Laughs]

When was the last time you saw your film?
God, I don't know. When it didn't turn out to be what I thought would happen, I got a little pissed off about the whole thing.

Does it help, though, that it's been rediscovered? It has to be more popular now than ever before.
It makes me think of Jack the Ripper: It's been an unsolved crime for a long period of time. And you'd think somehow—*somehow*—we'd get lucky and stumble onto something. That always kind of bothered me that they couldn't come up with one thing. The other thing is with the fingerprint stuff: You know, I sent my suspect letters saying he had won things.

Like the motorcycle offered as a raffle prize in the ads for your film? [See figure 3.2]
No, this was long after the film, when I was trying to refind out where the hell he was, and the gal at the Astoria Hotel where [the suspect] had been staying told me that he lived at a certain address. We tried to button him down. Also, she thought he was a little weirdo and I wish I had talked to her more about that, because I wanted to know why they think he was weird. But he had something stored there, so that private detective and I, they got me in a box. They put me in a room with, Christ, there's, like, a hundred of these packages in there and all they had on them was numbers, so I had to get the hell out of there.

That's interesting. Beyond being the director, and well after the fact, you played amateur detective.
Yes. He sent me three postcards. And they were the kind you buy at the post office: the kind that the Zodiac Killer had used. And the detectives I had worked with stole that whole portfolio I had. I had the postcards, other stuff in there, people I talked to, this and that, so I lost all that stuff. That kind of just welled me up.

Did that snuff out your enthusiasm for tracking him down?
It did, because I had nothing on him anymore. I didn't realize [what the detective was doing]. He had me and my wife go in another room so he could steal that portfolio out of my briefcase. So he did. I think it turned up. I think somebody talked to some friend of his. I think he passed away and she had that stuff.

I don't want to call it a hobby, but in your efforts in trying to find the Zodiac Killer, are we talking about a year of your life? Or years, plural? Or was all this concentrated into a matter of months?
I don't remember. I was trying to make a living also. I had to get back on my feet.

After the film, what business did you go into?

I'm having a hard time placing things where they belong, but I know I had a very, very busy bar and a restaurant in the San Fernando Valley. And I had guys from the Magic Castle—you'd come in and have to wait, and we were doing real damn good with it. Except my partner was doing some other things in there that you shouldn't do or whatever, so I had to sell that out. I started making heat lamps for food service that are now sold all over the world. So I'm always doing something.

After the film and after your investigative files were taken, I'm guessing it all just became a piece of your past that you forgot about or perhaps didn't think about. But as the years went on, the movie found a new audience and has become a cult favorite, and now it's even preserved on Blu-ray.
Really, I think there's more people digging into [the investigation]. It was a pretty good effort to catch a criminal. It's hard to tell if it's the end of this thing.

Where did you find Hal Reed? He's so much fun to watch.
Hal had worked in a couple of films for that producer. I know one of them was with a bunch of dogs. I forget the name of that movie. What do you call those long-legged dogs?

The Doberman Gang.
Yeah, okay. Hal had done a couple of films with those guys and I thought he would be good for what we were doing. And he was cooperative and he did a pretty good job on it. I don't know what happened to him. I guess he passed away.

Yes, in 2010.
Gosh, he never smoked, he never drinked, and I did both, and I'm still here! Jesus.

He was the lead in your other movie, but I guess you lost touch with him after that, when you left the film business?
No, I would see him from time to time. He had a rope-making company in some state.

And then the other lead, Bob Jones, who played his friend, Grover...
I knew Bob. He had worked with me on Pizza Man and some other chains. I was supposed to go public with Pizza Man and that would've been about, I think, $3.5 million, but something went haywire with that thing. Life is full of these little things.

Whatever happened to Bob?
He passed away in northern California a long time ago, maybe twenty years ago. He was selling real estate for a couple of guys. He was quite a character.

Lastly, I'd like you to clear up something for me. I've seen several online reviews that interpret Grover as being the original Zodiac Killer, and that it's only after he dies that Hal Reed's character picks up the torch. But I've always read Grover's "I'm the Zodiac!" admission as pure impulse in the heat of the moment with the police, and that Hal Reed's character is the only Zodiac Killer. Which is correct?
Oh, it's Hal Reed, all the way.

Special thanks to Scott Hanson for his assistance in setting up an interview with his grandfather, and to Joe Ziemba of Alamo Drafthouse and American Genre Film Archive.

REFERENCES

Graysmith, Robert. 1987. *Zodiac*. New York, NY: Berkley Books.
Poggiali, Chris. 2017. "This Is Not the Zodiac Speaking: A Conversation with Tom Hanson." *The Zodiac Killer*. American Genre Film Archive/Something Weird Video Blu-ray.
Rossen, Jake. 2017. "A Pizzeria Owner's Bizarre Plot to Capture the Zodiac Killer." October 31. Accessed December 2, 2018. http://mentalfloss.com/article/509038/pizzeria-owners-bizarre-plot-capture-zodiac-killer.
Ziemba, Joseph, A. 2018. Email interview with the author, November 26.

SECTION TWO
ZODIAC AND NARRATIVE

Chapter 4

Zodiac and the Melding Criminal Minds of David Fincher

Jeremy Carr

> If there is one key word for the entire story of the Zodiac mystery, it is obsession.
> —Robert Graysmith (1986, XII)

A serial killer's significance is often dependent on the degree to which he or she is pursued. Once a murder has been committed, if no law enforcement entity or individual investigator begins an inquiry, that inaction diminishes the crime, in the public sphere, as an unimportant breach of behavioral or legal custom. By that same token, a homicide detective without a killer to pursue ceases to fulfill a key requisite of their own occupation; while a world without psychopaths would, of course, be desirable, for the law officer, that absence would render their profession insignificant. Similarly, the impact of a serial killer movie is largely contingent on this unifying, if opposed, interplay, where an active homicidal antagonist is the zealous subject of a lawful, probing protagonist. It is a symbiotic relationship where one individual or group gains relevance and confidence by their conditional interactions with a conflicting party.

This is something David Fincher understands as well as any modern filmmaker, and few have delved as thoroughly and regularly into the physical and psychological depths of this reciprocal union as he. It's a two-way dynamic most exhaustively explored in his 2007 film *Zodiac*, the quintessential example of this complex chemistry, which features (presumably) one stalwart killer and no less than three inquiring minds, united in the common goal of identification and hopeful apprehension, yet diverging in methodic approach, private desire, and ultimately, individual impact. This essential narrative construct has been seen frequently in Fincher's work, from his gritty 1995 breakthrough *Se7en* to his 2011 adaptation of Stieg Larsson's *The Girl with the Dragon Tattoo* and his 2017–19 Netflix series, *Mindhunter*. The serial killer(s) at the bloody heart of these associated thrillers may play the role of instigating force, but it is often the hero of the Fincher crime film who reveals the director's interest in the expressed passion and inborn obsession of a man possessed. In *Zodiac* and elsewhere, it is a fine line between objective duty and crazed infatuation, and when that line is crossed, these characters, once so clearly on the right side of the law, begin a precarious path toward personal liability, familial estrangement, and professional complication. By focusing first on the proficient and previously grounded, Fincher's morality tales detach from the central adversary and eventually prove the hero to be an ominous, potentially hazardous counterpart.

Fincher's attachment to the Zodiac spree stems from his childhood, growing up in the San Francisco Bay area during the time of the killer's erratic reign. Born August 28, 1962, Fincher remembers, "If you grew up there, at that time, you had this childhood fear that you kind of insinuated yourself into . . . . What if he showed up in our neighborhood? You create even more drama about it when you're a kid because that's what kids do" (Levy 2006). The inspired imaginings of a young boy, perhaps, but this recollection nevertheless suggests an early instance of the complementary paranoia and fascination that correspond so distinctly to the serial killer phenomenon. Although there is no immediate cause for concern, the curious temptation to participate remains, even at this prefatory stage in one's life. It illustrates, with personal acuity, an innate desire for one to associate with the killer, to assign the encircling drama, no matter how peripheral, into a direct and local alarm, reveling and recoiling at the excitement, the horror, and the ambiguity.

Zodiac screenwriter James Vanderbilt also had a long-gestating interest in the Zodiac Killer, having first read in high school one of the books on which his film adaptation would be based, Robert Graysmith's 1986 best seller, *Zodiac: The Shocking True Story of the Hunt for the Nation's Most Elusive Serial Killer* (Graysmith also penned the 2007 follow-up, *Zodiac Unmasked: The Identity of America's Most Elusive Serial Killer Revealed*, from which Vanderbilt also gleaned inspiration). It was with Vanderbilt, "of whom Fincher requested a script re-write to include more factual information," as Brian Eggert notes, "that the director spent more than a year researching details of the case to prepare. He read thousands of pages of evidence; he interviewed survivors, loved ones of victims, and policemen involved in the investigation; he talked to the prime suspect's family; he reviewed the site of every crime. His obsession would eventually mirror that of his film's characters, who succumb to their own terrible need to know" (2015). Finding further incentive in Alan J. Pakula's 1976 Watergate exposé *All the President's Men*, Fincher also saw in *Zodiac* a supplemental conjoining thread: "[T]he story of a reporter determined to get the story at any cost and one who was new to being an investigative reporter. It was all about his obsession to know the truth" (Zodiac Production Notes). It would seem the frightful fancies of a youthful interest had borne the fruit of an ardent adult endeavor, transferred from schoolhouse possibilities to occupational practicalities, all without ever losing that visceral preliminary value.

Just as the reporter in Fincher's connective scenario is one who finds a point of interactive fixation and proceeds accordingly—this to say nothing of the demanding film director or, in the case of the *Zodiac* narrative, the detective—one critical aspect of the investigative relationship is how the killer interacts with, and responds to, the pursuing individual or individuals (if representative of a larger organization). While not unique in his zest for sensational proclamations, Zodiac had a particular penchant for prodding investigators, tempting them with clues, offering up confessions, and at once promoting and obscuring the hunt with enigmatic puzzles and tantalizing threats. Engaging with the authorities by teasing information they may soon be able to retrieve on their own, but for now remains just out of reach, this interaction is never fully satiated for either party, and is often just enough to provoke mounting frustration on both ends. When the Zodiac of Fincher's film boasts about his "needling" of "the blue pigs," mocking and deriding law enforcement efforts, his aim is to generate an investigation that becomes more than a professional duty, introducing in addition a personal vendetta, reaching out in the hopes of enhancing inner vexation and, ideally, inducing errored, prejudiced judgment in the process. In his writings to journalists and in his disdainful comments regarding police, Zodiac found a way of contesting individuals by aggravating their occupation, their livelihood, their sense of purpose, and leaving no realm of their life—personal or professional—safe from intrusion and preoccupation. He was as fanatical about their work as they were by his.

This outreach was likewise the result of Zodiac's fondness for publicity, for self-promotion and a quest for fame (or at least infamy). In other words, to make himself known and to, in effect, force a police response, is to both do what he does successfully and in secret, but also to make people aware of the end result. He is, in this sense, cognizant of his own dependency on official reaction—he is nothing without shaken recognition. Zodiac sustains his individual worth by promoting his identity, his persona, and his myth. Accordingly, as Adam Nayman argues, *Zodiac* the film is itself "less a movie about a serial killer than it is a movie about the idea of a serial killer" (2017), which aligns with the work-in-progress of Zodiac as a murderous adversary, evolving over time and honing the public perception of his crime and character, even going so far as to take credit for crimes he did not commit in order to boost his looming legitimacy. The embellishment and the resulting feedback prompt a reticent popularity that sweeps a city, a state, and a nation, so at the heart of *Zodiac*'s project is, Nayman continues, the charting of a "slippage between reality and pop culture that turned a murderer into a multimedia star" (2017).

Driven by Zodiac's perplexing cryptograms and enticing references, the public zest for the case is enacted early on in Fincher's film, as the initial outreach from the killer triggers a response extending from professional agencies like the FBI, CIA, and naval intelligence, to a recreational captivation of the general populace, inciting speculation, paranoia, and an almost casual commitment to the cause. The progression is first seen in a sequence capped off by the entrance of a North Salinas high school teacher, who with his wife crack the Zodiac code when these established institutions fail. Graysmith did not consider the murderer an expert in codes and ciphers, however. Rather, he posited Zodiac worked from the example of others; he was a novice, like this suburban couple, like Graysmith himself. The hunted and hunters were mirroring each other, notes the cartoonist turned amateur sleuth, "feeling their way toward a resolution" (Graysmith 1986, 58). Fincher presents this tentative enchantment in additional scenes of spectators glued to their television sets, forgoing their family at home and their duties at work while absorbing the enthralling news reports. As evinced in a parade of assorted witnesses, proffering up false confessions, advice, and frenzied theories, the Zodiac sensation had, according to Fincher, crept into the community's "collective unconscious" (Fincher 2009). If not his literal murders, the menacing abstract wave of the Zodiac specter spread throughout the region, in a social expansion of the killer's presence and an interest in his undertakings. It is a surge masterfully coordinated by Fincher, who appreciates the balance of pace and headlong momentum as an engrossing link to the characters in the film and their peculiar fervor, where audience response is directly affixed to the depicted outbreak of public enchantment.

But this intrigue goes both ways. "The thing that's fascinating for me about *Zodiac*," notes Fincher, "is I believe his compulsion and his addiction was not ultimately about maiming people or murdering them, it became about communicating with the *San Francisco Chronicle* and that became far more gratifying and far more seductive then what he started out doing" (2010). Indeed, the media's role in promoting the killer and serving as a conduit through which he could communicate—and insult—is an essential component of the *Zodiac* film. And it was a curious back-and-forth at that. In his true crime text, Graysmith outlines the remarkably two-sided exchange between Zodiac and Bay area publications, from the first Zodiac letter sent to the *San Francisco Chronicle* on August 1, 1969, to the *San Francisco Examiner*'s plea to the killer the following October; from a challenge issued by the Examiner—a cipher from Dr. Marsh of the American Cryptogram Association daring the killer to send in his real name—to an April 1970 letter in which the Zodiac notes the "score": "Zodiac—10, SFPD—0." While this robust media association certainly has its drawbacks, as when a news program in Fincher's film announces for all to hear Zodiac's plan to "pick off the kiddies," the two-way communique becomes mutually encouraging in its antithetical, ongoing correspondence. As the *Chronicle* editorial board deliberates the published placement of Zodiac's note, the quest for civic awareness crosses with a zest for salacious prosperity, jointly overriding any fleeting apprehension in the name of two-fold publicity. "Zodiac coverage soon vaults to page one," notes Tony Macklin. "And a legend is created out of fear and fascination. Zodiac and the media feed off each other. And so, modern journalism was born" (2007). The Zodiac-media rapport, buoyed and mirrored by the receptive, inquisitive spectator of *Zodiac*, supplies a way of maintaining this contentious relationship, confirming the unified existence and the continued immersion of all involved.

Such concerted audacity, though, such a brazen shared alliance, was bound to spark the interest of even those for whom Zodiac's actions were not a dominant part of their profession, as in the case of Robert Graysmith. To embody the primary figure in his *Zodiac* tale, Fincher looked to Jake Gyllenhaal. Initially impressed by his brooding turn in *Donnie Darko* (2001), Fincher saw in Gyllenhaal a naive yet possessed quality, a dichotomy that routinely comes through in the actor's *Zodiac* performance. Underscoring his guileless interest while also slighting his capacity for scrupulous research, the repeated "Boy Scout" epithet grounds Graysmith as one who has good intentions, but one who is also in over his head. It is a moniker, in any case, that works all the better to accentuate his accumulating obsession, which drives and devours an otherwise sane man. Shunned because of his professional status (a mere cartoonist) and seldom afforded priority of information as a result, Graysmith is additionally representative of *Zodiac*'s emphasis on rank and a consequential access to knowledge (see, effectively, access to Zodiac), an external hindrance eventually usurped by individual devotion.

Always with Zodiac as a central focus, Fincher's film posits three different levels of engagement, three different degrees of revelation, and three different individual outcomes: the detective work of Mark Ruffalo's Inspector David Toschi, the criminal reporting of Robert Downey Jr.'s Paul Avery, and Graysmith's side investigation, which soon consumes his day job to say nothing of his life away from work. In each occupation, there are varying measures of allocated information and generally deviating grades of dedication. For Graysmith, his outsider status is not only a vital part of his character's relationship with the viewer (as a regular person simply fascinated by the subject matter), but the fact he is not a law enforcement official, nor even a professional journalist like Avery, also tenders the novelty of his doing something outside the structures of "proper" engagement. By going where he shouldn't go, seeking information he shouldn't be privy to, and interacting with witnesses in an occasionally inappropriate manner, Graysmith is inquisitive beyond his pay grade. But there is no denying the efficacy of his procedural progress, connecting the dots, solving the cipher, and so on. All the same, given his lack of traditional involvement, he is routinely met with skepticism, even downright hostility. His idealism stands out from the prevalent cynicism while, at the same time, his own motivations are suspect, as if his mere interest in Zodiac was itself a dubious characteristic. Some, like Avery, are put off by the notion that there could be something personally satisfying in his work beyond a paycheck or occupational responsibility. "What do you want out of this?" questions Graysmith's apparent ally, who refuses to see why the Zodiac case would hold such allure for one who has essentially nothing invested in the matter. "This is good business for everyone but you." Graysmith is thus encouraged, in both word and deed, to stay in his place, and his limited station results in forced measures to work independently, placing him away from the norms of the official investigation and dispensing him onto a pariah plane analogous to Zodiac himself.

Regardless, in the face of his unauthorized position, Graysmith refuses to give up on the Zodiac case the way so many others had. Graysmith writes in his first Zodiac book, "I thought, 'Well, wait a minute. Nobody is sharing, all the different jurisdictions, all this information. They are not going to tell each other, even within departments. What if, as a private citizen, I went around and got all the information?' Well, it took a full 10 years. I put it all together" (2007b). But again, comparable to the presumed social ostracization of the Zodiac Killer, this desire took its toll on Graysmith's personal and professional life. As seen in *Zodiac*, he is driven to distraction well before he meets his future wife, Melanie (Chloë Sevigny)—he is a rambling, preoccupied mess on their first date and will remain that way for much of their union—and soon, his impulses, his intensity, and his tactics become morally ambiguous (at one point pushing a false statement just so it fits his constructed narrative). Whereas his zealous curiosity is scorned by Melanie, Fincher comically illustrates Graysmith's fixation as he enlists his three small children to help piece together parts of the Zodiac puzzle, remarking to the undercover offspring, "Don't tell mom about our special project." In reality, Graysmith was less cheerful, writing, "As far as the personal relationship [with my children] that was not good. Zodiac was number one, that just took over" (Graysmith 2007a). Spurred by such a reflective observance and the secretive nature of Graysmith's endeavor, Fincher draws a persistent parallel between the protagonist's interest in Zodiac and the killer's own private rage, exposing and associating what they each do away from the watchful eyes of others.

A tagline used in promoting *Zodiac* declares, "There's more than one way to lose your life to a killer," and certainly, how Graysmith in particular engages with Zodiac becomes a portentous aspect of his mental and physical well-being. "It's a very eerie and exciting thing to see a cipher start to come apart" (1986, 54). But it's hard to leave well enough alone, as Graysmith finds out. The mutual dependence, unwittingly formed between him and Zodiac, hits uncomfortably close to home. It's a self-sacrificial tendency shared with the killer, putting himself out there, unable to resist regardless of the consequences, almost asking to be confronted and subconsciously inviting the confrontation as a way of ultimate engagement. And to what aim? "What's harrowing," writes Nayman, "isn't the question of what Graysmith stands to lose by chasing leads, but rather what he might find if he succeeds. The film makes a point of showing that while the Zodiac's victims were chosen at random, Graysmith willingly puts himself in the crosshairs" (2017). His name is out there, articles have been written about his research; the media, as much as it has served the purposes of Zodiac, now plays into Graysmith's potential peril, and in the process, he puts his family in jeopardy. Graysmith, who upon reading the screenplay for *Zodiac* reportedly said, "God, now I see why my wife divorced me" (Cole 2015), though he also mused, "In the end, it wasn't all bad. I think, had I to do it over again, I probably would do it. Probably would. But it does grip you. It takes over your life" (Sorenson 2014).

Despite the earnestness of his exuberance, others routinely deride Graysmith's ambitions. For this sequestered investigator, though, the Zodiac case is more than some derivative endeavor; it is a means of forging his own identity, of establishing his own self-worth. And that, as Gyllenhaal shows, can be a grueling, overwrought process. Incessantly scrawling related names and places, seeing evocative signs of Zodiac everywhere, and hording a library of newspaper clippings and archival material, Gyllenhaal's breathless Graysmith is engrossed in all-consuming passion project—"Nobody has more zodiac crap than you do," comments his exasperated ex. Haunted by this irresistible, lingering mania, Gyllenhaal's performance is appropriately anxious, jittery, and animated, with wide, wild eyes, and a corresponding visualization manifest in kinetic editing patterns, emphasizing Graysmith's fitful mental state. Under Fincher's similarly enthused direction, Gyllenhaal aptly expresses the thrill of discovery, the renewal and excitement that accompanies the arrival of each new letter, and the satisfaction of directly working with Zodiac via his enigmatic submissions. At one point allowed neither pen nor paper to take notes, Graysmith absorbs a prodigious amount of material, letting the bombardment of detail seep into his mind until he comes unleashed at a nearby diner and begins to manically scribble down his observations.

The production design of *Zodiac* is also significant, particularly Graysmith's home toward the end of the film, as it abounds in unboxed remnants of his prodigious research, as if his mind were literally poured out upon his living room floor. He is blinded, though; he can't see the way others see him. He has entered an area already occupied by Zodiac, an area where one's behavior is removed from the "normal" world around him. And yet, when finally afforded the opportunity to see, face-to-face, the prime Zodiac suspect, Arthur Leigh Allen, played by John Carroll Lynch, Graysmith is speechless. And when met with the revelation that Zodiac takes credit for other murders reported in the newspaper, Graysmith almost seems disappointed. There is a shared appeal in the potential vastness of Zodiac's capabilities, an ongoing breadth that gives them both more incentive to continue.

In conjunction with personal interest, an underlying motive in Graysmith's plight is his genuine desire to assist, to be part of the investigation in a way that exceeds his professional standing or even the role of a middling citizen. In that, his unaffected exhortation of just wanting to help and his relentless desire to participate in the probe places him apart from most others in *Zodiac*, where inquisitive action is more often derived from vocational duty. "I need to know who he is," Graysmith says in the film. "I need to stand there. I need to look him in the eye . . . and I need to know that it's him." And why? "Because nobody else will." Two others who voice such an accommodating desire are Zodiac's Lake Berryessa victim, Bryan Hartnell (Patrick Scott Lewis), and Brian Cox's pretentious media personality, Melvin Belli. But they do so only in efforts of self-preservation, in the case of the former, and reasonable self-interest, in the case of the latter. Whereas these two men appear to lend the supposed killer a sympathetic ear, their aims are more manipulative than caring (in a sense, Belli's plugging of his own media brand overlaps the self-promotional connect of Zodiac). Graysmith is different, though. His motivations are, for lack of a better word, pure. He truly does want to help, not the killer, at least not directly, but the authoritative bodies with which he associates.

This motivation would later find a parallel in the David Fincher produced and intermittently directed *Mindhunter*, where in the first episode, chief protagonist Holden Ford (Jonathan Groff) is involved in a hostage negotiation and proclaims to the suspect (and genuinely believes), "Maybe I can help." From this impetus, and the avid curiosity that extends from such yearning, is the criminal profiling focus of the Netflix series. Ford's establishment of nonthreatening communication springs from an innate desire to understand, not dominate, his subjects, to listen to the people so many others simply dismiss. This progressively evolves into the formation of the FBI's Behavioral Science Unit, where inquisitiveness and a quest for insight is front and center. Its aim is to delve into the psychology of motive, to find a reason beyond the randomness, a rationale, and to imagine what it takes to commit even the most heinous of acts. Understandably, this isn't always a pretty place to be, having such empathy for the disturbed, but, echoing *Zodiac* as an obvious precursor, Ford nevertheless contends, "It's a riddle, but it can be solved."

Relatedly, one's occupation is indispensable to the way in which David Fincher draws parallels between the "good" and the "bad" of his serial killer tales. Although Graysmith is the lone example of one whose job is not reliant on the pursuit or capture of the serial killer target, contrary instances abound in Fincher's work, most notably in *Mindhunter*, which is in essence about a job wholly devoted to the existence of serial killers, and what is more, of relating to them. Taking place in the late 1970s, the series gauges what had become a new breed of criminal, emerging with striking regularity in a post-Charles Manson United States, but *Mindhunter* is even more preoccupied with the profession that also materialized from the phenomenon. As new investigative techniques are implemented and innovative psychological studies are explored, those who take part in the endeavor—primarily Ford, his partner Bill Tench (Holt McCallany), and Professor Wendy Carr (Anna Torv)—combat the established benchmarks of their profession. As with Graysmith, however, there is also the grave possibility of getting too close, of advancing an unwieldy and unhealthy infatuation with such behavior. Even Tench forewarns, "If we understand it we'd be aberrant too."

Also, like Graysmith, Ford tends to insinuate himself into the investigation. At various times in *Mindhunter*, Ford's occasionally improper efforts—pursuing conviction too vigorously, compromising stages of interaction, identifying too intently with a guilty party—risk straining the balance between objective and subjective analysis. Obfuscating the material at hand, dominated by his passions, Ford wants answers so bad his procedure can become misdirected; letting his immersion overpower his discernment, growing too considerate, he is almost complicit after the fact. Aware of this connection and its conceivable dangers, he acknowledges, "I can't let these guys rub off on me," a cautionary statement reiterated by Tench, who notes, "If what we're doing doesn't get under your skin, you're more screwed up than I thought, or kidding yourself." Akin to Graysmith's overriding fervency, Ford jeopardizes his relationships, resulting in miscommunication (or a lack of communication altogether) and romantic severance. Unlike Graysmith, though, at least as far as *Zodiac* shows, Ford's association with such deviant content exposes the volume of his own hidden desires, in effect transcending the barriers between his private and professional life and leading to compulsive anxiety and sexual confusion.

Setting aside the prospect of an investigator-killer personality overlay, a narrative and thematic concentration corroborated in *Zodiac* and *Mindhunter*, when Fincher met with Joe Penhall, a cocreator of *Mindhunter* and one of its writers, the director discussed aspects of the story he was interested in and aspects he hoped to avoid. Curiously, one of the features he wished to sidestep would in fact be one of the more compelling aspects of the series, and one of the recurring motifs of Fincher's work generally: "The notion that a fine line separates the FBI agent from the serial killer." "I felt that it was well trawled," stated Fincher, "I felt that it was a literary conceit and really had nothing to do with why I think people are interested in serial killers. I don't think people are interested in serial killers because they're so much like them, I think they're interested in the aberrant because it's so hard to understand" (2017c). But for Ford, understanding isn't necessarily the problem. For him, the affinity is perhaps too easy. If one wants truffles, he argues, one must "get in the dirt with the pigs," but his contact with affirmed predators is routinely disputed, generating unsettlingly casual relations, pointed parallels that even the killers note (Richard Speck, played by Jack Erdie, calls Ford the crazy one), and, as a result of his unconventional ideas and methodology, his own cast-off condition.

In order to truly understand one's enemy, Fincher did find intriguing the notion that "one had to develop even for short periods of time—even if they were faking it—empathy for people who heretofore would have been beneath our contempt. They had to figure out how to have human conversations with those who are subhuman" (Fincher 2017a). Profilers would, of course, be specifically dependent on this associative insight. "They have to imagine every permutation," Fincher states. "What if the killer does this? What if the victim does this?" (2017b). Although *Zodiac*'s Paul Avery says one can't think of Zodiac's murders in normal police terms, that is in fact what law enforcement officers do on a regular basis, here and elsewhere in Fincher's work. Recognizing patterns, formulating a sequence of events, posing rhetorical question of who does the killer kill, how, when, and where, they apply their own logic, biased and idiosyncratic, combined with the discernment of anticipating action based on past immersion. But this, too, can work both ways, as an inverse intuition. Cameron Britton's Edmund Kemper, *Mindhunter*'s serial killer key, has a professed interest in police work, gleaning insight into their operations from cop dramas on television, and Zodiac has an obvious knowledge of police procedure.

In that *Zodiac* is a film plaited by the time- and life-consuming actions of professional and amateur enquiry, it is consistently lavished with an attention to occupational detail, cross-cutting between diverging and collaborative entities and moving across jurisdictions and county lines. In recurrent montages of day-to-day, entwined investigation, this emphasis on inquest simultaneously develops character, for like Zodiac himself, the men who seek the killer's identity are defined by what they do. The personal and professional trajectory of Downey's Avery is a cynical contrast to optimistic Graysmith, for instance. The writer's descent into substance abuse is a striking deteriorating counterpoint to Graysmith's advancement, as the Zodiac case becomes the downer to Avery's existence just as it has provided an insatiable upper for Graysmith (the two, or rather three, are united in that Avery's reclusive boathouse looks to be in similar disarray as Leigh's rodent infested trailer, which is perhaps only a few breakdowns removed from Graysmith's boxes and boxes of clutter).

Toschi, by comparison, stresses by-the-book procedure, as opposed to Graysmith's unsanctioned excursions, though even he becomes as jaded as his newspaper counterpart. Used to the bloodshed, he adopts the necessary objectivity of his profession, treating the abnormal as normal, but there is just as much danger in complacency as there is in becoming too enamored. Running through what appears to be the botched robbery of a taxi driver, Toschi puts himself into the mind of the killer, getting into his shoes as a way of identifying and speculating. But as all three languish in moments of drought and disappointment, with nowhere to turn, scrounging for clues, they end up wanting more from Zodiac, just so they have more to go on. It is a problematic, unsettling dependency. As Kemper states in *Mindhunter*, referring to the proficiency of serial killers generally, "You're never going to find them if they don't want you to."

So, while *Zodiac* often features a flurry of sudden activity, concisely summarized in superimposed, ephemeral newspaper headlines, those sequences can be followed by days, weeks, months, and even years of stagnation, envisaged in the time-lapse erection of San Francisco's Transamerica Pyramid, underscored by Marvin Gaye's "Inner City Blues." The temporal extension of *Zodiac*'s case history, augmented by the effect such allowance has on its main characters, subsequently makes the film, as Kent Jones writes, "a movie about getting sucked into the vortex of obsession, as the expanding distance in time from the actual event makes an abstraction out of the investigation itself and turns the case into an urban legend—or in this case, fodder for a Nixon-era cop movie" (2008). "I can't tell if I wanted it to be Allen so bad because I thought it was him . . . or I want this to be over," states Toschi in *Zodiac*, and for the San Francisco detective, the mystifying and frustrating inaction of the killer leads to escalating frustration, especially when Hollywood takes over the investigation and turns the spree into fodder for Clint Eastwood's Dirty Harry Callahan. "It's quite a challenge. I never let a day go by without remembering Zodiac," notes Toschi in Graysmith's book. "Now that I'm the only one working on it, it's gotten to be more personal. I've got eight filing cabinet drawers filled with Zodiac data—including the names of more than 2,000 potential suspects. I don't know if I'll ever get the case solved, but I'm sure as hell trying. I feel he's out there. I feel he's going to surface" (197).

Discouraged but undaunted, Toschi and Graysmith are adamant in their severed yet allied efforts. In Fincher's film, an economic connective pan links both characters, unbeknownst to each other, as they revisit the fateful intersection of Washington and Cherry, where Zodiac killed the cabbie and was nearly identified. The disparities and similarities between Graysmith and Toschi are crucial contrasts for cracking the Zodiac case, as each character feeds from the work of the other, even if it's from occasionally oppositional plates. Fincher would show a comparably conflicting approach to collaborative investigation in the initially involuntary but instantly capable partnership of Mikael Blomkvist (Daniel Craig) and Lisbeth Salander (Rooney Mara) in *The Girl with the Dragon Tattoo* (2011). Their solitary quests exceed past antagonistic introductions to affirm an unlikely alliance, certified by kindred spirits and personal motivations. For both, like for those in *Zodiac*, a curiosity must be gratified, there must be the righting of a wrong, even if it means putting one's life in danger. It's an intrinsic, spontaneous sensation shared by their film's own devious executioner. Investigating what is revealed to be a legacy of animosity and violence, Mikael uncovers the culprit, Stellan Skarsgård's Martin Vanger, who admits to likewise working on instinct. "We're not that different, you and I," he dryly observes. "We both have urges; satisfying mine requires more towels."

In *Se7en*, Morgan Freeman's Detective Somerset is a grizzled, grim, and thoughtful counterpart to Brad Pitt's detective Mills, an eager, impulsive newcomer, also experienced but not in a city like the one in which the film is set (a foreboding disclaimer uttered by Somerset). Their contrasts are plenty: one's life of solitude, one's marriage; one's penchant for Chaucer and Dante, one's preference for beer and basketball; one's occupational optimism verses one's disillusionment—"You meant what you said about catching the guy," remarks Somerset, seemingly surprised by Mills's zealousness. Still, they do suffer the same weight of waiting, in their case at the behest of what John Doe (Kevin Spacey) does and when he decides to do it. Like *Zodiac*'s protagonists, they are at the mercy of their target, needing him to act in order for them to move forward, needing him to reveal further clues while dreading what may constitute the next crime scene. Angered by John Doe's apparent intentionality, that he is dogging them in the same way Zodiac taunts his pursuers, Mills also feels the killer is laughing at him and his partner, interpreting the antipathy as a personal affront (that a self-possessed John Doe gives himself up and isn't captured adds insult to injury).

Embodying the same professional resignation seen by Toschi, the two detectives of *Se7en* must get past the initial shock of John Doe's gruesome approach to focus on the revelatory details. What they don't account for is the drive and determination of the killer, a conviction symptomatic of the indigent setting, one that is not wholly dissimilar to their own. Somerset and Mills are clearly averse to their crime-ridden turf, and so when John Doe enters the picture as a self-appointed moralizer, the perimeter between his adjudication and that of the officers is notably blurred. Just as Somerset and Mills are disturbed by their surroundings, enforcing laws to combat the degradation, John Doe enacts his twisted punishment, embellished by elaborate, grisly sermons. In the end, the killer's atonement is in seeking out his own castigation (though more aggrandizing, his envious admissions recall Zodiac's mocking confessionals). But a reciprocated consideration is also seen in Somerset's recognition of John Doe's will, his concept of "the big picture," and his innate humanity: "It's dismissive to call him a lunatic," says the pensive detective.

"There is," also remarks Somerset, "nothing wrong with a man taking pleasure in his work." The comment has its application to the cops, reporters, and the killers who populate the criminal cinema of David Fincher (*Mindhunter*'s Kempler dubs his murderous deeds a "vocation" while John Doe calls his exploits "my work"), and it aligns with the director himself, in his rigorous perfectionism. Evoking the thoroughness of Graysmith's quest and John Doe's attention to detail—"Methodical, exacting, and most of all, patient," according to Somerset—Christopher Orr contends, "It's difficult to think of a more perfect pairing of director and project than *Zodiac*, which attaches Fincher's legendarily painstaking methods to a story about procedure and obsession" (2007). Employing precise expository detail to advance individual and narrative development, Fincher's film abounds in the thorough depiction of technique and the delineation of tangible evidence to distill the horrific methods of the monster into manageable, comprehensible connotations. "While nominally a police procedural film," *Zodiac* is at its heart, observes Mike Miley, "a film about filmmaking; it is less about the obsessive process of tracking a serial killer than about the obsessive process of creating meaningful work" (2010). Contingent on the accumulation of records, interviews, and quantifiable confirmation, Fincher's meticulous administration of authentic action and detail affirms a legitimacy that engenders immersed curiosity. "For obsession in *Zodiac* is not an end in itself," adds Miley, "rather, it becomes the point of origin, the catalyst for artistic creation" (2010).

In *Zodiac* and the three supplemental works considered here, Fincher's formal proclivity is for bleak visuals and a preponderance of charts, maps, files, and reports, using documentation as a way of seeing, analyzing, and engaging with the trail left behind, reconstructing a timeline, fixing the threads, and building graphic connections. Like the comics and ciphers and symbolically staged crime scenes so vital to the iconography of films like *Zodiac* and *Se7en*, here is a director incorporating redolent imagery as a way to establish and communicate pictorial relevance. "What many viewers found seductive about *Se7en*," argues Nayman, "was the way that its visual style basically enshrined the point of view of its Lecteresque antagonist. As framed by Fincher and photographed by Darius Khondji . . . *Se7en*'s world seemed exactly as corrupt and corroded as Kevin Spacey's John Doe suggested."

But while Nayman contends the filmmaking in *Se7en* is "perfectly aligned with its villain's perceptions" and that "there is no such identification in *Zodiac*" (2007), the rendering of Graysmith's increasingly overwhelmed and overwhelming mental state does correlate to how the artist related to Zodiac, which was, in the beginning, based on imagery, a raptness with the "purely visual qualities of Zodiac's symbol" (1986, X). "Like detectives," states Miley, "artists attempt to represent reality in an understandable form, to impose meaning through the organization of details. *Zodiac* dramatizes this artistic process.... The film chronicles an artist's obsessive attempt to render reality intelligible in the hopes of discovering a unified meaning to existence" (2010). Such pictorial pull is conveyed by Fincher in the repeated emphasis of graphic representation: the killer's criminal symbolism, the perceptible images with their inscrutable meanings. As Sam Dickson observes, "Prior to any denotative or connotative meanings found in the text, or of any figurative importance read from the killer's evocation of the idea of 'zodiac,' the detectives are most interested in the very shape of the signifiers. The written evidence—letters read as images—becomes a surrogate for the lack of visual or sonic evidence . . . the detectives are searching for the real beneath the confusing symbolic (cryptograms) and imaginary (psychologising narratives) leads produced by his letters" (2016). And in the solving of these puzzles, Fincher does in fact bring one closer to the wavelength of Zodiac, using this visual language as a gateway into his disturbed, albeit advanced, psychology.

While Fincher also speaks of an intentional detachment in *Zodiac*, pointing to the film's opening suburban street tracking shot or the impassive taxi cab killing, and the film often appears visually controlled, rigorous in its compositions, striking a stable illustrative balance to offset some of the more gruesome moments of the picture, there are also sequences of active filmic involvement. See, for example, the analytical point of view adopted during the questioning of Arthur Leigh Allen, where the nonchalant performances are counteracted by the viewer's own suspicions, guided by Fincher's camera, looking for clues and tell-tale signs of culpability. As the characters exchange cautious glances, fostering assumptions and evoking skepticism, the spectator plays along with the mulling progression through a series of close-ups and sightline matches. "The cops aren't studying Allen's personality," remarks Jones, "but the array of possible evidence he's laying out as he speaks. There's no giveaway of abnormality (beyond a faintly unpleasant prissiness), no Lecterish mind-melding. The drama of the scene is in the intensity of studying, surveying, sizing up within the limits of the law" (2008).

Still, the unsettled mystery remains. "Some of the most obsessive characters in cinema are artists, cops, and serial killers" (Miley, 2010), and *Zodiac* features all three. But while "these characters engage in repetitive toil in the hopes of reaching a point of completion," none, he argues, achieves satisfaction. "This makes the conflict of the film informational: there is a truth the characters and the audience want to know but cannot discover" (Miley, 2010). And this is in large part why Graysmith is such a relatable protagonist. Fundamentally admirable and decisively endearing, his perfectly plausible tenacity sprouts from a commendable inability to leave the case alone, or to allow it to remain incomplete. He thrives on the mystery but cannot bear the thought of that mystery persisting. "What drives this conflict is the modernist belief that the truth exists," writes Miley, "we just have to look harder in order to find it. This need to impose or discover meaning in the world can lead to obsession, with the obsessed believing that fixating on the subject will reveal meaning. To abandon the obsession is to accept the presence of meaninglessness in the world" (Miley, 2010). While professionally detached from Avery and Toschi, Graysmith's outcast post gives him the conveyed credibility of an average person in an average position, a linkage that makes his exhilaration more acceptable and understandable. Indeed, as shown in John Mikulenka's 2003 documentary, *Hunting the Zodiac*, the furtive ambiguity of the Zodiac case still resonates with true crime aficionados the world over, in no small part because of this enduring incompleteness. To that end, *Zodiac* endorses a persuasive, encouraging response, a feeling that, as Orr states, "the truth might be just around the corner, that one more scrap of evidence, one more phone call, could make all the pieces of the puzzle fit together at last." Like Graysmith, Orr adds, "Fincher has madness in his method; unlike him, he has found what he was looking for" (2007).

REFERENCES

Cole, Michael. 2015. "*Zodiac* (2007) Movie." *The Zodiac Revisited*. Accessed May 10, 2018, http://zodiacrevisited.com/zodiac-2007-movie

Dickson, Sam. 2016. "*Zodiac* and the Ends of Cinema." *Senses of Cinema*. Accessed May 7, 2018, http://sensesofcinema.com/2016/feature-articles/zodiac.

Eggert, Brian. 2015. "*Zodiac*." *Deep Focus Review*. Accessed May 10, 2018, https://deepfocusreview.com/definitives/zodiac.

Fincher, David. 2010. "Killer Talent: A David Fincher Profile (Part 3)." Interviewed by Trevor Hogg. *Flickering Myth*. Accessed May 10, 2018, https://www.flickeringmyth.com/2010/10/killer-talent-david-fincher-profile_13

———. 2017a. "David Fincher Knows Exactly Why We're All So Obsessed With True Crime." Interviewed by Eliana Dockterman. *Time*. Accessed May 13, 2018, http://time.com/4966408/david-fincher-mindhunter

———. 2017b. "David Fincher Is Still Fascinated by Serial Killers." Interviewed by Adam Grant, *Esquire*. Accessed May 13, 2018, https://www.esquire.com/entertainment/tv/a12775936/david-fincher-2017-interview-mindhunter

———. 2017c. "David Fincher: 'Moviemaking is a rat f*ck, every day is a skirmish.'" Interviewed by Matt Thrift, *Little White Lies*. Accessed May 13, 2018, http://lwlies.com/interviews/david-fincher-mindhunter-netflix-true-crime-series

Graysmith, Robert. 1986. *Zodiac: The Shocking True Story of the Hunt for the Nation's Most Elusive Serial Killer*. New York, NY: Berkley.

Graysmith, Robert. 2007a. "Robert Graysmith Discusses *Zodiac*," interviewed by Brad Brevet, *ComingSoon.net*. Accessed May 13, 2018, http://www.comingsoon.net/movies/news/515318-robert_graysmith_discusses_zodiac

Graysmith, Robert. 2007b. "Q&A: *Zodiac* Writer Robert Graysmith", interviewed by Karen Breslau, *Newsweek*. Accessed May 13, 2018, https://www.newsweek.com/qa-zodiac-writer-robert-graysmith-95629

Jones, Kent. 2008. "An Open-And-Shut Case: Why David Fincher's *Zodiac* Is the Film of the Year." *Film Comment*. Accessed May 10, 2018, https://www.csus.edu/indiv/s/starkj/coms192/zodiac1.pdf

Levy, Emanuel. 2006. "Fincher: Brilliant *Zodiac*." *emanuellevy.com*. Accessed May 7, 2018, http://emanuellevy.com/comment/finchers-brilliant-zodiac-preview-6

Macklin, Tony. 2007. "Man in the Dark: On David Fincher's *Zodiac*," *Bright Lights Film Journal*. Accessed May 7, 2018, https://brightlightsfilm.com/wp-content/cache/all/man-dark-david-finchers-zodiac/#.W51D2KZKiUk

Miley, Mike. 2010. "Deciphering the Indecipherable: Procedure as Art in Fincher's *Zodiac*." *Bright Lights Film Journal*. Accessed May 10, 2018, https://brightlightsfilm.com/wp-content/cache/all/deciphering-the-indecipherable-procedure-as-art-in-finchers-zodiac/#.W51D26ZKiUk

Nayman, Adam. 2017. "Unsolved Mystery." *The Ringer*. Accessed May 7, 2018, https://www.theringer.com/2017/7/25/16077982/zodiac-ten-year-anniversary-david-fincher-great-film-93d9cf2f70f6

Orr, Christopher. 2007. "The Movie Review: *Zodiac*." *The Atlantic*. Accessed May 10, 2018, https://www.theatlantic.com/entertainment/archive/2007/07/the-movie-review-zodiac/63807

Sorensen, Jeff. 2014. "An In-Depth Analysis of Zodiac the Film Vs. The Real Zodiac Killer Case." *UPROXX*. Accessed May 13, 2018, https://uproxx.com/viral/an-in-depth-analysis-of-zodiac-the-film-vs-the-real-zodiac-killer-case

"*Zodiac* Production Notes." 2007. Paramount Pictures. *MovieWeb*, February 14. Accessed May 7, 2018, https://web.archive.org/web/20070927225954/http://media.movieweb.com/galleries/3158/notes.pdf

Chapter 5

Subverting the Investigator as Hero

Masculinity and Failure in David Fincher's Zodiac

Theresa Rodewald

Time Magazine lists the Zodiac killings as number two on its list of "Top 10 Unsolved Crimes," trumped only by Jack the Ripper. Until today, the case continues to fascinate and captivate people in and outside of the United States as Zodiac's signature symbol, letters, and ciphers have inscribed themselves into cultural memory. His representation in popular culture spans from film and television to books, music, and even video games. In academia, the Zodiac has made his way into a variety of fields with philosopher Andrew Winters aptly summarizing that "although Zodiac has not been caught, most of us have already met him" (2010, 17). In this way, David Fincher's 2007 feature *Zodiac* is part of a long-standing tradition that feeds off and into the Zodiac mystery. In contrast to most movies about the Zodiac, Fincher's film shifts its focus away from the killer and onto the investigators: *San Fransisco Chronicle* cartoonist Robert Graysmith (Jake Gyllenhaal) on whose book the film is based, police inspector David Toschi (Mark Ruffalo), and investigative journalist Paul Avery (Robert Downey Jr.). Genre and storytelling conventions lead the audience to expect the capture of the Zodiac or at least for his identity to be revealed, yet neither of these things happen. While Graysmith's book provides a solution to the mystery of Zodiac's identity, Fincher's film is more cautious and denies its audience certainty in the matter. Therefore, the film is not just an adaptation of Graysmith's book but also an account of a failed crime investigation.

Zodiac's focus on the investigators' ultimately unsuccessful struggle to catch the killer is of interest here as this chapter strives to examine the film with regard to masculinity and failure. The study of masculinity in movies began as a continuation of feminist film studies and their analysis of representation and spectatorship. Today, however, work on the subject covers almost all areas of film studies (Gallagher 2017). Contemporary film scholarship examines masculinity in relation to genre-specific representations of men, such as the Western hero (Bordin 2014) or the gangster (Larke-Walsh 2010). Masculinity is also studied with regard to acting and performance (Peberdy 2011), or social roles such as fatherhood (Hamad 2013).

While *Zodiac* has been subject of scholarly research, its conjunction of masculinity and failure has not yet received thorough attention. Luis M. García-Mainar regards *Zodiac* as a proponent of what he describes as "the introspective realist crime film," a subgenre concerned with the social dimension of crime as well as aesthetics of realism (García-Mainar 2016, 2). Sarah Casey Benyahia focuses on *Zodiac*'s transgression of genre boundaries and the fact that the film does not offer a clearcut solution of the case (Benyahia 2012, 77). Allison Young argues that in spite of the failed police investigation, *Zodiac*'s "spectacle of process" assigns meaning to police procedure as such (Young 2010, 168). In contrast to that, Michele Schreiber is primarily interested in the intersection of masculinity and digital filmmaking techniques in Fincher's films. With regard to failure, she maintains that *Zodiac* shows "the ultimately futile investigative efforts of its male protagonists," a notion that does not differentiate between failure and futility (Schreiber 2016, 4).

Recurring features of these readings revolve around the fact that the case is never solved as well as *Zodiac*'s cinematic construction of the ensuing confusion and frustration (Benyahia 2012, 79; García-Mainar 2016, 143; Schreiber 2016, 4; Young 2010, 152). Accordingly, they also reflect on questions of audience expectations and knowledge (Benyahia 2012, 84; García-Mainar 2016, 147; Young 2010, 168). Genre is discussed insofar as *Zodiac* is seen as a character study of policemen and journalists, rather than a serial killer movie (Benyahia 2012, 87; García-Mainar 2016, 143). The cinematic representation of time passing often plays an important part as well (Benyahia 2012, 79; García-Mainar 2016, 142; Schreiber 2016, 7). Furthermore, Graysmith's obsession and how he seems to pay for it with the estrangement of his wife and children is a commonly discussed topic (Benyahia 2012, 83; García-Mainar 2016, 145). While these observations are extremely insightful, they do not as of yet include an exploration of masculinity and failure.

In order to close this gap, the reading of *Zodiac* offered here inspects the investigators' failure to solve the case from the perspective of genre conventions around heroism and masculinity. Subsequently, this chapter analyses how genre, cinematography and acting intersect to depict Graysmith, Avery, and Toschi as well as the Zodiac Killer. Since Graysmith is the film's main protagonist, he will also be the focal point of analysis. Comparing *Zodiac* to a number of other crime film genres like private eye and detective movies shows that it resists simple classification and undermines genre-typical depictions of masculinity and success. It will be argued that Graysmith is an unusual crime film protagonist because his underlying motivation is to belong and be acknowledged, that is to reach personal closure, rather than to enable justice.

A brief account of conceptions of failure outside of cinema reveals that "proper" masculinity is often synonymous with successful masculinity and associates failure with broken manhood. Similarly, crime films commonly associate failure with defeated heroism and compromised masculinity. Since the case in *Zodiac* remains unsolved, this chapter explores if and how failing to convict the killer reflects back on Graysmith's masculinity. It concludes that in *Zodiac*, failing appears less as the investigators' fault and more as an existential problem, a reflection on the relationship between society and crime.

ZODIAC AS A PRIVATE EYE FILM

As a crime thriller, *Zodiac* operates within genre conventions that prominently feature masculinity. In *Detecting Men: Masculinity and the Hollywood Detective Film* (2006), Philippa Gates argues that the way the detective movie tends to delineate narrative, characters, and themes into opposites allows for a thorough examination of positive (detective) and negative (villain) conceptions of masculinity (8). How these positive and negative conceptions of masculinity are defined and represented varies across the different subgenres of crime film and changes with time. What is interesting about Fincher's *Zodiac* in this context is that it evokes a number of different crime films. The first part of the movie focuses on the investigation conducted by Toschi and his partner Armstrong (Anthony Edwards) and includes elements of the police film. Contrary to most proponents of the genre, *Zodiac* presents police work in a more realistic way; instead of chase scenes or shootouts, there is an overwhelming amount of information, witness' statements and suspects (Leitch 2009, 215).

While Toschi and Armstrong are undeniably police men, describing Graysmith's position as an investigator is more difficult. Comparing *Zodiac* and its protagonist to the private eye film is quite compelling because they can be read as a rejection of the hard-boiled detective. In terms of narrative, *Zodiac* clearly departs from the private eye formula: there is no political conspiracy that involves corrupt police officials, the criminal on the loose is a serial killer, not a powerful businessman and above all there is no seductive, double-crossing and yet tragic *femme fatale* who the detective first falls in love with to then reject (Leitch 2009, 195).

Still, there is a distinctive *noir*-feeling about Fincher's film: its earthy, at times sepia-like color palette, the neon-lit, rainy streets of San Fransisco and the predominance of nighttime scenes are (mainly visual) features that *Zodiac* shares with the private eye film (193). Therefore, it is all the more interesting that *Zodiac*'s protagonist Robert Graysmith stands in such sharp contrast to the tough and hard-boiled private detective. In his analysis of the private eye film, Thomas Leitch states that the hard-boiled detective owes as much to amateur sleuths like Sherlock Holmes as to the Western hero which makes him something of urban cowboy (193). Accordingly, every case is first and foremost a test of the hard-boiled hero's masculinity (197). Leitch observes that by solving the case, the private eye often reaffirms and defends his tough, that is, violent and hegemonic, masculinity at the cost of the female and gay characters whom he leaves "demystified, disempowered, defeated, and dehumanised" (198).[1]

As opposed to that, *Zodiac*'s protagonist Graysmith is a divorced husband and father who likes puzzles and is so innocently naïve that few people take him seriously. Graysmith is not violent at all; his biggest flaw and most defining feature is his obsession with the Zodiac case. Although this obsession makes it impossible for him to combine his investigations with his family life, Graysmith does not reject other people. On the contrary, he tries to alleviate his outsider status and strives for acknowledgment from and community with them. As opposed to the hard-boiled detective, Graysmith looks up to other men. In fact, the relationship between him and his fellow investigators Avery and Toschi can be read as a buddy dynamic, that is, a relationship between opposites that gradually shifts into mutual respect (Benyahia 2012, 82). The hard-boiled detective on the other hand is a loner by choice (Leitch 2009, 197).

Graysmith's wish to belong is a defining aspect of his character which the film establishes during the opening titles. After dropping his son off at school, Graysmith enters the building of the *San Fransisco Chronicle* where he works as a cartoonist. In the crammed elevator, people engage in polite conversations but Graysmith is not involved in any of them. His desire to belong is effectively introduced when he enters the newsroom. The camera pulls back in a tracking shot that centers on Graysmith who faces the camera. As he passes a group of men around Paul Avery, who chatter and laugh amiably, he tilts his head in their direction while avoiding eye contact. Graysmith's body language indicates that he feels drawn to them and tries to listen in to their conversation. Tellingly, no one waits for him at his desk. Later, when the first Zodiac cipher is passed around the conference room, Graysmith, who has started copying it, is sent out almost immediately. These scenes illustrate that to people around him, Graysmith is not a part of the *Chronicle*'s inner circle but a tolerated bystander.

On a visual level, the first editorial sequence underlines Graysmith's outsider status through costume. While almost all men in the conference room are dressed in blue or white shirts combined with black ties or suits, Graysmith wears a brown suit and a plaid shirt in a similar color. Visually, this sets him apart from his colleagues while simultaneously blending him in with the brown wood panels around him. Thus, Graysmith appears invisible and isolated in his alterity. In contrast, Paul Avery simply stands out. His yellow-green waistcoat and green shirt separate him from his colleagues as well as the wood panels. While visually different, he is socially integrated and his jokes are received with laughter. Not surprisingly, the editorial sequence ends with Avery asking his colleagues out for a drink at "Morti's." The next shot shows Graysmith walking past the bar and peering through the door so that he is literally positioned outside looking in. While the color scheme of the exterior is dusky, blueish, and cold, the lights inside the bar appear yellow and warm, further underlining Graysmith's status as an outsider who would like to belong.

ZODIAC AND THE UNOFFICIAL INVESTIGATOR FILM

While evoking the *noir*-aesthetic of hard-boiled detective movies, *Zodiac* dismisses most of the genre's narrative conventions. Fincher's depiction of Graysmith as an outsider might seem closer to the unofficial detective or amateur sleuth in the tradition of Sherlock Holmes or Hercule Poirot. With regard to masculinity, the sleuth is not as narrowly defined as the private eye because, as Leitch puts it, unofficial detective films are primarily concerned with questions of knowledge (2009, 170). The amateur detective does not have to be tough so much as smart and often he is an eccentric that people tend to underestimate (170). At first glance, Graysmith seems to fit this mold perfectly: his work colleagues do not even notice him and only after he correctly predicts that the Zodiac will not include his name in the first cipher, Avery starts paying attention to him. Similarly to Avery, Toschi takes note of Graysmith after he surprises him with his insight into the investigation. They have their first conversation after a screening of *Dirty Harry* which Toschi has already forgotten by the time they meet again.

On closer examination, however, there are a number of major differences between the unofficial detective film and *Zodiac*. The eccentric amateur is often pitted against a mystery as opposed to a criminal (Leitch 2009, 170). A defining feature of Fincher's film, however, is the Zodiac Killer himself; the mystery revolves around his identity, not around the methodology of his crimes. In addition to that, unofficial detective films adapt an atmosphere of calm safety in the face of crime. The omniscient detective inevitably solves the mystery which serves to counterbalance all threats of social disruption and violence that crime usually evokes (173). These threatening elements are further contained by an emphasis on the detective's cozy domestic lifestyle and everyday rituals (174).[2]

Zodiac introduces Graysmith performing a domestic ritual: together with his son, he is brushing his teeth and getting ready to leave for work. The audience is witnessing an ordinary morning, a "ritual" made all the more believable because Graysmith is late for work and constantly double tasking, for instance, when he finishes a cartoon while stuck in traffic. Yet, there are two aspects already hinting at the fact that this comfortable domesticity is misleading. The first shot of Graysmith's face is as a mirror image which is revealing because the metaphor of the mirror is often used to express questions of identity and illusion. In Graysmith's case, the mirror image suggests that there is more to him than meets the eye, it points at the complexity of his personality and foreshadows that he is not the omniscient sleuth one might take him to be. Secondly, the cross-cutting between Graysmith arriving at the *Chronicle* and the first Zodiac letter making its way to the editor align him with the Zodiac murders. This connection leads the audience to expect that Graysmith will eventually solve the case (Benyahia 2012, 81). As the film progresses, it becomes clear that Graysmith's domestic rituals do not act as a counterweight to the killer's horrendous crimes but are gradually invaded by the case (for instance, when Graysmith has his children help him check some of the case data) until they cease to exist because his wife Melanie (Chloë Sevigny) leaves him and takes the children with her. Similarly, the film's narrative leads "from an optimistic revelation to another dead end," thus continually frustrating audience expectations (81).

GRAYSMITH AS "CRIMINALIST"

Zodiac's intriguing mix of crime film subgenres, and its unusual detective Graysmith seem to converge in what Philippa Gates calls films featuring a "criminalist," a hero who is not so much tough as smart (2006, 158). This genre presents a more realistic and complex depiction of masculinity, it focuses on the relationship between the detective and his adversary and features serial, seemingly random murder as the crime (158). This description fits *Zodiac* because the "relationship" to the Zodiac seems to take up more space in Graysmith's life than his marriage. Above all, however, the film draws an important parallel between the two men: Graysmith as well as the Zodiac are outsiders. It seems that both, the Zodiac as well as Graysmith, want to be acknowledged, they both work alone and the film strongly suggests that Graysmith gets as close to the killer as anyone because of these shared characteristics.

Despite this parallel, however, *Zodiac* does not suggest that they are the same so much as each other's opposites. The Zodiac does not want to belong so much as dominate; in sending letters and ciphers to newspapers, he strives to demonstrate his superiority. Here, the act of murder is an absolute expression of power, the power to take someone else's life. Graysmith on the other hand wants to belong and hopes that by supplying the police with information, he will earn the acknowledgment of those he looks up to. When Avery asks him what he "want[s] out of this," Graysmith does not even understand the question. While the Zodiac's desire to be seen acknowledged expresses itself in dominance of and violence against other people, Graysmith seeks community with them. While Zodiac's impulse is destructive, Graysmith's impulse is social—they are like two sides of the same coin.

Graysmith is an interesting detective-protagonist because he is neither an amateur sleuth nor a hard-boiled private detective. Instead, he starts out as a bystander and through his obsession with the case gradually becomes a Zodiac expert. With regard to masculinity, Graysmith's underlying character drive is the desire to belong. His outsider status sets him apart not only from the private detective but also from most crime thriller investigators because more often than not, the detective is content with his outsider status. Indeed, a common feature of buddy cop films is the wayward cop who does not want a partner at first, as is the case in *Lethal Weapon* (Richard Donner, 1987). Similarly, the amateur sleuth might be an eccentric like Hercule Poirot or Sherlock Holmes, or a loner like Same Spade or Jack Gittes but he seldomly struggles to be acknowledged. Thus, detective films tend to reject personal relationships as points of weakness suggesting instead that the detective needs to be alone to solve the case (Gates 2006, 34). *Zodiac* evokes this idea when Graysmith's obsessive quest for the Zodiac becomes so all-encompassing that Melanie decides to leave him. When Graysmith finds the note she has left for him, he crumbles it up in frustration and anger which turns out to be the next vital clue: the name of Linda del Buono (Clea DuVall), the sister of Darleen Ferrin (Ciara Hughes) who was murdered by the Zodiac. Yet, neither this nor any other clue lead Graysmith to actually solving the case. They help him assemble a theory about Arthur Lee Allen (John Carroll Lynch) being the Zodiac but the identity of the killer is never confirmed. Devoting his life to the Zodiac case does not automatically lead to success. Fincher's film thus undermines the seemingly natural connection between effort and accomplishment that is present in so many detective films. After all, *Zodiac*'s most obvious and interesting divergence from the majority of crime films is that the case remains unsolved.

NOTIONS OF FAILURE

Ideas associated with failure and failing are not surprisingly quintessentially negative: failing is often a statement about someone's identity as in "being" a failure. Failing is associated with lack of effort or laziness and is frequently connected to futility and a sense of defeat. At the same time, however, there are ideas around failing "better" where failure appears as another step on the way to eventual success.

In his book, *Born Losers: A History of Failure in America* (2005), Scott A. Sandage explores how failure became a mode of being, an identity. He argues that the notion of failure as a deficient self is intertwined with the rise of capitalism in nineteenth-century America: failure was "something made, not someone born—until the market revolution" (Sandage 2005, 11). Thus, failure is a by-product of capitalism, a system under which, according to Sandage, hard work does not automatically warrant success (15). This relationship, however, is usually disguised and instead, failure appears to result from lack of ambition and striving (18).

In *The Material Culture of Failure*, Timothy Carroll, David Jeevendrampillai, Aaron Parkhurst, and Julie Shackelford also ask why failing usually appears so disastrous and shameful. Modern society's aversion to failure, they argue, is embedded in the competitive spirit of capitalism (Carroll et al. 2017, 3). Tracing what they call the "cultural line of evolutionary thought," they argue that failure is often part of a worldview where everything one sees is that which has succeeded (2). Consequently, failure is only bearable when aligned with a sense of intentionality which in return is tied to ideas of duty, responsibility, and blame (2). As opposed to Sandage, however, they are not primarily concerned with these ideological roots of failing and instead regard failure as something inherently productive (5). According to Carroll et al., failure produces change and is connected to discovery and processes of learning, as in learning from past mistakes (3). As a result, they define failure as "the gap that follows the collapse of one mode of life and precedes the development of a new one" (2).

A somewhat radical approach to the study of failure is Jack/Judith Halberstam's book *The Queer Art of Failure* (2011). While sharing Sandage's idea of failure as an ideological tool of capitalism, the author proposes to embrace failing as an alternative way of being (Halberstam 2011, 11). Halberstam reads failure "as a refusal of mastery, a critique of the intuitive connections within capitalism between success and profit, and as a counter hegemonic discourse of losing" (11). Approaching failure from the angle of queer studies, Halberstam aims to "queer" notions of success and failure, that is, to make them strange and point to the meaning-making processes behind them.

Still, the idea of failure as something inherently negative that reflects back on a person's identity is quite persistent, not least because it is constantly reproduced in cultural discourse. Thomas Patrick Oates analyses the representation of failure and masculinity in sport documentaries. He argues that success frequently appears as a foundation of normative masculinity while inversely, failure entails failing to be a "proper" man: "[b]ecause sport defines success in hyper-masculine terms, failed players are often portrayed as failed men—lacking toughness or hunger, demonstrating unwillingness to accept a place within a rigid hierarchy" (Oates 2014, 222). Oates regards success and failure as features of hegemonic masculinity, a term coined by R. W. Connell that refers to sociocultural practices which serve to maintain the suppression of women as well as men who fall outside of its norms (217; Connell 2005, 77). Because striving for success legitimizes the abuse of professional athletes, Oates argues that the depiction of failure can be a mode of resistance (Oates 2014, 217). Making failure visible can help reveal the abusive system behind professional sport and show that physical and psychological punishment do not inevitably lead to success but to suffering (219).

Oates makes two interesting observations. First, he connects failure to notions of normative masculinity and second, he argues that depicting failure can help subvert these notions of manhood. While *Zodiac* does not go as far as Oates's sport documentaries, the film is an account of a crime investigation that fails to identify and catch the killer. In terms of genre, not many detective films deny their audience the closure of finding the culprit because by solving the mystery, the detective wraps up the case as well as any social issues it might have raised (Gates 2006, 24). As a result, the audience can rest assured that "as civilized beings, we retain a mastery over the world in which we live no matter how complex, violent, or chaotic it seems" (20). Therefore, failing to solve the crime is often connected to a sense of defeat: the killer gets away, justice does not prevail and what remains is a sense of futility (265).

With regard to masculinity Gates observes that a detective who fails to solve the case is not a proper hero (172). As opposed to Oates's reading of failure in sport documentaries, the unsuccessful detective is not so much a failed man as the wrong man for the job. Failing to detect can be a way of criticizing outmoded forms of masculinity rather than reaffirming features of hegemonic masculinity. Gates argues that detective films of the 1990s and early 2000s not only featured a new kind of hero who embodied a new kind of masculinity (the criminalist, cf. above) but also suggested that the hard-boiled detective was no longer suited to solve contemporary crime. Gates reads the portrayal of Detective Dave Kujan (Chazz Palminteri) in *The Usual Suspects* (1995), Detective David Mills (Brad Pitt) in *Se7en* (1995) and Officer Bud White (Russell Crowe) and Detective Jack Vincennes (Kevin Spacey) in *L.A. Confidential* (1997) as a critique of the anti-intellectual, tough detective. It is their lack of knowledge and sensitivity that prevents them from solving the case (Gates 2006, 173).[3]

In a way, Polanski's *Chinatown* (1974) can be read as an early proponent of detective films that represent tough and hard-boiled masculinity as doomed to fail. A brief account of *Chinatown* is interesting because just like *Zodiac*, the film deals with a failed crime investigation but in quite a different way. Although detective Jake Gittes (Jack Nicholson) solves the case, Leitch calls the film "a record of unrelieved failure" (2009, 202). While Gittes does get to know the killer's identity, he is unable to persuade the police to arrest him just as he is unable to save the life of his love interest Evelyn Mulwray (Faye Dunaway) (202). The truth that Gittes uncovers is so monstrous that it is hard to believe: wealthy businessman Noah Cross (John Huston) raped his daughter Evelyn and fostered a child with her. Cross also killed Evelyn's husband Mulwray (Darrell Zwerling) to cover up his involvement in a scheme to inflate the value of land he has purchased by manipulating the city's water supply. Leitch argues that Cross's crime "reveals the catastrophic sexual and social power of patriarchy gone mad" (210). Cross is depicted as both a socially and sexually deviant monster as well as a powerful man who controls an entire city. He succeeds in his plans while the private detective knows the truth but is helpless to do anything about it (213). According to Leitch, Gittes fails because he is a perfect specimen of the private eye: he looks at the world in black and white, he delineates people into suspects and innocent victims and he is a violent and emotionally stunted man (214). Essentially, failure in *Chinatown* amounts to a critique of the private eye film and its representation of masculinity.

MASCULINTIES IN *ZODIAC*

While films such as *Chinatown* or *Se7en* reject tough masculinity by showing that its proponents are suited to solve crimes, *Zodiac* depicts its main protagonist Graysmith as a reverse tough guy. The character embodying most aspects of tough and violent masculinity is the antagonist, the Zodiac Killer. He is anxiety-provoking, brutal and violent, directs his aggressions toward women and seems unable to express emotions other than anger. It is true of course that most filmic (serial) killers exhibit features of violent masculinity. Yet the fact that Graysmith stands in such sharp contrast to the violent hard-boiled detective, sets *Zodiac* apart from most proponents of its genre.

This characterization of the Zodiac corresponds to another feature of serial killer movies. Gates remarks that because his preferred targets are women, the serial killer's violence can be read as "a backlash against the loss of power experienced by dominant males" (2006, 162). Following this line of argumentation, the serial killer appears as another take on the cowboy which makes him "the ultimate hero of American culture" (163). In this rendering of the American myth, the frontier hero has gone mad, his need to assert dominance through violence has reached a pivotal moment (serial murder) and there is no place for him in (or even at the margins of) society. This monstrous hero voices the most extreme form of the American ideal of individual freedom. As Gates notes, most serial killer films tend to dampen this criticism by strongly aligning the audience with the detective-hero (164). Although *Zodiac* definitely offers alignment with Graysmith, it is still possible to read the Zodiac as a distorted version of the Western hero and a critique of unrestrained individualism not least because he successfully avoids capture.

As has been shown above, Graysmith and the Zodiac are two sides of the same coin, they are each other's opposites and represent two opposed types of masculinity. Graysmith is somewhat naïve and neither hard-boiled nor violent while the Zodiac reveals the destructive toxicity at the core of tough masculinity. Thus, *Zodiac* maintains the classic detective film division between good and evil and presents the Zodiac Killer as society's other. Interestingly, this "other" and his masculinity are neither marked as effeminate or homosexual as is the case in private eye films (Leitch 2009, 198), nor as seemingly weak and inconspicuous as in films featuring the criminalist (Gates 2006, 161). The partial identity the film reveals but never confirms is that of a white man with a crew cut, someone who is not defined by conventional and highly problematic markers of otherness such as foreignness or homosexuality (161). However partial and elusive this identity might be, it still seems to stand in opposition to the ideals of 1970s counterculture. While the Zodiac-based serial killer in *Dirty Harry* is more of a long-haired hippie who arguably embodies conservative America's fears of the counterculture, Fincher's Zodiac seems to look more like a conservative himself.

Taken together, the characterization of the Zodiac and of Graysmith make for an account of modern (or contemporary) masculinity. Angry, tough, and violent white masculinity is associated with the killer and thus rejected while a more sensitive masculinity characterizes the protagonist. Since *Zodiac* is based on Graysmith's book, his version of events underlies the film's narrative. Graysmith is convinced that Arthur Lee Allen is the Zodiac. As a child molester who lives in a trailer at edge of town, Allen fits the mould of social outcast, of monster and "other" perfectly. This characterization of the Zodiac is more in line with crime film genre conventions that depict the killer as sexually and socially deviant. What is interesting here is that *Zodiac* leans toward Graysmith's more conventional narrative without confirming it. At the end of the film, the Zodiac remains elusive, invisible, and uncaught. Contrary to audience expectations, "the bad guy" (and his masculinity) is neither contained nor defeated, punished, or even clearly defined. Withholding a clear identification of the Zodiac Killer also withholds a clear delineation of society's other, of evil. In Fincher's film, evil is threatening, violent, and disturbing but also elusive and ungraspable and cannot be contained or extracted but exists among us. *Zodiac* seems to admit that the killer's "murderous abnormality" was and is nothing less than part of society.

FAILING TO DETECT IN *ZODIAC*

Zodiac is an unusual crime thriller because the criminal succeeds in most of his crimes while the group of men on the "right" side of the law fail to catch him. The main difference between the Zodiac and his pursuers is that he works alone while they collaborate. In fact, it seems that Fincher's film suggests a connection between Zodiac's success and his solitary method of working. In a way, he uses the cracks and fissures of collaborative effort to remain undetected. The slow communication (or complete lack thereof) between police departments, for instance, works in his advantage. The same is true for the amount of evidence and witnesses that the police have to work through; the film even shows that a piece of crucial evidence would have almost been lost among the many flood of accusations and statements. Despite their efforts, official police detectives are eventually unable to come close to this individual that uses society's rules against itself.

Contrary to *Dirty Harry*, however, Fincher's film is not a critique of institutional justice. *Dirty Harry* strongly suggests that if Harry Callahan (Clint Eastwood) were to follow police procedure, the killer would remain on the loose (Gates 2006, 184). In the end, he catches Scorpio (Andy Robinson) but is so disgusted with the justice system that he leaves the police force. *Zodiac* on the other hand is a very different representation of legal justice. The slow process of police work is less a critique of the state's power and its "violation" of individual freedom and more a metaphor for the elusiveness of certainty and truth.

Zodiac does not suggest that the investigators' lack of heroism, their embodiment of masculinity, or their position in society prevent them from catching the killer. They are "good" men that the audience feels and roots for but still they fail to solve the case. *Zodiac* thus offers a subversion of heroic masculinity and effort: these attributes are no guarantee for catching the criminal. Failing to solve the crime is less the investigator's fault and more of an existential problem, a worldview according to which not all crimes can be solved.

In most serial killer films, the seemingly random and motiveless crimes of the killer harbor a secret pattern that brings order into chaos and helps resolve the case (Gates 2006, 170). In *Zodiac*, the killer's pattern remains unclear and unresolved. Since assigning a pattern to random and motiveless crimes serves to restore order, the lack of clarity and deduction in Fincher's film suggests a lack of clarity and order in the world.

CLOSURE IN *ZODIAC*

Although this worldview seems decidedly bleak, *Zodiac* offers closure to its characters and audience. Graysmith attains closure by arriving at the the conclusion that Arthur Lee Allen is the Zodiac. The fact that he cannot prove his theory does not turn him into a broken man like Jerry Black (Jack Nicholson) in *The Pledge* (Sean Penn, 2001). Instead, he works his theory into a book which becomes a critically acclaimed best seller and prompts George Bawart (James Le Gros) to interview Mike Mageau (Jimmi Simpson). Mageau identifies Arthur Lee Allen as his attacker and the film ends with this final, incriminating clue. To Graysmith, writing the book is also a way of finally moving past his obsession with the case. Writing becomes a cure and in a way, the threatening and violating power of language in the Zodiac letters is now opposed by its healing qualities.

In addition to the sense of closure facilitated by his book, the ending of *Zodiac* also alleviates Graysmith's underlying desire to belong. During their last conversation, when Graysmith presents his final Zodiac theory, Toschi conveys a silent sense of acknowledgment. Half way through the scene, the dynamic between Graysmith and Toschi shifts when Graysmith steps out of his role as the amateur and into the role of Zodiac expert. While previously Toschi dismissed most of Graysmith's deductions, he now cautiously starts to follow his thought process. Visually, this transition is emphasized by framing Graysmith standing up in a low-angle medium shot and Toschi sitting down in a high-angle medium close-up. While high angles are often used to minimize the subject, this particular shot does not depict Toschi as powerless but visually manifests Graysmith's expert position.

For as long as Graysmith thoroughly explains his theory, the scene relies on dialogue to convey the facts of the case. Afterwards, however, close-ups draw attention to the actor's faces and the display of emotions upon them. While Toschi does not verbally agree with Graysmith, his facial expression suggests otherwise. Following Graysmith's decisive clue (that Arthur Lee

Allen lived close to Darleen Ferrin's workplace), Toschi's facial expression is more open than previously. There is a small smile on his face and he looks almost astonished. He shakes his head and mutters: "Jesus Christ." When a waitress places the bill in front of him, he turns to look down at the table as if to hide his expression. The smile is wiped from his face. After Graysmith inquires about his opinion, Toschi covers his mouth with his hand, looks down on the table, and shakes his head as if keeping himself from talking. When Graysmith points out that he is not asking him as a cop, Toschi's facial expression is closed, his jaw is set, and his gaze firm as he replies: "But I am a cop." This short exchange can be read as Toschi believing Graysmith's theory but due to his lack of tangible evidence being unable to verbally concur with it. In his role as a representative of the law he cannot merely believe but has to prove beyond doubt. Contrary to Clint Eastwood's Harry Callahan, he cannot sidestep police procedure. Correspondingly, he counters Graysmith's suggestion ("Just because you can't prove it doesn't mean it's not true") with the statement "Easy, Dirty Harry, finish the book." Before leaving the diner, Toschi thanks Graysmith for their early breakfast, a statement that could be read as a thank-you for conveying a Zodiac theory that, although unprovable, puts his mind at ease. By shifting its focus from social to personal closure, *Zodiac* loosens the detective film's grip on the need for institutional justice. Thus, the film manages to combine a relatively bleak worldview with a sense of closure.

CONCLUSION

This chapter explored how masculinity and failure intersect in Fincher's *Zodiac*. The film defies simple classification and is difficult to categorize. As has been shown above, *Zodiac* mixes a number of different crime film subgenres. While the first half of the movie evokes the police film, the period after the time jump leans more toward the unofficial detective film. *Zodiac's* aesthetic evokes private eye films while the characterization of its protagonist simultaneously rejects the hard-boiled detective's tough masculinity. Particularly the portrayal of Robert Graysmith as an outsider who would like to belong and whose obsessive quest for the Zodiac does not end in a satisfying revelation, departs from genre conventions. While he fails to solve the case beyond doubt, he does not do so due to lack of trying. Graysmith devotes his life to the case, willingly sacrificing his career as well as family to catching the Zodiac. Still, the film allows Graysmith to attain closure as his Zodiac theory receives a silent approval from Toschi and his book becomes a bestseller. Although the Zodiac investigation fails in terms of the criminal justice system, the investigators' efforts are not futile, as futility implies not only a lack of results but also pointlessness. Thus, *Zodiac* challenges conceptions of success and failure as well as genre-specific expectations around heroic masculinity.

In a nutshell, this chapter argued that in *Zodiac*, failing to solve the crime does not reflect back on the protagonists' masculinity so much as on more existential questions. To some extent, the film depicts an uncertain world in which simple answers do not exist. Failing is, therefore, neither a form of punishment nor a personal deficiency. With regard to masculinity, *Zodiac* can be read as a critique of violent and tough masculinity. As opposed to films like *Chinatown* or *Se7en*, *Zodiac* does not locate this problematic masculinity in the detective himself but in his "other," that is, the criminal. At first glance, this form of critique seems less complex because it adheres to the simple dualism of a good detective and an evil criminal. That is why it is so significant that the investigators fail while the criminal gets away with his crimes. Although violent masculinity is mainly associated with the Zodiac, the fact that he evades capture can serve to show that his violent features are part of society, that is, that they can neither be pinpointed nor extracted from it. Fincher's *Zodiac* arguably redefines the meaning of failure in crime films. Instead of acting tool for criticizing the failed investigator, failing in *Zodiac* is a way of reflecting on the relationship between good and evil and on the ways in which we create narratives around them.

NOTES

1. The private eye film often depicts its villains as effeminate and/or homosexual (Leitch 2009, 198).
2. A perfect example are Holmes and Watson's domestic squabbles and the way in which 221b Baker Street is described in minute detail.
3. Of course, failing to catch or convict the criminal is not limited to a critique of the detective's masculinity but can just as well act as a means of social criticism.

REFERENCES

Benyahia, Sarah Casey. 2012. *Crime*. London, New York, NY: Routledge.
Bordin, Elisa. 2014. *Masculinity and Westerns: Regenerations at the Turn of the New Millennium*. Verona: ombre corte.
Carroll, Timothy, David Jeevendrampillai, Aaron Parkhurst, and Julie Shackelford. 2017. *The Material Culture of Failure—When Things Do Wrong*. London, UK: Bloomsbury.
Connell, R.W. 2005. *Masculinities*. Berkeley, Los Angeles, CA: University of California Press.

Gallagher, Mark. 2017. "Masculinity in Film". Oxford Bibliographies. Last reviewed April 28, 2017. Accessed April 19, 2019, http://www.oxfordbibliographies.com/view/document/obo-9780199791286/obo-9780199791286-0048.xml.

García-Mainar, Luis M. 2016. *The Introspective Realist Crime Film*. London: Palgrave Macmillan.

Gates, Philippa. 2006. *Detecting Men: Masculinity and the Hollywood Detective Film*. Albany: State University of New York Press. ProQuest Ebrary.

Halberstam, Jack/Judith. 2011. *The Queer Art of Failure*. Durham, NC: Duke University Press.

Hamad, Hannah. 2013. *Postfeminism and Paternity in Contemporary US Film: Framing Fatherhood*. London, New York, NY: Routledge.

Larke-Walsh, George S. 2010. *Screening the Mafia: Masculinity, Ethnicity and Mobsters from* The Godfather *to* The Sopranos. Jefferson, NC: McFarland.

Leitch, Thomas. 2009. *Crime Films*. Cambridge, UK: Cambridge University Press. Cambridge Books Online.

Oates, Thomas Patrick. 2014. "Failure Is Not an Option: Sport Documentaries and the Politics of Redemption." *Journal of Sport History* 41 (2) Summer: 215–223.

Peberdy, Donna. 2011. *Masculinity and Film Performance: Male Angst in Contemporary American Cinema*. Basingstoke, UK: Palgrave Macmillan.

Sandage, Scott A. 2005. *Born Losers: A History of Failure in America*. Cambridge, MA: Harvard University Press, 2005. ProQuest Ebrary.

Schreiber, Michele. 2016. "Tiny Life: Technology and Masculinity in the Films of David Fincher." *Journal of Film and Video* 68 (1) Spring: 3–18.

Time. n.d. "Top 10 Unsolved Crimes". Accessed July 19, 2019, http://content.time.com/time/specials/packages/article/0,28804,1867198_1867170_1867159,00.html.

Winters, Andrew M. 2010. "Man Is the Most Dangerous Animal of All: A Philosophical Gaze into the Writings of the Zodiac Killer". In *Serial Killers: Philosophy for Everyone, Being and Killing*, edited by S. Waller, 17–28. Malden: Wiley-Blackwell.

Young, Allison. 2010. *The Scene of Violence: Cinema, Crime, Affect*. Abingdon, New York: Routledge-Cavendish.

Chapter 6

Performing the Zodiac
Piffle, Paradox, and Self-Promotion
Daniel R. Fredrick

Playful raconteur, intimate newspaper correspondent, scathing critic of police incompetence and 1960s society—these are a few of the positive traits of the Zodiac Killer's rhetorical ethos. In his letters, the Zodiac Killer takes special care to construct a paradoxical performance that will not only convince the police to engage in his murderous games, but also to sell himself—his brand if you will—for societal consumption. To that end, the Zodiac writes for dual audiences (primarily the police and secondarily the readers of newspapers), balancing a personal agenda (to toy with and torment the police) with a public agenda (to develop a following). His pursuit is rife with piffle and paradox; with piffle, because much of his reasoning is either absurd or based on watered-down historical or religious references. His arguments, like his unbreakable codes, are built on nonsense; with paradox, because the Zodiac's rhetorical purposes are incompatible. For example, he desires both invisibility (from law enforcement) and visibility (published articles), clinging to anonymity while crying out for exposure. He seeks praise for his cleverness, strangely enough, from those (the police) whom he believes too stupid to recognize it.

METHODOLOGY

This chapter will use the tools of classical rhetorical theory to analyze the rhetorical features (e.g., ethos, logic and style) of the Zodiac Killer's letters and how Fincher situates those elements in his film *Zodiac*. Rhetorical theory is an analytical approach I believe quite apropos considering the Zodiac's intense cravings to persuade the public and the police that he is the greatest gamer and killer of all time. Additionally, the methodology takes shape in content analysis and viewing of Fincher's film to interpret and evaluate the character and the letters of the Zodiac in light of the elements of rhetorical theory.

Zodiac and the Anti-Ethos

In Aristotelian rhetorical theory, there are three primary modes of *pisteis* or proof—*logos* (rational demonstration), *pathos* (emotions), and *ethos* (the character of the speaker himself). All three are in play in any communicative act, but of the three, *ethos* is the most important to the Zodiac. Usually *ethos* is referred to as one's credibility, or something somewhat akin to literature's idea of "persona" (Cherry 1998, 252). However, defining ethos is not so simple, for many Greek rhetorical concepts have no real English word equivalents. The concept of *ethos* can be further complicated in that a writer or speaker can invent a whole range of variations in ethos; put another way, one's *ethos* can fluctuate given the audience, mental state of the writer, or moral and practical purpose of the communicative act. In other words, *ethos* is about the impression one makes to an audience (Schutrumpf 2007, 38). In the world of fiction, these variations are an integral part of creating characters. Consider quickly the dialogue titled *Gorgias* by Plato. Plato—the author—is playing all the parts. He is concurrently Socrates, Gorgias, Polus, and so on. He constructs a different *ethos* (attitude, prose style, and motive) for each character. Because of a writer's creative license, rhetoricians understand well that trying to pinpoint the authenticity of a text based on style consistency is highly problematic because good authors such as Plato, or any author who is thoughtful at best, manipulative at worst (like the Zodiac), can create a believable *ethos* no matter what. This focus on believability was one major criticism Plato had of rhetoric teachers (sophists). If rhetoric was merely a tool to create belief, then, condemningly, sophists were skilled at making the true appear false and the false appear true. The Zodiac shares this sophistic trait in that, in his own moral outlook, he positively views the murdering of innocents.

As the Zodiac constructs his ethos throughout his letters, he reveals a persona who is deeply conflicted. Is he a playful raconteur, or social critic? Is he just a sociopath, or a critical thinker clever enough to invent uncrackable ciphers? Indeed, although his letters make claim to an authentic self, one that is egocentric, steadfast, authoritative; still, he comes across as vulnerable in the sense that he is at times juvenile (calling cops "pigs"), silly (referring to cops as "blue meanies"), and needy (begging the citizens of San Francisco to don Zodiac pins). To establish an authentic *ethos*, the Zodiac begins most of his letters with a greeting that spells out his self-titled "stage" name: "This is the Zodiac speaking." Not to be too painstaking here, but the general pronoun "this" actually gives life to the letter. In other words, this very artifact, this piece of paper represents the Zodiac himself. But this point of minutiae in no way is an attempt to be wry. There is an important distinction in rhetorical studies between the written word and the spoken word, and yet, there is also no distinction. What the Zodiac is doing in announcing that he is speaking through the letter is engaging intuitively in a long historical motif, the idea that one can engrave living, oral language onto a tangible surface, in this case a printed page. Handwritten letters (rather than typed documents) are more personal, allowing his *ethos* to materialize. It is the same hand that murders with knife or pulls a trigger as the one that crafts the letter. To engrave language onto a surface is to establish not only authority but to symbolize that the writing is eternal. (For this reason, the Ten Commandments are written in—not on—stone rather than papyrus, clay, or slate). It is a commonplace, then, for a writer to want to establish his eternal life in his written texts, and the Zodiac is highly conscious about an afterlife and sets out to attain it. Recall that one of his stated motives is to collect slaves for his afterlife, a paradox here because this motive makes murder work, rather than mere fun, which is also a contradictory motive.

We must take note then that the Zodiac's letters are not only a key part of his identity and *ethos*, but they are actually his ticket to eternal life. Lovers of literature will immediately connect this trope to those in Shakespeare's works. In his eighteenth Sonnet (Shall I compare thee to a summer's day), Shakespeare argues in the concluding couplet that "As long as men can breathe, or eyes can see,/So long lives this [that is, Sonnet 18], and this [Sonnet 18] gives life to thee" [i.e. gives eternal life to the beloved as long as the poem's 'container' whether that container is archived in a library or on a flash drive etc.]. Similar tropes that imbue the artifact with (literary) eternal life go back even to the time of Homer, when the Cup of Nestor "speaks" with the inscription "I Am Nestor's Cup" (Watkins 1976, 25).

And so, the Zodiac, we might argue, kills to get published, to attain at least a text-based immortality. He never states this reason explicitly, but it is implied in his incessant demands to be published on the front page of major newspapers, and when he is "buried" in the back pages, he is furious. The Zodiac's stated reason for killing, to acquire slaves for the afterlife, is secondary, I purport, if truly a reason at all. Why? Because the Zodiac could still acquire those slaves even if remaining anonymous. And so, we see another paradox. He wants to remain anonymous, but when anonymity could prolong his hunt and acquisition of more and more slaves for the afterlife, he prefers publicity, a fan base, to see (hear?) his voice on the front page of major newspapers. Thus, it is by way of the power of *logos* (not *logos* as in *pisteis*), that is, the written word, which allows the Zodiac to break the boundaries of anonymity, to remain unnamed and uncaught, while basking in the public eye. Showcasing his *ethos*—his identity (albeit disguised)—in the paper allows the Zodiac to reap all the benefits of engaging with his audience while keeping cover. One of the benefits is that the Zodiac does not have to face a hostile audience, or worse yet, face arrest and execution. In short, getting published, especially on the front page, would confirm his ego-centric, anti-*ethos* while keeping himself masked. Anonymity then is key because it is a way for the Zodiac to thwart audience judgment.

We should remember that in many rhetorical texts, the use of anonymity was always a way to hide one's true identity from the judgments of audience. Benjamin Franklin became a woman, Silence Dogood; while Mary Anne Evans became a man, George Eliot. It is interesting to note that the Zodiac, unlike Franklin and Evans, takes on not a human persona, but a celestial one. He is the "Zodiac," a word that calls to mind a being that is astral, otherworldly, cosmic. The Zodiac might as well call himself *the universe*. This puffed-up ethos will come through as well in David Fincher's film *Zodiac*.

THE ANTI-ETHOS OF THE LETTERS

In Fincher's film *Zodiac*, the Zodiac's *ethos* slowly emerges, first in oral language (the phone call to police) then in written (the letters). The Zodiac is present, but faceless (and therefore anonymous) in the opening murder scene, and interestingly it is the telephone voice of the Zodiac we first hear rather than the words of his epistles. In most horror films, it is monster's voice or actions (chasing and slashing) which causes horror. A villain's letters are rarely the focus, and difficult to translate their horror in a film. Fincher leads us toward understanding the Zodiac's *ethos* by first presenting the Zodiac audibly. Here is how Fincher introduces the Zodiac's *ethos*: It is a dark night at lover's lane in Vallejo, California, where Darlene Ferrin and Mike Mageau have parked their car. Donovan's "Hurdy Gurdy Man" (who brings songs of love) is playing on their radio, yet another man, the Zodiac, is approaching their car who brings a song of gunfire. Fincher's film has been praised for its historical accuracy, and the film shows

Mageau injured and moving toward the back of the car after the Zodiac begins shooting, which is exactly as the Zodiac reports the event in one of his letters, facts which make his *ethos* credible. In the next voice-over, the viewer *hears* rather than reads the Zodiac's message of the killings to the police. The Zodiac confesses that he shot the teenagers, yet did not refer to himself yet as the "Zodiac." In brief, the Zodiac's *ethos* in the film is first presented as a cliché, a bogeyman with a creepy voice. Donovan's "Hurdy Gurdy Man" is supposed to contribute to this creepiness while setting the time frame of the murder, the late 1960s.

The Zodiac's voice and his creepy, baritone, sociopathic sound when he says "goooood bye," however, is not as frightening as the actual content and style of the letter he wrote to the *San Francisco Chronicle* on July 31, 1969. The Zodiac desperately needs credit for this murder and attempted murder, so he offers up facts regarding the crime scene about which only the police investigators and the killer himself would know. He selects the following pieces of information to distinguish between his human identity in relation to his literary identity. (Literary here does not mean literary in the sense of great books and great authors, but merely the idea that the Zodiac puts pen to paper): the ammo used, the number of shots fired, and the final layout of the victims. Specificity is an important element in establishing proof because it not only provides accuracy but also evidence (Miles et al. 1991, 35).

The Zodiac's description of the boy's back and direction of his feet are specific to the actual police report (and what Fincher shows in the film); therefore, the retelling of the specifics provides the evidence that the Zodiac is the killer. The Zodiac even mentions that the girl's feet were "to the west." Not only does the direction of the feet establish further proof that the Zodiac committed the murder, but his fixed focus on the feet, as if they are a type of compass, reveal the Zodiac's attitude toward his victims; feet are symbols of servitude being the lowest part of the body. We should recall that other letters note how the Zodiac kills to collect servants for the afterlife, and, even more revealing, one of the major themes of the collective letters is a demand of servitude from readers, namely that authority figures and the general population ought to pay homage to him by both publishing those letters and granting those letters special attention. If these facts are not enough to establish proof of his identity and his *ethos*, the Zodiac also notes the girl's "patterned slacks" and the location of the bullet strikes. For example, the boy was shot in the knee. One idea so far is that the Zodiac is aware at least intuitively of the central role of captivating and establishing credibility with his audience, a key idea in rhetorical theory (Clason 2010, 44).

Fincher's attempt at establishing his own credibility as filmmaker must focus on audience as well. To that end, Fincher eases us into an awareness of the Zodiac's true *ethos* by introducing the Zodiac in typical horror movie fashion, presenting to us a faceless figure, an awful voice. If the viewer first saw the face *of the letter*, there would not be much horror. A piece of paper is unlikely to cause tension or fear. Fincher thus gives us the ominous, faceless figure, the gunshots, the screaming victims, and that awful, soulless voice. The Zodiac's oral communication via phone, however, is only the start. Fincher, once he eases us into the Zodiac's *ethos*, can develop the Zodiac's anti-ethos further by showing us the Zodiac's texts. The Zodiac, I argue, *is* the letter, a more authentic identity and *ethos* that Fincher introduces about nine minutes into the movie. The letter first appears after a faceless attendant wheels in a giant bin of mail across the newsroom. The music score during this scene—with all eyes on the letter—is in the frenetic jazz style of late night talk television—a rolling snare drum, cymbals shaking, electric organ whistling. It is jazz, but it is also chaotic, not droning and monotone like Donovan's "Hurdy Gurdy Man." It is as if the letter itself has just come out from behind Johnny Carson drapery. It is a strange way to introduce a murderer.

In the film, the excitement of the coming letter is contrasted with the dullness of cartoons presented to Templeton Peck (John Getz), the managing editor at the *San Francisco Chronicle*. These cartoons are presented to Peck by Robert Graysmith (Jake Gyllenhall); Peck mundanely selects for publication a "not-so-horrid" cartoon. The irony with this juxtaposition of the cartoon and the Zodiac letter is that Peck will soon come across the letter, which is truly horrid. The letter is first scanned by a secretary who brings the letter to Paul Avery (Robert Downey Jr.) and Peck who are having a ridiculous conversation. Avery is boasting about his weekend adventures, something about fondue and nudity. Peck quips that *that* is a crime, and probably the beginning of a "crime wave." The secretary then hands him the Zodiac's letter, a confession of a real crime and a crime wave that will begin, and never be solved. Fincher portrays the staff at the *San Francisco Chronicle* as slightly vapid, an assessment that the Zodiac will confirm in his letters.

We now hear the message of the Zodiac through the voice of staff members at the newspaper. The letter is read out loud at what looks like a routine Monday morning meeting. The initial reading of the letter is even more mundane, and then is cut short, most likely because its content is too disturbing to the first reader. Fincher's camera offers a close up of the letter, including a focus on the penmanship as well as the misspelling of *Christmass*. This is what they read:

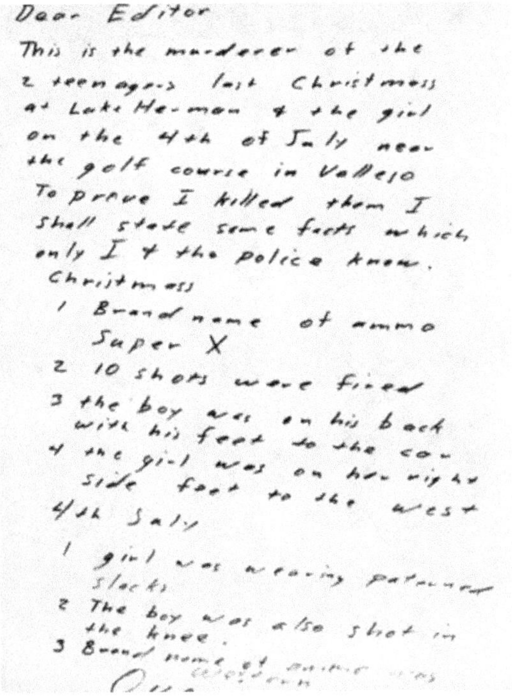

Dear Editor
This is the murderer of the
2 teenagers last Christmass
at Lake Herman & the girl
on the 4th of July near
the golf course in Vallejo
To prove I killed them I
shall state some facts which
only I & the police know.
Christmass
1 Brand name of ammo
Super X
2 10 shots were fired
3 the boy was on his back
with his feet to the car
4 the girl was on her right
side feet to the west
4th July
1 girl was wearing patterned
slacks
2 The boy was also shot in
the knee.
3 Brand name of ammo was
Western

Figure 6.1 The August 1, 1969, letter received by the *San Francisco Chronicle* (copies with slight variations were received by the *San Francisco Examiner* and *Vallejo Times-Herald*). "Zodiac Killer: The Letters." SFGATE, 13 Feb. 2012, www.sfgate.com/news/slideshow/Zodiac-KillerTheLetters-37941.php.

When he gets to item 4, the details become too much for the first reader; he must stop reading; he is in shock; the letter is passed to Peck who continues reading.

In the film the following is highlighted:

on to kill again, untill I end
up with a dozen people over
the weekend.

It is a long text to be read on screen. But Fincher realizes that the letter *is* the Zodiac. The letter is a bona fide character, imbued with *ethos*, getting a decent amount of screen time. (The irony is that in his last letter [April 26, 1978] the Zodiac wonders who will play him in the movie about him. No one it appears to the viewer, yet interestingly, three different actors play

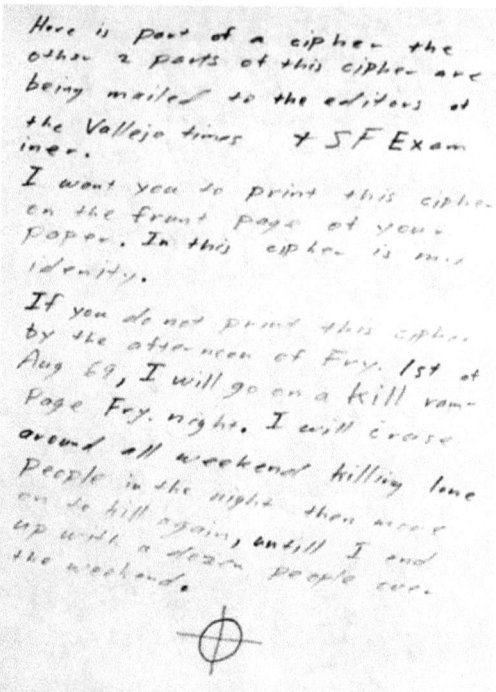

Figure 6.2   The second portion of the August 1, 1969, letter received by the *San Francisco Examiner*, the *San Francisco Chronicle*, and *Vallejo Times-Herald*. "Zodiac Killer: The Letters." SFGATE, 13 Feb. 2012, www.sfgate.com/news/slideshow/Zodiac-KillerTheLetters-37941.php.

him in the film. The letters will be the star.) In addition, the letter contains a cipher which, as a key part of the movie, I feel, should take central focus as it stylistically stands out far more than anything else in the letters. The cipher gets the attention of Avery, who, on the way out of the meeting, jokes that the first person who cracks the Zodiac's identity contained in the cipher gets twenty bucks. The cipher, a unique stylistic device, functions as an impressive and intriguing hook. Its rhetorical power comes from its ability to draw in and unify an audience by way of creating a game, a mental activity for the audience to experience and dramatize together. Similar "audience-bridging" techniques are used in forensic rhetoric—to get judges and jury to engage in similar experiences. The Zodiac's cipher shows that he is well aware of the importance of captivating an audience, and offering them a game increases his appeal (Blatner 2000, 68). The cipher is important, not only for engaging the audience, but also for highlighting the Zodiac's intelligence, one of the main features of *ethos* in Aristotelian theory.

THE ROLE OF INTELLIGENCE IN THE ZODIAC'S ETHOS

Ethos in Aristotelian theory has three main characteristics: intelligence, moral character, and good will. Interestingly, the letters of the Zodiac synchronize with this traditional tripartite schema. It is, of course, pointless to analyze the Zodiac's *ethos* in terms of moral character and goodwill for obvious reasons, so we must realize that the Zodiac must overcompensate for his lack of morality and lack of goodwill by underscoring his intelligence. Indeed, the Zodiac thrives on intelligence. No other item in the entire case establishes the Zodiac's superior intelligence than the cipher, first published on July 31, 1969, to the *San Francisco Chronicle*. The cipher entices and invites police, detectives, computer scientists, historians, teachers, and perhaps even the casual crossword puzzler, to take a shot at cracking the code. In other words, the Zodiac's cipher offers a game to a wide, diverse audience. The reward is too good to resist: the revelation of his identity. The cipher is akin to lottery jackpots that are over half a billion dollars; it attracts everyone, even those who do not regularly have any interest in playing. Again, the reward is too tempting to pass up. But decades later, even if Donald and Bettye Harden found patterns enough to tease out phrases such as *I like killing* and so forth, the Zodiac's identity has never been found; the code never fully cracked.

But it should be a truism universally accepted that killers do everything they can to *avoid* being caught. The Zodiac should be deemed as no different. To run headlong into ciphering the code is to sniff along in hopes of a red herring? Craig P. Bauer, professor of mathematics strongly believes that the Zodiac's messages in the ciphers would not reveal the killer's identity (2017, 171). Think about this: almost half a century later, with mind-boggling technology at our disposal, the Zodiac's cipher has still not been cracked. Hitler's enigma machine was cracked; the Rosetta stone unlocked Egyptian hieroglyphs. And yet, this crazed killer's made-up cipher has eluded geniuses. Bauer notes two main problems which may explain why the Zodiac's ciphers are impossible to crack using computers, technology, or even human genius and grit. One, that the Zodiac's spelling errors derail computer abilities to properly find messages (2017, 191), and two, that the Zodiac's humor was a central part of his method. Indeed, Bauer even reminds us that in the "Z13" cipher, numerous names are possible, and the most likely one is "Alfred E. Neuman," the goofy cover boy of *Mad* magazine (2017, 182).

Regardless of its insolvability, the cipher is the only joyful element in the letters. It allows the Zodiac to entice his audience by entertaining them, rather than horrifying them. The cipher also allows the Zodiac complete control of his audience because he has the answer key (assuming there is an answer). The Zodiac indeed seems to intuit one of the key views of the orator in the ancient world, that the speaker could manipulate his audience to his will. Some rhetorical theorists even believed that orators were so persuasive that they could force suicide on their audiences as in the ancient example of Hegesius, the death orator (Fredrick 2012, 2). And yet, the Zodiac fails to realize one of the basic tenets of Ciceronian rhetorical theory: that the audience, not the speaker, actually wields the ultimate power (Arena 2013, 196). To be sure, the audience of the Zodiac did wield publishing power over the Zodiac. To elaborate, the Zodiac demanded that the cipher be printed *on the front page* of the *San Francisco Chronicle* with a dire warning that if it did not appear there, he would kill again. The Zodiac gave the publishers a one-day notice. He warned that he would cruise around and seek a dozen victims. At the bottom of his letter, he signed off with his trademark symbol. Unfortunately, for the Zodiac, the cipher did not make the front page. In a sense, the Zodiac learned the hard way that audience (the journalists and the police) held the greater power. Fincher emphasizes this specific power of the audience over the Zodiac right after barraging the viewer with multiple excerpts of the letters. The next scene cuts to Graysmith in disbelief, asking Avery, if it is true that the papers are no longer going to publish the Zodiac's letters.

Ethos as a Game

The cipher is important for it reveals a key part of the Zodiac's *ethos*: he's a gamer. Forcing others to play his games and to play by his rules adds a child-like or immature dimension to his character. To illustrate, in the letter dated November 29, 1966, the Zodiac sets up clues with his victim Miss Bates. As he stalks her, he cryptically says, "It's about time." Bates has no clue what he means, but soon finds out what he meant, "It's about time *to die*." In the same letter, he warns that the "the game" will not stop. Furthermore, the whole point of coercing the *San Francisco Chronicle* to publish his letters is to engage in a murder game. If they publish, he stops murdering, and therefore the newspapers, if they play the game properly can prevent him from murdering more victims. This gaming is not necessarily a part of any classical rhetorical theory, but it may resemble the worst kind of sophistic ethic, using the tools of persuasion for self-serving purposes. Zodiac employs deception and dishonesty to urge his audience to deliberate on his letters. The gaming strategy, however, is more akin to the political game of shifting the blame onto your opponent. Because The Zodiac's letter was not featured on the front page, the Zodiac is forced to "move his piece" so to speak and commit a murder (that's the rule of the game), but when he does kill someone, the blame is no longer on him. The general population back then may have wondered (as we might today) why the papers, having the power and the knowledge to print the Zodiac's letters—a small price to save lives—are not complying. Would giving the Zodiac what he wants—front page coverage—be a type of giving in to his terrorism? Were the police engaging in zero tolerance for negotiating/giving in to a criminal's demands? Regardless of the reason, there would be no doubt many who may have sensed the situation was far more complex and may have been open to such questions as whether or not it was possible or even preferable to negotiate with the Zodiac as many modern investigators speculate when dealing with terrorists (Miller 2011, 145).

The games the Zodiac sets up, however, are not all as strong as the cipher. For example, a couple of years later, on March 22, 1971, a card arrives from Lake Tahoe which offers a game clue. The Zodiac's twelfth victim was stalked around "in the snow" and the Zodiac "peek[ed] through the pines." But these are weak clues, far less engaging than the cipher. These clues are especially weak because they are "post" killing. In other words, the Zodiac avoids predicting his crimes. There are no pre-clues to his murders such as "I will be in Tahoe in the woods in March." To understand the complex *ethos* of the Zodiac, then, viewers must be aware that the Zodiac uses a literary *ethos* not only as a part of the game, but he also possesses a real, human *ethos* (a guy who is really guilty) and is therefore doing everything he can to mislead authorities as to his true, human identity.

Ethos and Inartistic Proofs

Ethos, remember, is a type of proof. That is, *ethos* is a type of evidence. It is different than forensic evidence that can be found at a crime scene or examined under a microscope. Yet, the Zodiac knows that his primary audience (the police, the journalists) highly values forensic evidence, so he must offer to them facts and artifacts to establish greater credibility to his *ethos*, both in terms of assuring his identity as well as promoting his intelligence. The inartistic proofs are both a game and an argument. In the August 4, 1969, letter, for example, the Zodiac explains that he did not have to open the car door because the windows were down, and therefore the victims made it easy for him. Again, the details establish the authenticity of his testimony because he is both a witness and the perpetrator while the blame shifts away from him; as he notes regarding the crime in the opening of Fincher's film, had the victims kept the windows up, maybe they could have sped off? As he fires the gun at the boy's head, the boy flips into the back seat, writhing out of the firing line, which is why the boy ended up getting shot in the knee. More important than the details, however, is how the Zodiac challenges the paper's narrative of the same story, especially the point that, after he shot the victims, he sped away from the crime scene like a maniac. Not true, argues the Zodiac. He was, on the contrary, slow and careful, a rendition that highlights his calm, rational, intellectual side. He's not maniacal, he's mellow, more like a chemist than a mad scientist. The paper was wrong on other accounts as well. The police claim it was a well-lit night, but the Zodiac points out he needed to tape a pencil flash light to the barrel of his gun. The Zodiac likes direct confrontation—in words, but not in person.

But it is not just his ability to debate, to utilize logical demonstrations such as the law of non-contradiction (a thing cannot be and not be at the same time), that increases his *ethos* of intelligence. Rather it is his scientific know-how. The Zodiac emphasizes his knowledge of things that appear in inartistic proofs during criminal investigations. Put more simply, the Zodiac shows off his scientific prowess in many of the letters. For example, he explains how a beam of light will help him because it creates a pinpoint target, and thus all he had to do was "spray them [victims] like it was a water hose." Notice that there is almost a need to instruct others in this excerpt (misspellings are from the original):

> What I did was tape a small pencel flash light to the barrel of my gun. If you notice, in the center of the beam of light if you aim it at a wall or celling you will see a black or darck spot in the center of the circle of light about 3 to 6 inches across. When taped to a gun barrel, the bullet will strike exactly in the center of the black dot in the light.

This is the language of instruction, and it ties into the one of the duties of a communicator in rhetorical theory. According to Cicero, there were three offices (or obligations) on the part of an orator: to teach (*docere*), to move (*movere*), and to delight (*delectare*). The Zodiac elevates his ethos of intelligence with his systematic teaching style. The passage above strongly suggests a killer who is thoughtful, philosophical, practical, and prepared. Is there any wonder why the cipher has never been cracked?

Fincher's film also highlights the Zodiac's attempt to raise his *ethos* of intelligence by using inartistic proofs especially in the letter dated October 13, 1969. This letter begins with the assuredness of his identity, the introductory line that came to be his signature greeting: "This is the Zodiac speaking." In this letter, the Zodiac establishes solid proof by including a tangible piece of forensic evidence: the blood-stained piece of Paul Stine's (the taxi driver) shirt. The shirt piece, lying across the letter, symbolically dons the Zodiac; it clothes his written *ethos* in the garb of his victim. It is the identity of the victim (Paul Stine's DNA is found on the clothing) that confirms both the identity of the letter as well as the Zodiac. His murderous relationship with his victims is now an essential part of constructing his own *ethos*.

In the film, this letter which contains the bloodied shirt also contains other elements that contrast the intelligence of the Zodiac with the idiocy of the police. The Zodiac, to explain, was at the scene of the crime and would have been caught by the police if the police had focused on him. The problem, however, is that the police were too busy revving their motorcycles to take notice of suspicious bystanders. The idea here is that the Zodiac portrays the *ethos* of the police as a bunch of unthinking, macho brutes. The antithesis is striking. He is smart; they are stupid. He is calm and exact; they are boisterous yet lax. This strategy, to battle one's own *ethos* against another, was coined the rhetoric of "polarization," and although it was usually a fundamental part of political smearing, we see that the tactic is a basic, visceral tactics of the Zodiac (King and Anderson 1971, 248).

The most unnerving part of the Zodiac's intelligent *ethos* that Fincher underscores is his announcement that he will target school children. At first, this appeal seems to be more about *pathos*, about inciting fear and horror. The Zodiac warns that he will "Wipe out a school bus some morning." But this warning I argue should be seen in light of the Zodiac's desire to appear intelligent rather than menacing. Why? Notice how the Zodiac's procedure in the killing will be calmly planned and calmly executed. He will "Just shoot out the front tire + then pick off the kiddies as they come bouncing out." The description reminds us of a carnival BB gun game. The cops in the film panic and rush out of the office just as the Zodiac intends them to do. They jump to begin some kind of prevention; however, the Zodiac is a puppet master; he does not reveal specifics about these killings such as what neighborhood? What school district? Morning or afternoon? So, one might ask, to where are these keystone cops slipping and sliding? If the Zodiac had provided more detail, he would have allowed his puppet to have too much information which could be used to improve their game preparation. Yet even this threat—to shoot school children—is too much information. The Zodiac never wrote in advance about whom he was going to kill, and he never did target school children.

Role of Audience

Rhetoric in a large sense is the art of affecting an audience, moving them to act, or influencing an emotional state. In the history of the discipline, ethics were intimately bound to the rhetor, yet many of the persuasive strategies of the discipline can be used regardless of whether one is ethical or not. In the case of the Zodiac, he motivates his audience through threats and stimulates fear by offering terror. With this in mind, the Zodiac is better seen as an anti-rhetor. The effects of the letters were that its messages, ciphers, and clues were completely baffling to the editors of the papers and forced Californians to preoccupy their thoughts with paranoia. To emphasize how the letters were baffling to everyone, Fincher offers a montage of the reading of the letters, a synopsis where excerpts from the letters roll and bleed into one another as a type of auditory "Ken Burns" effect. In the middle of Fincher's film, about an hour in, we hear the fading in and out of the following excerpts:

April 20, 1970 (The cipher is not included):
> This is the Zodiac speaking
> By the way have you cracked the last cipher I sent you?
> I am mildly cerous as to how much money you have on my head now. I hope you do not think that I was the one who wiped out that blue meannie with a bomb at the cop station. Even though I talked about killing school children with one.

April 28, 1970 (Greeting Card)
> (The film does not include the part about the bomb in this letter).
> I would like to see some nice Zodiac butons wandering about town. Every one else has these buttons like, (inserts peace sign) black power, Melvin eats bluber, etc. Well it would cheer me up considerably if I saw a lot of people wearing my buton. Please no nasty ones like Melvin's

June 26, 1970
> This is the Zodiac speaking.
> I shot a man sitting in a parked car with a .38.
> (Zodiac symbol) -12 SFPD-0
> The map coupled with this code will tell you where the bomb is set. You have untill next Fall to dig it up. (Zodiac symbol).

July 24, 1970
> This is the Zodiac speaking.
> I am rather unhappy because you people will not wear some nice (Zodiac symbol) buttons. So I now have a little list, starting with the woeman + her baby that I gave a rather intersting ride for a couple howers one evening a few months back that ended in my burning her car where I found them.

After each major character in the film narrates an excerpt, Graysmith asks Avery if the paper is really not going to publish anymore of the Zodiac's letters? Fincher is flushing this scene with an overwhelming amount of the Zodiac only to have the characters reject the Zodiac. It is a cathartic moment as the viewer gets a bit of revenge on the killer. Avery argues that the Zodiac is a fraud, that the letters are bogus. Recall that in most of the letters, the Zodiac works tirelessly to confirm the authenticity of his *ethos* and identity. But Avery shrugs off the Zodiac's attempt to prove he committed the crimes, asserting that the Zodiac is composing the letters by lifting information from previously published newspaper accounts of other crimes. For example, Avery illustrates this point by showing Graysmith similarities between the newspaper account of the Kathleen Johns story, the woman who was abducted with her baby in a car, and the Zodiac's letters. The problem is that the newspaper was published long before the letter. What is interesting to note is that Fincher is paradoxically diminishing the *ethos* of the Zodiac at this point in the film right after he increased the *ethos* by spotlighting multiple letters. To Avery, at least at this point in the film, the letters are not authentic. In a couple of scenes later, Fincher makes us feel as if the Zodiac can read Avery's mind, for Avery becomes the Zodiac's next target. There is a noticeable parallel between the changing nature of the film's attitude toward the Zodiac and his connection to the crimes and the overall nature of the Zodiac's claims in his letters. Fincher, for example, seems ambivalent about whether or not the Zodiac committed the Johns crime, and it is on this point that Avery completely finds the Zodiac to be a fraud. The nature of the letters shift as well, from the earlier letters working to establish an authentic *ethos* to later letters working to confuse the readers. In other words, in rhetorical terms, the early letters can be classified as heuristics for ethos and the later letters can be classified as *eristic*.

When Avery receives a Halloween card from the Zodiac, his scoffing at the Zodiac's authenticity quickly turns to fear and paranoia; knees knocking, Avery asks for permission to be armed. In the next scene, as Avery fires away in a shooting range, Graysmith is nearby, reading the paper to him, pointing out that other journalists are now wearing buttons that read, "I am not Paul Avery." What Fincher does here is show how all the characters are now wrestling to establish or preserve their own *ethos* in counter-distinction to Avery. Unlike the Zodiac, these journalists have lost interest in claiming who they are and shift to establish who they are *not*.

At this point in the movie (about 75 minutes), there is a refocus on acquiring evidence against the Zodiac. The heuristics to determine his authenticity are, interestingly, a focus on the rhetoric, that is, the writing. For example, Avery brings up an unsolved case in 1966, which introduces the viewing audience to a letter dated November 29, 1966. This letter seems like it was penned by the Zodiac but does not claim explicitly to be authored by him. According to police, the literary analysis has all the telltale signs, specifically the plea to be published: "This letter should be published for all to read it." The message is typed in all caps. The letter is also double stamped with postage just like the other envelopes used by the Zodiac. Fincher goes so far even to showcase the engravings on a desk from Riverside City College. The writing is formed more as poetry than prose and tells of a murder wherein blood spurts "all over her new dress." The next line, "Oh well it [the dress] was red anyway," highly suggests this is from the Zodiac because it is flippant, perhaps even silly. A literary or author analysis is still common both in English and rhetoric classes as well as crime investigations where the focus is on various rhetorical features such as those that are lexical, syntactic, structural, or content-specific (Abbasi and Chen 2005, 68). Of course, greater knowledge of a writer's rhetorical practices could enhance further lexical, syntactic, structural, and content-specific features of one's writing. For example, the Zodiac's heuristics may be a feature that could identify him.

Heuristics

Heuristics, or invention, is one of the five cannons of rhetoric. The Zodiac takes special care to explain how he selects those he will kill and how he will kill them. Focusing on this rhetorical process could enhance author analysis. In the November 29, 1966, letter, for example, the Zodiac explains how he chooses his victims. At night, he wrestles and mulls over the possibilities. We learn that he is a passive stalker, observing the potential victims that cross his path on a daily basis. He could choose the blonde that babysits near the store and takes the dark alley home, or a girl who spurned him in high school. He brainstorms; he's contemplative. He is also egomaniacal. He could choose anyone he feels like choosing. One of his stated motives for killing (July 31, 1969, to the *San Francisco Chronicle*) was that he needed slaves for the afterlife; it is crazy, but it is part of his heuristics. Who would be a decent slave? An adult more than a child for sure. Maybe that is why he never killed children? Children fare poorly at basic labor and chores. Furthermore, as the Zodiac states in the letter on April 20, 1970, there is more glory in killing a cop than a kid because the cop can shoot back. However, he never shot a cop. A cop would also make for a bad slave, for they possess too much authority. Two other heuristics were mentioned but never developed by the Zodiac, that killing was "fun," and that humans were the most dangerous game. But his victims did not fight; they were easier targets than cops, for example.

Some of the details in the letters show heuristics which help him thwart the police. For example, the Zodiac knows how to conceal his fingerprints with "airplane cement coated on [his] fingertips" (October 13, 1969). One of his more subtle heuristics is to tell the police that he purposely engages in dissuasion; that is, he plants false clues, a practice which would raise the suspicion of all pieces of forensic evidence. In the same letter, he tells that he wiped down the cab for this purpose. In the letter dated November 9, 1969, the Zodiac retaliates regarding the "lies" about him, so his heuristic is to reinvent the rules of the game. For example, he will not "announce" the murders while working harder to conceal his identity. He will make the murders appear as if they are "routine robberies, killings of anger, and faked accidents." The heuristics are flexible. The Zodiac goes with the flow. He adapts to maintain the upper hand.

This deliberate attempt—to rig the game by leaving false clues, that is, by creating his letters more as sources for debate and confusion (*eristic* rhetoric)—should call great attention to the cipher, which the Zodiac designed before he announced that he would purposely be deceptive. The cipher, after all, is still one of the only viable remnants of the Zodiac's legacy. Strangely, in the film, Fincher gives the cipher very little attention, and yet, the Zodiac claims that his real name is revealed in the cipher. It would seem that all focus should gravitate toward cracking the code, and in the letters, the Zodiac pushes his readers to return to it. For example, he often hopes that the police are doing just that, sitting at their desks puzzling with the cipher. Is the cipher too engrossing to be bogus? It is a key part of the letters. No game is fun if it never concludes, and one wonders if there was a part of the Zodiac that wanted to get caught? Or maybe he did not expect the cipher to be too difficult? Then again, maybe the cipher was a way to get revenge on the police by giving them busy work for failing to publish him? From a rhetorical perspective, the cipher is a blended heuristic-eristic puzzle, which allows the Zodiac to construct a sophistic argument, one that serves himself while entertaining his audience. It is a complicated element in the letters, one that engages in fallacy and yet, paradoxically, functions as authentic, forensic proof. These paradoxes create an *ethos* that is hard to pin down, and, as history has shown, hard to uncover and solve.

Cipher aside, an equally powerful and more fearful heuristic is the Zodiac's knowledge of bomb making. In the October 13, 1969, letter he outlines all of the items he will need, boasting that he can buy them "on the open market" and therefore will avoid being traced, unlike if he sent photos which could be traced back to the developer. In short, the Zodiac's use of heuristics could be a way to identify him, whether he is brainstorming his choice of victims or outlining weapons of destruction.

THE STYLE OF THE ZODIAC

No rhetorical analysis would be complete without a study of style, for it is style that that affects the hearts and minds of audiences. I emphasize style as key, for content requires context to affect the heart and mind. For example, if one were to read, "I will cut off her female parts and deposit them," the content here is horrifying in the context of the Zodiac's letters. However, if the context were from a coroner's report, there may be queasy stomachs, but few, if no one, would be horrified.

As a general feature of the Zodiac's style, one might say it is conflicted. There is at times modesty, a reservation to avoid being vulgar. In the November 29, 1966, letter, as noted above, he claims he will "cut off her female parts." Since every part of a woman is female, we of course know he is referring to the sexual parts. Why not be vulgar here? Why not use schoolyard terms, or even medical terms as if to portray a mad doctor? Perhaps the reason is one of publication. Does the Zodiac choose modesty to keep things clean for the publisher? In other areas where he engages in euphemism, it is often to toy with the police. For example, he refers to the murders as "good times" (August 4, 1969), as "my thing," or as doing "in" the people in the North Bay area (October 13, 1969). These euphemisms allow the Zodiac to avoid vulgarities that might restrict the letters from publication, but also downplay his *ethos* as a murderer while raising his ethos as a social critic against the police.

For example, in the spirit of the counterculture in the bay area during the late 1960s, police were not always seen as the heroes of society, and even had the reputation as being donut-eating brutes. Notice the slapstick nature of the crime scene from the letter dated October 13, 1969. The Zodiac claims to speak directly to the police officer in real life and then recreates this discussion in the letter. "Hey blue pig I was in the park . . . The dogs never came within 2 blocks of me." The police, he admits, nearly got him, but they "pulled a goof." As being questioned by an officer, the Zodiac tells us that he made up a story about a man running and waving a gun, a description that made the fooled officers burn rubber as the Zodiac slipped away into the woods. This story reminds us of a typical slapstick comedy chase scene, where the culprit accidentally runs into the police, and the culprit helps the police by saying, "He went that-a-way." The Zodiac then escalates the discussion with derogatory labels and mocking language. "Hey pig, doesn't it rile you up to have your nose rubbed in your booboos." The term "booboos" of course highlights the Zodiac's perception of the immaturity of the police (the ones who peel rubber), and as a result makes himself appear parental. But there is more here. Rubbing your nose in something reminds us of a cruel method of toilet training puppies. In this view, the Zodiac is not the parent but the master, and the police are "owned." The relationship between orator and audience illustrates dominance and submission, the sharpest kind of antagonism. Rhetorically, the Zodiac finds a literary audience (rather than live audience) to be sufficient enough to construct an argument about his own worth and identity.

In addition to these stylistic devices, the Zodiac's style has other elements of form. For example, at times (November 29, 1966), he writes in all capital letters. On other occasions, the medium of his message is not a letter, but a car door at Lake Berryesa. He will even use greeting cards (and possibly the desktop in the library). But his most interesting use of style is to manipulate alphabets into his cipher such as the notorious word: AENOOKOMOTNAM. This manipulation is sophisticated and, as of yet, impossible to crack. The cipher stands in sharp contrast to the low-brow moments in many of his letters. It is hard to believe that the same person who took such great care to design a sophisticated cipher (and some of it works because parts have been cracked by very intelligent people) is the same person who rants that the police have "fat asses" and "fart and fiddle" around (March 13, 1971). The mixing of sophistication and vulgarity creates jarring inconsistencies in the style, making an author analysis very challenging.

In Fincher's film, the Zodiac's rhetorical style as a writer focuses mostly on the form of the penmanship. Penmanship is useful in that writing with a pen is a physical activity that is unique (compared to typing which renders all letters uniform no matter who is typing). The penmanship analysis leads them to a key suspect, Richard Marshall, who is assumed to draw up movie posters. This idea in the film takes on special emphasis because the Zodiac's last letter on April 24, 1978, shows the Zodiac wondering who will play him in a movie? Is the reference to movie a mere coincidence or could Marshall be the Zodiac? And so, in the film, the *ethos* and identity of the Zodiac again take center stage over any of the Zodiac's actual stylistic features such as euphemism, antithesis, or low style (e.g., vulgarities). Although the Zodiac's letters are shown close up on screen and although many lines of them are read (albeit without any dramatic delivery), it is only the penmanship that plays any major role in Fincher's film. It is the penmanship, the handwriting analysis, that induces horror. And we see how Fincher accomplishes this near the end of the film when Graysmith is in Vaughn's house discussing Marshall's creation of the movie posters, for the penmanship on the posters is a match to the letters.

Suddenly, Graysmith is stunned when Vaughn says that he himself made the posters, not Marshall. Graysmith is shocked because he considers the penmanship the ultimate stylistic proof (also forensic proof), far more convincing than any other elements of rhetorical style or even content. As Vaughn encourages Graysmith to join him in the basement to look for the film release of *The Most Dangerous Game*, Graysmith panics, remembering that the Zodiac mentioned having a basement, which are rare in California (November 9, 1969). Hearing footsteps above, Graysmith rushes for the door, awkwardly getting out. The viewer is left with some confidence that Vaughn is the Zodiac, but not for long. The movie ends with Mageau identifying Arthur Leigh Allen, and Fincher further supports the idea that Allen is the Zodiac by having Graysmith stare down Allen as Allen works in a hardware store.

What we see Fincher doing at the end of the film is abandoning the letters altogether. The Zodiac went from a voice, a stereotypical horror character, to the letters and all their complexities. Then Fincher dismantles the Zodiac's *ethos* by replacing a focus on the letters with a focus on other things. In a sense, Fincher frees the Zodiac's *ethos* from the letters by humanizing him as a criminal, as an ordinary clerk. But if he is not locked in the letters, where is he? Fincher leaves us bewildered just as the case has bewildered police for half a century. Fincher's film seems to settle on Allen, but the viewer also suspects Marshall, suggesting the depth of difficulty in finding the Zodiac, or, the Zodiacs if they were possibly working together. The film thus concludes with a total dismantling of the Zodiac's *ethos* and identity. In short, the Zodiac is no longer the *letter*; he is someone, somewhere; a guy who makes posters for movies, a guy in a photo lineup, a guy in a hardware store, and more than likely, fifty years after the murders, a guy who is dead yet who may be finally answering for those crimes.

REFERENCES

Abbasi, Ahmed, and Hsinchun Chen. 2005. "Applying Authorship Analysis to Extremist-Group Web Forum Messages." *IEEE Intelligent Systems* 20 (5): 67–75.

Arena, Valentina. 2013. "The Orator and His Audience: The Rhetorical Perspective in the Art of Deliberation." In *Community and Communication: Oratory and Politics in Republican Rome,* edited by Catherine E. W. Steel and Henriette Van Der Blom. Oxford: Oxford University Press.

Bauer, Craig P. 2017. *Unsolved!: The History and Mystery of the World's Greatest Ciphers from Ancient Egypt to Online Secret Societies.* Princeton: Princeton University Press.

Blatner, Adam. 2000. *Foundations of Psychodrama: History, Theory, and Practice.* New York: Springer Pub. Co.

Cherry, Roger D. 1988. "Ethos Versus Persona: Self-Representation in Written Discourse." *Written Communication* 5 (3): 251–276.

Clason, Susanna Shelton. 2010. *Forensic Rhetoric: The Force of Closing Arguments.* El Paso, TX: LFB Scholarly Publishing LLC.

Eckart, Schutrumpf. 2007. "Ethos in Persuasion and in Musical Education in Plato and Aristotle. In *Influences on Peripatetic Rhetoric: Essays in Honor of William W. Fortenbaugh,* edited by David C. Mirhady. Boston, MA: Brill.

Fredrick, Daniel R. 2012. "Pathos: Its Role and Scope in Ancient Rhetoric." *Journal of Teaching and Education* 1 (6): 1–4.

—. 2006. "Learning an Art of Refutation: Five exercises from Cicero with Sample Student Essays." *Issues in Writing* 16 (2): 123–161.

King, Andrew A. and Floyd Douglas Anderson. 1971. Nixon, Agnew, and the "Silent Majority": A Case Study in the Rhetoric of Polarization." *Western Speech* 35 (4): 243–255.

Miles, Robert, Marc Bertonasco, and William Karns. 1991. *Prose Style: A Contemporary Guide.* Upper Saddle River, NJ: Prentice-Hall.

Miller, Carl. 2011. "Is It Possible and Preferable to Negotiate with Terrorists?" *Defence Studies* 11 (1): 145–185.

Watkins, Calvert. 1976. "Observations on the 'Nestor's Cup' Inscription." *Harvard Studies in Classical Philology* 80: 25–40.

Chapter 7

Allegories of Obsession

David Fincher's Zodiac *and Edgar G. Ulmer's* The Black Cat *(1934)*

George Toles

In David Fincher's *Zodiac*, much attention is given to the Zodiac Killer's fascination with the 1932 film adaptation (directed by Ernest B. Schoedsack and Irving Pichel) of the Richard Connell story, "The Most Dangerous Game" (*Collier's*, January 19, 1924). The plot of the film concerns a complacent big game hunter and author, Bob Rainsford (Joel McCrea) who, through the connivance of another hunter, Count Zaroff (Leslie Banks), is shipwrecked in the course of an ocean voyage on Zaroff's private island. Rainsford's interests closely match up with those of his refined and decadent host, and—in symbolic terms—it seems that Rainsford (even without Zaroff's efforts to destroy his ship) has been drawn magnetically into Zaroff's sphere because of the two men's shared obsession with the hunt as a game. Rainsford, in this regard, has much in common with *Zodiac*'s most persistent hunter, Robert Graysmith (Jake Gyllenhaal). Zaroff's conception of sport in his jungle preserve has long ago swollen into madness. The challenge of killing animals has been replaced for him by the challenge of pursuing and destroying human prey, selected for their resourcefulness and skill. In the spirit of *Zodiac*'s steady proliferation of odd, forking paths and circuitous routes to discovery, I am going to propose another horror film of the early 1930s as a suggestive key to Fincher's narrative design. I take that design to involve the slow transformation of an intricate procedural film (with many quasi-documentary elements) into an allegory of obsession. Edgar G. Ulmer's *The Black Cat* (1934), though vastly different from *Zodiac* in style and narrative terrain, resembles it in its delineation of the process whereby a central character's obsessive derangement becomes our only means of access to external reality. The phenomenal world takes on the lineaments and disposition of his monomania. *The Black*

Cat, whose allegorical intentions are forcefully declared, will make the less pronounced workings of allegory in *Zodiac* more intelligible. A comparative analysis of the two narratives is likely to yield strange fruit.

The Black Cat displays obvious similarities, at the level of plot and character, to *The Most Dangerous Game* (1932). A central male figure who is both victimized and arrogant is caught after a storm in an island-like fortress by a sinister double, whose shared attachments and inclinations have led, in his case, to an overmastering, destructive preoccupation. Madness is initially concealed by a veneer of elegance and a courtly, jousting rationality. The fortress mansion of *The Black Cat* is a maze in much the same way that Count Zaroff's Gothic estate (and its surrounding jungle and swamp, where the man hunt will take place) proves to be. The Ulmer film tarries for only a few minutes in a realm that might warrant the term "realistic"—a train station in Hungary; the honeymoon couple relaxing in their compartment at the beginning of a journey. *Zodiac*, by contrast, must be pried loose from its grounding in carefully grounded, period-sensitive realism. Expressionist elements for a considerable portion of its length remain subordinate to the solid milieu of a San Francisco newspaper, various media outlets, the homes of ordinary citizens, the work environments of specialists with expertise, and the sturdy trappings of a police investigation. Many critics have identified obsession as a significant theme in *Zodiac*, but aside from discussing the manner in which the unsolved case absorbs the attention and life energy of its investigators (especially cartoonist, Robert Graysmith)—to the point where other commitments wither away—their treatment of it has been superficial. How is obsession in *Zodiac* to be distinguished from the single-mindedness and persistent "strong need" that are typical of most film protagonists? *The Black Cat*'s Werdegast's emptying of the world he barely inhabits for his own increasingly senseless, arid attempts to reclaim what he never understood or possessed may shed a surprising, spectral light on Graysmith's prolonged unraveling in *Zodiac*, and the ways in which the film's viewer is implicated in it.

Shortly after the newlywed Alisons in *The Black Cat* begin to exchange loving banter in the privacy of their train compartment, they are interrupted by a request to share their space, because of a ticketing error, with the cordial, apologetic psychiatrist, Dr. Vitus Werdegast (Bela Lugosi). In spite of his training in mental disorders, Werdegast soon reveals himself as someone mired in past torments and confusions. He alternates between appearing poignantly and disconcertingly unstable. After he is observed stroking the hair of Joan Alison (Julie Bishop), who has fallen asleep, he attempts to explain a portion of his tragic history to her husband, Peter (David Manners). He is a former prisoner of war who suffered a long World War I captivity, which continued for an indefinite period in its aftermath. Fifteen years after he was violently separated from his wife, he continues to mourn her loss. He has never located her or the man he believes abducted her, a man who also unquestionably betrayed Werdegast to "the enemy," and ensured his imprisonment and torture. Eventually, we discover that Poelzig (Boris Karloff), his nemesis, has returned to the very place in Hungary where Werdegast's tribulations occurred. Werdegast too has "returned," as he declares to Peter Alison, with a limitless hunger for vengeance. Werdegast's destination is the rural castle town of Visegrad, once a scene of immense wartime carnage and now a mass burial site for the slaughtered soldiers. Directly above this old battlefield and graveyard Poelzig has designed a gigantic modern home and fortress for himself. The Alisons are headed to the same town, for carefree marital sightseeing.

Within a minute of Werdegast's taking his seat in the train compartment, his haunted vision seems to usurp the "ordinary appearances" of the train, the young couple's warmly contented mood, and the passing countryside visible through the night-enshrouded train window. The railway promptly transforms, in a brief montage, into an emanation of his demented, driven consciousness. A few actions prepare us for the transition. A piece of the doctor's luggage is jarred loose from a rack above the Alisons by the train's lurching movement and nearly falls on the couple. "Better to be frightened than crushed," Werdegast amiably remarks after helping Peter catch and reposition his heavy black valise. Following this mishap, the doctor and couple introduce themselves. With little more than a fixed Lugosi stare as he announces, somberly, his intention to visit an "old friend," and the raising of a shade on the train compartment window, which reveals a swirl of white steam and Werdegast's dim reflection in the glass, Ulmer makes us feel that all the objects and ensuing actions presented to us are projections of the doctor's haunted consciousness. Reality is sufficiently there to allow for continued cause and effect action, but we are never again certain of the demarcation line separating Werdegast's experiences from his fixations and recurring fantasies. The night journey montage contrasts markedly with the film's opening presentation of a lively, crowded Budapest train station, in which we observe bakers making and selling delicacies and passengers anticipating a pleasurable departure. The montage of frantic nocturnal motion establishes the landscape of allegory that will be the only ground available for the characters to occupy until film's end. Following the image of steam and Werdegast's reflected face, we observe the silhouette of a train, viewed from below, with lighted passenger windows, then a phantasmal engineer and his fireman shoveling fuel into the engine firebox. The square opening of the firebox, filled with burning light, rhymes with the illuminated windows of the train that were shown before it. The screen of light henceforth displayed to us as *The Black Cat*'s outer world will always burn with Werdegast's hallucinations of the past recaptured. After our glimpse of the engine compartment, Ulmer switches our placement and view to the churning pistons below it. The steam we began with converts before our eyes into driving gusts of rain. Then a combination of light and rain enter the frame from the opposite side asserting "weather" as mentality, beheld from an unmoored vantage point.

An indefinite amount of time has elapsed before we are brought back again through the window frame to the train compartment. Time is both going forward and at a standstill, frozen, as it has been for Werdegast since his war imprisonment. The doctor continues to sit beside the window framing the train's movement. But now the direction seems not toward the future, but into the mausoleum past of the doctor's dark memories. The doctor's gaze is no longer aimed outside. For an instant he acknowledges the presence of the camera, and by extension the spectator, as though we were fellow-travelers in the compartment. Then there is a disconcerting perceptual shock as the point of view replaces *us* with a shot of the sleeping Alisons. A close-up of Werdegast's face in profile, tenderly soft-focused, marks the turn of his gaze away from us, the camera, and the couple, and narrows his concentration to the unconscious Joan. She is shown to us from his perspective, no longer joined to her husband, though in the previous two shot they leaned together in sleep. The camera moves in tandem with Werdegast's hand, which reaches out (also in close-up) to touch, ever so lightly, the top of Joan's head and the curls of her hair. Melancholy violins accompany his gesture, and the music seems to combine the heartache of memory with reawakened obsession. Werdegast's hand resembles a hypnotist's during his furtive caress. He appears to enter a trance himself as he strokes the hair and, in some obscure fashion, takes possession of Joan. The music and Werdegast's sense of helpless memory enthrallment may link the viewer to his dream experience.

As Werdegast leans back into his seat and shifts his attention to Peter, we receive another perceptual jolt with the cut that reveals the forgotten husband. He is not still asleep, as we have assumed, but rather staring directly at the doctor. It suddenly seems likely that he has been a witness to Werdegast's entire, secret, fetishistic ceremony. His expression is stern and reproachful. The viewer can hardly avoid the sensation of having been caught in the act, with Werdegast. Somehow his transgressive fit of abandon has become one that we have at least partially sanctioned. As seasoned movie spectators, we regard it as a viewing prerogative to partake of the freedom of the unobserved predator, for as long as he remains unobserved. But Peter's unflinching, prolonged stare at Werdegast, reinforced by his silence and attitude of judgment, render us complicit in "taking advantage" of the sleeping bride.

Werdegast, however, is not unsettled in the least by Peter's authority as the aggrieved husband. He gently asks for Peter's indulgence. He only touched Joan's hair because of her resemblance to his wife, who was torn away from him almost twenty years ago. He has not seen her since. The doctor speaks with pointed brevity about his three years of being tortured in a prisoner-of-war camp. His fifteen years of postwar existence are left strangely blank, as though he has retained no impression of them. He bitterly notes that while few survived the travails of captivity and torture, he did, and has now "returned." The grave should have claimed him, but has not. He still regards with astonishment his right to move freely among the living. As Werdegast partially divulges his identity to Peter, his claim to Peter's wife seems strangely to displace the husband's own. Peter's suspicions and uneasiness seem to dissolve, as in a dream. The "atmosphere of death" which envelops the composed, yet helpless doctor engulfs and does away with the hitherto dependable world of honeymoon travel and intimacy. The couple has ceded its right to a separate journey, and even a separate volition. Werdegast invades the couple's reality sense and the viewer's with the same thoroughness and speed that he has invaded their train compartment, with its locked door. Although Werdegast shares only a small portion of his story with Peter, Peter cannot withstand its grim, incantatory power. A miasma of long-ago atrocities, in World War I and its desolate aftermath, unfastens Peter the listener and his slumbering bride from their attachment to their own time and—very soon—to each other.

When the Alisons and Werdegast disembark together at Visegrad, the rainstorm has become monumental. They hire a small bus to take them to their respective accommodations, and its driver—as though hatched from Werdegast's psyche—immediately launches into a continuation of the doctor's previous account of war terrors in the region. The downpour that accompanies his tale appears to be washing away all the appearances and illusions of the present tense. We notice that Werdeegast's eyes are closed in the rear seat, suggesting that the bus journey is both happening and being dreamed. The bus's lurching forward movement and the driver's tale usher us more fully into the past which rises up all around the passengers in thick, spectral forms—Werdegast's past. Without warning, the bus suddenly overturns, killing the driver. Ulmer's story logic persuades us that the eruptive force of unappeased, unavenged former crimes against Werdegast is what causes the bus to overturn not far from Poelzig's fortress home and what returns Joan to unconsciousness. (She has been mostly mute or "dead to the world" in sleep since Werdegast's first appearance.) Werdegast returns to complete alertness after his half-sleep on the journey. His towering servant/assistant (as wrapped in silence as Joan) materializes in this emergency and is told to carry Joan's injured, insensible body to the large Bauhaus mansion nearby, built on the ruins of Fort Marmarus. Werdegast's enemy, the torturer-wife thief turned architect, Poelzig, has brazenly established his home on the very spot beneath which countless war victims rest, buried in a mass grave and all but forgotten. This mansion, which literalizes repression, proves to have a sleek, defiantly modern interior: it is a vast, ornate, and labyrinthine mindscape. Whether the mind it represents is Poelzig's or Werdegast's remains an open question. What is clear is that the Alisons have been swallowed up in Werdegast's obscure campaign of vengeance.

In some ways, Werdegast resembles the tutelary spirit or daemon of allegory, whose task it is to bring to life psychic truths lodged within the consciousness of an ordinary couple (especially the wife), pursuing their superficial pleasures. These truths are rooted in a past which the couple has forgotten. It is as though they need to be reunited to an old sorrow if they are to draw closer to life, and closer to the beings—as opposed to the masks—that they actually are. But Werdegast proves a stymied, unfit guide for such a redemptive enterprise, consumed by fear and implacable, bloodthirsty obsession. It is too late for him to separate himself from the death vapors that sustain and poison him. Although he is not an adversary of the Alisons, he can only lead them in the direction of his own insuperable losses. Every event for him is a repetition (or reenactment) of some aspect of the traumas that devastated and depleted him. (At one point Werdegast appears to kill a fearsome cat belonging to Poelzig by flinging a knife at it. It screeches off-screen, suggesting that Werdegast has succeeded in dispatching it. But the cat returns unharmed in subsequent scenes, available for Poelzig's caresses. It becomes a symbol of his indestructible evil, or more accurately, Werdegast's fixation with that idea.) There is no possible release from the circle in which past suffering chimes the hours, and where propitiation is demanded in the form of mirror image torture. Poelzig, the host, will be the victim of his guest's former punishment. Poelzig seems to be both planning further persecution of his own, and awaiting Werdegast's revenge with a kind of masochistic rapture. He appears hopeful but uncertain that Werdegast will summon the strength to don his own former robes as ice-cold Tormenter. Can Werdegast be the one to seize authority, to give commands, to wield the flaying knife?

In a world where good things have become impossibly scarce, Joan (and the lost, in all likelihood dead, wife she reminds Werdegast of) is the only link with untaintedness, the sole image suggestive of vitality and deliverance that has not decomposed for him. Otherwise, only the ever-present siren song of revenge against Poelzig keeps him at a slight remove from the grave. There are few films in which the utter derangement of space and time is so swiftly, irreversibly effected. Werdegast, in the train compartment, asks the Alisons "May I?" before raising the shade that will expose the nocturnal scene passing by. "Certainly," Peter replies off-screen. Once the blind is lifted and Werdegast encounters his reflection in the glass, everything that remains in the narrative issues from his calcified, distorting gaze.

In Fincher's *Zodiac*, the metamorphosis of external reality into an Expressionist mindscape is not, of course, as conspicuous or thorough as in *The Black Cat*. However, by the point in the narrative where the "false climax" occurs—Robert Graysmith's visit to the old, dark house of theater employee Bob Vaughn (Charles Fleischer) during a rainstorm—a melding of Graysmith's obsessive, life-emptying perspective and the spaces his "private investigation" lead him to has been achieved. I will present a detailed analysis of the Vaughn meeting, including its allegorical dimensions, later in the chapter. But I would like to begin my reading of *Zodiac* with an examination of the interview scene with Arthur Leigh Allen (John Carroll Lynch) in the Union Oil Refinery break room, conducted by a team of three police officers—Sgt. Jack Mulanay (Elias Koteas), Inspector William Armstrong (Anthony Edwards), the primary questioner, and Inspector Dave Toschi (Mark Ruffalo). It is in this episode that the previous concerns of the film and its affiliations with both the procedural and the crime thriller are subtly revised and inverted. The spectator's emotional understanding of what is at stake in the case drastically shifts as a "guilty party" stripped of all grandeur materializes before us.

The setting for the Allen interview is drab, impersonal, and disproportionately large for the intimate give-and-take of interrogation. The refinery break room is a grungier, more disordered version of the cafeteria space in Torrence where the Don Cheney interview took place a day earlier. (Cheney's disclosures during that talk lead the police team to Allen.) The circle of chairs that the four men occupy throughout their tense exchange seem at first to be a makeshift "island" in the fluorescent-lit frozen sea of the break room. Reference is made at the beginning of the scene to a "busted" coke machine. The sly implication here is that anything broken in this dreary environment will probably never be fixed. We observe other concession machines set against the walls, offering Hot Foods, snacks, and cigarettes. As Allen, dressed in a rumpled blue laborer's outfit, is accompanied down the corridor adjacent to the break room, Fincher emphasizes his approaching feet on the dark-tiled floor, alongside those of a fellow-employee walking beside him. Fincher supplies an unattached, mobile point-of-view shot through the meshed window where the police are waiting before this hallway walk concludes. We seem to be covertly scanning the three officers from behind a diamond-patterned wire strip covering a portion of the break room windows. This shot reinforces our sense that the "holding area" we are about to be enclosed in has cage-like attributes. And the cage is subjectively highlighted by being attached to the gaze of the as yet unrevealed suspect. We may be tempted to align ourselves with the perspective of a wary suspect being guided into a trap. The visual concentration on Allen's feet give him a hulking, threatening quality before he is fully exposed in the doorway. Our initial likely reading of his overall appearance—when we are finally shown the archetypal "ordinary Joe" embodied by actor John Carroll Lynch—will briefly contradict the prior intimations of ominousness.

We are past the midpoint of the film, but we are confident that the narrative is not yet ready for a conclusive verdict on a suspect. (We may, in fact, doubt that such conclusiveness is an aim of the film.) Although Allen may prove to be peculiar and capable of disturbing, depraved action, he lacks the stature and aura of a resourceful, intellectually adept killer. As soon as Allen sits down and begins to respond to questions, he appears completely out of his depth and unprepared for the inquisition being sprung on him. His air of incompetence extends even to the sound of his voice, which slides into a nervous, artificial register during his first few sentences. He declares that he stopped reading about the Zodiac "because it was *too morbid*." Fincher structures the ensuing exchange so the viewer is rewarded with a veritable cascade of incriminating revelations. From our initial sense that bumbler Allen lacks the capacity to conceal anything of consequence from the men who press him for information, we are led with a growing excitement to a near certainty that the Zodiac is *here* and has given himself away. We have penetrated, with remarkable ease, his highly improbable, maladroit, "working stiff" disguise.

I recall during my first viewing of the film that I felt (however preposterously) shrewd and discerning as Leigh Allen, without prompting, clumsily provides more evidence against himself than the police questioners know how to ask for. As Allen continues to smear himself with guilt, the initially distant walls of the break room seem to press in and tighten around him and the astonished trio of officers. Allen makes offhand references to "knives in [my] car with blood on them," as well as a prior interrogation by another officer about one of the Zodiac murders. He also acknowledges his proximity to the Riverside killing location "around the same time" as the murder happened, makes knowing references to "The Most Dangerous Game," and gives no more than half-hearted denials to the accusation that he spoke to a friend about "killing school children." ("That's horrible. That's a horrible thing to say.") None of these admissions were the result of clever tactical maneuvers on the part of the team of officers, or intimidating pressure being brought to bear. Rather, we appear to be in the presence of a hopelessly incautious prattler, with no sense of how to protect his own interests. One can hardly avoid regarding him as a person who cannot keep secrets, or be discreet even about his own misdeeds. Allen is equally "caught out" in his body language. When he makes a self-conscious effort to display physical composure, he tensely crosses his legs and leans back. His dark shoe boot thrusts into the frame to accentuate his anxiety.

The point in the interrogation scene which I think most closely parallels Werdegast's gesture of stroking sleeping Joan's hair in *The Black Cat* (where the doctor is caught by an awake, staring Peter while indulging his unmanageable obsession) is Allen's hyperclear attempt to conceal his Zodiac wristwatch from scrutiny, followed by his willingness to let Dave Toschi—who mentions the watch—hold and examine it. The viewer has been previously alerted by another Zodiac investigator, journalist Paul Harvey (Robert Downey Jr.) to a crucial linkage of the watch to Zodiac's drawn emblem. Dave Toschi notices the watch first, and, tracking his discovery, the viewer becomes mindful of Allen touching it. We also cannot fail to see Allen trying to cover it with his hand when Toschi directly alludes to it. After unfastening it and surrendering the watch to Dave and the other two men to inspect, Allen divulges, with a trace of defensiveness, that it was "a Christmas gift from my mother two years ago." At this juncture, the viewer may well feel as persuaded as Dave and his colleagues that Allen's identity as the Zodiac is close to being established. It seems as baldly obtrusive as the Refinery employee name tag that Leigh Allen displays, clipped to the breast pocket of his uniform.

My original claim about this scene was that it marks a major shift, in several respects, both in the nature of the film's world (and our attendant reality sense) and our intimate involvement in the theme of obsession. It is here that the allegorical framework begins to assert itself, rising up before us in a manner akin to Fincher's speeded-up depiction of the Transamerica Building being constructed. The intensely accelerated motion of this "process" compresses the long period of building to a shimmer of moments. The concluding sight of the building finished and alight at night is at once marvelous and vexingly empty. As the Allen interview proceeds, various forms of subtle sound underlay and distortion are introduced. The voice echoing effect in the talk magnifies, and a persistent, whirring industrial wind sound accompanies the speakers' words. We hear occasional refinery noises in the background, and when a buzzer blares at the conclusion of the questioning, there is a rapid resurgence of ordinary "people presence" noise, including footsteps and snatches of conversation in the corridor bordering the break room. When Allen leaves the room, the sound of the metal door opening and clanging shut (like a jail cell) is sharply emphasized, replacing the actual sight of his departure. The wire mesh on the break room windows is reintroduced, and behind it the three officers are framed together, as though it were they who were suddenly enclosed and made captive. An Expressionist thumping heartbeat becomes audible as Allen glances at the group while passing by them in the outside hallway.

We have strayed some distance from realism in the soundscape—appropriate, given the abrupt intensification of the listeners' attentiveness to Allen's sluice gate disclosures. He is not merely relating more than his examiners counted on hearing, but his ways of smearing himself with guilt (vocally, behaviorally)—to repeat a metaphor I employed earlier—manages to take possession of his auditors' imaginations, and of course the film viewer's in tandem. The preliminary excitement of having unexpectedly stumbled into the Zodiac Killer's presence, of having "netted" him almost beyond doubt with his startling avowals and a clinching object—the Zodiac wristwatch—is followed, in short order, by a sense of severely curtailed possibility. The viewer must contend with the prospect of a Zodiac Killer bereft of Adversary mystique and intellectual agility (gone is the philosophizing, well-read John Doe of *Se7en* [1995] and the Byzantine identity labyrinths of *Se7en* and *Fight Club*, 1999). This suspect, for all the mystification he has engendered, has no plot-building acumen. Allen is a Zodiac candidate of shreds and patches, whose pathology is grubby and incoherent. If he is indeed the master of codes, puzzles, ambidextrous handwriting, and shape-shifting identity, these reputed accomplishments suddenly feel dispiritingly aimless and blunt-edged. In such a narrative as the one opening up in the break room, Sherlock Holmes has no Moriarty worthy of his pursuit. We are not yet willing to settle for such an unveiling; a ghastly, fumbling mechanism of perverted deeds, one all too suitable for Hannah Arendt's designation, "the banality of evil."

The break room interview then is both electrifying and depleting. The search for the Zodiac, after so many confusing signals, dead ends, and enigmatic connectives seems to fold in on itself and flatten out. In the scene immediately after the Allen interrogation, the three officers have a completely encouraging follow-up discussion in the home of Allen's brother and sister-in-law. In their warmly lit living room, the strikingly "normal," middle-class couple present no resistance to any of the team's suspicions of Allen's guilt. They concur with the officers' findings, support the claim that Allen was a child molester, and promise to look for additional damning evidence. (We learn that Leigh Allen, like the Zodiac, misspelled "Christ-mass" on a card he sent them "two years ago.") Leigh's brother John agrees to conduct a search of the suspect's apartment. Convergence and the movement toward certainty have an undeniable appeal, but what works against that appeal is the simultaneous removal of obstacles and our dwindling faith in the Zodiac's prior uncanny elusiveness. "Excessive clarity" is an unwelcome guest in an investigation that has thrived on intricacy. The Zodiac watch, given to Allen by his mother as a Christmas gift, speaks too loudly of a psychological solution to a formerly vast riddle.

But perhaps we should resist the urge to attach the watch to either the Zodiac brand label or the potentially suffocating relationship between mother and son. Beneath these clues that demand instant careful attention once they come to light is an obvious but neatly unstressed linkage with time itself. After the misleading speed up of time, as Allen emerges as a figure worth settling on as the "gathering place" for Zodiac iniquity, time abruptly slows down again, with obdurate lethargy, when Allen's handwriting disqualifies him from further consideration as a suspect. The "collapse" of the Leigh Allen edifice of guilt comes swiftly on the heels of the officers' two exultant interviews with Allen and his family members. It is precisely here in the film narrative that obsession turns from a movie-familiar version of valiant, admirable persistence to an allegorical trope of enervating fixity. Obsession—from the Latin obsessus: a siege, blockade, a blocking up. There is a parallel with Werdegast's eighteen-year wait, after the irreparable time of loss and torture in *The Black Cat*, to the dreamlike time of return and confrontation with the moldering, malevolent Poelzig.

Most movie protagonists are animated by a powerful drive or need, which is tinged with obsessive elements. Obsession, however, is rarely cast in a negative light if a protagonist's efforts—whether in pursuit of love, vengeance, artistic recognition, the solution to a mystery, or a victory on real world or mythic battlefields—are crowned with success. Instead of being a morally compromised, unpalatable obsessive, the hero who surmounts all obstacles and refuses to quit seems justified in his or her perseverance toward a difficult, elusive goal. Single-mindedness is so often deemed preferable to weak-minded compromise, diffuse aims, and the caution dictated by authority figures or stultifying "group think." Even in cases where the protagonist does not prevail, redemption of various sorts can be achieved in a final reversal or burst of striving, which emotionally validate an obsessive's nobly doomed enterprise.

Obsession built around "besieged" or "blocked up" psychic states are generally far less palatable. Tales delineating such obsession parallel classical allegories in their positing of equivalents of Vice or Sin figures, though there is a major difference when the central character is imbued with the Vice throughout his or her journey. The conception of Sin in allegory is predominantly static, and it typically inhabits a landscape which mirrors that stasis. The creature or human identified as Despair, Envy, Avarice, Sloth or Rage might be encountered in a cave or wilderness waste where confinement, separation from vital, forward motion (morally speaking) and blind, helpless repetition are one's necessary fate. The shared attribute of all these personified negative drives (which keep one complacently distant from the light of God's love and mercy) is a state of paralysis. One is stuck or mired or circling in a frenzied emptiness that the sin personage mistakes for purposeful action. The cave or desert realm in which they operate becomes, for them, synonymous with reality. One can lure pilgrims and questing knights into contagious embroilment, but the Vice can never be edified by his or her contrasting, spiritual struggle. The Vice figures are invariably obsessive in their overdetermined "oneness." Avarice, say, cannot be freed from the hypnotic wheel of his dead craving, the appetite for more of the poisonous wealth and futile counting of coins that locks him in place. Movies customarily make it easy to separate salutary obsessions from the dark implications of the mire. *Zodiac*, by contrast, like *The Black Cat*, is interested in dramatizing obsession both as an inviting, potentially expansive "way of being" in a world that seems constricting in its visible alternatives, and at the same time as a process of dangerous disengagement, a haunting and withering of the quester's consciousness.

Once Allen is shown to us bedecked in incriminating behavior and then frustratingly, somewhat unpersuasively removed from the list of viable suspects, the Zodiac pilgrimage begins to acquire the delusive fog and mire of the allegorical landscape. There is often a point in the knight's or struggling believer's journey when the original, luminous goal—the Holy Grail, for example—becomes confused and tainted with a debased substitute. The light grows dim, the trail is lost, and the knight, without realizing it, is lost as well. What is fascinating about Allen's partial fading from view in *Zodiac* and fitful, finally obsessive reemergence is that he so thoroughly disallows both grandeur and larger-than-life consequence in the decades-long attempt to uncover the solution to the puzzle. Other suspects are considered, but none emerges with more imposing force and clarity than Allen. His image lingers, disquietingly, in the first time viewer's memory, but not as something spacious and transfiguring. He stays stubbornly rooted in the mundane. To the extent that we are granted access to them, his urges are as pointlessly chaotic as his trailer living quarters, which Dave Toschi eventually receives permission to search. Yes, more and more data can continue to surface and be organized, but all of it (where Allen is concerned) brings us back to his hulking, pathetic ordinariness. His sickness is so much smaller than the story it has engendered. It is as though the Minotaur in the labyrinth turned out to be a rabid squirrel.

When Robert Graysmith becomes the central focus of the film—the lone wolf, ex-cartoonist investigator who refuses to give up—we can hardly avoid the impression that all the scraps of information this bleary-eyed cave dweller obsessively accumulates—are "enigmas seen in a mirror." Attempting to explain to his wife, Melanie (Chloe Sevigny) "what it's going to take for [him] to be done with this," Graysmith, late in the film, memorably declares: "I need to know who he is. I need to stand there and look him in the eye and know it's him." He finally gets his chance to confront Leigh Allen in a hardware store in 1983, but the large, balding, initially friendly but soon tight and resentful clerk wearing the misspelled name tag "Lee" with whom Graysmith exchanges a lengthy, silent, appraising look, is not knowable. He certainly has not become monumental since our first encounter with him. His presence does not supply a gratifying repository for Graysmith's endless time of digging. The contact affords no tingle. This undistinguished stranger, who seems perfectly suited for his clerking position in Ace Hardware, is the same man whose Motor Vehicle birthday documentation had brought on Graysmith's most triumphant experience of epiphany. The small photo on that document proved far more galvanizing than the "match up" with the living person.

Jamie Vanderbilt's shooting script for *Zodiac* contains stage directions for this meeting which specify an epic, decisive, frankly melodramatic "unmasking." "His [Leigh's] face transforms. And we see how terrifying the man could really be. They hold each other's gaze for what seems like forever . . . Getting what he came for. Knowing for sure. Graysmith turns and walks out the door" (189). None of Vanderbilt's descriptive detail and the impact he prescribes for this ocular showdown corresponds to the scene that Fincher shot. The unsettlingly pitiful yield of the long-delayed eye-to-eye inspection is prepared for by Fincher's inclusion of a prominent red-lettered sign advertising "Featured Items" in Ace Hardware, right before Allen is revealed to us. We first spot a man clad in a sleeveless orange work vest with his back turned to the camera. He swings around to face Robert, a prospective customer, and the Zodiac Killer smoothly fuses with a sales clerk. Allen is not wearing the Zodiac watch that the screenwriter suggested highlighting. The ominous music that underscores Robert's entrance into the store, anticipating an occasion of "great pitch and moment" dwindles away as the face-off begins, and in its place we hear a snatch of a pop song on the store radio and the rising noise of the commonplace milieu where the "Zodiac" works. Graysmith strikes me as taken aback by the staggering lack of proportion between his own mental investment in the case and this resolutely ponderous store employee. Graysmith neither arrives at a conclusive identification nor feels in touch with a human equivalent of his own incessant striving. Any creative enterprise, as well as any search for truth (however imbued with moral passion) can take an unfortunate turn into something arid and impoverished. Without the seeker being aware of it, his energies for attachment to any aspect of life apart from it can be leached away.

The progress of the Zodiac investigation has an unlikely endpoint: Graysmith's loss of connection even with the human reality of the figure he has pledged, like a parody of Count Zaroff, to "hunt down" with data, and behold at last with trembling, righteous certitude. Graysmith reminds me of the third brother in a fairy tale, trying to avoid the perils and blunders that have halted the advance of the two who have gone before him, seeking the prize. We witness journalist Paul Harvey's descent into paranoia, rage, and the permanent fog of drugs and alcohol. Dave Toschi, "brother 2," is defeated (in Graysmith's view) by his excessive adherence to protocols, procedures, and the bureaucracy of police departments. And he is further hindered by his celebrity and the envy-induced allegations that he has forged documents. Graysmith regards his own path through the Zodiac wilderness as freer, but as we attend to him, he gradually sinks into a lightless realm of faint signals, ciphers, and conspiracy-saturated disorder. The quest becomes a frighteningly inhuman abyss of perplexity. The vital substance at the outset was obviously supplied by recent victims, a still active perpetrator, and questions having to do with purpose and consequence. All of these moral matters fade away. Graysmith's mind is elsewhere, entranced by minutiae that seem crucially related to the original atmosphere of immanent evil, but are now tracing out patterns in a human vacuum. The emotional trajectory of everything in *Zodiac* is toward death: the death of connectedness as a mass of little connectives ferreted out from text and testimony take its place; the death of actual seeing and hearing; the death of the present tense, of daylight stimuli, of interests with no bearing on the case. Graysmith's vocation is to become entirely, and unwittingly, a man of shadow, like the abstract figure he relentlessly chases. Every apparent gain seems to advance the mirroring of quester and delusive object. To *see* the unbalanced Zodiac necessitates Graysmith's parting company with his own sense of balance.

In *The Black Cat*, once Werdegast rescues unconscious Joan from both the bus accident and the unearthly storm, he transports her to the living quarters of his despised persecutor, Poelzig. Once admitted there, Joan leaves the "present tense" of her new marriage and becomes part of a mausoleum of longing. Whatever, in fact, has some bearing on present tensions is forfeited to the past, whose ghosts are adamant and unshakable. The unexpiated enormities of war, torture, long imprisonment, the obliterated Werdegast family and other betrayals writhe beneath the stilted tranquility of resumed peacetime norms. This vertical positioning of present and past is literalized in Poelzig's sleek, future-proclaiming Bauhaus home, which rests upon the ruins of the fortress in which so much evil was authorized and effected by Commandant Poelzig. Poelzig's dwelling, for which he has been the architect, is an immense act of will—a devil's pact—which proclaims mastery of the past. No matter how close Poelzig remains to his old horrors, they cannot touch him. (The Zodiac's resumed acts of letter writing, after prolonged silences, is a similar assertion of detachment and imperviousness.) The Poelzig mansion is emphatically unreal, without persuasive material substance, like Poe's House of Usher. Along with his revenge-obsessed victim and mirror image, Werdegast, Poelzig is trapped in a cycle of deadening repetition and reenactment. It is as though his spectral edifice has been built solely to allow for the arrival of its one essential guest, Werdegast, who was Poelzig's Supreme Victim. But for Werdegast to gain admission, he must bring Poelzig *another* version of Werdegast's lost wife—in the form of Joan.

In the film's dream version of the "awful truth," Poelzig, unbeknownst to Werdegast, has wooed, won, and killed Werdegast's lost wife, and now shares a bed with Werdegast's daughter. Her destiny—since Poelzig can only repeat his steps, as in an old ritual (echoing Werdegast's monomaniacal fantasy of retribution)—is to be killed, and displayed in a dungeon glass cage, like her mother. Until she arrives at death fruition, she seems a weak simulacrum of flesh and blood. She is an even more somnambulistic version of Joan, the *new* wife being readied for "possession" and sacrifice. Like Joan, she seems always on the verge of unconsciousness. Both women resemble the men who control them in their lack of agency and effectual will. Poelzig initially impresses the viewer as someone who might be real, after a fashion, but he makes fuller sense as a demented projection of his former victim—a creature of allegory and stasis. (What sort of persecutor does one conjure when stretched on the rack?)

The world I am invoking here has perhaps even more in common with Fincher's *Fight Club* than *Zodiac*, but it bridges the two movies' preoccupation with digging up oneself in the transfixing, then frightening guise of another—or a Superhuman other. In *Fight Club*, until the narrator's final awakening to the frenzied splitting within him, everything of significance in the narrative seems to settle down inside one character's head (Tyler Durden) and be locked there. The narrator's discovery that he *is* Tyler, to the extent that Tyler has any standing at all—and his renunciation of this debilitating fantasy of selfhood brings about a vast unscrambling of the viewer's reality sense. In *Zodiac*, Graysmith's kindred feat of projection (so that Zodiac "Tyler" suffuses every nook and cranny of his inner world, displacing the abiding, present "thereness" of things unrelated to it), is neither strongly highlighted, nor finally undone. What the viewer's obsession turns into in *Zodiac* is an attempt to piece together conclusively the Zodiac puzzle for oneself, no matter how coarse, dreary, and ill-fitting the particulars prove to be. Moving alongside Graysmith, we become sharers of his need to see and know. In the event of his success, it is Graysmith's psyche (he hopes), not the *face* of his nemesis, that will come to rest, with gratifying intelligibility.

Commandant Poelzig turns up, after Werdegast's endless attempt to track him down, in exactly the place where Werdegast lost contact with him, so many years ago. He ironically demonstrates that he has never *been* hidden. He is enclosed now in a house that goes far into the earth, a house that jostles at its foundation with the unfinished burials of the war dead. Poelzig himself seems tied to these nameless corpses by invisible chains. Perhaps his semblance of being is but another incomplete interment. When Werdegast arrives at his doorstep, bearing Joan as a kind of propitiatory offering, Poelzig seems to revive from a deathlike sleep. Werdegast summons Poelzig back to an imitation of life because he needs him for his own story to have a rational ending. All of his afflictions have been designed, like the Commandant's dwelling, by one malevolent plotter, the supreme, all-knowing architect of misfortune. The environment Werdegast stumbles upon at last in his mental storm is one immense knot of depravity and woe.

After Werdegast is admitted by servants to Poelzig's Bauhaus stronghold, bearing unconscious Joan, covered by a coat, he sees to it that she is assigned to one of Poelzig's upstairs bedroom, where he can properly examine and tend to her. There is ample stairway distance in the mansion between upstairs and dungeon. The upstairs is for those who rest, in different realms of unconsciousness. The dungeon is for those more committed to death, though the bodies Poelzig has chosen to exhibit there reveal no signs of decay. It is an art gallery ruled by obsessive stasis.

As Dr. Werdegast, in his physician role, ministers to Joan on the bed, her husband, Peter, is seated on the other side of her, occupying a similar position to that he adopted in the train compartment, while Joan slept. (It is as though her injuries in the bus accident have taken her back inside the dream which enshrouded her on the train.) As Peter watches Werdegast touch Joan and prepare an injection of hyoscine for a still heavier sleep, his earlier grounds for objection to the doctor's "caressing" hand have been removed. The hand has become that of a concerned healer. Yet, despite this alteration of circumstances, the hair-stroking images from the train emerge, obsessively, into view once again, though played in a different key. The "return" of the hair touching occurs during a congested bedside gathering. We begin with a shot of Peter reaching out to his wife's hair with solicitude. Then, timed to coincide with the stark entrance of Poelzig, the unambiguous depiction of the husband's gesture is displaced by a second shot of a hand stroking hair. In this close-up image, the owner of the hand is rendered unsettlingly equivocal. Poelzig's apparitional arrival, silently pressing open a door without a handle that evokes a coffin lid, concludes with him looking intently and unwaveringly at the recumbent Joan, as though she has emerged from *his* just ended dream. Before his appearance at the door, we have watched Poelzig, in ghostly silhouette, raise the upper half of his body in his bed in another upstairs chamber. (A lighted intercom has announced the arrival of Werdegast in his home.) The side of the bed he takes up is dark. Beside him lies another sleeping woman, more clearly lit than Poelzig, that we assume is his wife. A wide, high window, covered by diaphanous material, stands facing Poelzig's bed, and its lighted squares carry suggestions of a movie screen. As his dark outline traverses his bedroom floor and leaves the room, a match cut on action transforms him into a female servant entering Werdegast's chamber, bearing a large, transparent bowl filled with sparkling water to the doctor. The momentary shape-shifting confusion caused by the editing linkage of Poelzig and the woman happens in an ominous silence. The merging of these figures, combined with the prominent, glowing liquid, in which Werdegast washes his hands in extended close-up, has the effect of tying all the elements in the environment together, as though the interchangeable hands, faces, hair and movement all attest to the attunement of every isolated element to a sovereign, dictating will. But what is the nature of this will, and where is it located? The hands that wash, administer medicine and care, and reach out protectively and tenderly seem to be supplying cover for the hands that seek control and erotic gratification.

The juxtaposition of the hair stroking (by a disembodied hand) with Poelzig's immediately obsessive gaze at Joan manages to appropriate the stroking gesture for himself. The act feels like an emanation of his covetousness, which is overtly connected with Werdegast's earlier caressing of the hair on the train. Poelzig becomes the manifestly sinister agent of Werdegast's chaotic desires. When Peter caught the doctor in the act during the train episode, Werdegast attempted to explain to the riled husband and himself that his fetishistic conduct was in truth only an attempt to honor the "sacred memory" of his wife, whom Joan resembles. Poelzig is summoned from his deathlike sleep by Werdegast to become, in effect, a second, blameworthy "dreamer" of Joan—one with malicious designs, and who must be stopped. The "dreaming" wife whom Poelzig left behind in his own bed is, we soon learn, Werdegast's daughter, whom he *dreams*—too late, too late— of rescuing from Poelzig, before Werdegast's own ordained tragic ending comes to pass.

In both moments of surreptitious hair caress, a testing of a woman's metaphysical status seems to be taking place. Does this tantalizingly familiar being dwell more plausibly in the realm of the living or the dead? Werdegast, in the coils of fantasy and delusion, hopes that she can be counted as one alive, and externally present, as opposed to another guilt phantom inside his head. Her reality would demonstrate that he is still in touch with life in the world beyond his ravaged memory. And yet, without her equally strong affinities with death and loss, he wouldn't be able to focus on her at all. Poelzig—whether acting in his own right or in accordance with the demands of Werdegast's projections—is eager to add Joan to the list of his victims. It is her death potential that rivets and energizes him.

Poelzig bears only scant resemblance to the brute fortress commandant of Werdegast's long obsession. He strikes us instead as an effete wraith, with an androgynous voice that nearly coos its threats. His regime of torture now seems limited to seducing/enslaving female "mates," and mounting them in glass dungeon display cases once he has vampirized their female life-force for his own sustenance. Once again, this manifestation of the Poelzig plot against captive women is best understood as a projection of Werdegast's consuming "fifteen year" vision of Poelzig luring his wife away from him, of replacing him in her affections by unfathomable sorcery, and bringing her to a monstrous, sordid end. Female vitality seems the key to the survival of the mansion erected over a charnel house. A ghastly mime show of conjugal adaptability and compliance is played out in the massive Bauhaus echo chamber. In *Zodiac*, Melanie extends to Robert the possibility of a humanly connected existence that might be recovered if he breaks free from his enclosure in the Zodiac burrow. Linda, the prisoner who is his final interview subject in the film, reinforces Melanie's identification of Robert's blindness and advancing illness.

Werdegast's time in the vaporous Poelzig dwelling is on one level an attempt to win a "chess game" with Poelzig, on another to overcome his overwhelming fear of cats, on a third to exorcise war traumas by creating a narrative of Poelzig's marital atrocities that equal in scope all the mental torment that he has endured. He brings his obsession to a fitting climax by making Poelzig replicate the stance of the torture victim, then stripping off the perpetrator's flesh in a final paroxysm of punitive rage. Of course, Werdegast must first prove that Poelzig has "skin" to lose, rather than being no more than a shadow cast on the dungeon wall. Is Werdegast contending with a flesh-and-blood persecutor, or is Poelzig a delusional projection? Werdegast's putting the blade to his foe's skin, with the intent to peel it away, serves in his inflamed mind as a final proof. With everything around him in ruins, Werdegast decides to blow up the mansion of his dead host, after releasing Peter and Joan from their imprisonment. "Redeemed marriage" is allowed to start over again outside Werdegast's shattered psyche. He tells the couple as they are about to break free of his mindscape: "I was only trying to help." The series of explosions Werdegast sets off, visible from the grounds of the Poelzig estate, eerily conjure up the battlefield of a "war without end." (James Whale's *Bride of Frankenstein* [1935], released the year after *The Black Cat*, imitates this apocalyptic explosion at its ending—this one set off by the despairing monster—and other Universal horror films followed suit.)

I have spent so long on the allegorical contortions of *The Black Cat* because they seem connected to *Zodiac*'s most obscure, least admissible and sane objectives. *The Black Cat* replicates the hysterical rampage and hunt of *The Most Dangerous Game*, the film which is repeatedly alluded to throughout *Zodiac*, but never screened. The sickness and obsession depicted in that narrative are identified as likely contributing incitements to the Zodiac Killer. The melodramatic pageant that unfolds in the Zodiac's hidden consciousness is "locked away" from Graysmith's ceaseless probing. The movie in Zodiac's head is the movie that Graysmith and the viewer long to see, but can't. In *The Most Dangerous Game*, everything meaningful in the jungle/castle landscape emanates from Count Zaroff, and reality is only restored when Rainsford mirrors and defeats him. In *The Black Cat*, the Zaroff figure is severed in two: Werdegast the dreamer, and Poelzig, the dreamed object, grow indistinguishable as the narrative proceeds. Ulmer's film is an allegory such as Melanie Klein might have devised: a stymied psyche attempting to know itself through frenzied splittings. Eve Kosofsky Sedgwick (2011) has compellingly characterized the Kleinian narrative of conflict-raging development as

> relations among multiple, semi-anthropomorphic objects treat[ed] in terms of deities and demons . . . able in themselves to damage and be damaged, to renew and be renewed. The traffic of projection and introjection is the vehicle for the primitive defenses of the paranoid-schizoid position—but also for the forms of reality orientation and creativity, through the treatment of the good internal object, that can mitigate or transfigure those defenses. (2011, 30–31)

In *The Black Cat*, the world vapors forth from Werdegast's "ember and ash" consciousness. This internal fog encloses him in an "atmosphere of death" and fosters a repetition compulsion that delusively feels like progress.

Melanie Klein's account of the psyche, according to Sedgwick, bespeaks "a ratio or relation between an internal object [hopefully working for good] and an ambient surround" (2011, 31), which both supports and suppresses it. *Zodiac* sets out to persuade us that its events are as firmly rooted as any fact-gathering documentary in a solid, recognizably real world. But Fincher's meticulous recreation of the Zodiac investigation (incorporating its veritable horde of obsessed seekers) resembles the frenetic "splitting" of the stymied Klein psyche. Fincher presents us with a great many characters, but their shared obsessive focus on the Zodiac's incoherent itinerary and strange doings gradually causes (for the viewer) a *Fight Club*-like coalescence of the many into one. The many Zodiac suspects are similarly engaged in recurrent splitting, with a resultant need—within the trackers—to have them coalesce and *resolve* as one.

In the late scenes of *Zodiac*, and most powerfully in Robert Graysmith's inconclusive yet oddly terrifying visit to the old, dark house inhabited by his namesake, *Bob* Vaughn, we see a merger of a plausible final two [Ur-perpetrator and Ur-obsessive tracker] into one. This encounter might be regarded as the false climax of the "objective" story Fincher is telling, but the true climax of the allegory of obsession superimposed on it. Graysmith and the Zodiac suspect attain a Werdegast-Poelzig degree of mirroring that is the most important revelation of the episode. The narrative segment commences after Robert's wife, Melanie (an increasingly inaccessible good internal object, akin to Werdegast's Joan), asks him why he consented to do a television interview about his most recent "findings" about the Zodiac, thereby endangering his family's safety. Just before this exchange, Robert receives a telephone message about someone named "Linda" whom he hasn't been able to locate because she is in prison. Robert excitedly presents this discovery to Melanie, unaware that the information also contains clues (if he could focus on them) about inaccessibility and imprisonment within his own marriage. Robert impatiently thrusts aside Melanie's concerns and seizes the first opportunity to leave for his scheduled meeting with Vaughn.

Graysmith waits for Vaughn's car to arrive under the brightly lit marquee of a movie theater. It is raining heavily. When Vaughn's car pulls up and the two men briefly confer through the rain-streaked car window about where they should have their talk, the viewer is swiftly alerted to something ominous in Vaughn. We are initially deprived of a view of his face, and when it is at last briefly shown to us, he is obscured by shadow. Graysmith agrees with peculiar alacrity to have the meeting at Bob Vaughn's house rather than a nearby coffee shop. When Vaughn suggests that Graysmith should "follow [him]" to his conveniently located home, Graysmith again immediately agrees. This dangerous invitation and the possible victim's naïve acceptance of it conspicuously resemble a well-furrowed horror movie scenario. The movie plot familiarity of the set-up is strongly reinforced by the proximity of the movie theater directly behind Graysmith, as well as the rainstorm, in which Graysmith gets drenched as he and Vaughn make their arrangements. It is also hinted that the subsequent visit might play out as a movie in Graysmith's head. When the two vehicles arrive together at Vaughn's imposing home, the edifice takes on haunted house associations as the men run side by side toward the front door, in the continuing downpour.

From inside the hallway, we watch the pair come through the front entrance simultaneously, a blended entity. As they stand in the cluttered hall close to the door, Vaughn troublingly pauses to lock it. At almost the same moment we catch sight of a large standing mirror in the hallway, which prominently reflects, and thus doubles, the image of Vaughn. The mirror further enhances our sense of a lack of clear boundary distinctions between Robert and Bob. Graysmith declines to take off his jacket—after a bit of coaxing from his host. Vaughn, who seems to have an undisclosed agenda of his own, leads him through another hallway passage that brings them to a large, windowless kitchen. In spite of the lack of windows, the kitchen is initially a less disquieting space than the tight front hall. A tray of fruit on a kitchen counter seems to bid the visitor a friendly welcome, and the warm light promises a measure of coziness after the rainstorm. One might easily fail to notice that the door on the kitchen's rear wall has no knob.

Graysmith sits at a table divided from the kitchen proper by a counter barrier. We become conscious of two separate realms in the kitchen as Vaughn moves around in the more spacious rear area making tea while Graysmith remains seated, passive and waiting. A movie poster for a 1937 film, *Conquest*, in which Napoleon is romantically conquered by Greta Garbo's Polish countess and then conquers her in turn by a pragmatic act of betrayal, is prominently displayed on the kitchen's back wall. It creates a rhyming effect with the movie poster seen in Graysmith's apartment during his quarrel with Melanie. Graysmith's vintage poster is for the Edward G. Robinson film, *Illegal* (1955), about an upright lawyer who takes on many crooked clients and gradually becomes "one of them." Perhaps, given the fact that Graysmith is dutifully following in the wake of other failed questers, it is worth noting that *Illegal* is a remake of a much better film, *The Mouthpiece* (1932). A brief discussion about the 1932 movie, *The Most Dangerous Game* ensues, in which we are given time to wonder who the hunter and the hunted are in this private meeting. The *Conquest* poster in Vaughn's sector of the kitchen, combined with his freedom of movement and domination of the talk, subtly establishes him as hunter, even before any strong signals of insidious design are introduced.

When Graysmith introduces the topic of the Zodiac—still hunched in his chair at the table—Vaughn, facing him from the other side of the counter divider, turns away to assume a profile position. His affability has vanished. He grows instantly perturbed and resentful, as Graysmith brings up the name of Rick Marshall, a former projectionist at his theater, who (at the moment) is Graysmith's primary suspect. Vaughn pointedly insists that he has no communication with him "these days," though the extent of their former closeness remains in doubt. Another startling mood reversal occurs within an instant. As Graysmith tentatively speaks of a "connection," Vaughn reveals himself, almost eagerly, as a fellow-obsessive. He alludes to the Zodiac symbol, and no sooner has he done so than he crosses the barrier to Graysmith's narrow section of the kitchen. He briefly disappears into the darkness behind his visitor, then reemerges with subtly unnerving closeness beside Graysmith, holding a small coil of film. He shows Graysmith the standard academy leader countdown, which, like Allen's watch in the earlier interview, precisely matches the Zodiac sign. We have swiftly moved from references to a specific film, *The Most Dangerous Game*, to a symbol hidden within *all* film reels. The prelude to the experience of film screening and viewer imagining is connected to the Zodiac case, the *secret* mechanism of projection, and the obsession potential encoded in movie narratives. We are given a point-of-view shot, from Graysmith's perspective, of the Zodiac symbol on numerous film frames.

Once Graysmith completes the inspection that Vaughn has forced upon him, he discovers Vaughn once again returned to the other side of the counter barrier. The conversation then turns to a secret film canister that Rick Marshall presumably left in Vaughn's keeping long ago. According to Graysmith's source, Vaughn was told never to open it. Vaughn surprisingly confirms the rumor, offering a purring, confidential "Yes" to Graysmith's query. What follows are two achingly vulnerable shots of Graysmith, who has never appeared so childlike and beseechingly in need as he does here, at the prospect of opening the canister that "Zodiac" has prohibited anyone from seeing. One might well contrast this expression with Graysmith's stony demeanor when Melanie confronted him earlier about "family safety." He coldly added, "Are you done?" before abandoning her yet again for his consuming crusade. Graysmith's plaintive "May I see it?" to Vaughn is countered with the shattering "snatch back" of Vaughn's perhaps sadistically teasing offer. Not only did Vaughn honor Rick Marshall's demand to refrain from looking in the forbidden box, but Marshall returned to retrieve it seven years ago. Yet another quick emotional reversal, this one shocking and seemingly decisive, occurs when Vaughn shifts from withholding any canister knowledge to confessing, almost brazenly, that it was he and not Rick Marshall who drew the possibly incriminating movie posters. Graysmith has already indicated that the Zodiac's handwriting and the poster artist's were close to a match.

The most significant, confounding, and increasingly fear-inducing portion of the scene commences at this juncture. Graysmith tries to compose himself in the face of this all-too-immediate, unanticipated peril by gazing at the posters in his notebook and declaring his intention to leave. ("I won't take any more of your time.") Vaughn moves past the divider once more, positioning himself in a dark basement doorway directly behind Graysmith. We are given a two-shot view of Graysmith's apprehensive face in close-up, looking toward us, and Vaughn out of focus in the background, where Graysmith can't observe him, and where our own interpretive powers are also impaired. Vaughn urges Graysmith—from behind—to stay in the house until he has checked his basement records on *The Most Dangerous Game*'s ancient play dates at his theater. Graysmith suddenly recalls, at the same moment we do, Dave Toschi talking to him once about basements in relation to the Zodiac Killer. He pointed out that not many Californians have them. Vaughn switches on the basement light—perfectly timed with Graysmith's shuddering realization that the Zodiac may just have materialized behind him, and announced his presence. Graysmith turns around at last to face this metamorphosed Vaughn, as Vaughn, ambiguously poised between information yielding and half-unveiled threat, acknowledges his own possession of a basement ("I do"). By this stage of the scene, we may well have assigned Vaughn the capacity to read Graysmith's thoughts.

As we hear Vaughn's off-screen steps on the cellar stairs, his voice lightly calls out, "Coming, Mr. Graysmith?" as the camera remains on Graysmith's seemingly paralyzed form, still seated at the table. An ominous, whirring sound (as if issuing from a wind tunnel) arises on the soundtrack, replicating the agitation and panic of Graysmith's inner state, as well as repeating a sound we hear during the Allen refinery interview. (Fincher may well have borrowed this surrealistic "noise within" from the Coen brothers *Barton Fink* [1991]. Whenever Barton opens the door to his hotel room, a similar sound arises.) Instead of seizing his opportunity to flee, however, Graysmith surprisingly adopts the sheepish pose of a child obliged to do what his authoritative elder dictates. There is no question that Graysmith considers himself in real danger, but he helplessly pursues Vaughn down the basement stairway. The unavoidable question to raise about this decision is "Why?" Graysmith, at this point, appears simultaneously to be a compliant victim-in-the-making, consenting to a highly conceivable slaughter (an ironic fate), and an obsessive whose determination to "see more"—maybe including an unequivocal eye-to-eye encounter with the Zodiac, or at least to gain a sprinkling of new, "telling" facts—overrides any ability to look after his own well-being. The stairway includes, near the bottom, a visible phone on the wall, a second potential escape route that Graysmith disregards. In the course of his slow descent of the steps, Fincher begins to emphasize, by cunning deployment of sound and visual elements, the melding of the two figures. Vaughn is both a dreadful new suspect and an obsessive hoarder-investigator, like Graysmith. His moldy files and sprawling collection of artifacts put us in mind of Graysmith's own apartment. Vaughn ushers Graysmith into an underworld space that seems to be a shared unconscious. Like Poelzig's dungeon in *The Black Cat*, which is as much a projection of Werdegast's as a literal den of horror, the Vaughn cellar is uncannily Graysmith's psychic home: terrifying not because of its strangeness but because of its deep familiarity. Graysmith in all likelihood longs to see Vaughn standing in the midst of his laid bare secrets, allowing Graysmith to *know* that this grubby, mild-mannered hoarder is indeed the Zodiac, who can tie all threads together. But the man who emerges beneath a single, lit, hanging light bulb at the far end of the basement's dark dream passageway is chiefly menacing as a reflector of the one who follows. Vaughn confronts Graysmith starkly with a version of his own unaffiliated emptiness. Or rather, his affiliation with a matching emptiness.

In *The Logic of Sensation*, a monograph on the painter, Francis Bacon, Gilles Deleuze evocatively describes an encounter between visible and invisible in terms which directly apply to the death-driven consolidation of Robert and Bob in the echo-filled night room below Vaughn's home: "When visible sensation confronts the invisible force that conditions it, sensation releases force as something that might destroy it, or become its ally or friend" (2005, 48). The "invisible force" in the episode is the fractured and dispersed presence of the Zodiac. Graysmith could be approaching it in the form of Vaughn—beneath the accusing finger of the bare bulb—but at the clinching moment Vaughn is engaged in a task identical to Graysmith's work. He is searching for the scrap of information about *The Most Dangerous Game* screening, which will settle a question. But his position, so recognizable from other horror movies, is that of a maniac poised to spring, amidst all the disquieting clutter. Graysmith is filmed as a stalking predator himself as he silently moves closer to Vaughn, closing the gap. Vaughn may even be at a disadvantage here, distracted by the record book he appears to be consulting.

Graysmith is brought to a halt by increasingly definite sounds of movement in whatever room is directly above him, suggesting that there are one or more additional inhabitants of the house, stealthily assuming their positions for a planned assault on him. It is fitting that the Zodiac now appears, however illogically, to be everywhere and precisely nowhere. To the extent that Vaughn is in league with the invisible force released by Graysmith's act of following him "into the depths," the spectator invests him with the means and the knowledge to destroy this troublesome pursuer. But as the two men's echoing voices strive to unite and it is possible for us to comprehend that Graysmith is facing a pathetic blankness within himself, it seems that the right sort of realization might make the "invisible force" in this "shared unconscious" an "ally or friend" (Rodowick, 103). The anxiety that Vaughn engenders is in part due to our quickening sense that he is a fellow-obsessive solitary, stuck in his own catacomb of pointless data.

What makes this bloodless scene in which no significant discoveries are made so horrifying for a first-time viewer is the unbearable excess of multidirectional "not knowing," coupled with the equally unbearable excess of potential revelation. We seem to lose touch with the established *character* of Graysmith as he becomes part of this palpable, palpitating knot of malignant intentions. We also lose touch with Vaughn's precise position on Graysmith's projection screen. The disquietingly nondescript eccentric might at any instant become a plausible release point for the inconceivably monstrous. What a screening room Vaughn's basement unconscious becomes. D. N. Rodowick, in his 2017 study *What Philosophy Wants from Images*, describes Hugo Munsterberg's sense of the cinema phenomenon as "a machine for picturing the world, as the projected image of our own internal resources for registering the world and making it meaningful" (104). I find it stunning how viewer's mind and registered world (this viewer's mind, at the very least) are pressed to the breaking point by this *Zodiac* episode of obsession unmasking in its lair. Call it a triple lair, jointly occupied by Graysmith, Vaughn, and the "caught" spectator, beholding her own obsessions. Our meaning-making efforts are met with a mirroring that, in effect, shatters (briefly) the "internal resources" that we bring to our task.

How polite Graysmith and his double are with one another as they arrive at the climactic moment of mirroring, and never has politeness done more to intensify fear. "You're sure no one else is in the house?" Graysmith asks, with quiet deference. Vaughn, deflecting the question with a gesture of permission we can't persuade ourselves is genuine, replies with equivalent softspokenness: "Would you like to go and check?" As Graysmith fumbles with a "Thank you" and turns to bolt up the stairway in panic, Vaughn (never more apparitional) appears to set off in a separate basement direction. Could there be a second flight of stairs? When Graysmith reaches the kitchen, the only menacing presence he uncovers as he hurries through it is the piercing whistle of Vaughn's tea kettle brought to a boil. We cannot imagine Graysmith being able to break free of the house without further opposition. It may occur to us as Graysmith struggles vainly to open the front door that Vaughn locked it just after they came in together. Graysmith turns around and again faces Vaughn at close range, doubled this time in a literal mirror reflection. Adopting a victim pose—back pressed against the curtained door, his demeanor all childlike pleading—Graysmith seems unable to take the situation in hand. We are given another unreadable close-up of Vaughn as he decides on an appropriate action. We cannot avoid believing, for a few moments, that he is reaching in his pocket for a knife. Instead—in a deflating joke that the first-time viewer cannot respond to with laughter—the knife turns out to be a key, and Vaughn, relinquishing his advantage as a controlling adversary, opens the door and bids Graysmith a pleasant, slightly patronizing "Good night" as his guest runs back to his car in the rain. The reduction of stature and menace in Vaughn, coupled with the viewer's confusion and disappointment, repeats the deflating pattern established in the Allen interview scene.

What follows is a short, close range interior shot of Graysmith driving his vehicle. The windshield wipers work against the spattering rain, the whirring sound from inside the house (and Graysmith's head) returns, and a light from an unspecified source illuminates the driver's face in profile. Though he is alone in his car, he does not *seem* to be alone. In the next shot, he is already back at his apartment. We feel the temporal compression. Graysmith rushes up the exterior steps, rhyming with his very recent ascent of the basement stairs at the Vaughn house, approaches another door, which rhymes with Vaughn's front door. This one Graysmith must open with his own key. He mumbles while engaged in this action about the possibility of a split Zodiac: "Rick Marshall as killer, Vaughn as letter writer." His apartment is dark and unoccupied when he comes into it, extending the mirroring of Vaughn's lonely dwelling to Graysmith's equally desolate, vacated home. His movement through the estranged domestic interior returns us, emotionally and viscerally, to the Vaughn cellar from which we just escaped. The lights Graysmith switches on in his children's bedroom reveal made-up beds. A follow-up mobile point-of-view shot in his own bedroom exacerbates the sensation of abandonment and isolation. When Graysmith enters the kitchen, again linked to the Vaughn kitchen he recently "made himself at home in," he discovers a piece of paper containing a pair of messages, one on each side. The first he sees is a note from his wife explaining that she has taken the children to her mother's, and demanding that he not call her there. He responds to this message with angry frustration, crumpling the paper in his hand. As he continues standing by the phone, uncertain of what to do next, he recalls the earlier phone communication that he had received just prior to leaving the apartment to meet Vaughn. That message is scrawled on the other side of the paper, justifying his straightening out the rejected sheet and reconnecting with it. Here Graysmith discovers the name "Linda," another female friend of one of Zodiac's victims.

We promptly cut to Graysmith's visit to prison, where he manages to interview her. His choice to pursue "Linda" rather than his wife, Melanie, has seemingly been made for him, as though he now possesses no will separate from the case. And his detachment from family matters is reinforced by the interview itself. This stranger across the table has effortlessly displaced whatever concern may have arisen in him at the loss of his family. Fincher makes Graysmjith's anxiety about "peripheral matters" involving his other existence an ellipsis. Graysmith will only see Melanie once more in the film, when she appears like another ghost to present him with a crucial piece of information about Leigh Allen's birthday. No emotional reattachment is established on that occasion. The face of Leigh Allen on his driver's license, magnified with the accompanying "guilt-laden" birth date, effaces the competing reality of residue from Graysmith's evacuated personal life. Graysmith instantly remembers that Zodiac announced he would kill again on his birthday, but he is unable to remember any of the ties that once linked Graysmith to Melanie.

During his brisk prison interview with Linda (Clea DuVall), she commences by informing him that he has the self-consuming "look" of a Zodiac obsessive. The suspect she describes to Graysmith, who is himself now an incontestably haggard *inmate* of obsession, resembles him in certain particulars. "He wasn't into people, I can tell you that." At a party Leigh attended, "he sat alone in a chair, didn't talk to anyone. Creeped me out. Darlene [the soon to be victim] was scared of him." Graysmith's breakthrough coffee shop discussion with Dave Toschi, which comes close on the heels of Graysmith's acquisition of the clinching Allen birth date, at first glance might seem to mark a human resurfacing from his private dungeon. But, of course, the sole topic of conversation between the two men is the resurrected suspect, Leigh Allen, the dullard who is also a heap of pathologies. They discuss his activities and whereabouts at various distant times with minute attentiveness and accuracy. At the high point of their exchange, Graysmith sets a salt-and-pepper shaker quite close to each other on the dinner table in order to demonstrate how *near* Leigh Allen lived to his first victim, Darlene. He lived in his "mother's basement," not "fifty yards away" from the person he may have killed. The viewer may well be alert at this point to the fact that Graysmith craves to dwell in the closest possible proximity to Allen's long-ago footsteps (every minute action from those faraway days is Graysmith's "present tense"). All he can attend to with genuine attachment and concentration are the surviving items of Leigh Allen's itinerary in that vanished but somehow brightly flickering swatch of the past. Graysmith has been almost wholly absorbed, like Werdegast, by this shadowy, pathetically limited alter ego—a fellow "basement" dweller—and nothing but the lines and dots fastening him to Zodiac have the clarity of something real.

Frank Kermode's famous distinction in *The Sense of an Ending* (1968) between modes of time—*chronos* (passing time) and *kairos* (significant time)—has a clear bearing on our experience of time in *Zodiac*. The initial apprehension of significant time, in the Zodiac's early manifestations, with the promise of a meaningful revelation pattern, is slowly degraded to *chronos* time. Time merely passes, leaks away. For the obsessive in his cave, there is no escape from chronicity, no disclosure (despite Graysmith's published book and most fervent hopes) of reality at a higher, grander, redemptive pitch. With Graysmith, as with Werdegast in *The Black Cat*, there are only phantoms of his own obscure torment, beckoning from a lonely mirror. (The torment may have begun as a simple desire to graduate from cartoon illustration to the grown-up journalist intuitions and intrepid exploits of his senior colleague, Paul Avery.) The capitulation to the inefficacious sovereignty of obsession is "the most dangerous game" of both narratives. And Robert Graysmith, the last avatar of the futile quest for "release" from the Zodiac mystery, can echo Werdegast's sad appeal for clemency from Joan before blowing himself up: "I was only trying to help."

REFERENCES

Deleuze, Gilles. 2005. *Francis Bacon: The Logic of Sensation*. Translated by Daniel W. Smith. Minneapolis, MN: University of Minnesota Press.

Fletcher, Angus. 1982. *Allegory: The Theory of a Symbolic Mode*, Ithaca, NY: Cornell University Press.

Kermode, Frank. 1968. *The Sense of an Ending*, London: Oxford University Press.

Miley, Mike. 2010. "Deciphering the Indecipherable: Procedure as Art in Fincher's Zodiac." *Bright Lights Film Journal*, January 31. Accessed August 1, 2018. https://brightlightsfilm.com/deciphering-the-indecipherable-procedure-as-art-in-finchers-zodiac/#.XKy9BZhKiM8.

Rodowick, D. N. 2017. *What Philosophy Wants from Images*. Chicago, IL: University of Chicago Press.

Sedgwick, Eve Kosofsky. 2011. "Melanie Klein and the Difference Affect Makes." In *The Weather in Proust*, edited by Jonathan Goldberg, 123–43. Durham, NC: Duke University Press.

Vanderbilt, Jamie. 2006. *Chronicles* (Final Shooting Script for *Zodiac*). May. Accessed July 20, 2018, http://www.screenplaydb.com/film/scripts/Zodiac.PDF

Wartenberg, Thomas E. 2012. *Fight Club: Philosophers on Film*. London: Routledge.

SECTION THREE
ZODIAC AND MEDIA

Chapter 8

The Dantesque Desires of David Fincher's *Zodiac*

Martin Kevorkian

David Fincher's *Zodiac* thoroughly concerns itself with issues of mimesis. The script explicitly calls out the ambiguous popular culture competition between originals and copies, as when cartoonist and amateur sleuth Robert Graysmith (Jake Gyllenhaal), seeing Inspector David Toschi (Mark Ruffalo) for the first time, observes that "He wears his gun like Bullitt," to which journalist Paul Avery (Robert Downey Jr.) insists, "No, McQueen got that from Toschi." The film sustains a chicken-and-egg relationship with films including *Bullitt* and *Dirty Harry*, highlighted both broadly and in several visual details. The Zodiac himself emerges as not only variously imitative of books and films and even the police, but as an envious figure from Dante's *Inferno*, a resentful killer of young lovers. The connections of Fincher's *Se7en* (1995) to Dante and deadly sin have been well explored, as in Jeremy Tambling's Lacanian-inflected analysis (Tambling 1999), but the carryover of John Doe's Envy to *Zodiac* has not been remarked, and yet this subsequent film is permeated with the traces of envy, the desire that imitates desire. For Dante, as for theorists from Aristotle to René Girard, desire is fundamentally mimetic, a mimesis that readily leads to conflict. David Humbert has recently focused upon conflictual desire in *Violence in the Films of Alfred Hitchcock: A Study in Mimesis* (2017), and I argue that Fincher's work is no less attuned to this dynamic of rivalrous imitation.

Se7en spotlights the deadly sin of Envy, assigning that attribute to the killer John Doe (Kevin Spacey) and reserving its revelation to the very end. The final act of *Se7en* bears explication by way of Girard's commentary on

> the second half of the Ten Commandments, which is entirely devoted to prohibiting violence against one's neighbor.

Commandments six, seven, eight, and nine are both simple and brief. They prohibit the most serious acts of violence in the order of their seriousness:

You shall not kill.
You shall not commit adultery.
You shall not steal.
You shall not bear false witness against your neighbor.

The tenth and last commandment is distinguished from those preceding it both by its length and its object: in place of prohibiting an *act* it forbids a *desire*.

You shall not covet the house of your neighbor. You shall not covet the wife of your neighbor, nor his male or female slave, nor his ox or ass, nor anything that belongs to him. (Exod. 20:17)[1]

As Girard explains, this final prohibition offers protection against all of the acts of violence listed before it; rather than representing a miscellany in afterthought, this final commandment highlights the compendious generativity of this one principle, the danger of envy: "Mimetic desire does not always result in conflict, but it frequently does so for reasons that the tenth commandment makes evident": the conflict arises over the "object I desire in envious imitation of my neighbor" (Girard 2001, 10). John Doe's Envy completes the loop by driving Detective Mills (Brad Pitt) to perform an act of vengeful wrath: the violent conflict over the neighbor's wife precipitates reciprocal killing. The character John Doe may be read as a highly focused and stylized version of the Zodiac, abstracting and infusing a series of killings with specific meanings. In *Zodiac*, a tipster who knew leading suspect Arthur Leigh Allen reports that, when Leigh was asked how he expected to get away with "hunting people, like that book . . . he said, 'It would be easy because there'd be no real motive to the thing.' He said he'd write letters to the police, call himself Zodiac to mess with them." John Doe, in contrast, creates and boasts of an elaborately motivated scheme of twisted pedagogy (one honed to a point of extreme literal emulation of the books he studies). And yet, as per the witness above, the Zodiac has revealed two sources of motive: an imitation of actions in a book, and a possible sense of rivalry with the police. These motives, of following a literary script and in seeking to mess with the police, both place him close to John Doe, who is immersed in the literature of sin and who reaches out to tell the police, "I just had to call and express my admiration." Even calling himself the Zodiac—though the suspect is here said to treat the name as a kind of arbitrary throwaway to sow confusion—bears a whiff of John Doe's medievalism, as Graysmith discovers that "the zodiac alphabet" can be traced to the Middle Ages. And, on the most basic level of serial killer math: as Avery explains to Graysmith, only seven attack victims can be confirmed for the Zodiac, and that number, seven, is attested by the consensus of those who have studied the case.[2] In these senses, the character of John Doe emerges as a copy of the Zodiac; and thus the later film, *Zodiac*, as a copy of *Se7en*; *Zodiac* as a copy of a copy of own source material.[3] One that perhaps seeks to outdo *Se7en* as a faithful mimesis of its subject matter, and to do so by remaining even more intently focused on the principle of mimesis itself.

Studies of *Zodiac* to date have noted the film's fascination with (and dependence upon) technologies of simulation (as in Amy Taubin's *Nerds on a Wire* [2007] and Michele Schreiber's *Tiny Life* [2016]); the present chapter aims to map *Zodiac*'s obsession with technological mimesis onto its characters' structural embroilment in Dantesque desire. Fincher's meticulous attention to technological simulation manifests itself within the first ten seconds of the movie: the company credits for "Paramount: A Viacom Company" appear with the scratches and speckling of a worn, projected film, accompanied by the noise of a crackling soundtrack. On a common-sense level, this credit presents itself as an impossible image, hearkening back to an analog archive that predates Viacom ownership (which arrived with the multimedia conglomeration of the 1990s). The logo "Viacom" name here appears in the same typeface that used to grace the Paramount logo when it was "A Gulf + Western Company" (in a style that appeared in the late 1960s and persisted through the 1980s) and similarly appears without the digitally animated stars that zoom into the frame of current Paramount releases, but rather shows a static constellation set against a majestically drifting backscreen of clouds. That is, *Zodiac*'s company credits evoke the old Gulf + Western aesthetic, as if the film had been shot at the time of the events depicted (starting with the first scene, which announces, in plain reportorial Courier, that we are witnessing a 1969 occurrence). The WB logo immediately follows and receives similar visual noise treatment, while reproducing the same subtitle and style, "A Time Warner Company," that, for instance, introduced audiences to *Bullitt* in 1968. While this aesthetic may indeed help to transport us to a different time, I would suggest that these special treatments are not meant to fool us entirely or even primarily. Rather, the technical noise and iconic nostalgia read as deliberate effects, no less so than, say, *The Matrix*'s (1999) notable digital doctoring of the WB logo, which subjects it to an ominous green flicker that alerts us, even before the action commences, that something is up, that someone is tampering with our ordinary perceptions. Indeed, *Zodiac* does operate on a bit of a "Matrix" principle of revealed deception, of imitation understood as such; within *The Matrix*, we come to recognize that "the Matrix" itself projects a kind of throwback simulation, with retro cars, nostalgic neon signs, and old-timey beat cops. In *Zodiac*, these opening seconds already invite us to reflect upon the paradox of what we are seeing, an evidently digital simulation of an analog (copy of the) past, an imitation of an "original copy" of an old film. The company credit, moreover, simulates an original which is itself an emblem par excellence of Hollywood (re)production—Paramount and its star system as the last of the big studios. *Zodiac*'s company logos establish a complex dynamic between original and copy, authentic and simulated, which the first projected narrative words deepen: "What follows is based on actual case files." While the film thoroughly dramatizes the analog paper knowledge of those case files (even highlighting the degree to which the police departments involved lacked access to such transitional technologies as telefaxes), within our current viewing frame, the term "files" may take on a doubled reference.[4] As Schreiber and others have emphasized, *Zodiac* was among the first films "to be shot directly to a hard drive" (Schreiber 2016, 4). The story may be based upon case files; the images we see have been captured, stored, and reproduced entirely by means of digital files, files designed to emulate for us an authentic documentation of the original events.

Bridging the company credits and the opening scene, Three Dog Night's "Easy to Be Hard" continues the hiss and pop soundtrack and floats into a July 4, 1969, Vallejo evening. The song poses a question, named as a paradoxical question of "evil," with which *Zodiac* will wrestle: "How can people be so cruel?" The lyrics point to the deadly sin of pride as the nominal cause of coldness to be found "especially" among people "who care about evil," and who thus sacrifice personal ties in their would-be noble crusades for justice, emotional investments that make them "proud." Surely the film dramatizes such sacrifices, as the obsessive protagonist Robert Graysmith commits himself to an amateur investigation of the *Zodiac* killings, a pursuit which separates him from his family. And yet the lyrics also hint at an even broader motive for the story's actions, one both driving the hauntingly extended investigation and offering a key to the mystery of the killings, a key which the first scene similarly makes available from the very start: "You know I'm hung up on you." Graysmith is hung up on Zodiac, and the desire to know, to know what only the killer knows; in a mode that can even be more directly taken for envy, the Zodiac is hung up on the first victims we meet, the young lovers Darlene Ferrin and Mike Mageau, *Zodiac*'s initial doomed Paolo and Francesca figures.

We first see Darlene picking up Mike for the purposes of what we can soon infer to have been planned as an adulterous assignation. Mike reveals as much with his nervous question to Darlene, in response to a menacing Mustang circling the site of their would-be tryst: "Was that your husband?" Darlene's first answer is "No," and, then, a perhaps too-anxious performance of certainty: "It was nothing." Her façade slips when the car returns: "Oh, shit," as if in recognition of a reckoning that has fallen due. We later learn from Darlene's sister that the returning agent of judgment is likely someone

Darlene did know: not her husband, and yet cast into a structurally similar position with regard to her affairs, someone whose presence is incompatible with and hostile to Darlene's habitual casual dalliances with "a lot of boys . . . even though she was married." At a party that Darlene throws, "this guy showed up in a suit . . . and just sat in a chair all by himself all night long. Didn't talk to anyone. And Darlene told me to stay away from him. She was scared of him." No party boy he: the older man in the suit, the envious representative of patriarchal law, excluded by and drawn to the bond of young love, wreaks his resentful vengeance. He steps (or, more precisely, lumbers, as one witness describes his gait as "lumbering") into a long-running role, one made famous Francesca's husband, Giancotto Malatesta (aka "Gianne lo Sciancato" or Lame Johnny) whose murderous violence Dante immortalizes in *Inferno* V. The role suits him, and he repeats his performance, violently sending another couple to their own punitive underworld. On the shore of Lake Berryessa, a young couple, contemplating "an entire hidden city" beneath them, find themselves the object of an interloper's gaze: "I think he's watching us," worries the young woman; "Well, we're very good-looking" quips her boyfriend. Perhaps the Zodiac is drawn to their desirability; perhaps he is drawn to their desire. As Toschi's police partner, Inspector William Armstrong (Anthony Edwards) later observes, the original series of confirmed Zodiac attacks conforms to a pattern: "all lovers on lovers' lanes."

And, as one may well suppose, there is more to the pattern: the story of young lovers murdered by an envious older man is not unique to Dante, nor to *Zodiac*. What Dante's version usefully highlights for the purposes of taking a next step in a reading of *Zodiac* is the degree to which the entire scenario is mediated.[5] Dantesque desire is desire mediated by entertainment, by narrative. Fincher's film is about that mediation. The famous literary exemplar of Paolo and Francesca serves as both a useful and dramatically pertinent illustration. In the most basic love triangle, a subject imitates the desire of a model, and can be drawn into rivalry by vying for the object of the model's apparent or presumed desire.[6] But sometimes the model of desire is not even another person, but rather a text, one that incites a structure of desire. As John Freccero explains, Francesca confesses to Dante that—not merely despite but in fact strictly because of its similarity to cliched medieval romances—the love tryst with Paolo was "neither spontaneous nor predestined. It was suggested by their reading of the romance of Lancelot. In Hell, Francesca seems to be disabused of her romantic illusions. What appeared to have been love at first sight was in fact love by the book. Book and author seduced the lovers, just as Lancelot and Guinevere were seduced into adultery by the traitor Gallehault."[7] Hence Francesca's bitter recrimination of the text that defeated them on the day of their first illicit kiss: "A Galeotto, that book!" (Pinsky 1994, 43). Galeotto here names Gallehault, who acted as "messenger between

Lancelot and Guinevere," and whose name "has become a synonym for 'pander' or 'go-between' " (Freccero 1994, 314). The crucial critical move of Dante's Francesca is to identify a text itself as such a mediating go-between. Fincher's *Zodiac* offers a veritable catalog of such texts, books, and films that not only describe the desires of *Zodiac*'s characters but may be seen to have mediated those desires by offering models for imitation.

Zodiac's staging of the first depicted killing, when viewed in light of details later emphasized in the film, bears several marks of such model texts. In the Zodiac's first letter to newspapers and police departments, he declares, "I like killing people . . . because man is the most dangerous animal of all," and in a follow-up letter, he specifically glories in his technical prowess of having used a flashlight aligned with his gun barrel to hit his targets in the dark, without need of a gun sight. Graysmith immediately recognizes and puzzles over that phrasing, "Dangerous animal. Dangerous animal. What dangerous animal? How do I know that?" He eventually makes the connection to the 1932 film, *The Most Dangerous Game*: "I knew that I heard that from somewhere. The Most Dangerous Game. It's a movie about a count who hunts people for sport. People. The Most Dangerous Game." Journalist Paul Avery, who somewhat reluctantly allows Graysmith to partner with him in the investigation, makes a further connection, when Graysmith informs him that the hunter is one Count Zaroff: "Zaroff? With a Z?" implying that Zodiac may derive at least part of his sense of self by identifying with the murderous count. Much later in *Zodiac*, the leap to the1932 film becomes something of a red herring, leading Graysmith to believe he has found himself in the presence of the killer, film aficionado Bob Vaughan (Charles Fleischer). And yet along the way, the Count Zaroff narrative very closely attaches itself to the suspect upon whom *Zodiac* comes the closest to settling as being the Zodiac: Arthur "Leigh" Allen.[8] When being interviewed by police, Leigh acknowledges his admiration for the tale of Zaroff: "The Most Dangerous Game. That's why you're here, isn't it? It was my favorite book in high school." When Leigh says, "That's why you're here," in one sense, he is mistaken: this particular set of police had no idea of his fascination with what the short story that he terms a "great book." But in another sense, Leigh may be exactly correct: insofar as that text has inspired his actions as the Zodiac, "The Most Dangerous Game" is indeed responsible for bringing him and the police investigating his actions to this very crossroads.

Yet the nexus in the Zodiac's letters, between man as the most dangerous animal and his own proficiency as a hunter, does not exhaust its allusive reach in referring to Richard Connell's short story "The Most Dangerous Game" (1924) and the 1932 film it inspired. As others have observed, the phrase "the most dangerous game" also features prominently in a 1961 episode of *Alfred Hitchcock Presents*, "Museum Piece," which contains the story of a man who had "invented a foolproof gadget for night shooting," namely, "A spotlight mounted on his 22 in such a way that his shot would strike the exact center of light," the precise boast of the Zodiac who wrote that "When taped to a gun barrel, the bullet will strike exactly in the center of the black dot in the light" (*ZodiacKillerFacts.com,* 2016). In "Museum Piece," much as in Zodiac, the initial dramatic event—one that precipitates years of fallout, investigation, and quest for retribution—centers upon a night hunter who comes across a pair of young lovers (one of whom guiltily mistakes him for the other's stern father, much as Mike had thought the Zodiac might be Darlene's enraged husband) and shoots one of them.[9] The Zodiac, that is, may well style himself as a Count Zaroff, but he appears to have augmented his aim (and even borrowed his targets) by means of television tips brought to him by Hitchcock.

While fictional hunters may fuel the Zodiac's taste for blood, we overlook a crucial aspect of the Zodiac's identity if we fail to observe his emulation of models from the other side of the law. Fincher's film suggests throughout that the Zodiac is, from the start, locked into a mimetic rivalry with the police. When we first hear what turns out to be the Zodiac's voice, calling to report the killing, we are seeing a cop, whose face remains above the frame, striding impassively onto the murder scene. For a moment at least, the shot seems ambiguous, as we match faceless voice to the faceless body with which the film juxtaposes it: is the voice we hear that of the cop, calling in the crime? Or, has the killer returned to the scene in the costume of a cop? No: and yet, Fincher's framing of the faceless cop, with the Zodiac speaking, offers an image of how the Zodiac would like to see himself. Though he does not dress up as a cop to revisit the victims, I would suggest rather, and nevertheless along these lines, that the killer first approached the scene in the trappings of a famous fictional law man. In his 1969 attack, *Zodiac* shows him stalking the lovers in a Ford Mustang much like the one iconically identified with the 1968 film, *Bullitt.* Mike calls attention to the specific vehicle when he says that he saw "that car" previously at Mr. Ed's drive in, where a famished Darlene passed on a chance to eat, mysteriously deeming the scene "too crowded" (right after she has seen the Mustang parked there). Fincher comments that originally a Corvair, the same model driven by Darlene, was considered for the attacker's vehicle, but that choice was set aside so as not to make the Zodiac's car too "ironic" of a "doppelganger" with the victim's car. By avoiding one strange doppelganger, one that would identify the killer with the lovers, *Zodiac* creates a more intriguing and telling doppelganging, that of killer with fictional cop. Zodiac drives Bulllitt's car to perform his act, and then, immediately phones in to report the crime, as if eager to join the squad. If, as Avery avers, McQueen as Bullitt got something from Toschi, and it further appears that the Zodiac got something from Bullitt, then the Zodiac is already the copy of the copy of the cop who will investigate him.

As the film progresses, Zodiac's mediation by Toschi becomes a firsthand rivalry, albeit one still caught up in fantasies of fictional representation, ideally a text in which he might appear as a model rather than imitator: "That city pig Toschi is good but I am better. I'm waiting for a good movie about me. Who will play me?" The Zodiac's statement about waiting for a "good movie about me" implies his dissatisfaction with *Dirty Harry* (1971), which had been released before he penned this note; his slight is understandable, as the film deifies the cop who vanquishes the "Scorpio" killer. Fincher's film even ambiguously hints that Dirty Harry, like Bullitt, may have got something from Toschi—or, perhaps, in this case, Toschi got something from Dirty Harry (even if Toschi doesn't like the film either, for different reasons, particularly its scorn for "due process"). In the scene prior to the special SFPD screening of *Dirty Harry*, we see Toschi investigating Leigh's trailer park residence; he gets there in a Ford Galaxie 500, the same car that Dirty Harry drives. *Zodiac* time stamp's the investigation of the trailer as September 14, 1972, while *Dirty Harry* was released on December 23, 1971.

But if the mimetic status of Toschi vis-à-vis Dirty Harry remains subtle and ambiguous, the mimetic link between the Zodiac and Toschi becomes increasingly clear. Toschi later observes that, of all the suspects, Leigh was the only one ever to write to him: "Dear Dave, if ever I can be of help to you, just let me know." In an earlier exchange, Graysmith has noted to Toschi, regarding serial killers, that "They like to help, sometimes." Toschi, wearily: "I know, Robert." Indeed, earlier the Zodiac has even sent a "key" for his own code to one of the police departments (something he did not do for the newspapers), to make extra certain that *they* receive his message. He craves communication with them as a fellow man of skill and craft, while also making a power move of showing himself to be a smarter version of them (via the insulting implication that they would need the key). Leigh, when interviewed by the police in person, offers that he is "willing to help in any way possible. I look forward to the day when police officers are no longer referred to as pigs." Leigh may imagine himself to be speaking with dry irony at this point, and yet his words may yet testify to a true desire to see himself alongside the police, assisting them in the noble act of investigation, and earning proper respect for it. The Zodiac's communications consistently evince a degree of identification with the cops, even as he insults them with a kind of forced arrogance: "I hope that you do not think that I wiped out that blue meanie with a bomb at the cop station." He compares himself to the cops while asserting his superiority to them; he taunts them because he seeks to rival them, presuming, for example, to know better than they how to do their jobs: "The police could've caught me last night if they had searched the park properly." In the clutches of mimetic rivalry, Girard has observed (borrowing from Dostoyevsky), "Men become gods in the eyes of each other": resentful victims of mimetic rivalry become obsessed with those who seem to have what they lack (Girard 1976, 53). As Cynthia Haven explains, with particular reference to Dostoyevsky's Underground Man, "Girard points out again and again how we imitate those we wish to resemble . . . whom we loathe and love, as they alternately fascinate and frustrate us. We are addicted to our obstacles, and go 'underground' to hide the derivative nature of our lives, even from ourselves" (Haven 2018, 103). Zodiac's own grandiose rhetoric of prospective self-deification (as in imagining that he is gathering slaves for an afterlife) might be read as a reflection of how he idolizes the police, and popular depictions thereof, like Bullitt. He sees them as gods and hopes to gain what his idolatry of them has convinced him that they possess. Though he mocks them, he does so to shore up belief in his own imagined potential for achieving godlike status, with wishful insistence asserting his superiority to the detectives whom he in fact views and emulates as godlike.

As suggested above, one crucial piece to the Zodiac's sense of identity, and identity as mastery, is his use of codes, a medium that he can deploy to flaunt his cleverness and bolster his feeling of superiority. In assembling his profile of the Zodiac, Graysmith his delved into the world of cryptography: "I've been doing research on the first cipher. Everything an amateur would need to create it can be found in these books. Now, I started thinking that if you can track these books then maybe you could track the man." Graysmith, in sleuthing mode, literally means that he hopes to pinpoint the Zodiac by means of library records, but tracking these books may also further allow us to track the imagined identity of the man who has tracked these exemplars. In *Se7en*—which, if nothing else, demonstrates alongside *Zodiac* Fincher's abiding faith in the power of library research!—Detective Somerset (Morgan Freeman) homes in on John Doe by tracking circulation records for Chaucer, Dante, and books related to the seven deadly sins.[10] Somerset poses in succession two questions that perfectly illuminate the double usefulness of the tracking of books in *Zodiac* as well: "What would he need to study to do the things he's done? What are his other interests?" *Zodiac* prominently displays *The Codebreakers* (1967) as the most monumental of the studies that Graysmith posits as sources for the Zodiac's skills and defining interests, and it may be taken to offer more than just instrumental knowledge. This book is, for example, not called How to Make and Break Codes, or something self-evidently in a user manual vein. Rather the title, *The Codebreakers*, traffics in the prestige and allure of *the* originators, the definite, genuine articles themselves, heroic models to emulate, and by whose light to see oneself as a master.

Assisting his father in his research to identify the Zodiac, Graysmith's son carries and plops down a stack of books: from atop the bulging tome of *The*

Codebreakers the child removes Dr. Seuss's *Yertle the Turtle* (1958), itself a tale of precarious stacking (the child's gesture in fact reveals the cover of *The Codebreakers* to the camera, as one tale of outsized ambition parts the curtains for another). Yertle, a turtle with serious delusions of grandeur, continually wishes to raise himself higher, to the absurd extreme of seeing the rising moon as a rival whose achievements he must outdo:

> "What's THAT?" snorted Yertle. "Say, what IS that thing
> That dares to be higher than Yertle the King?
> I shall not allow it! I'll go higher still!
> I'll build my throne higher! I can and I will!

Yertle eventually topples from his self-made tower, undone by a burping turtle beneath him. But this comic comeuppance seems less salient to *Zodiac* than Seuss's analysis of the delusive mimetic desire that led Yertle to such dangerous heights in the first place. Fincher's work, like Hitchcock's, seems similarly concerned with offering its viewers access to the mechanisms of delusion, a way of recognizing the idols that warp vision and destroy balance. As Humbert argues with respect to *Vertigo*, itself an analysis of mimetic scaling to untenable, unstable heights, "Vertigo is banished when . . . the lineaments of the real world are freed of distorting, self-divinizing desire" (Humbert 2017, 116). The Zodiac's vertiginous delusion appears complete in his boast that "I am now in control of all things"; he has ceded control to his mediators to arrive at this wishful pronouncement.

Nor are those who seek the Zodiac themselves entirely immune to mimetic mediations of desire. The *Codebreakers*, for instance, may serve as a model for Graysmith's desire as well: its author, David Kahn, was a journalist who set out to write a book about cryptology and ended up quitting his job in order to devote years of his life to completing it. Such a mimesis of a successful model is not inherently conflictual—any damage to Graysmith's life proceeds not directly from rivalrous interaction with a model for his investigation, but rather from the sacrifices made while pursuing the obsession that results from it. But while dramatizing Graysmith's trade-offs and domestic losses, *Zodiac* does not offer a sentimental distinction between true love at home and unhealthy devotion to work. Rather, in a mimetic vein, the film deromanticizes Graysmith's relationship with Melanie (Chloë Sevigny), which finds its initial spark not in love at first sight (though it does, classically, occur on a blind date), but in a love effect derived from a mutual thrill in the search for the Zodiac. When Graysmith apologizes during their first date for having derailed and extended the evening, offering that "You don't have to stay," Melanie replies, "Are you kidding? This is the most interesting date I've ever had." In the end, of course, she doesn't stay with Graysmith. As she says later, with sadness, "It was just the date that didn't end," the date defined by the figure of the Zodiac. Their relationship, at its outset, mirrors or reverses the attack victims' position as objects of the gaze and violent attention of the Zodiac: rather than a couple whose enactment of desire attracts the envious desire of a killer, Graysmith and Melanie become a couple when their passion is ignited by the danger of pursuing the Zodiac. In the cases of both the victims of attack and pursuers of the attacker, however, the Zodiac (in person or in prospect) destroys a couple's relationship: in the first case, the killer engages in violent mimetic conflict that ends with the death of the woman (whether she is the object of his desire or rather the rival and obstacle to his desire); in the case of the amateur investigators, the figure of the Zodiac created in the wake of those killings becomes the object of Graysmith's passion at the expense of Melanie and home life (thus again, in effect, winning the "affection" of the man and vanquishing the woman who would rival him as focal point for desire).

After the film's opening depiction of the Vallejo 1969 attack, and immediately following the establishing shot—overlaid with title credits—of the Ferry Building that locates us in San Francisco four weeks later, Fincher treats us to a warm domestic scene that seems the diametrical opposite of the shocking violence we have just witnessed. The first frames of this domestic scene, which introduce us to Graysmith, present a charming tableau of father and son brushing their teeth (6:33). Showing both Graysmiths wearing a green shirt with brown pants, and displaying the pair both in left-facing profile with right elbow jutting to hold toothbrush in mouth, the tableau at first suggests a charming duplicate. Upon closer inspection, the visual doubling of father and son reveals a possible triplicate: in the background, behind the child in the restroom, we may discern a third figure in green—a toothy monster also in left-facing profile, with white foam dripping from the corner of his mouth (does this monster use toothpaste, too?). The father-son doubling presents apparently innocuous—indeed salutary—mimesis; the older generation models excellent oral hygiene for the latter. But the way their doubled poses match the looming monster on the wall may give one pause. Behind copycat morning ritual of Graysmith elder and younger, the frame gives us the visually rhyming poster for *The Beast from 20,000 Fathoms* (1953). The advertisement for the movie promises a "MASTER-BEAST OF THE AGES—RAGING UP FROM THE BOTTOM OF TIME!" and that "YOU'LL SEE IT TEAR A CITY APART!" A silly monster flick, we may suppose (Ray Bradbury writing credit notwithstanding), and yet, in these promotional declarations of menace, we may discern the outlines of a social reality beneath such myth. It is indeed the conflictual mimetic contagion of a "CAST OF THOUSANDS!" that can tear a city apart. While the monster inhabits the realm of myth, the true "master-beast" raging up from the bottom of time, from the foundation of the world, is mimetic violence.[11]

The toothbrushing scene's doubling of father and child offers a moment of heartwarming relief in the rhythm of the film, an emotional counterpoint to the chilling violence of the attack that precedes it, and yet it, too, neatly stages another classic scenario of mimetic conflict. If Mike and Darlene and the Zodiac recall Paolo and Francesca and Giancotto, here father and son and monster recall the possibility of Oedipal strife, here understood mimetically. From a Girardian perspective, Oedipal conflict is merely a special case of mimetic rivalry: it has its origins not in the child's allegedly natural desire to sleep with the mother and thus wish to kill the father, but rather in a tutelary desire, a desire in the child to imitate the father which results in conflict when the model of desire, the father, becomes obstacle to the desire's fulfillment. In Fincher's tableau, the mother is absent; this framing pares the scene down to the seed, the imitative behavior that can ultimately produce the monster.[12] Finished with toothbrushing and whisking his son off to school, the father poses a frank question: "You don't like having a new little brother?" "No, not really" confesses the child. "Oh. That's honest"—Graysmith applauds the son's forthright admission that a new arrival poses a threat, as potential rival, to the existing status situation in the family; no one welcomes a new competitor for the affections of the person one admires. *Zodiac* commits to that honesty about the power of mimetic behavior.

The media framing of another domestic scene at Graysmith's home extends *Zodiac*'s exploration of mimetic dangers. A television reporter is confirming that "the Zodiac Killer has come to San Francisco"; the monster, and the monstrous wave of panic that such reports will spread, has arrived to threaten the city. Noticing that his son has entered the room, Graysmith stands to switch off the television; as he rises, the camera moves to bring into the frame a movie poster on the wall above Graysmith's television. As Graysmith moves to short circuit the channel of fear, a relevant and competing text comes into focus: *The Wrong Man* (1956) starring Henry Fonda as the mistakenly accused Manny Balestrero and Vera Miles as his suffering wife. As in *Zodiac*, a cheerful domestic scene early on hints at a principle that may generate strife: we see Manny at home with two young boys who "compete for his attention" as Humbert (2017) observes (85). Specifically, the younger boy has provoked his brother, albeit playfully, by mimicking on the harmonica a Mozart piano piece that the older son attempts to master: the competition takes place in a contextually determined arena, as both boys vie for the approval of their father, a professional musician. But in *The Wrong Man*, the gravest danger comes not from conflictual mimesis, the monster that tears us apart, but the mimetic contagion of accusation, the force that unites us as a monster. As Humbert notes, *The Wrong Man* makes clear "the contagious desire, with the encouragement of others, to take action and to find a culprit," as dramatized in the detectives' "mimetic and reciprocal incitement," of both one another and the witnesses, to point to Manny as the guilty party (Humbert 2017, 81, 86). And Vera Miles as the wife knows how this works: "They've got it fixed against you"; a collective entity has arrived at unanimity to predetermine the outcome for the scapegoat. Vera Miles happens to be the same actress who did the voicework for the trailer to *The Beast from 20,000 Fathoms*. In that trailer, Miles poses the grave rhetorical question, "Who knows what waits for us in nature's no man's land?" In *The Wrong Man*, Miles as Rose finds herself in a version of this pitiless landscape. But what *The Wrong Man* shows us is that this no man's land is not natural but rather man-made, as the contagious violence of social order imposes itself as the inescapable "nature" of things. Miles in the trailer for *The Beast from 20,000 Fathoms* warns of "the leviathans that roamed the deep from the dawn of time"; the leviathan of *The Wrong Man* is that of Thomas Hobbes, the collective artificial man capable of reordering the war of all against all into a persecution of all against one. *Zodiac* shows us that Graysmith is not immune to the intoxicating spirit of accusation. At one point having arrived at the conclusion that film buff Rick Marshall is the Zodiac, he interviews Darlene Ferrin's sister, Linda (Clea Duvall) with feverishly coercive excitement, demanding that she remember the name he has deemed correct:

GRAYSMITH: Rick?
LINDA: No, I don't think so.
GRAYSMITH: Are you sure?
LINDA: Yeah.
GRAYSMITH: How can you be sure? It was long ago. Think hard.
LINDA: I am thinking hard.
GRAYSMITH: It was Rick.
LINDA: No, it wasn't.
GRAYSMITH: It was Rick. It was Rick Marshall.
LINDA: No.
GRAYSMITH: Just say it.
LINDA: It wasn't Rick.[13]

Unlike the witnesses in *The Wrong Man*, Darlene's sister actively resists the contagion of accusation with which Graysmith at this juncture seeks to infect her. Similarly, Inspector Toschi underlines the dangers of the will to closure: "Do you know what the worst part of this is? I can't tell if I wanted it to be Allen so bad because I thought it was him . . . or I want this to be over." An enthusiastic Graysmith tells Toschi, "Just because you can't prove it doesn't mean it's not true," to which Toschi gives a cautionary reply: "Easy, Dirty

Harry." Hanging in Graysmith's living room, Hitchcock's *The Wrong Man* posts a dialectical note to self: "It doesn't have to be true for you to prove it."[14] Similarly, "Museum Piece," a possible source for the Zodiac's use of a flashlight for his more accurate targeting of shooting victims, centers dramatically on the inaccurate targeting of an accusation of murder. A father, making the plea that his son is innocent, the "town is ready to lynch him"; that is, the town finds itself in the throes of a mimetic frenzy that leads to lawlessly violent acts of would-be justice. The district attorney replies with confidence (much like the representatives of law and order continually reassure Manny Balestrero), "If he's innocent, he'll go free." He is innocent, and he does not go free. Graysmith has decorated another wall with an entry from the manhunt genre: *I Died A Thousand Times* (1955), billed as the "story behind the terrifying 60-day hunt for desperado 'Mad-Dog' Earle," also known as the "Million-Dollar Killer." What is "terrifying" about the manhunt in "Museum Piece" is the contagion of certainty that attaches itself to that hunt's innocent target. Surrounding himself with such reminders, Graysmith has chosen an environment that mediates his desires to perform his own manhunt, perhaps to whet that desire and yet also to temper its excesses. In further resonance with *The Wrong Man*, on display in Graysmith's home is a poster for *Illegal* (1955), starring Edward C. Robinson as a district attorney who has helped secure the death sentence of an innocent man. This net of allusions exists in tension with Graysmith's quest for certainty. Ultimately, Fincher's engagement with cinematic exemplars presents a model of positive mimesis: *Zodiac* is a film thoroughly mediated by films that warn against the dangers of mediation.

NOTES

1. See also Girard 2001, 7.

2. Avery enumerates the murders: "There's three in Vallejo, one in Berryessa, the cabby. That's it." So, five murder victims and two survivors, one each in Vallego and Berryessa, for a total of seven attack victims. In another version of this echo, Graysmith focuses on a clipping whose headline reads, "I've Killed Seven."

3. Though I would not suggest that *Se7en* presents itself as "a Zodiac story," it can be read, especially retrospectively in light of *Zodiac*, as the director's first relationship to the essential material of a serial killer investigation that bears several marks of the Zodiac. From this perspective, *Se7en* abstracts and transposes the Zodiac killings from the San Francisco area to Los Angeles—to the site of imaginative movie-making, as it were—rendering it as a stylized parable for the present day. *Zodiac*, on this account, represents a deepening of Fincher's relationship to the source material, and a restoration of the story to its original location and time, with all aspects of setting treated with aspirations to documentary fidelity.

4. Gitelman 2014 offers a pertinent context for considering Fincher's project in *Zodiac* as a thorough meditation on the media and mediations of documentary knowledge.

5. For René Girard's influential anti-romantic reading of *Inferno* V, see Girard 1978, 1–8.

6. There is something to be said on this score regarding Paul Avery's having written, to the Zodiac's apparent displeasure, that the killer was a "latent homosexual." Following the course of mimetic desire in a love triangle, the rival of the subject (in this case, the Zodiac) would be the one with whom the subject would be drawn into violent conflict: the point would be to kill the rival in order to isolate the object of desire. On a structural level, then, Avery's speculation makes sense of the Zodiac's attack pattern, with the repeated result that "Boy lived, the girl didn't. Again." As Armstrong observes regarding the two graphic attacks with which Fincher's film opens, "he only manages to kill the girls. Mageau lives, Ferrin dies. Hartnell lives, Shepard dies. He gets so caught up with the women, he forgets to finish the men." In these encounters, from the standpoint of conflictual mimesis, the girl suffers the fate of the rival, even if the desire for the boy remains "latent" and distorted as non-fatal attack. Incidentally, the report that the "Boy lived, the girl didn't. Again" also describes the outcome of *Se7en* and John Doe's final machinations against Mills by means of fatal assault on his wife (Gwyneth Paltrow).

7. Freccero, who was a colleague of Girard's when the latter wrote his essay on "The Mimetic Desire of Paolo and Francesca," supplies this note to Robert Pinsky's verse translation of *The Inferno of Dante* (1994, 313).

8. Taubin (2007), for one, finds that "As close as *Zodiac* comes to solving its mystery is a simple shot/countershot sequence in which Graysmith goes eyeball to eyeball with his prime suspect, Arthur Leigh Allen (played with impassive menace by John Carroll Lynch)."

9. In this episode, with story by William C. Morrison and teleplay by Harold Swanton, "the most dangerous game" takes on a different valence, as it refers not to the prey of a lawless count hunting for sport, but rather to the shooter being tracked by the law: "I remember the excitement of the manhunt. The most dangerous game." Fincher's *Zodiac* recounts both thrills: both that of the Zodiac (as he boasts in his letters of the "fun" he derives from killing) and of those who hunt him.

10. When an incredulous Avery asks Graysmith how he had figured it out, Graysmith replies in pointedly matter-of-fact tone, "I went to the library." Later, asked a similar question by a reporter, he answers, "I just read a lot of books at the library." Graysmith, like Somerset in *Se7en*, find himself most in his element when using the resources of the public library.

11. See René Girard's (1987) study of violent origins.

12. In myth, as technically designated by Girard, the imagined monster obscures the actual scapegoat who suffers the blame for destructive social energies. Girard's critique of such acts of unifying foundational violence serve to call into question the allure of such myths, myths of justified monster hunts. At the end of the toothbrushing scene, Graysmith asks his son why he swallowed the toothpaste: "It was minty," explains the child. Toothbrushing is good for you, but you can't swallow the

toothpaste, the father insists. Oral hygiene is a purification ritual that can go wrong; the need for cleaning should not be displaced by an appetite for cleansing for its own sake. Don't eat the toothpaste, even if it is minty. Even in the pursuit of justice, one mustn't, like the Zodiac or John Doe or a hasty accuser, develop a taste for cleansing violence.

13. Paradoxically, this moment, portayed as Graysmith's peak of wrongheadedness, make *Zodiac*'s strongest bid for being right that Leigh is the killer. Despite Graysmith's badgering, the sister finally produces her verdict, "It was Leigh," and the film (perhaps wishfully, in quest for its own approximation of certainty) stages this remembering as uncoached and unmediated.

14. In both *The Wrong Man* and in *Zodiac*, we see a witness pick with certainty the fourth man in a lineup. If *Zodiac* leans quite heavily on the idea that the pick is correct, it nevertheless keeps in play the ghostly uncertainty of mistaken accusation. As a producer for *Zodiac* puts it in a commentary track for the director's cut, the film presents a story of "slow persistence driven by unknowing," unlike, say, the deadly certainty that drives Dirty Harry, in which the identity of the killer is apparent for most of the movie. *The Wrong Man* unsettles confidence in such certainty. *The Wrong Man* is also a significant model for *Zodiac* within the Hitchcock canon because, as Matthew Sorrento (2010) emphasizes, "this was Hitch's only film explicitly based on a true story."

REFERENCES

Freccero, John. 1994. "Introduction." *The Inferno of Dante: a New Verse Translation*, translated by Robert Pinsky. New York: Farrar, Straus, and Giroux.

Girard, René. 1976. *Deceit, Desire, and the Novel: Self and Other in Literary Structure*. Baltimore, MD: Johns Hopkins University Press.

—. 1978. "The Mimetic Desire of Paolo and Francesca." In *To Double Business Bound: Essays on Literature, Mimesis and Anthropology*, 1–8. Baltimore, MD: Johns Hopkins University Press.

—. 1987. *Things Hidden Since the Foundation of the World*. Palo Alto, CA: Stanford University Press.

—. 2001. *I See Satan Fall Like Lightning*. Maryknoll, NY: Orbis.

Gitelman, Lisa. 2014. *Paper Knowledge: Toward a Media History of Documents*. Durham, NC: Duke University Press.

Haven, Cynthia L. 2018. *Evolution of Desire: A Life of René Girard*. East Lansing, MI: Michigan State University Press.

Humbert, David. 2017. *Violence in the Films of Alfred Hitchcock: A Study in Mimesis*. East Lansing, MI: Michigan State University Press.

Schreiber, Michele. 2016. "Tiny Life: Technology and Masculinity in the Films of David Fincher." *Journal of Film and Video* 68 (1): 3–18.

Sorrento, Matthew. 2010. "*The Wrong Man*: Hitchcock 101." *PopMatters*, June 21. Accessed August 16, 2018, https://www.popmatters.com/127052-hitchcock-101-day-eight-1956-1958-2496178877.html.

Tambling, Jeremy. 1999. "'We Are Seven': Dante and the Serial Killer" *Paragraph: A Journal of Modern Critical Theory* 22 (3): 293–309.
Taubin, Amy. 2007. "Nerds on a Wire." *Sight and Sound* 17 (5): 24–26.
ZodiacKillerFacts.com. 2016. "The Zodiac's 'Electric Gun Sight.'" April 26. Accessed April 9, 2020, https://zodiackillerfacts.com/tag/museum-piece/.

Chapter 9

The Zodiac Strikes a Blue Chord

Evoking Art-Horror in Music

Andrew M. Winters

INTRODUCTION

If you are reading this, then it is likely you have already heard or read about the Zodiac Killer (hereafter, "Z"). As a quick refresher, Z is confirmed to have begun a killing spree on the eve of the Winter Solstice (December 20) in 1968, having started by shooting David Faraday and Betty Jensen in Benicia, California. While Z claimed to have killed thirty-five people, police have only confirmed seven victims—two of whom, Bryan Hartnell and Michael Mageau, survived. While Z was most active in 1969, it is possible that he, and I am presuming that Z is a *he*, started as early as 1963 and did not finish until 1971.

In addition to his identity remaining unknown and him having never been caught, what sets Z apart from other serial killers was his use of letters to blatantly taunt the police—the only other serial killer to do so was Jack the Ripper. It was Z's demands for his letters to be published in mainstream presses that allowed Z to reach celebrity status. Not only did the public know of Z's actions from the police reports, but they also gained access to his intentions to gather them as slaves for the afterlife.

Between August 1 and August 8, three letters were received by major news presses based in the Northern California area, including the *Vallejo Times Herald*, *San Francisco Chronicle*, and *The San Francisco Examiner*. For the details of these letters, I refer the reader to Robert Graysmith's *Zodiac* (1986). Graysmith was a political cartoonist working at the *San Francisco Chronicle* when the Zodiac letters had arrived. His book served as the basis for David Fincher's 2007 film *Zodiac*.

On April 24, 1978, Z allegedly sent his final letter to the *San Francisco Chronicle*. While the letter's authenticity is in dispute, the letter states,

> Dear Editor, This is the Zodiac speaking I am back with you. Tell herb caen I am here, I have always been here. That city pig toschi is good ' but I am smarter and better he will get tired then leave me alone. I am waiting for a good movie about me. who will play me. I am now in control of all things.

Yours truly:

SFPD- 0

Even if it is a forgery, we *do* have a "good movie" about Zodiac (David Fincher's *Zodiac* [2007]) and we know who plays Z thirty years after the letter's delivery: Richmond Arquette (Zodiac 1 & 2), John Lacy (Zodiac 4), and Bob Stephenson (Zodiac 3). Fincher's 2007 film emphasizes Graysmith's role in tracking Z. Whereas many other Zodiac-based films focus on the horrendous nature of Z's actions, Fincher's film emphasizes the anxiety that Graysmith, law enforcement, and the public experienced while attempting to determine Z's identity. While I presume that most of the chapters in the present volume discuss the film in even more detail, we should recognize that Z's influence has gone beyond the screen.

In music, for example, numerous bands have used Z's letters and actions as the source of inspiration for their lyrics, titles, and imagery. In this chapter, I explore the emotional effect these bands have had by using Z as a source of inspiration. In particular, I look at their capacity to evoke the feeling of being, what Nöel Carroll has labeled, *art-horrified* (Carroll 1990). In doing so, I argue that those bands that have explicitly used Z's letters as lyrics are more effective in evoking the audience's feeling of being art-horrified than those bands that have only used Z as inspiration.

The chapter unfolds as follows: The first section discusses the ways in which film evokes the feeling of being art-horrified. The second section argues that music can also produce a similar feeling in the audience. The third section looks at specific cases of music in which Z serves as a source of inspiration. In particular, I look at examples from subgenres of metal to argue that Z's own words are more effective in generating the feeling of being art-horrified than only using Z as a source of artistic inspiration.

ART-HORROR AND THE POSSIBILITY OF THE REAL IN FILM

On a regular basis, and especially around Halloween, we entertain ourselves with things that we ordinarily think of as being horrific and, if real, those things would certainly be a threat to our well-being. Yet, we find this form of entertainment to be desirable, if not outright enjoyable. If we did not find the horror genre to be desirable, then it is unlikely that the market for horror would be so profitable. But the horror genre grosses over a billion each year at the box office and accounted for almost 10 percent of the box office market in 2018 (*The Numbers.com*) and interactive horror attractions (e.g., haunted houses) bring in over $500 million each year (*American Haunts.com*). Given the profitability of the horror market, we have some reason for thinking that the horror genre is desirable.

These numbers illustrate a strange feature of us—we appear to desire the undesirable. Carroll refers to this feature as the *paradox of the heart* (Carroll 1990, 10). In an attempt to better understand our paradoxical nature, Carroll offers an account of horror involving an emotional response to the horrific. The *evaluative theory of emotion* that Carroll employs involves having some feeling of agitation being caused by the feeling subject's evaluation of her situation (Carroll 1990, 27). Carroll goes on to describe the particular emotion tied to our desire for engaging horror as *art-horror* as follows, which I have modified for clarity:

> Assuming that "I-as-audience-member" am in an analogous emotional state to that which fictional characters beset by monsters are to be described to be in, then: I am occurrently art-horrified by some monster M if and only if:
> 1. I am in some state of abnormal, physically felt agitation
> 2. Caused by
>   a. The thought: M is possible
>   b. The evaluation: M is a threat
>   c. The belief: M is impure
> 3. Resulting in the desire to avoid contact with M.

While additional debate is warranted regarding whether M must be external to the character beset by M or if M is something that does not currently exist, art-horror involves M being both threatening and disgusting.

This account appears to apply accurately to those things with which we entertain ourselves when desiring something from the horror genre. Most of the monsters in the horror genre are only the things of nightmares. In our day-to-day experiences, we do not concern ourselves with aliens springing from our chests; monsters using claw-adorned gloves to hunt our children in their dreams; or creatures stirring from ominous waterscapes. But when watching horror films, it is the thoughts that the alien, Freddy Krueger, or the creature is possible, that they are potential threats, and that they are disgusting that lead us to desire to avoid them (and oddly draws us to their respective films).

In the case of horror films that incorporate serial killers, we know that they are not just possible, but that they are real. We have seen them, read their testimonies, and met those who have survived their attacks. Furthermore, we know that they are a threat to our safety. News coverage becomes rampant with warnings when a suspected serial killer is on the prowl; curfews are put into effect; and extended law enforcement resources are used to prevent any additional killings. Due to these reasons, the feeling of agitation that is experienced while watching a film about Richard Ramirez in *Night Stalker* (2009), John Wayne Gacy in *Gacy* (2003), or Z in *Zodiac* (2007) is due to them having existed and them having been genuine threats. To what extent, however, should we think of serial killers as being impure?

While serial killers are not of the same ilk as fictional monsters such as the alien, Freddy Krueger, or the creature from the black lagoon, they are certainly different enough from most of us that they fall into a different category from those who are not serial killers. The neuroscientist James Fallon (2013) has reported that a serial killer's brain is more likely to have physiological differences from a statistically normal brain, including lower orbital cortex activity (which is thought to be involved with ethical behavior, moral decision making, and impulse control). The forensic psychiatrist Helen Morrison (2004), who has interviewed more than eighty serial killers, identifies a range of common traits that serial killers exhibit. These traits include the lack of personality structure, having above-average intelligence, being psychologically incomplete human beings, having an uncontrollable addiction to killing, and having the emotional age of an infant. While both Fallon's and Morrison's works are not fully accepted within their own fields, there is a wide range of literature indicating that there are significant physiological and psychological differences between serial killers and us (see Baron-Cohen (2011); Blair (2003); and Blair (2006)).[1]

Like the monsters in horror films, we are also drawn to serial killers due to, what I have deemed, the *macabre-interest* (Winters 2010). We are drawn to the horrible and the real possibility of the horrible existing draws us more than when the monster is only a feature of our imaginations. While the thought of someone like Freddy Krueger hunting us in our dreams makes *Nightmare on Elm Street* (1984) an unsettling film, films that portray the threat as someone who is more similar to someone with whom we would come into contact while awake is even more unsettling. Dr. Hannibal Lecter from *The Silence of the Lambs* (1991) was inspired by a Mexican surgeon, Alfredo Ballí Treviño, who was convicted of murdering and chopping up his lover in 1959. Norman Bates from *Psycho* (1960) was based on Ed Gein, also known as the Butcher of Plainfield. After watching films like *Silence of the Lambs* and *Psycho* when the audience leaves the theater, or their couches, they may be able to shake the fact that what they watched was *just* a movie. Yet, knowing that those characters were based upon people who existed, and frequently reading in the news about similarly troubling individuals, the audience is left with a sense of discomfort that cannot be shaken in the same way that we can when watching a film entirely based on fiction.

Something similar can be said for Z who is not without his own range of cinematic influence, serving as the basis of the character Zodiac in *The Zodiac Killer* (1971), *Zodiac Killer* (2005), and *Zodiac* (2007). While these films are more likely part of the mystery, crime, and thriller genres, the presentation of Z as someone who exists makes them more haunting and unsettling than if he was only a fictional character. This is evident in those cases in which Z only serves as inspiration for a character. In *Dirty Harry* (1971), Z was the inspiration for the character Scorpio. In *The Exorcist III* (1990), he provides the background for the character Gemini. In these films these characters are certainly threatening, menacing, and impure, but they become even more unsettling when we understand them as being based on a person who exists (or, more likely, *did* exist).

Directors are aware of the effect that basing their films on real events has on their audiences. For example, exorcist films that are allegedly based on real exorcisms are more effective in generating the feeling of discomfort when the audience is told that the film is based on those real events (no matter how loosely based). For example, *The Exorcist* (1973) was inspired by an exorcism on a 13-year-old boy in 1949. *The Exorcism of Emily Rose* (2005) was inspired by an exorcism of a 16-year-old girl who had been displaying symptoms for over seven years. *The Conjuring* (2013) recounts a year-long paranormal investigation in the 1970s. Outside the exorcist subgenre, serial killers, such as Ed Gein, serve as the basis of horrific characters such as Leatherface from *The Texas Chainsaw Massacre* (1974). While each of these films on their own would be effective in generating the feeling of art-horror, by knowing that there were real events that inspired those stories, the audience is put at greater unease given the possibility of confronting those threats in their own lives outside the sanctuary of the movie theater or the safety of one's own home.

Contrast the ways in which films that are based on real events can evoke the feeling of horror to those that are entirely fictional. In the case of *Alien* (1979), very few of us who are currently living are likely to be put into a deep sleep for interplanetary exploration. We can feel safe knowing that the horrors to be found on Earth are not the kind that will spawn from our chests. While some of us may have encountered Freddy in our sleep, even if he did succeed in killing us, we were able to awaken safely in our beds—despite the possibility of waking in a pool of our own sweat or urine. And, yes, there are creepy things in the deep waters, but they would rather be left alone than pursue us like the creature from the black lagoon. Perhaps one of the most outlandish examples is the alien clowns in *Killer Klowns from Outerspace* (1998) who have arrived on earth in a spaceship that looks like a large circus tent. Their attempts to ensnare humans in cotton candy-like cocoons makes the threat merely laughable. While some people may think of clowns as being creepy, which is more representative in *It* (1990), clowns are typically not known for harmful antics (setting Gacy aside). The point here is that in thinking about the films that best evoke the horror effect will be those films that are more closely grounded in our everyday experiences.

Summary

The aim of this section has been to illustrate how we are drawn to horror as a means of having the feeling of being art-horrified. More importantly, this section makes the case that those films that have been based upon real events are more likely to evoke the unsettling feelings that we strive to obtain when viewing horror films than those films that are based on purely fictional characters. While Carroll is likely to suggest that horror films require the monster to be fictional, the current focus is not on what makes a film part of the horror genre. Instead, my aim is only to make the case that those films that are based on real events are more unsettling, and thus more effective in generating the feeling of being art-horrified, than those that are purely fictional. If it turns out that a film's capacity to produce the feeling of being art-horrified is both necessary and sufficient for a film being part of the horror genre, then the horror genre is more complex than we had initially imagined. But, to reiterate, what makes a film part of the horror genre is not my present concern.

In the case of films dealing with Z, those films that have incorporated Z's letters and actions are more effective in making the audience unsettled than those films that merely allude to or were inspired by Z. This is certainly the case for Fincher's *Zodiac*. While watching Jake Gyllenhaal's portrayal of Graysmith, we become sympathetic to the anxiety and obsession that comes with attempting to halt the seemingly unending murders. And while we at least know that Z is human, his monstrous portrayal of us as slaves for his own afterlife allows Fincher's film to present us with a horrific understanding of reality. Unfortunately, little attention, if any, has been given to the ways in which Z has influenced music. Before addressing how Z can evoke similar reactions in the audience in music as he does in film, I will discuss how the feeling of being art-horrified can occur in music.

ART-HORROR AND MUSIC

Similar to there being films and books that are aimed at generating the feelings of horror and terror, there are also genres of music that have this aim. Even the names of some subgenres of metal, punk, and electronica are intended to make people feel uncomfortable. Among these include, brutal death metal, death rock, batcave, satanic black metal, grindcore, powerviolence, horror punk, and witch house. Notable bands such as Slayer and Cannibal Corpse have utilized horrific imagery for the sake of evoking a horror-like reaction in their audiences (or at least deter the uninitiated). For example, Tom Araya, vocalist and bassist for the thrash band Slayer, notes that the use of satanic imagery was employed to scare people (Feniak 2006). George "Corpsegrinder" Fisher, vocalist for the death metal band Cannibal Corpse, has stated that Cannibal Corpse's music is like a horror film in audio form (Divita 2017).

It is little surprise, though, that music would have an emotional effect on us. The discussion regarding music's impact is not a new one. As early as around 500 BCE, Pythagoras (c. 582–500 BCE) was looking at how the mathematical relations underlying musical scales were also found in nature (Ferguson 2008, 65). These relations were believed to also be exhibited by the human soul, indicating that there was a commonality between both humans and music that could be described using the same mathematical relations. This relationship between music and the human soul led the Pythagoreans to believe that the kind of music a person listened to would impact that person's moods (Anderson 1983). For example, a myth recounted by Boethius (477–524 CE) has Pythagoras treating an enraged male by having him listen to a particular scale that Pythagoras believes was more pleasing to the young man's soul than what he was initially listening to (Godwin 1987, 30). By changing the young man's *tune*, Pythagoras was able to change the young man's dispositions.

Given the relationship between music and the soul, some early Greek thinkers adopted the technique of considering music's educational and therapeutic roles. Notably, Plato (c. 429–347 BCE) saw the soul as being constructed in three phases (*Timaeus* 35A–37C). In the first, the *demiurge* (Craftsman) mixes Same, Other, and Being to create the stuff of which souls are made. He then uses the soul-stuff to make a musical strip, using the cosmic scale to tune the soul. Last, he divides the stuff to create the paths upon which Same and Other will move.

One of the results of Plato's origin story is to see that both the human soul and the world soul are tuned in the same way, using the Pythagorean musical ratios. This understanding of the soul led Plato to prescribe specific scales to treat and educate different kinds of people. Specifically, he maintains that music's purpose is to educate a person's soul (*Laws* 2.659e). In educating a person through music, Plato believed that you also adjust the person's emotional states.

In addition to the classical Greek thinkers, intellectual figures during the Romantic Era, such as Friedrich Nietzsche (1844–1900), Georg Wilhelm Hegel (1770–1831), Johann von Goethe (1749–1832), Arthur Schopenhauer (1788–1860), Søren Kierkegaard (1813–1855), and Immanuel Kant (1724–1804) discussed extensively the relationship between music and the emotions. In particular, their discussions centered on whether the relationship should be best understood in terms of *absolute music* or *program music*. On the absolute music view, instrumental music is not intended to represent or illustrate anything, leading some critics such as Kant to dismiss instrumental music as being only for enjoyment since it contained no lyrical content (Kant 2000, 206). Spiritualists, such as Wilhelm Heinrich Wackenroder (1773–1798), have instead argued that since instrumental music does not have lyrical content it allows the listener to transcend to higher planes of existence that are not constrained by the formal structure of language.

Instrumental songs from within the metal genre do have the capacity to evoke emotional states and teach us something about ourselves in ways that are at odds with Kant's assessments. Their atonal nature, change in time signatures, and implementation of minor, or blue, chords evoke feelings of angst and unease. For example, Cannibal Corpse's instrumental "From Skin to Liquid" from their 1999 album *Gallery of Suicide* is haunting in its unpleasant time changes and eerie guitar leads. While the song would make for a good soundtrack to a horror film, the feeling of horror is further realized when we learn that it is a band named "Cannibal Corpse" playing a song titled "From Skin to Liquid" from the album *Gallery of Suicide*. So, while we could certainly adopt an absolute music approach to analyze the way in which the song evokes the feeling of being trapped in a horror film, I believe that a programmatic approach is more appropriate for understanding the capacity for music from the metal genres to evoke varying emotional states. In particular, it is due to the lyrical and thematic content of the metal albums and songs that they have the capacity to generate the feeling of being art-horrified. For this reason, I will be tending to the lyrical content of a wide range of songs and bands to better understand the influence Z and his letters have had on the metal genre.

Summary

In this section, I have shown how the feeling of being art-horrified that occurs from viewing horror films can also be experienced from listening to some forms of music. While the music itself may certainly produce feelings of discomfort and unease, the feeling of being art-horrified is more likely to be the result of the lyrics and imagery used. For this reason, a programmatic approach, instead of a pure music approach, will be used to understand the effect of listening to bands that have used Z as a source of influence.

ZODIAC KILLER IN MUSIC

Z has been used by multiple bands as a source of inspiration for lyrical content. Some bands have even had their songs associated with Z without their intention. For example, the rock band Grateful Dead's song "Dire Wolf" from their 1970 album *Workingman's Dead* was written in 1969 in the San Francisco Bay Area when Z was committing his murders. While not initially intended to be an account of Z, Jerry Garcia aligned the lyrics with the perspective of one of Z's victims. He says,

> I wrote that song when the Zodiac Killer was out murdering in San Francisco. Every night I was coming home from the studio, and I'd stop at an intersection and look around, and if a car pulled up, it was like, "This is it. I'm gonna die now." It became a game. Every night I was conscious of that thing, and the refrain got to be so real to me: "Please don't murder me." It was a coincidence in a way, but it was also the truth at the moment. (Ashes 2012)

The Grateful Dead are a generally more accessible group to the mainstream with their use of dancing "Jerry Bears" and general message of peace and love. But where there is something in the mainstream, there is likely a more sinister, unfiltered version in the underground. And Z's influence on the underground music scene is no exception.

Underground music is often associated with images of the macabre, violent, and grotesque. The tale of Z's killing and, more importantly, his cryptic writings have been the subject matter of many songs ranging from death metal, horror punk, death rock, doom metal, electronic dance music, and hip hop. In using Z as a source of inspiration, many of these bands evoke emotional states consistent with those produced by films in the horror genre. Similar to those films that use Z in their plot lines, however, music that clearly use Z's writings as lyrical content, and not just inspiration, more effectively evoke the experience of being art-horrified.

I have separated these areas of inspiration in terms of the *thematic influences*, *lyrical influences*, and *direct influences* to make the case that those bands that have used Z's writing as a direct influence are more effective at evoking the sense of art-horror than those bands that have merely used Z's letters and actions as a source of either thematic or lyrical influence. As a point of clarification, by "thematic" and "lyrical" influence I mean that while those bands have appropriated Z's letters and actions as a source of inspiration, we would not be able to identify Z's influence without them explicitly telling you that those bands have used Z as a source of inspiration or them having used clear indicators that the album or song is making a reference to Z.

Thematic Influences

In the case of the Japanese horror punk band Balzac, they have performed and released albums under the name Zodiac. They released the EP *Zodiac Killer* (2004), established the Zodiac Fan Club, produced a box set *Zodiac Is Alive* (2009), and released the album *Paranoid Dream of the Zodiac Killer* (2007). So, they have certainly found musical inspiration from Z. The music on its own is not particularly horrific, being reminiscent of the famed horror punk band Misfits, and most of their music is best described as traditional punk. Their music may be uncomfortable to listen to for those who are not familiar with punk beat style drums or heavily distorted guitars, but those who are already comfortable listening to punk music will unlikely have any experience of being art-horrified when looking at the album titles.

In looking at the criteria for what is involved in being art-horrified, there may be some sense of abnormal or physical agitation—but this is more likely due to the punk style of music and not the thematic usage of Z's works. To those who are not familiar with Z, they may view the album titles as being nothing more than metaphors. In which case, then, there is no real sense of agitation resulting from the thought of Z being possible, Z would not be perceived as a threat, or the belief that Z is impure. So, in being exposed to the materials presented by Balzac, there is no real sense of being art-horrified.

A similar analysis would hold for the San Francisco punk band the Zodiac Killers, who employed Z's actions and letters for the purposes of thematic influence, playing shows with cross-hair adorned sun glasses and having albums titled *The Most Thrilling Experience* (1999), *Have a Blast* (2001), and *Society's Offenders* (2003). But the song titles on these albums do not provide any indication of Z's influence—it is only when you know that the band playing these songs is the Zodiac Killers that the audience may attempt to make a connection between Z and a song entitled "Microwave Slave," "My Boyfriend Is a Masochist," "Gonna Kill," or "Sick Mind." But, like most punk, the Zodiac Killers are effective in producing a feeling of discomfort or shock, but there is certainly no feeling of art-horror in the same way that other bands' usage of Z's actions and letters may create. Put simply, their use of Z results in something shocking but not horrific.

As I indicate above, both Balzac, while playing under the name Zodiac, and the Zodiac Killers have either album or song titles that indicate the influence Z has had on their artistic expression. Additional bands have used Z as a source of influence for their song titles. For example, the German electronic body music ("EBM" to the initiated) band Synthetic Adrenaline Music (SAM) on the self-titled album, *SAM*, from 2006 has the instrumental titled "Zodiac Killer." When listening to the song, though, it is high energy trance music, which may produce a sense of agitation in those who are not familiar with EBM. Yet, the music is the source of agitation and, given that there are no lyrics, the listener would not have any sense of agitation resulting from anything dealing with Z when listening to the music itself. It is not until the listener becomes aware of the song title that there is any connection with Z. While this may impact how the person experiences the song, it does not produce any sense of art-horror. Similar to the discussion about Cannibal Corpse's song "From Skin to Liquid," SAM's music may be uncomfortable, but it is not until the listener becomes aware of the song title that the listener would begin contemplating the possibility of Z being a threat or impure, further motivating the need to look at music from a programmatic perspective instead of adopting a purist approach. For this reason, I will look to some examples of bands that have used Z as a source of inspiration for their lyrical content.

Lyrical Influences

The Northern California based heavy metal band, Machine Head has a song titled "Blood of the Zodiac" on their *The More Things Change* (1997) album. The ominous title and listening to the heavy metal music certainly creates an uncomfortable listening experience. The lyrics are also dark, further creating an uncomfortable sense of agitation in the listener. So, this song seems to be a good starting point of a band that is able to use Z's influence to generate the first necessary condition of being art-horrified. When looking at the lyrics, though, it is unclear as to whether or not Z is the source of the agitation or if it is simply the music and lyrical content that is creating the agitation. The lyrics entertain the possibility of a blind man asking an angel for help. The angel, however, has her own struggles and does not wish to be worshipped. Rather than looking to religion, the man had used addiction to help him cope with life. In his own desperation, he attempts suicide. In his self-pity he feels that he is not heard, but also rejects the world that he believes misunderstands him. Through his rejection of society he loses touch with reality. The lyrics state,[2]

> A blind man asked an angel could you please help, but was told take me from this altar. I won't falter, but I might fall. This bitter man would understand

through all his life, a needle had been his savior, been his god so he tried to make a change tried to rearrange gun at his side, suicide. I can't help feel I been mistreated. Won't you listen to me? Despise all that I say, all that I feel, all that I want to be burned. Blistered and raw, tearing apart all that is sane to me. A wise man, half pariah, half messiah, came to seed. Rain down blood like fire born desire. Racist breed his dominance of ignorance was rhetoric that made no sense. Some believed in all the lies, but in my mind I know what's wrong. Way too fucking strong. Taste the revenge on my tongue. And now is my time to rise and now is our time to rise our time to rise. Ignorant, indignant promises made in vain rise. I can't feel like you rise, I can't see like you rise, never be like you rise, time for all us to rise.

In reading the lyrics, it is not obvious that there is any connection to Z. Initially, upon reading the lyrics, the listener may think that the song is about overcoming drug addiction or the ending phrases serving as indicators of awaiting resurrection, which may have either addiction or religious undertones. In either case, it is not clear that this is a song about Z. It is certainly possible that the song is to be sung from the perspective of Z and perhaps what had led Z to become a serial killer—but this is artistic speculation.

If a listener ends up having the experience of being art-horrified because of listening to the lyrics, then it is possible that, if we believe Z to be any of the men mentioned in the lyrics, Z is the source of agitation. But, it is not clear in which ways we should think of Z as being possible, a threat, or impure on the basis of the lyrics. It is possible that Z is the blind, bitter, or wise man (if not any combination of the three). In which case, then, there does not appear to be any clear desire of wanting to avoid contact with Z on the basis of listening to Machine Head's song. For these reasons, while the song is certainly haunting, it is not clear that the discomfort the audience experiences is the result of anything dealing with Z.

The Los Angeles-based death rock band, Christian Death, song "Zodiac (He Is Still Out There)" on the album *Born Again Anti Christian* (2000) is more poetic in its portrayal of the mental states Z might have had. The song certainly has in common with Machine Head's the uncomfortable sound and title, but the Christian Death lyrics are clearer in identifying Z's perspective from which the lyrics are based. Rather than providing the entire lyrics here, I will offer a summary of the lyrical themes that occur in the song.

The song starts off with, who is presumably Z, identifying his pariah status and the experience he has when feeling a victim claw at his skin. The experience is seductive while he places his hands over his victim's face. Z recognizes that while he tortures his victim that his anger is only enhanced by the fear he sees. The song's refrain explores the ways in which he becomes lost in the seductive act of killing.

If we accept that the "I" in the song's lyrics references Z, then the song becomes even more disturbing. We see from the perspective of the killer how he views us. It is quite clear that he is a threat to our well-being since he finds it seductive and is not hesitant in his willingness to bring us harm. Since he finds such comfort in performing this kind of act, it is even more indicative of why we should want to avoid someone like Z. So, while both Machine Head and Christian Death use Z as the basis of their lyrics for songs including "Zodiac" in their respective titles, Christian Death's ability to be clearer in the role of Z in the lyrics makes it clearer that Z is a source of the agitation being experienced by the listener. This assessment, however, requires the assumption that the "I" is Z, which indicates that there is still room for ambiguity regarding the protagonist, and, being familiar with Christian Death's other works, there is certainly the possibility that the song is not about Z at all.

Allowing for the possibility that both Machine Head and Christian Death are appealing to Z in their lyrics, both bands generate the sense of unease in an indirect way similar to how films such as *Exorcist III* and *Dirty Harry* use Z as a source for their own unease. This is also like Slayer's song "Gemini" from their album *Undisputed Attitude* (1996), in which they use Z as inspiration for their lyrics detailing Z's thoughts and experiences of being mentally ill, in which he believes that in killing his victims he is preparing himself for a kingdom in the afterlife.

Slayer has more than once used serial killers for inspiration of their song lyrics with the intention of scaring their audiences. For example, "Dead Skin Mask" off their 1990 album *Seasons in the Abyss*, which is based on Ed Gein, and "213" from their 1994 album *Divine Intervention*, which is based on Jeffrey Dahmer, both of whom are individuals we would want to avoid. Slayer's use of Z in "Gemini" allows us to be exposed to the thought process of someone who is clearly a threat to us, exists, and is impure—thus evoking the sense of being art-horrified. Whereas the song title is not clearly about Z, we know that Gemini is the character in *Exorcist III* who is based upon Z, but this information is needed to make the connection between Slayer's song and Z.

Direct Influence

So far I have considered the ways in which bands have either used Z as the basis of their overarching themes or lyrics. While both approaches have the capacity to make the audience uneasy, bands that have used Z as the basis for their themes are ineffective in producing the sense of being art-horrified (and if they do, it is not directly due to Z's influence). Instead, they appear to be more shocking than horrific. Bands that have used Z as the basis of their lyrical content appear to be more effective in generating the sense of art-horror in a similar fashion to films that have used Z as a source of inspiration. While these songs can be menacing and uncomfortable, they become even more so when we realize that they are based on Z. Given that the source of the art-horror in these contexts comes directly from the lyrics being inspired by Z, and not just the thematic elements, there is reason to believe that if Z is the basis of the lyrics themselves, then lyrics that are not just inspired by, but are directly based on Z's letters and actions, might be more effective in producing the sense of being art-horrified in the listener.

On their album *Poetry for the Poisoned*, Tampa-based power metal band Kamelot has two songs that make reference to Z. The first, "Dear Editor" directly uses Z's April 24, 1974, letter as its lyrical content, in which Z tells the audience of his interests in being ahead of the cops and that he hopes that there will be a good movie made about him (it is the same letter I have used in the beginning of this chapter). The song makes use of a somber piano riff against the backdrop of rain, enhancing a loathsome experience. The letter is then read by a voice that has been pitch shifted, providing an unsettling effect for the listener. It certainly has a chilling effect. The result is that we come to feel further agitated by knowing that Z had actually written the letter, indicating his desire to harm us, that he feels like a god, and that he is someone we ought to avoid. Thus, meeting the conditions for being art-horrified. More importantly, as a result of the band using Z's words as the source and not just inspiration for the lyrics, there is little ambiguity that Z is the source of the agitation and desire to avoid someone like him.

Unfortunately, the second song that references Zodiac, "Zodiac," that immediately follows "Dear Editor" adopts an artistic interpretation of Z that ends up reducing the horror effect resulting from "Dear Editor" with the lyrics only portraying the kind of desire Z felt before attacking his victims. It is unclear who the "I" and the "she" are referring to. Similar to Machine Head's "Blood of the Zodiac," it would not be clear that the song has anything to do with Z if it were not for the song title. While "Zodiac" is not as effective in generating the sense of being art-horrified as the preceding song on Poetry for the Poisoned, "Dear Editor" does show us how the use of Z's actual words can be used to generate the sense of being art-horrified in a way that is more effective than those songs that are merely inspired by Z.

The Japanese stoner doom metal band Church of Misery provides additional insight to how the use of the Z's actual words can generate the feeling of being art-horrified. Similar to Slayer, yet less cryptically, Church of Misery has regularly used serial killers as the basis of their lyrical content, including figures such as the Bender Family, John Haigh, Harold Shipman, and Tommy Sells. Knowing the band's penchant for using serial killers as the basis for their lyrics, the somewhat upbeat tone of their song "Sick of Living," which first appeared on the compilation album *Stone Deaf Forever* (1999), makes it even more unsettling once attention is given to the lyrics. In particular, the lyrics are suggestive in attempting to convey the pleasure Z experiences when killing someone.

While some of the lyrics are additions of the band, there are direct lines from the well-known 408 cipher sent to the *San Francisco Chronical*, *San Francisco Examiner*, and *Vallejo Times-Herald* on July 31, 1969. For example, "I like killing people because it is so much fun" is the famous line that Z had adopted from Richard Connell's 1924 short story "The Most Dangerous Game." The following lines of the letter "To kill something give me the most thrilling feel" indicates Z's desire to kill, which is illustrated by earlier examples of lyrics that use Z's letters to suggest that he finds killing to be seductive.

It is not clear, though, if this is a sexual rush, although in the cipher he does indicate that he compares killing to an orgasm (the cipher has a more explicit expression for this comparison). The line expressing Z's depression, but unwillingness to die, comes from a phrase carved into a desk at the Riverside City College library, but there is disagreement as to whether those lines are from Z (Graysmith 1986, 82). The last lines alluding to Z's desire to collect slaves for his afterlife are the most horrific. While the earlier lines are certainly disturbing, these last lines allow us insight to how Z views his prey. No longer are they individual persons, but Z has reified us into objects for his own collection. By including these lines from Z's cipher, we get a more complete picture of Z as a deviant individual who exists and is certainly a threat to our well-being.

At this point, it would seem that this is the most effective use of Z's words to evoke the feeling of art-horror. In adding their own lyrics, however, Church of Misery tampers some of the horror effects. In particular, the lines asking the listener to consider what it must feel like to kill prevent the listener from having the more potent experience than if they had only included Z's lines.

Fortunately, there is a band that has only used Z's words as their lyrics. The Chicago-based death metal band Macabre, like previously mentioned bands, have used serial killers as the basis of their thematic and lyrical material. (They actually call their style of music *murder metal*.)

In the song "Zodiac" from the album *Sinister Slaughter* (1993), Macabre uses Z's words without any additional contributions or modifications. They may as well have reprinted the July 31, 1969, cipher in the CD inlay. Similar to previous bands, Macabre's music is menacing and is an uncomfortable listening experience (even for those who are accustomed to this genre). Furthermore, the thematic elements play into the sense of agitation, but the lyrics being solely from Z's own letters provides the audience with an aural experience that is horrifying in a way that the other bands I mention are unable to accomplish. The selection of words indicate just how menacing Z is, how deviant his desires are, his intentions to collect us for the afterlife, and his ability to not be caught by the "meanies in blue" makes Z a more unsettling figure than previous bands have accomplished. Therefore, Macabre has accomplished evoking the experience of being art-horrified in the listener in a more proficient way than the other bands.

Summary

In this section I have looked at the ways that Z has influenced many bands in the underground. The bands I specifically looked at include Balzac, Zodiac Killers, SAM, Machine Head, Christian Death, Slayer, Kamelot, Church of Misery, and Macabre. These bands are not just from the United States and span a range of time from the 1980s through current time, indicating that Z's influence has been both global and spans many generations. In looking at these bands, I have argued that Z's influence on music is similar to his influence on film. In particular, the incorporation of Z's letters and actions as a source of thematic, lyrical, or direct influence has the capacity to evoke the experience of being art-horrified in music in a similar way to how the incorporation of similar materials in film has the capacity to evoke the feeling of being art-horrified in the viewing audience.

By looking at individual instances of how the aforementioned bands have used Z as a source of inspiration, I have made the case that those bands that use Z as a direct influence are more effective in producing the feeling of being art-horrified than those bands that merely use him as a source of either thematic or lyrical influence. This result is due to those bands that use Z as a source of thematic influence end up being more shocking than horrifying. Those bands that use Z as a source of lyrical influence, while certainly providing some sense of being art-horrified, appear to leave the lyrics as being ambiguous, which may be unsettling but not clearly horrific as a result of Z's influence. Those bands that have used Z's actual words as the lyrical content provide us with a complete picture as to how Z is a genuine threat and impure in his desire to collect us to be slaves for the afterlife, indicating that Z is something that we desire to avoid, which, in accordance with Carroll's conditions for being art-horrified, is the very definition of what it means to be horrified.

CONCLUSION

In the summer of 1969, Z introduced himself to the world. Since then he has been the focus of fascination and horror, serving as the source of influence in film and music. While significant discussion has been focused on his role in inspiring many films, little attention has been given to Z's influence on music—especially the underground music scene. My aim in this chapter has been to illustrate the significant impact Z has had on music. In doing so, I have adopted a programmatic approach to the music that has taken Z's letters and actions as a source of inspiration (instead of adopting a pure music approach). The result has been that Z has been able to provide us with a horrific image of us being a source of his collection. The bands that have been most effective in providing us with this image are those that most accurately employ his letters. Like Fincher's film *Zodiac*, by better understanding how we are seen by Z and more accurately understanding how the events unfolded around Z's actions, we gain better insight to the mind of a killer. By exposing ourselves to how we are seen by such a killer we have a better understanding of ourselves. While this may certainly be frightening and we may wish to only be exposed to horror for the sake of entertainment, sometimes a better understanding of reality is needed so that we can make more informed choices as to how we live. Unfortunately, the better we understand reality the more we may come to realize that it is not pretty.

NOTES

1. A caveat: I am not suggesting that anyone who has a psychological or physiological trait that varies from the statistical norm should automatically be identified as being impure; it is a challenge enough to clearly define what is meant by "pure." There does, however, appear to be a correlation between those who possess physiological and psychological traits and the likelihood of those individuals engaging in monstrous activities. So regardless of what the underlying cause may be as to why serial killers engage in the behaviors that they do, we can think of them as being putatively impure due to their willingness and ability to engage in actions such as necrophilia, vorarephilia, rape, and murder.

2. Due to copyright and licensing issues, I am unable to replicate the exact lyrics here. For these reasons, I will only be offering a summary of the lyrics. For the curious, please use lyric sites such as AZLyrics.com, genius.com, or lyrics.com. For the brave, please listen to the songs on your favorite streaming platform.

REFERENCES

Anderson, Gene H. 1983. "Pythagoras and the Origin of Music Theory." *Indiana Theory Review*, 6 (3), 35–61.
Ashes, Light. 2012. "Dire Wolf 1969." *Deadessays.Blogspot.Com*. October 02, 2012. Accessed March 23, 2019. http://deadessays.blogspot.com/2012/10/dire-wolf-1969.html.
Balzac (as Zodiac), *Zodiac Killer*, Evilegend, 2004, compact disc.
Balzac (as Zodiac), *Paranoid Dream of the Zodiac*, Gan-Shin, 2007, compact disc.
Balzac (as Zodiac), *Zodiac is Alive*, Evilegend, 2009, compact disc.
Baron-Cohen, Simon. 2011. *The Science of Evil: On Empathy and the Origins of Cruelty*. New York, NY: Basic Books.
Blair, R. James R. 2003. "Neurobiological Basis of Psychopathy." *British Journal of Psychiatry* 182 (1): 5–7.
Blair, R. James. 2006. "The Emergence of Psychopathy: Implications for the Neuropsychological Approach to Developmental Disorders." *Cognition*, 101: 414–442.
"Box Office History for Horror." 2019. *The Numbers—Where Data and Movies Meet*. Accessed 24, 2019, https://www.the-numbers.com/market/genre/Horror.
Cannibal Corpse, "From Skin to Liquid," Track 7 on *Gallery of Suicide*, Metal Blade Records, 1998, compact disc.
Carroll, Nöel. 1990. *The Philosophy of Horror: Or, Paradoxes of the Heart*. New York, NY: Routledge.
Christian Death, "Zodiac (He is Still Out There)," Track 2 on *Born Again Anti Christian*, Candlelight Records, 2000, compact disc.
Church of Misery, "Sick of Living," Track 11 on *Stone Deaf Forever*, Red Sun, 1999, compact disc.
Connell, Richard. 1925. "The Most Dangerous Game." In *O. Henry Memorial Award Prize Stories of 1924*. Garden City, NY: Double Day.
Divita, Joe. 2017. "Corpsegrinder: Cannibal Corpse's Music Is Horror in Audio Form." *Loudwire.com*. November 07. Accessed March 21, 2019. http://loudwire.com/corpsegrinder-fisher-cannibal-corpse-interview/.
"Facts." n.d. *American Haunts, Representing the Best Halloween Attractions in America*. Accessed March 24, 2019. https://www.americahaunts.com/ah/facts/.
Fallon, James. 2013. *The Psychopath Inside: A Neuroscientist's Personal Journey into the Dark Side of the Brain*. New York, NY: Penguin.
Feniak, Jenny. 2006. "Tom Araya: Slayer's Lyrics Are 'Just Words And They'll Never Interfere With What I Believe'." *Blabbermouth.net*. July 09. Accessed March 21, 2019. http://www.blabbermouth.net/news/tom-araya-slayer-s-lyrics-are-just-words-and-they-ll-never-interfere-with-what-i-believe/.
Ferguson, Kitty. 2008. *The Music of Pythagoras: How an Ancient Brotherhood Cracked the Code of the Universe and Lit the Path from Antiquity to Outer Space*. New York, NY: Walker.

Godwin, Joscelyn. 1987. *Harmonies of Heaven and Earth*. Rochester, VT: Inner Traditions.

Graysmith, Robert. 1986. *Zodiac*. New York, NY: St. Martin's Press.

Grateful Dead, "Dire Wolf," Track 3 on *Workingman's Dead*, Warner Bros, 1970, compact disc.

Kamelot. 2010a, "Dear Editor." Track 3 on *Poetry for the Poisoned*. Ear Music.

Kamelot. 2010b. "The Zodiac." Track 4 on *Poetry for the Poisoned*. Ear Music.

Kant, Immanuel. 2000, 1790. *Critique of the Power of Judgement*. Edited by Paul Guyer. Translated by Eric Matthews. The Cambridge Edition of the Works of Immanuel Kant. Cambridge: Cambridge University Press.

Macabre, "Zodiac / Identity Unknown," Track 5 on *Sinister Slaughter*, Nuclear Blast, 1993, compact disc.

Machine Head, "Blood of the Zodiac," Track 10 on *The More Things Change*, Roadrunner Records, 1997, compact disc.

Morrison, Helen; Goldberg, Harold. 2004. *My Life among the Serial Killers, Inside the Minds of the World's Most Notorious Murderers*. New York, NY: Harper Collins.

Plato. 1989a. *Laws*. Translated by A.E. Taylor. In *Plato: The Collected Dialogues*, edited by Edith Hamilton and Huntington Cairns.Princeton, NJ: Princeton University Press.

Plato. 1989b. *Timaeus*. Translated by Benjamin Jowett. In *Plato: The Collected Dialogues*, edited by Edith Hamilton and Huntington Cairns. Princeton, NJ: Princeton University Press.

Slayer, "Dead Skin Mask," Track 5 on *Seasons in the Abyss*, Def American Recordings, 1990, compact disc.

Slayer. "213." Track 9 on *Divine Intervention*. American Recordings. 1994, compact disc.

Slayer. "Gemini." Track 14 on *Undisputed Attitude*. American Recordings. 1996, compact disc.

Synthetic Adrenaline Music, "Zodiac Killer," Bonus Track on *SAM*, Pro Noize, 2006. compact disc.

The Zodiac Killers, *The Most Thrilling Experience*, Rip Off Records, 1999, compact disc.

The Zodiac Killers, *Have a Blast*, Rip Off Records, 2001, compact disc.

The Zodiac Killers, *Society's Offenders*, Rip Off Records, 2003, compact disc.

Winters, Andrew M. 2010. "Man is the Most Dangerous Animal of All: A Philosophical Gaze into the Writings of the Zodiac Killer." *Serial Killers: Being and Killing*. Hoboken, NJ: Wiley Blackwell: 15–28.

Zodiac. Directed by David Fincher. Culver City, CA: Phoenix Pictures, 2007.

Zodiac Killer. Directed by Ulli Lommel. Lommel Entertainment, 2005.

Chapter 10

Algorithmic Anxiety

Data Hegemony and Mediated Murder in David Fincher's Zodiac

Jake Rutkowski

About an hour into *Zodiac* (2007), the terror of an enigmatic serial killer with no discernible motive or pattern holding the news media hostage and claiming victims seems, suddenly, like a lot of fun. The procedural gives way to a digital composite sequence as we see news clippings and excerpts of the killer's letters superimposed over scenes of investigators getting to work on the case. This work includes San Francisco PD's lead inspectors Dave Toschi (Mark Ruffalo) and Bill Armstrong (Anthony Edwards) making frequent stops at the offices of the *San Francisco Chronicle*, such that the lines between law enforcement and investigative journalist become increasingly and deliberately blurred. The craftwork enabled by digital composite technology accentuates this notion of crossed boundaries, as in when the lettering on the *Chronicle* building seamlessly flips into the ink titling on a front-page newspaper excerpt. High-resolution cameras and microscopes scan the killer's letters, turning, lens to lens, to face the audience. Analysis is the central act of the film, becoming a literal matter of life and death.

But again, there's the fun. Sly and the Family Stone's "I Want to Take You Higher" bops over the proceedings. The Zodiac begins playing with his own influence, introducing new media through taunting greeting cards and requesting that city residents wear buttons with his trademark cross-hair logo on them. In other words, the Zodiac Killer expands his brand. He is fascinated with the market value of his murders, professing to police that he's "mildly curious how much money you have on my head." The Zodiac has an acute awareness of what captures an audience. He offers a multimedia, interactive news experience that changes in scope and platform at a dizzying pace. In this way, he seems just as likely to pitch a new digital media outlet as he is to claim another victim. The cacophony of information, the zeal with which it is presented, and the acute awareness of how this mania may be profitable all combine to emulate the irrational, dissonant nature of news media in the new millennium. What's more, it dramatizes a shift in influence over the work of journalism, from finding a narrative to relaying data. *Zodiac* is a film that calmly picks at the state of media in its moment, and presages an age of data hegemony. As such, it anticipates the dramatic fracturing in meaning-making that we are now witnessing eleven years later.

With help from Gramsci, I define "data hegemony" here as the ubiquity of digital systems of information exchange, and the function of these systems as tools for maintenance and oversight of a cultural status quo (Saba 1982). Data provides a superstructure of power balances buttressed by host/client relationships across a number of services and platforms, from banking information to social interaction. The fissures in this structure have begun revealing themselves more frequently of late, and examples of the perils of data hegemony can be found in even the most mainstream points of reference. For one, multiple instances of breaches, mistakes, and overreach in the operations of

Figure 10.1 The three ciphers mailed to the *San Francisco Examiner, San Francisco Chronicle,* and *Vallejo Times-Herald.*

the U.S. security state come to mind (Scott 2013). As do a number of stories around the 2016 U.S. presidential election. Between the Clinton campaign's trust in the faulty decision-making algorithm Ada (Wagner 2016), the false promises of statisticians and media oddsmakers (Robinson 2016), and the ongoing investigation into web-based disinformation practices organized by Trump's team (aided by the Russian government and the social media data-sharing firm Cambridge Analytica) (Rosenberg, Confessore, and Cadwalladr 2018), there are clear material consequences to seemingly neutral and invisible forces like data and algorithms.

Perhaps surprisingly, data hegemony is nothing new in journalism. In *Manufacturing Consent: The Political Economy of Mass Media*, Noam Chomsky and Edward S. Herman warn of the problems with privatized media distribution, problems we still see today. Their "propaganda model" is broken into five factors of media filtration, the most relevant to *Zodiac* being the size, structure, and profit orientation of media firms, reliance on information from "expert" sources either participating in or beholden to government and business, and public denigration of the media from those in power ("flak") to keep outlets in check (Herman and Chomsky 2002, 2). For the most part, innovations in data collection and storage have greatly honed each of these tools. James Bridle, for example, notes the havoc on stock markets brought on by Automated Insights, an automatic writing software used by the AP (Bridle 2018, 123). Even in cases where it seems the model has been bypassed altogether, such as the WikiLeaks project, there are still questions of motive. Just as data has at times been seized by those seeking to operate outside of the propaganda model, the Zodiac too seizes the means of media production, and manipulates and distributes complex dataflows with an acute awareness of how newspapers operate and of what conversations dominate public opinion.

Zodiac is especially relevant to this discussion of digital media, as it made nascent strides in the field of digital film production. And Fincher invites analyses of film's transitioning from analog production, as he often uses digital cameras, CGI sequences, and computerized effects in his films. Michele Schreiber (2016, 3) argues that Fincher's films reflect concerns over corporeality and physical existence in a digital age. In service of this argument, she points to the details of *Zodiac*'s digital production and its effects on the "texture" of its sense of time and authenticity. Schreiber (6) also uses the same digital composite scene with which I open this chapter as her primary example of the ways in which technological concerns dominate the film. David Bordwell and Kristin Thompson (2015, 18) also note the tension between digital and analog that the film embodies, noting that it showed "that high-resolution capture could in many respects rival 35mm film while harboring its own artistic possibilities." Sam Dickson unpacks the film's fears in erasing the very past it seeks to reconstruct, a sort of meta-murder, and the postmodern crisis of epistemology that ripples out from this. He concludes that "it is at once anxious concerning the loss of indexicality with the passing of celluloid, while at the same time obviously animated by the capabilities of code to remediate older cinematic visions. The digital cinema in one of its earliest inceptions offers us a curious hybrid form of historicist imagery, enacting an open, transitional process of remediating its analogue past" (2016). If, according to Benjamin, a machine's involvement in the production of art leads to a shattering of tradition and a stripping of its "aura" (that ineffable air of authenticity and authority lent to art in its representation of reality) then *Zodiac*'s aura is dead where it stands (1988, 221).

Compilation, distribution, and analysis of data is a central concern in *Zodiac*. There is a near-fetishistic obsession with information in the film, as close zooms on documents, clues, and note-taking often dominate the frame. This obsession is accentuated by Robert Graysmith's (Jake Gyllenhaal) own downward spiral, which becomes one of the leading dramatic strains of the third act. While there are primary examples of data analysis that I will unpack in this chapter, from the process of cracking the "Zodiac Code" to the actual criminal investigation, the film also presents metadata in the form of intertextuality and genre code-switching. Pop culture literacy becomes its own form of data collection, influencing both the *mise* of the film and the investigation itself. The film cycles through genres, from newspaper picture to detective thriller to blunt-force horror, demonstrating the complexity of its data filtration. Draped over each of these genres (both in the canon and in *Zodiac*) is the pall of the Gothic and its traditions in buried truths, mind-bending mania, and uncontained terrors. A sense of transience dominates the film's structure, as it is an episodic telling of a story across thirteen years of investigation with no concrete sense of closure in the end. This lack of centering is also underscored by a motif of facelessness, as there are several instances of dialogue spoken by characters off-screen, never to be revealed to the viewer in full (not to mention the obvious fixation on identifying the killer throughout the investigation, and Graysmith's primary motive to "stand there . . . look him in the eye, and . . . know that it's him"). *Zodiac* is defined by its datapoints and the attempts at sifting through mountains of information. It mimics the acts of creation and analysis in an age of digital reproduction, and does so with the sort of anxiety that comes with charting new territories. In this chapter, I'll detail how *Zodiac* provides a distinct summation of its contemporaneous transitional moment in its representation of an increasingly nebulous information superstructure. As such, the film anticipates the dramatic fracturing in meaning-making that we are now witnessing eleven years later.

ENCODING EPISTEMOLOGY

The first time that the viewer is presented with the Zodiac Killer's code, the infamous string of glyphs that comes accompanied with a threat that if it is not published and decoded then the killer will strike again, it is put through a gauntlet of institutionalized ways of seeing. First, in a newspaper conference room, it is passed around and debated over in a frenetic rush of forty-seven cuts while the team decides whether or not to publish the letter per the killer's demands. Graysmith even jumps right into jotting down and decoding the cipher then and there. The letter then moves into a criminal lab, where it is displayed in clinical, high definition detail. The color scheme is all sterile whites, and the camera focuses on the analyst's gloved hands setting up the paper on his workstation. A fluorescent bulb buzzes on, a choice in sound design that calls attention to the film's digital refinements, as this is the sort of background noise made worse by the "signal-to-noise" impurities that arise from HD digital camera filming, and getting the right effect would likely require some postproduction non-diegetic sound work (Holben 2004). The camera also hovers on the analyst's machinery, clearly displaying the words "POLAROID MP-3 LAND CAMERA / Multipurpose Industrial View Camera," a copy camera with no features beyond focusing and reproducing images (*Photrio* 2009). This one technical detail reveals two larger undercurrents: a commitment to historical detail, and the intelligence industry's inability to do anything beyond copying and distributing the Zodiac's screeds. We leave the lab and enter a revolving door of authoritative offices working on the code (police, reporters, military, FBI, CIA), but after all of this professional analysis, it's a history teacher and his wife, amateur puzzle enthusiasts, who crack the code. Already, the gatekeepers of the status quo are powerless to understand this new amorphous way of sharing data.

The nature of the code itself presents a clear metaphor for an algorithm generated by an opensource, digitally maintained information archive. As a CIA official notes, it has "symbols from at least 7 different sources: Greek, Morse Code, maybe semaphore, weather symbols, astrological signs." So, the killer uses data from many sources to create and proliferate a code. A bit further into the Zodiac fervor, after the killer claims another victim and the story begins permeating everyday life in San Francisco (with every radio and TV station covering it and police helicopters circling overhead), we are walked through a process of looking for patterns, a central act in detective work, according to a book Robert found in the library. But veteran beat reporter Paul Avery (Robert Downey Jr.) cautions, "you can't think of this case in normal police terms." Juxtaposed conversations about the case details unfold between two duos, Toschi and Armstrong and Graysmith and Avery, each set of dialogue feeding off of the other. The boundaries between journalist and detective continue to collapse, and Toschi reaches a chilling conclusion: "he's breaking the pattern." It is this random generation of data and results that vexes all parties throughout the film, and which lends itself most to description as a system that is algorithmic but largely illogical. A computer with a virus perhaps, or a program that is being used for a purpose not suited to its original intent. Whatever the results or influences, it is clear the ownership of epistemology rests solely with the Zodiac Killer. As he writes in a later letter taunting Toschi directly, "I am waiting for a good movie about me. Who will play me? I am now in control of all things."

This hegemony over narrative-building is most present in the Zodiac's sense of iconography and mythos. He creates his own vision of life after death, one that hinges on the commodification of human life, as we learn that the killer believes his victims to be his "slaves" that will accompany him in the afterlife. His vision then becomes tied to his personal branding. Moments after this first cipher is translated, a second letter is pored over at the editorial board offices of the *San Francisco Chronicle*. The primary piece of information that's gleaned from this letter, via the paper's EIC, is that the killer "gave himself a name." The camera tilts and zooms onto this second letter to reveal a phrase at the top of the page: "This is the Zodiac speaking." Self-definition and ownership of the details of his story follow the Zodiac Killer throughout the film. The myopia of his pursuers and their inability to see that he is a storyteller first and foremost leads them down a decade-long-plus investigation with no real sense of closure.

DIAGNOSING A HEADACHE

Immediately after Toschi reaches his epiphany that the Zodiac has begun breaking his own pattern, the killer's violent message moves to televised news for proliferation. The killer has contacted local morning news show *A.M. San Francisco* and proposed to speak in a live phone interview, so long as celebrity lawyer Melvin Belli (Brian Cox) is there to mediate. Belli agrees, and the police arrange to trace the call during the TV spot. In what feels like a darkly realized version of a call-in therapy program, he has his cast, his platform, and his audience. The interview becomes its own news event, reporters flock to the scene, and our protagonists remain glued to their televisions. Later, television is established as the medium for narrative reification, when Toschi wonders aloud if a lead that Paul publicizes on the evening news is real. "It's very real," Bill replies sardonically, "You know how I know? Because I saw it on TV." The first words spoken on air by the killer are the phrase that has by now become something like a catchphrase, its repetition helping to build his brand, "This is the Zodiac speaking." He is acutely aware of how the media helps to create his image, casting a wider net and now bringing in name recognition both through his own nom-de-gore, and by utilizing an attorney who has represented celebrities and high-profile defendants like Jack Ruby (and who has starred in an episode of *Star Trek*, as noted in the film). Troubling this brand recognition slightly is the variable note that the Zodiac on the phone may also be known as "Sam," a divergent fissure in the Zodiac mythos that foreshadows the tenuous grasp of the facts inherent to the scene's ultimate outcome: the caller is not the Zodiac, but a patient at a local mental hospital. Again, the media's attempts at data collection and proliferation lead only to more confusion and dead ends. The Zodiac is able to maintain absolute control of narrative as his image becomes self-sustaining and the panic continues without his direct engagement.

It is also in this television scene that we encounter something like pathology, as the caller creates an angle for the Zodiac that begets a sort of psychosomatic need to commit murder. He claims that killing helps to rid him of his "headaches," and emits a primal scream that cuts through the audio track, which he explains is one such headache. The medical tenor of this conversation recalls the clinical discussion of motive and desire in the final minutes of *Psycho* (1960). However, the caller is very particular about the help he needs being "medical, not mental." This addition to the Zodiac characterization, whether it comes from the actual killer or not, gets at the social malaise on which the murderer preys.[1] In *Heroes*, Bifo Berardi (2015, 2) declares, "I don't care about the conventional serial killer, the brand of secretive sadistic psychopaths who are attracted to other people's suffering and enjoy seeing people die. I'm interested in people who are suffering themselves, and who become criminals because this is their way both to express their psychopathic need for publicity and also to find a suicidal exit from their present hell." In other words, Berardi is diagnosing a "headache," the transference of one's own suffering into a cataclysmic communal suffering. In addition to this television scene, I cannot help but compare Berardi's words to the opening minutes of *Mindhunter*,[2] Fincher's latest work, in which an analyst for the FBI delivers a lecture to recruits about an uptick in random acts of violence, citing David Berkowitz as his example. "Where do we go," he asks, "when motive becomes illusive?" Though Berardi is overtly disinterested in serial killers, his subjects still share the burden of an absence of meaning with the Zodiac. In fact, it's plausible that the spectacle of ephemeral, mediated moments of bloodshed has supplanted the methodically built machinations of the serial killer altogether.

The other way in which *Heroes* helps give a language to the notion of data hegemony in *Zodiac* is the examination of the financial market's impact on our understanding of the world. Berardi (78) locates a severe downturn in the mental health of the public brought on by the irrationality and decentering of capitalism in a market controlled by a "deterritorialized financial class," a practice that he refers to as "semiocapitalism." As he notes, "semiocapitalism occupies the sphere of randomness of value, as well as the sphere of randomness of law and of moral judgment" (76). The Zodiac Killer functions in the same way as semiocapitalism. He is a deterritorialized killer. He defies definition despite presenting a very calculated set of signs, inspires others to claim responsibility for his acts, and frustrates timelines and evidence and motive. He even short circuits common sense, as in the scene in which Toschi and Armstrong grill two beat cops who in all likelihood witnessed the killer fleeing the scene of Paul Stine's murder, but neglected to stop him for questioning because he didn't match the racial profile of the suspect. The irrationality that the killer inspires mimics that of the late stage capitalist market and its operatives, per Berardi's reading. This irrationality and deterritorialization are accelerated by the invisible processes guiding data hegemony. There is an air of authority and control lent to the tightly organized algorithmic functions of our digital age, but, as we are learning in real time, these data-driven environments can easily breed isolation, obfuscation, and corruption. The film shows an evolution in the mediation of this disconnect through another television scene, shifting genres from televised news to video games.

When Graysmith visits Paul Avery to introduce his idea for a book on the Zodiac Killer, he finds his old friend living on a houseboat, drug-addled, and antagonistic. Avery sits him down in front of a game of Pong running on a television with no one operating it, an endless pixelated serve with no volley, a repetition of beeping tones providing an unnerving soundtrack. "My own kids would kill me for one of those," Graysmith says admiringly. The image of a disgraced journalist sitting zombified in front of a computerized novelty—with no real understanding of how it works, no agency in utilizing it, and the implication that it cost a lot of money—gets to a core thematic concept of this chapter. *Zodiac* expresses a distinct anxiety over the sustainability of critical thinking in an increasingly digitized future, and the ability of journalists and other vestiges of a tangible media age to continue to make rational sense of a rapidly growing information environment. For the most part, in the face of this algorithmic force, all turns to madness. Avery's response to Graysmith's proposal for the book underscores the irrationality. "I've been thinking," Graysmith begins, "somebody should write a book." Avery, only half-listening, replies, "Somebody should write a fuckin' book, that's for sure. About what?" This investigation has stripped almost everyone who touches it of their sense and their reputation. The book becomes the only constant. It is also the only concrete result of the investigation. And its salability is used as a placeholder for the passage of time, as its appearance in paperback on an airport sales rack in the final scene signals how far into the future the story has jumped. It is also, of course, the genesis for the film itself, as James Vanderbilt's screenplay is an adaptation of Graysmith's eponymous book. As a liminal figure himself, neither detective nor journalist, Graysmith is able to escape relatively unscathed and reap whatever profits can be gained from the Zodiac investigation. Before Graysmith can leave this plane of irrationality, he must face the trial of entering Bob Vaughn's basement, and it is here that several themes and motifs come to a head with a sense of urgency.[3] The subterranean paranoia that unfolds speaks to the film's communication with a larger Gothic tradition, a notion that Dickson introduces and upon which I will expand. This scene also presents the last instance of a running motif throughout the film: the faceless figure.

"HE WISHES TO REMAIN ANONYMOUS, I WISH TO REMAIN INFAMOUS"

Vaughn speaks to Graysmith in his basement primarily under heavy shadow. His interest is piqued when he discovers that his theater screened *The Most Dangerous Game* (1932), a story that figures heavily in the Zodiac investigation, just nine weeks before the first killing. He steps into almost complete darkness, his face nearly invisible, and asks Graysmith if he thinks the Zodiac saw the film in his theater and was "inspired." Again, the aural stimuli turn to madness, as the floor creaks above (there was previously no indication that there was anyone else in the house) and Vaughn's teapot begins to scream upstairs. He then shuts off the light that's directly above him and briefly disappears into pitch blackness. This specific and deliberate act is a direct perversion of Robert's prime directive, to "look [the Zodiac] in the eye and ... know that it's him." He stalks Robert back up the stairs to the front door, and suddenly appears reflected in a mirror behind his guest. Mirrors are another medium for obfuscating truth and bending reality in the film, as is addressed in the analysis of the "Modesto incident" scene below.

Facelessness and shadow provide nice metaphors for the detachment that pervades life in an age of data hegemony. As Bridle writes it, the history of computation is made up of invisible motives and unknowable processes guiding the majority of our everyday lives. He relays the story of the SSEC, IBM's answer to the ENIAC urcomputer, a giant computation device housed in a storefront display window as a shining beacon of the future at which passing shoppers could marvel. Originally intended for calculations related to prospective NASA missions, SSEC was quickly taken over by the military for Hippo, the top-secret program for producing simulations of the first hydrogen bomb. Bridle (32) writes that "the result of the calculations was at least three full simulations of a hydrogen bomb explosion: calculations carried out in full view of the public, in a shopfront in New York City, without anyone in the street being even slightly aware of what was going on." This is the essence of the media's relationship with data. Vast swells of knowledge and information processed at impossible speeds, managed by hegemonic forces geared toward violent dominance, commodified and presented in an alluring package. Today's media consumer is not exactly blind to these machinations. Facebook users, for example, know that the social media platform is not a trustworthy silo for the storage and protection of their data. Polling being as specious as it is in this age of data hegemony, recent reports show that 63 percent of the site's users don't trust it with their information (Neidig 2018). Nevertheless, the average citizen cannot do much to reverse this course without a massive cultural shift, a recalibration of hegemonic priorities. This notion, of the just barely visible influences that shape and direct our information infrastructure, is exemplified in *Zodiac*'s faceless exchanges. Of course, the overall communication flow between killer and investigators throughout the film is rooted in one-sided, decentralized opacity, as we really only "hear" from the killer in writing, through specious phone calls, and a number of false leads. And in the one instance where we do see a killer in broad daylight, he is entirely dressed in black, with a black cloth bag over his head as a mask. But the film doubles down on this obfuscation through a number of dialogue scenes or moments in which one speaker's face is either hidden by high back lighting, or not on-screen at all. The most extreme case of this motif is the scene that dramatizes the "Modesto incident."

In March 1970, a motorist and her infant in Modesto, California, barely escaped with their lives when a man posing as a Good Samaritan kidnapped them on the highway. *Zodiac*'s reenactment of this incident makes for the stuff of the best urban legends: a woman is driving late at night; a car barrels up behind her wildly, honking its horn and flashing its lights; the woman pulls over, the pursuing motorist tells her she has a wheel loose, and he offers to tighten it; he tightens the wheel, they both pull away, then the woman's wheel falls off; the Good Samaritan offers to drive her to a service station, and she quickly realizes she is doomed. This snippet of the Zodiac saga is composed in such a way in the film as to almost celebrate its sensational, camp qualities. A rhythmic, repetitive piano key steadily plunks away in the background, recalling John Carpenter's score for *Halloween* (1978). Once he has her trapped in his car, the kidnapper calmly tells the hapless motorist, "Before I kill you, I'm going to throw your baby out the window." A light briefly illuminates the woman's look of frozen shock right as the piano hits a discordant note, and the screen sharply fades to black. We learn almost immediately that she and her baby survived, badly shaken and bruised by a daring vault from the moving car, but virtually unharmed.

The scene lasts all of five minutes and serves almost exclusively as a moody counterpoint to the proceeding rollick of the Sly Stone-backed digital composite scene, but it carries a bevy of metaphoric value for the unknowable terror that permeates the film. The establishing long shot of the somewhat rural highway is an aerial view of a road stretching through open fields, a smattering of streetlights dotting the route. CGI clouds pass over the frame as the camera lingers. A highway is a tangible space for conveying information, goods, and people, an analog internet, and this highway is doubly shrouded, by darkness and cloud. The road is not exactly deserted, either. Cars whizz past frequently, setting up a victimization that unfolds in public, ephemeral view. When the assailant is first introduced, he is shown strictly through glass-like car windows and mirrors, as the camera stays put in the victim's car. In fact, the mirror gives the first clue that this Good Samaritan may not be what he seems. We watch in a rear-view mirror from the victim's POV as he turns a tire iron to tighten the wheel, so his actions are inverted, hard to decipher. His face is hidden by the blocking of the car, or washed out by headlights. We cannot see the attacker's face even when his victim is sitting directly next to him in his car, thanks to blocking and back lighting. The only evidence we are given that the Zodiac is the perpetrator in this incident is a snippet of a headline in the montage that follows, as the victim assigns blame to him. Here he is reified by the newspapers, hiding in plain sight.

Other faceless exchanges and shots are not as extensive but add up to form an overall mood of dissonance and detachment. The police officer who discovers the victims in the opening scene is barely seen from the waist up. The first Zodiac letter makes its way to the *Chronicle* offices in a montage that splits Robert's arrival with a series of mail-clerks sorting envelopes, their heads cut from the frame. Similarly, the waiter who takes Robert and Melanie's (Chloë Sevigny) orders on their first date does so with his head cropped out. Compared to the Modesto scene, these instances are rather innocuous. In fact, the examples even get playful at times, as in Paul and Robert's foray into the *Chronicle* archives to establish the timeline of the killer's media appearances. Paul is drunk and leading Robert through an interactive experience, shouting out directions for finding boxed evidence to a point that he already knows to be true: the letters have been arriving after details of the murders have already been published in newspapers, meaning that the writer is likely taking credit for crimes he did not commit. "He's in it for the press," Avery explains. There is some physical comedy in how Robert gets turned around among the stacks, and his and Paul's voices echo disembodied across the room as they call out to each other. The space in which this moment of levity occurs is central to another motif tied to the film's relationship with the information age: the archive scene. There are three such scenes across the film, two of which (this Paul/Robert scene, and Vaughn's basement) have been addressed in this chapter already. This space speaks to the film's Gothic themes of buried pasts and pursuits of knowledge that give way to madness, encapsulating Dickson's reference to *Zodiac* as an example of the "ontological Gothic," establishing a sense of what Caroline Joan "Kay" S. Picart and Cecil Greek term "Gothic criminology," and presenting an early analog version of what Bridle (by way of human geographers George Kitchin and Martin Dodge) refers to as "code/space."

THE GOTHIC ARCHIVE

In his analysis of the ambivalence and anxiety over the disappearance of physical signs and signifiers in *Zodiac* as an extension of its transitional status as a digital film, Dickson (par. 7) refers to Garrett Stewart's concept of the "ontological Gothic." Stewart establishes a trend in digital age cinema toward "paranoiac panic about narrative causality," a self-reflexive obsession with the "realness" of a story and the subsequent mania of uncontained fears exhibited by the films' endings (*Vanilla Sky* [2001] and *The Sixth Sense* [1999] are cited as examples) (ibid). As Dickson (ibid) paraphrases, "The 'continuous equivocation of the real' in this digital cinematic trend reiterates the conception of 'nothing' being there, playing out and reinforcing a disengagement with political and economic realities." Dickson locates nostalgia as evidence of Fincher's ambivalence toward this transitional moment, but there are other examples, like the "lens facing lens" moments or the way that cinema culture saturates the film. That said, the film most prominently signals its concern with materiality in Robert's monomaniacal engagement with archive materials. He keeps a scrapbook of sorts, documenting each headline about the Zodiac in a binder that he flips through casually in his living room. He is also a staunch advocate for that most symbolic of spaces that stands in direct opposition to the internet in its physicality: the library. Libraries become a running joke between he and Avery throughout the film, as Graysmith's bookishness is an object of playful scorn. The library also becomes a self-reflexive piece of the investigation, another piece of metadata, as Robert reveals to Toschi in their first meeting that all of the codebreaking books that could be used to crack the Zodiac's first cipher had been stolen from military base libraries in the area. This piques Toschi's interest and kicks off his and Robert's years-long clandestine collaboration on the case. Not long after this, Robert is led to Jack Mulanax (Elias Koteas) and his first of two visits to the Vallejo Police Department's criminal file archives.

Robert's trips to traditional archives (the *Chronicle*'s and the Vallejo PD's) are marked by some of the same signifiers: an initial buzz and illumination as his hosts lead him into the room and flick on the lights, a frenzy of searching and pulling of documents. In the first scene in the Vallejo archive, the camera is waiting in the room for Graysmith and Mulanax to enter. The door opens, and they are framed in the doorway against the light of the hallway and the darkness within, signaling the gravity of Robert's crossing boundaries into new investigatory spaces. Already his relationship with the material conditions of the investigation is troubled, as he is under strict instructions not to use any writing implements in the room and must keep any relevant information in his head. Herrmann-esque strings set the tone for the ensuing mania, as Robert must pore over and memorize the preponderance of raw primary sources to which Mulanax has given him access. The frame fills with scrolling text as the camera pans over the police files on the first murder. The soundtrack too becomes just as dominated by data, as Robert reads snippets aloud in a whisper and the monologue overlaps itself in a swirl of phrases. Audio from the opening scene further muddles the soundscape as it plays in conjunction with Robert's whispers in pieces. The unreality of the "Gothic ontology" surfaces when the sound of screeching tires from the Zodiac's getaway cuts in and jolts Robert out of a sleepy daze. Robert's second visit to the Vallejo PD later in the film presents a fatalistic counterpoint to this scene, and mania gives way to madness.

Some of the same beats persist between the two police department scenes. They share the same score, for instance, and both start with an establishing shot out front of the building. However, the rainy nighttime setting of the second establishing shot stands in direct contrast to the optimistic sunniness of the first. The rain serves as an important reminder of Robert's trip to ontological Hell in Vaughn's basement, as it pours on him in torrents that night as well and gives him the same bedraggled look once he is indoors in both scenes. And this time, there is no revelatory light, or cooperation from Mulanax. The urgency of the research becomes more pronounced. Robert is only given five minutes with the files, and the scene jumps right from the outside of the station to Robert standing across from the Sergeant in heavy shadow, wet and wild-eyed and unshaven, a file box to his right and a document in his hand indicating that he has already gone through the motions of pulling evidence from the archive. Unconvinced by Robert's evidence that first victim Darlene Ferrin knew Allen, Mulanax dismisses him. The film then jump-cuts to Robert's home, which has itself become a sort of archive, with boxes and papers crowding his living space, domesticity giving way to his obsession. The same methodical archive score plays as Robert frantically searches for more evidence on Allen. This moment represents the height of his madness, as his worlds have now bled into each other and his sense of space has been short-circuited.

Bridle's reading of "code/space" applies here. Code/space helps to define the relationship between "the built environment and daily experience to a very specific extent: rather than merely overlaying and augmenting them, computation becomes a crucial component of them, such that the environment and the experience of it actually ceases to function in the absence of code" (37). As we become more dependent on "smart" technologies, as our working and social lives become networked to invisible processes, most of our world becomes a code/space. This concept bears some frightening implications, not just in the lack of agency inherent to trusting in the keepers of code, but in the scope of the implied negation should the code ever give way. Graysmith's archival living space adheres to this code/space dichotomy: if it weren't for the Zodiac's code, and his subsequent invisibility, then Graysmith's domestic life would not be in such disarray. Indeed, his frenetic visit to his files at home is interrupted by a visit from Melanie, who has begun the process of separating from him. Although Graysmith's search eventually comes to an end and is channeled into the book, the fracturing brought on by his creation of a personal code/space is partially irreversible, as he never quite repairs his marriage. That, and the narrative remains uncontained. Though he does get to fulfill his one desire to "look the killer in the eye" in the penultimate scene, an encounter with Allen, no arrest is made. That, and we learn in the epilogue that prints from the Stine murder rule out Allen as a suspect. This lack of containment communicates not just with Bridle's code/space anxieties, but with the Gothic tradition as well.

The existence of buried secrets that refuse to remain buried is a central feature of Gothic literature, as outlined by Jerrold Hogle. Hogle (2014, 4) notes that one of the primary recurring features of the genre is "ghostly or monstrous figures, intermixing life and death as well as other incompatibilities, that loom forth in or invade [antiquated] settings, usually because of secrets from the past buried deep in memories or archives, and may be either supernatural or psychological in origin, at times even hinting at a personal or cultural unconscious." As shown above, *Zodiac* fits the bill for this aspect of the tradition, but another applicable and unique theoretical framework is Picart and Greek's concept of "Gothic criminology." The thrust of their argument is that American media, across a multitude of rhetorical genres (from popular culture to public policy), has increasingly framed stories of criminality and violence in Gothic terms, specifically in their invocations of evil and the "monstrous" (Picart and Greek 2007). Examples range from pedophilic priests to corporate entities to police departments to terrorists and so on. *Zodiac* does not just fit this model in its existence as a piece of popular culture that ascribes Gothic codifying to a serial killer story, it also dramatizes this act as a story about the news media's creation of a criminal monster. As is revealed in the *Chronicle* archive scene, this monster would not exist if not for the local media's sensationalist headline machine, and may not even be a single entity.

The Zodiac is a Gothic monster, an indefinable chimera empowered by strange glyphs with the distinct ability to tear at the fabric of all reason and reality. Avery loses all sense of self-preservation, readily volunteering to follow suspicious leads into dark alleys and eventually falling into destructive habits that push him to an early grave (the epilogue notes that he died of pulmonary emphysema at age 66, his ashes scattered in San Francisco Bay). Toschi loses Armstrong, who decides after years on the case to put in for a transfer, and his reputation, as he finds himself embroiled in a scandal surrounding accusations that he wrote some of the Zodiac letters himself. In a moment of desperation after raiding Allen's home does not yield any actionable evidence, he also undoes the rationality of his detective duties, remarking, "I can't tell if I wanted this to be Allen so bad because I thought it was him, or I just want all this to be over." He delivers this line from a stairwell surrounded by shiny marble walls, a few steps below his gruff but caring supervisor (Dermot Mulroney), his reflection standing faintly behind him in ethereal duplicate. As the country barreled toward its own fracturing brought on by the irrationality of the market accelerated by the semio-trading of digital transactions at the time of this film's release, so too do these characters become undone by an absence of ratiocination in the face of an unknowable and monstrous force. On the topic of *Zodiac*'s communication with genre and its place in a pop culture trend, the final layer of the film's systems of data filtration is its abundance of intertextual moments and the crucial role that media literacy plays in the investigation. And just as the archive space bleeds its way into Robert's everyday life, Toschi finds himself in a moment of hyperreality and witnesses his life converted into popular culture fodder in real time.

"THE ZODIAC KILLER IS OBSESSED WITH MOVIES"

Taking his observation on code/space a step further, Bridle argues that our very sense of culture now fits the concept of a built environment that would not exist in the absence of code. "Reading a book," he observes, "listening to music, researching and learning: these and many other activities are increasingly governed by algorithmic logics and policed by opaque and hidden computational processes" (39). *Zodiac* bears out this argument, as film knowledge permeates the world built by the killer and dominates everything from plot to production design. Pop culture is its own datapoint, a source for bits of evidence that guide the investigation. For one, the *mise* is dominated by a multitude of allusions to period-appropriate films like *All the President's Men* (1976) and *Chinatown* (1974), which Dickson cites as one piece of evidence for the film's nostalgia for its celluloid-era forebears. Film posters also occupy many frames in Robert's home and seem almost to set up an in-joke throughout the story, as titles like *The Wrong Man* (1956), *The Beast from 20,000 Fathoms* (1953), and *Illegal* (1955) appear on his walls at different points. There is, of course, the critical allusion to *The Most Dangerous Game*, which Robert is the first person to track. Other forms of popular media occupy the investigation, especially advertising and branding, as a Zodiac watch ad becomes critical to identifying Allen as a suspect, and the unique origin and purpose of Windwalker boots helps the detectives to focus on military-affiliated leads. Surprisingly, despite Robert's bookishness and artistry, it is Toschi who is most impacted by this milieu of popular culture, his interaction with it taking on a quality of a man entering a realm he will never fully understand.

As Dave Toschi exits the *Chronicle* offices after his first visit, Graysmith is in awe. "You know he wears his gun like Bullitt," he gushes to Avery. But Avery corrects him, "No, McQueen got that from Toschi." Already the detective's world is a feedback loop between simulacra and reality, a cultural code/space built on pop datapoints. Later, in what amounts to Avery's last interaction with Toschi, he calls out to the detective, "Hey Bullitt! It's been a year and a half, you going to catch this fuckin' guy or not?" This line of dialogue reifies and reiterates the collapsing of man and simulation. Just as Graysmith's domesticity gives way to the archive and Avery gives up all agency at an altar of pixelated ping-pong, Toschi's autonomy is replaced by a copy. For one, the piece of evidence used to accuse Toschi of generating his own fake Zodiac letters is the fact that he once wrote to a *Chronicle* writer asking for the return of a character based on the detective. "It was like writing fan-mail to himself, that's all," his wife explains to Graysmith. He clears his name later, but not before he is tried in the court of public opinion and kicked out of his department's homicide division. Prior to this incident, however, is the starkest example of Toschi's data-generated dissonance, when he attends a screening of *Dirty Harry* (1971).

After Toschi voices his dejection over Allen's exoneration, his boss suggests he take his mind off the case a little. In a twist of fate reminiscent of the "Great Clown Pagliacci" joke, he goes to the movies to see what happens to be a ripped-from-the-headlines pastiche of the Zodiac story. Scorpio, *Dirty Harry*'s ransom-demanding murderer, writes mass-proliferated threatening letters, like the Zodiac, and attacks a school bus full of children, like the Zodiac suggests he may do. The scene-within-the-scene is the reading of a ransom letter, blown up on an overhead projector and read aloud, a deliberate reminder of *Zodiac*'s preoccupation with data, mass communication, and analysis. Toschi becomes understandably agitated, watching a hyperbolic and cathartic version of his own frustrated investigation. He turns around and, impossibly close and almost surreally aloof, is his boss. He gets up and leaves the screening, a cardboard cutout of Eastwood's "Dirty" Harry Callahan looming overhead, his face (it's worth noting) cut out from the frame and his iconic .44 Magnum pointed directly at the passing real-life detective. Toschi is beset on all sides by a slippage of reality, and though he never quite gives up the investigation, he concedes that he cannot adapt to this environment. When Robert gives him words of encouragement in the theater lobby, Toschi brushes him off and heads for the door, replying, "Pal, they're already making movies about it." Film becomes a shorthand for fatalism, and the scene fades to black on a morose Robert left to ponder Toschi's words. When the film picks back up, it is for a third act in which the cartoonist ostensibly becomes the lead investigator on the case.

There are still unexplored avenues in this study of data hegemony and mass communication in *Zodiac*. For one, the faceless motif is met with a contrapuntal pattern of faces in medium close-up, as in the claustrophobic interrogation scene when the detectives finally meet Arthur Leigh Allen, and the madcap montage of farcical leads when "witnesses" and "confessors" begin coming out of the woodwork after the story hits a high point in its media frenzy. There is also perhaps an argument to be made for the film as a meditation on the nature of memory in this digitally mediated age, as nostalgia does play a heavy hand in the film's aesthetic and Toschi begins to dissuade Robert from investigating further by telling him that evidence gets spottier the longer the case runs dormant. "People get old Robert," he tells the still-enthusiastic Graysmith, "they forget." Nostalgia for a bygone era is especially applicable in a discussion of journalism's current state. On the topic of *All the President's Men*, Bob Woodward is in the news again with a new book, this one an exposé on the Trump administration called *Fear* (Vernon 2018). Perhaps the president does make one wistful for a time when American journalists did not sit quite so literally in the crosshairs, especially given the logical conclusion to this animus in the mass-shooting attack on the *Capital Gazette* offices in June of 2018 (Prudente and Dance 2018). Which is to say nothing of the war waged on the press by other keepers of a neoliberal status quo, especially those in Silicon Valley that traffic in the business of data hegemony. There's Peter Thiel, the digital marketplace and data surveillance maven who recently led a successful charge in defunding culture blog *Gawker* because it published unfavorable press about him (Denton 2018), and the ways in which Mark Zuckerberg's Facebook has supplanted access to thoroughly vetted journalism in some very harmful ways (Rosenberg, Confessore, and Cadwalladr, ibid). On this latter point, a synthesizing study of *Zodiac* in concert with Fincher's *The Social Network* (2010) is perhaps in order. Just as in the film, there's not so much a lesson to be taken from this investigation as there is a call to awareness, and a hope for critically minded engagement with systems of information-sharing and their superstructure of ownership. Looking the Zodiac in the face is all well and good, but where do we go from there?

NOTES

1. The nebulous identity of the interview subject underscores the universality of a violent societal deterioration. Judging by the projects that Fincher chooses to work on, the causal nature of social ills on mass murder and other acts of violence is a subject that has continuously captured his attention. From the bareknuckle boxing, chain bombing, cultural revolutionary nihilist cult of *Fight Club* (1999) to the exegesis on the uptick in serial killings outlined in the first episode of the recent Netflix series *Mindhunter* (2017), Fincher is preoccupied with connecting conditioning and destruction. Despite the actual killer's obsession with *The Most Dangerous Game* (1932) and the perverse sense of evolutionary superiority guiding his bloody hand, *Zodiac* makes the case for nurture over nature quite strongly.

2. A series with a story that starts, incidentally, in 1977, the same year that Berardi locates as the beginning of our great psychological fracturing (Berardi 2015, 5).

3. Though this chapter only concerns itself with two of the motifs that this basement scene presents, the scene also offers a third: the metaphysical dilemma posed by a "deal with the devil" in digital filmmaking. Vaughn is a satanic figure, as underscored by the apples that he hovers around throughout the conversation in his kitchen. This "Faustian bargain" imagery is also present in Robert's first smoky barroom conversation with Paul, and Paul's foray into dark back alleys to chase a mysterious lead.

REFERENCES

Benjamin, Walter. 1988. "The Work of Art in the Age of Mechanical Reproduction." *Illuminations: Essays and Reflections.* New York, NY: Schocken Books.

Berardi, Franco "Bifo." 2015. *Heroes: Mass Murders and Suicide.* Brooklyn, NY: Verso.

Bordwell, David and Kristin Thompson. 2013. *Film Art: An Introduction*, 10th ed. New York, NY: McGraw-Hill.

Bridle, James. 2018. *New Dark Age: Technology and the End of Future.* Brooklyn, NY: Verso.

Denton, Nick. 2016. "How Things Work." *Gawker*, August 22. Accessed September 22, 2019, http://gawker.com/how-things-work-1785604699.

Dickson, Sam. 2016. "*Zodiac* and the Ends of Cinema." *Senses of Cinema* 78 (March). Accessed October 22, 2019, http://sensesofcinema.com/2016/feature-articles/zodiac/.

"Forums: Polaroid mp3 view camera." 2009. *Photrio*, September 5. Accessed October 28, 2019, https://www.photrio.com/forum/threads/polaroid-mp3-view-camera.52455/.

Herman, Edward S. and Noam Chomsky. 2002. *Manufacturing Consent: The Political Economy of the Mass Media.* New York, NY: Pantheon.

Hogle, Jerrold E. 2014. "Introduction: modernity and the proliferation of the Gothic." In *The Cambridge Companion to the Modern Gothic*, 4. Cambridge, UK:

Cambridge University Press. Accessed October 11, 2019, https://doi.org/10.1017/CCO9781139151757.003

Holben, Jay. 2004. "Hell on Wheels." *American Cinematographer* 85.8 (August). Accessed October 1, 2019, https://theasc.com/magazine/aug04/collateral/page1.html.

Neidig, Harper. 2018. "Most Facebook users don't trust site with their data: poll." *The Hill*, April 3. Accessed October 5, 2019, https://thehill.com/policy/technology/381406-poll-most-facebook-users-dont-trust-the-site-with-their-data.

Picart, Caroline (Kay), and Cecil Greek. 2007. *Monsters In and Among Us: Toward a Gothic Criminology*, edited by Picart and Greek. Madison, NJ: Farleigh Dickinson University Press.

Prudente, Tim and Scott Dance. 2018. "'I Don't Know What Else to Do': Grieving Capital Gazette Journalists Cover the Massacre of their Own Newsroom." *The Baltimore Sun*, June 29. Accessed October 28, 2019, http://www.baltimoresun.com/news/maryland/anne-arundel/annapolis/bs-md-capital-staff-20180628-story.html.

Robinson, Nathan J. 2016. "Why You Should Never Listen to Nate Silver." *Current Affairs*, December 29. Accessed October 22, 2019, https://www.currentaffairs.org/2016/12/why-you-should-never-ever-listen-to-nate-silver.

Rosenberg, Matthew, Nicholas Confessore, and Carole Cadwalladr. "How Trump Consultants Exploited the Facebook Data of Millions." *The New York Times*, March 17. Accessed September 22, 2019, https://www.nytimes.com/2018/03/17/us/politics/cambridge-analytica-trump-campaign.html.

Saba, Paul. 1982. "The Concepts of Ideology, Hegemony, and Organic Intellectuals in Gramsci's Marxism." *Theoretical Review* 27 (March-April). Accessed October 10, 2019, https://www.marxists.org/history/erol/periodicals/theoretical-review/1982301.htm.

Schreiber, Michele. 2016. "Tiny Life: Technology and Masculinity in the Films of David Fincher." *Journal of Film and Video* 68 (1) Spring: 3–18.

Shane, Scott. 2013. "No Morsel Too Miniscule for All-Consuming N.S.A." *The New York Times*, November 2. Accessed October 22, 2019, https://www.nytimes.com/2013/11/03/world/no-morsel-too-minuscule-for-all-consuming-nsa.html?hp&pagewanted=all.

Vernon, Pete. 2018. "The devil's bargain in Bob Woodward's *Fear*." *Columbia Journalism Review* (September 12). Accessed October 2, 2019, https://www.cjr.org/covering_trump/bob-woodward-fear.php.

Wagner, John. 2016. "Clinton's data-driven campaign relied heavily on an algorithm named Ada. What didn't she see?" *The Washington Post*, November 9. Accessed September 18, 2019, https://www.washingtonpost.com/news/post-politics/wp/2016/11/09/clintons-data-driven-campaign-relied-heavily-on-an-algorithm-named-ada-what-didnt-she-see/.

Chapter 11

Gaming the Ripper Coast
Mapping the Radicalized Acts of the Zodiac Killer

David Ryan

Growing up in northern California in the 1970s and 1980s, my family neither strayed too far from walking into the woods to be assaulted and raped nor retreated into our safe homes to be stabbed, shot, and murdered.[1] I remember California's Ripper Era (1969–1986)[2] as a time of nourishment and terror, particularly reading about the serial offenses of the East Area Rapist, or better now known as the Golden State Killer (GSK), for he reportedly raped his first victim around 4:00 am in Rancho Cordova, California, a tree-heavy, river-adjacent suburb of Sacramento, in June 1976, just two miles from our home.

He continued to terrorize our community for three years, committing numerous burglaries and rapes. He added murder to his list of offenses when he confronted and killed a couple near the scene of his original crime in 1978. Unknown to us, he exited the region in 1979, traveling beyond the Sacramento Valley, adding to his list of offenses. He was active in central and southern California up until 1986 when, suddenly, the crimes seem to have ceased. The criminal tally: 13 murders, 50 rapes, and over 120 burglaries, according to the FBI (2016). After over forty-years of hiding in plain sight, former police officer Joseph James DeAngelo was arrested in 2018 in his Citrus Heights home just 10 miles from Rancho Cordova after the FBI uploaded his DNA profile to a genomics website that linked his profile to his relatives (*CBS News*, 2018).

When my father retired from the U.S. Air Force in the mid-1970s at Mather Air Force Base and settled in Rancho Cordova, little did we know our part of the West was already a seductive land for serial killers. The Golden State Killer's (GSK) first reported crime came seven years after the concurrent murder sprees of Charles Manson in southern California and the Zodiac in northern California in 1968–69. GSK's initial crime wave began a month before Son of Sam started searing New York City with his .44 Bulldog revolver. These coastal crimes occurred while we lived adjacent to the I-5 corridor in which Richard Woodfield accosted, robbed, and killed from 1975 to 1981 in northern California, Oregon, and Washington, earning him the "I-5 Killer" moniker.[3] Woodfield's tri-state spree took place while Kenneth Bianchi and Angelo Buono operated between 1977 and 1978 in southern California as the Hillside Stranglers and while the Trailside Killer David Carpenter prowled Marin, Santa Cruz, and San Francisco Counties, murdering approximately ten women from 1979 to 1981.

These crimes preceded the Night Stalker Richard Ramirez's murders in Los Angeles; Leonard Lake and Charles Ng's murder sprees in Calaveras County in 1984–85; and the work of the Speed Freak Killers (Loren Herzog and Wesley Shermantine) in San Joaquin County, both of whom were suspected in the deaths of over seventy people during the 1980s and 1990s. Though these jarring crimes filled many headlines, northern California was already *terra firma* for serial killers in the early 1970s, for Sutter County was pocketed with the twenty-five shallow graves of Juan Corona's victims while Ted Bundy was quietly killing thirty people from California to Florida from 1971 to 1976.

Up and down the Golden State, serial killers were writing California's history by chiseling their desires on the lives of their victims and swirling back into their communities, often hiding in plain sight with their dark stoicism and quiet anonymity. All of the serial killers mentioned above were captured with the exception of the Zodiac, and GSK was apprehended after forty years of evading the criminal justice system. All by himself, the Zodiac seems to have found a secret doorway out of our world and into our imaginations where he exists in alternating states of living and dead.

Though a handful of alert researchers have raised the larger question as to why so many serial killers plague the modern era (Hitchcock 270), fewer have formulated perceptible information beyond data collection (Hickey 280–81). The data does indicate that California has had more reported serial killers than other states (281).[4] But why? Does part of the answer lie in California's rapid population growth and spatial density? Perhaps the proliferation of media markets has contributed in some way? But how? Or was it always just easier to kill out west, a land seized and settled by transients, miners, pioneers, and immigrants seeking their fortunes?[5] There might still lurk in our mythogenic imaginations the uneasy feeling of murder in California's golden hills and valleys—where the stories about the criminal formations of Los Angeles and San Francisco construct a social history marked by sudden riches and swift poverty, of entrepreneurial invention and criminal enterprise, of John Sutter's gold strikes and the Donner Party's cannibalism—a duality that breeds quests for satisfaction and resentment.

Part of the explanation could lie in the northern state's long history of relying on Barbary Coast micro-economies to shape and build its social structures while disfiguring itself with bad social policy, such as California's deinstitutionalization of psychiatric care facilities from the 1950s to the 1980s.[6] In this historicist's scenario, California becomes an improvisational place of perpetual pleasure for some and fanciful injustice for others—a land dominated by the histories of Charles Crocker, Dominic Ghiradelli, William Randolph Hearst, Charles Manson, the East Area Rapist/Golden State Killer, and the Zodiac. The lack of a plausible answer to the identity of the Zodiac is one reason why popular narratives memorialize the killer and why a resilient but defeated criminal justice system sought help in its long hunt for both GSK and Zodiac.

METHODOLOGY: INSPECTING GAME THEORY

My inquiry takes some key principles of game theory to help theorize why the GSK remained free for forty years and why the Zodiac has never been apprehended even when hounded by their vigilant pursuers. This inquiry utilizes a model of inspection games[7] to frame serial killing as a series of *ludostrategic* choices between killer and police[8] but modifies the framework for mapping the aberrant, noncooperative, conflictive behavior of GSK and the Zodiac while utilizing David Fincher's *Zodiac* to illustrate key points. This interdisciplinary approach is based on taking aspects of historicism, game theory, and Fincher's well-structured narrative to conduct an intermedial analysis, one in which textual analysis assists in understanding nonliterary texts or historical phenomena because the framework and content of stories and narratives are often informed and shaped by these phenomena.[9] Fincher's film is based on Robert Graysmith's popular book, and the film's narrative is also heavily influenced by the social science of game theory. This intermedial analysis also uses content analysis of Fincher and screenwriter James Vanderbilt's narrative to illustrate organizational behavior and individual character choices.

For this inquiry, let's start with the primary criminal operator: the Zodiac. Because we lack definitive proof to his identity, the Zodiac has become a pop culture chimera who publicly stabbed and shot his victims, perceivably outwitted his pursuers, and disappeared into the tides of history. As Fincher and Vanderbilt utilize Graysmith's book, *Zodiac* makes an argument of *probability* by approaching the identity of the killer in two ways: first, we see the representation of the empirical acts of a male (or different male actors) engaging in four serial offenses; and second, we view the social impact of a series of letters that arrive to the media and law enforcement agencies after the crimes. Within this narrative frame, these two acts of crime and cryptography represent one part of an overall stratagem to navigate the *Serial Killer's Dilemma*, one where the serial killer desires to remain free to commit the very crimes that would cost him his freedom.

In the film's narrative, there is little characterization of the Zodiac beyond his/their strategic choices and the composition of the letters. For example, we see the Zodiac attack his victims, but we never directly *understand* his criminal identity beyond his race and gender. For example, in his first assault in the evening that opens the film, the Zodiac prowls a parked couple, and as he shoots them, he does not speak. In his second attack during the day, we hear his muffled talk from beneath his hood to the Lake Berryessa couple, but we also know that the story he tells them is pure misdirection; in the third attack, we see a silent, backseat killer violently shoot his cab driver to death, and in the fourth attack, we see and hear the Zodiac's chilling threats to a mother and her infant. As Fincher unfolds the Zodiac's scenes, we see a progression of verbal behavior that is meant to give a vocal shape to the voiceless letters that are read by other characters. What we see of the Zodiac is that he uses a gambit of quick and direct confrontations; he positions himself proximally to his isolated victims before attacking and exiting his crime scenes. Though these scenes are meant to give us a semblance of a human identity that connects to the rhetorical identity of the Zodiac in the letters, these actions speak to a strategy of short-term opportunism within a construct of long-term thinking that compose the *Serial Killer's Dilemma*—a series of choices created by a serial criminal's desire to stay free to commit the very atrocities that endanger his life and freedom.

To illustrate this dilemma, Fincher and Vanderbilt create a narrative sequence that illustrates a series of cause and effect relationships, for *Zodiac* actively shows us the serial offenses and connects these events chronologically to the arrival of the letters. The film treats the serial crimes and the outside-of-the-killing-zone letters as parts of a larger stratagem meant to resist the creation of reliable problem-solving schemas on the part of the Zodiac's pursuers. The letters (and the material sent with a few of the letters) offer some forensic proof of the authenticity of the letter writer's (partial) knowledge of the crimes while also presenting extraneous cognitive load puzzle-problems meant to confuse readers and stymie pursuers. Though amateur and professional sleuths have pointed their fingers at a few suspects, no one was arrested for the Zodiac's crimes. If we are to conclude things here, the Zodiac has effectively and successfully played the *Serial Killer's Dilemma*, one where a serialist attacks his victims and pollutes the contexts of his crimes in order to remain free to strike again.

In this inquiry, there is no attempt to sleuth the identity of the Zodiac because amateur, academic, and professional detectives have mined the facts and have contributed to the knowledge of these individual cases with mixed conclusions.[10] However, the film does strongly suggest that Arthur Leigh Allen is implicated in some way but offers no definitive answers beyond Graysmith's belief in his own case-building. Interestingly, the film does suggest that our understanding of the Zodiac is framed by a pluralism of conflicting facts and composite identities. For this reason, in the Zodiac's four scenes, Fincher employs different actors to portray the offender, and all of them are not the actor portraying Arthur Leigh Allen (John Carroll Lynch). Fincher's approach to the Zodiac's casting suggests that the public identity of the Zodiac is a witness-based composite, one based on varied accounts that have been accumulating over the years, and the complexity of this casting choice also suggests a triangulation between (1) the crimes attributed to the Zodiac, (2) the rhetorical identity of the Zodiac as composed by the letters, perhaps penned by someone other than Allen, and the (3) man law enforcement suspects is the primary killer.

In dramatic terms, we witness a singular middle-aged Caucasian male assault, wound, and murder people without fully understanding other aspects of his identity because the film works in a world where dramatic irony permits us only partial truths about human choices and actions. Fincher and Vanderbilt understand that human narratives can dramatize only a limited understanding of actual criminal identities, and for this reason, the film offers no secure platform for understanding Zodiac or his choices. Rather, we witness a series of separate crimes that are connected by the arrival of the suggestive letters and a narrative that binds them in a cause and effect relationship.

More thematically secure is that *Zodiac* offers insight into the norms of organizational behavior and the problems they face when challenged by radical acts of criminality. The film allows us to study organizational crisis response models by understanding the priorities of decision-makers when their rationality is challenged by acts of communication that utilize intimidation and fear. Fincher and Vanderbilt illustrate how these organizations use vertical processes to make decisions regarding threats to its norms and practices, assess the value of evidence, and make critical decisions regarding whether or not to cooperate with one another.

My inquiry accepts the film's arguments regarding the composite identity of the Zodiac (due to the different people involved in the crimes and composing the letters), and assumes for the sake of this inquiry that the letter writer had some knowledge of the murders. This inquiry uses Fincher's dramatization of the numerous dilemmas associated with the serial crimes attributed to the Zodiac to explain the known tactics and strategies. Here, the central question is: can understanding how the Zodiac Killer gamed and solved the *Serial Killer's Dilemma* promote the public good?[11]

GAME THEORY: INDIVIDUAL DILEMMAS AND ORGANIZATIONAL RESPONSES[12]

As Dixit and Nalebuff explain, Game Theory (GT) is a "branch of social science that studies strategic decision making" (xvi) by studying human behavior within cooperative, noncooperative, and conflictive task environments. Because GT is about understanding and employing strategic behavior, it is also about understanding the choices made within a spectrum of goals, objectives, tactics, and strategies.

In *Zodiac*, Fincher illustrates the organizational benefits and problems related to cooperation and communication, as small groups of men and women with dedicated specialties and missions are tasked with solving Zodiac's crimes. To better understand how organizations approach problem-solving as illustrated in the film, this chapter examines three key GT areas in relation to the *Zodiac*: (1) deterrence and compellence; (2) task environments; and (3) Zero Sum Games within a broader understanding of well-structured task environments.[13] But before we delve into these critical areas, let's explore how Fincher and Vanderbilt frame the Zodiac's criminal agency to understand how knowledge of gaming emerges as an important tapestry in *Zodiac*.

As a methodology, GT finds its origins in mathematical and economic models of inquiry, and practitioners and theorists focus on understanding the social interactions and communicative acts among people who make a series of decisions (in cooperative or noncooperative acts) contextualized by implicit and explicit rules and boundaries. In *Zodiac*, Fincher illustrates these boundaries in two fundamental ways: first, these boundaries serve as organizational constraints that define people within their narrowly focused vocations, whether they are journalists, the police, or a cartoonist. Second, the film argues that these social constraints hamper individual moral agents from resolving issues created by deviants who are neither bound by organizational values nor are their actions congruent with these values. For these reasons (among others), the film argues, Zodiac is able to elude his pursuers. Why? From a strategic point of view, when serial criminals understand the norms of group constraints and unbound themselves from these constraints to commit their crimes, they increase their chances to escape to offend again. Offenders, however, who rely merely on impulse and instinct (rather than long-term planning) or only seem to engage in short-term planning, are detained and incarcerated as is the case for many of the offenders listed earlier.

One reason why *Zodiac* is a compelling film is because it makes any number of arguments related to exploring and explaining how groups of people engage problem-solving activities. One important argument is that organizations dedicated to serving the welfare of the public are capable of engaging the day-to-day activities associated with well-structured *tame problems*, but they are often incapable of resolving *wicked problems*. Wicked problems are differentiated from tame ones in that they present altogether confusing, contradictory, conflicting, and incomplete information. In essence, they are ill-defined or ill-structured problems (Brown, et al. 2010, 4). For Fincher and Vanderbilt, when tasked with confronting wicked problems, organizations react by using linguistic norms and behavioral standards to classify and categorize these problems as if they were ordinary problems. However, this kind of categorical problem-solving breaks down because the Zodiac-as-a-wicked-problem uses *ludostrategic* choices in his poison letters by juxtaposing authentic and inauthentic information designed to confuse and confound his pursuers. The result is that the Zodiac's identity becomes a parataxic distortion that blends the crimes attributed to the serial killer with a literary identity that communicates partial forensic proofs wrapped in tantalizing lies.

What makes *Zodiac* a useful film for game theorists is that the narrative frames this composite identity not just as a *wicked problem* but as a *super wicked problem*. In theoretical studies, a super wicked problem has four variables (Levin et al. 2012, 124) that distinguish it from wicked problems: (1) *time pressure—perceived and real:* as Fincher and Vanderbilt conceive the story, the narrative boxes Zodiac's actions into time-sensitive segments; in his letters, the Zodiac threatens to go on rampages if his demands are not met *immediately*; because news and police organizations often labor under pressurized time constraints, the Zodiac's threats compel these organizations into a cognitive load of forced choice tests where they have to guess how to proceed in their search for clues; and the film notes the passage of time in years as fewer and fewer people pursue the Zodiac; (2) *those who cause the problem also seek to provide a solution:* the time pressure that the crimes and the letters create is meant to lower the effective response rate of the media and police, and this strategy is compounded when the Zodiac argues that his ciphers will reveal the solution to his identity—if his puzzles can be solved; meanwhile, he works to thwart his pursuers by contextualizing his ciphers with confusing, incomplete, and contradictory information; (3) *the central authority is weak or nonexistent*: as well-resourced as the criminal justice system and media are, they are ill-prepared to resolve the criminal gamesmanship of the Zodiac; the organizations seem to be making up responses as such problems occur and are portrayed as always behind and working in competition with one another; and (4), *irrational discounting occurs that pushes responses into the future:* while both law enforcement and media work separately to identify the killer, their resolve does not account for acts of collaboration related to long-term problem-solving; rather, both are trapped into making short-term decisions related to formulating the next edition of the paper or preventing the next murder; though not necessarily irrational, this sequencing pushes Zodiac's pursuers repeatedly into dead ends. It is only when Graysmith and Toschi agree to work outside of organizational boundaries do they more successfully piece together the clues.

For Fincher and Vanderbilt, there is no satisfactory solution to the problem of identifying the Zodiac because our perception of this composite figure is skewed by different proofs and evidence as well as filtered by our fears and imagination. This parataxic distortion of identity is further configured with Graysmith's perspective that Arthur Leigh Allen is involved with the killings, a perspective the film emphasizes when Graysmith (Jake Gyllenhaal) states to his wife midway through the film that he wants to "stand there and look [the Zodiac] in the eye." Later, in one of the film's two conclusions, he goes to the hardware store to engage Allen (John Carroll Lynch), and as Fincher composes the scene, each man stares at the other before Graysmith exits the store. Here, Fincher and Vanderbilt illustrate how Allen remains free while Graysmith resolves to write his book. However, as *Zodiac*'s self-referential narrative concludes seven-and-a-half years later in an Ontario airport breakroom, *Zodiac* argues that personal truths regarding identities are influenced by and are often conceived within storytelling narratives when an older Mike Mageau (Jimmi Simpson) fingers Allen as his assailant to a Vallejo detective. We shall return to further analyze this scene in the conclusion of this chapter.

COERCIVE GAMING: DESIGNING DETERRENT MOVES AND COMPELLENT COUNTERMOVES

The primary purpose of this inquiry is to examine how a few key principles of Game Theory are used to create thematic tapestries in *Zodiac*. As a method of inquiry, GT examines the relationships among strategy, tactics, objectives, and goals in competitive and noncompetitive contexts. Games are designed to be either cooperative or noncooperative, and cooperative games rely on forming alliances on mutually established goals. Groups, for instance, will form based on mutually understood or agreed-upon interests, objectives and goals and work or play against others in competitive contexts. Team members cooperate and collaborate because working together better ensures that they will achieve their goals. No doubt, *Zodiac* suggests that Graysmith is able to come to his conclusions only when he and Toschi cooperate with each other outside of their organizations. Additionally, the film suggests a degree of cooperation between Bob Vaughn (Charles Fleischer) and Allen as the letters relate to the killings. This implied cooperation thematically mirrors the more collaborative efforts of Toschi and Graysmith.

This motif of cooperation countervails the more dominant theme of noncooperation. In GT, noncooperative games suggest little or no cooperation and collaboration. For instance, noncooperative operators can engage in a loose kind of coordination where "you work over there, and I'll work over here, but we won't necessarily share resources or insights as we move about our tasks." This principle is how most organizations operate, and the film suggests that the Zodiac exploits this lack of cooperation when the letters (or parts of letters) are sent to different organizations, and they fail to share resources or actively piece together clues.

As *Zodiac* dramatizes the organizational environments of law enforcement and the media, the film illustrates how different individuals and teams formulate objectives as they work to constrain or stop others. Into these conflicting task environments arrive the gamesmanship of the Zodiac's cryptographic letters. There are plenty of efforts to interpret, explain, and analyze his letters, but one important variable to keep in mind is that the letters either are or become tools of a broader stratagem to successfully manage the *Serial Killer's Dilemma*. The letters make two kinds of threats—deterrent or compellent—as a tactic to help meet these outcomes. Schelling (1965) argues that both deterrence and compellence are coercive in nature and serve the same ends. For instance, compellence occurs when an agent coerces someone to give up something that the agent wants or needs while deterrent tactics dissuade people by threatening to take action against them. Either way, deterrence and compellence are strategic moves with planned courses of action with corresponding consequences (Dixit and Nalebuff 2008, 187).

Given these brief descriptions, the film frames the Zodiac's cryptic letters as a witches brew of compellent and deterrent messages designed to confuse pursuers by polluting the interpretive framework with warnings, threats, and promises. As strategies, deterrence, and compellence work not to inform and persuade but to manipulate and coerce audiences into making poor strategic choices. And as key operators (Avery and Toschi) fall out of pursuing the killer, only Graysmith stays on task at great personal cost. Though Toschi is reassigned, he cooperates with Graysmith later on. When Graysmith discovers more evidence, the film steers us away from identifying the Zodiac as a single person by suggesting Vaughn was involved in the letters and Allen is responsible for at least one of the attacks.

COGNITIVE STRATEGIES AND WORK: WELL-STRUCTURED AND ILL-STRUCTURED TASK ENVIRONMENTS

In fundamental terms, gaming environments are task-oriented environments, and task environments are problem-solving spaces. From a cognitivist's framework, gaming is a measurement of three intersecting practices:

interaction among participants, engaging the content the environment provides, and analyzing the data participants and audiences provide.

In this intersectional space are three kinds of problem-solving environments: (1) well-structured, (2) ill-structured, and (3) a synthesis of well and ill. In gaming, players understand the construct of a well-structured task environment. In chess, for instance, the board is a well-structured task environment because it has finite boundaries divided into an alphanumeric grid; and on this grid of sixty-four squares of alternating colors, each player begins with sixteen pieces that have specific names with well-defined moves. Chess provides players a series of cognitive problems based on spatial and temporal variables, and problem-solving is reliant on the skills, experience, and game plan of the operators. Chess offers controlling strategies to create structured tasks and rules to constrain the participants' behaviors. The chess environment is an *exemplar* of a well-structured task environment in which the participants are often identifiable, and their methods of play are revealed through their strategic choices. Though chess matches can end in resignation and stalemate, the purpose of chess is to have one agent prevail by forcing the opponent to resign or by capturing the opponent's king.

By contrast, an ill-structured task environment resembles more of the problems one encounters in real life. In these ill-defined areas, information processing is deeply problematized, for participants engage in a series of choices often not knowing what the objectives and goals—not to mention the problems—are. Rules and boundaries, if they exist, are often ill-defined or are poorly enforced or managed; directions for engagement are scant or vague, if they exist at all. Ill-structured task environments are a swirl of uncontrolled and unforeseen variables that involve incongruent data, contradictory ideas, or no information at all. The result is little consensus regarding problem-solving. In this environment, little makes sense.[14] Now, there are few if any examples of board or video games that are ill-structured, for most game, designers will compose task environments with rules of conduct with consequences and rewards in relation to specified objectives and goals. The third task environment is a convergence where certain variables are well-structured while others are ill-structured. No doubt, a large ill-structured problem may become seemingly manageable if and when well-structured cognitive approaches begin to solve smaller problems associated with the larger problem. For instance, law enforcement authorities collect evidence, theorize about suspects, eliminate prospects based on the evidence, and come to conclusions about motives and opportunities. Similar to cognitivists, game theorists work to understand a rational plan of action as operators move from premise to premise, situation to situation, and action to action within a context that values perseverance, completion, and prevailing; gamers learn and adapt as they develop strategic competencies and, if they are at it long enough, master a repertoire of tactics that enable them to carry out their objectives to meet their goals in the three different kinds of task environments.

Fincher illustrates these task environments in clearly defined actions. For example, the offices of the *San Francisco Chronicle* are a squeeze of activity, and the employees understand their social roles and are identified and constrained by their jobs. Fincher illustrates the norms of well-structured task environments by showing people's tasks, their allocated spaces (their desks, their rooms), and their time commitments to fill these places with work. When the editorial staff reads the Zodiac's first letter, Charles Thieriot (John Terry) asks reporter Paul Avery (Robert Downey Jr.) about a crime in neighboring Vallejo, and Avery responds with snappy sarcasm: "What? I cover crime in Vallejo?" He then exits the room to make a phone call to the Vallejo Police Department; thereafter, Graysmith is reminded a few times about meeting his deadline, and he retreats to his desk to be queried again about submitting his work. Afterward, Fincher uses a montage to illustrate that numerous organizations (CIA, FBI, Naval Intelligence) working to decipher the Zodiac's first letter. Though these organizations are game, it is the most efficient group of people who crack the cipher: a family of two, Donald and Bettye Harden (John Sarno and Gloria Grant).

There are many scenes where Fincher illustrates how vertical groups constantly press people to produce results. At the *Chronicle*, for example, the organizational hierarchy has well-defined areas of responsibility for its human agents, all of whom are pressed to meet regular deadlines. However, for law enforcement, *Zodiac* frames their work as ill-structured constructs where the pursuit of justice is constrained by poor communication, lack of resources, and narrow jurisdictional boundaries. After the Zodiac murders cab driver Paul Stine, we are introduced to Inspectors Toschi (Mark Ruffalo) and Armstrong (Anthony Edwards). They are tasked with capturing the killer by Captain Lee (Dermot Mulroney); however, what makes their task environment ill-structured are the many social obstructions that impede any sense of coherent progress. For instance, the ill-structured nature of their investigation means they have to spend time making distinctions between useful information and misinformation, decipher real leads from distractions, work with *bona fides* and false ones while traveling from place to place and coordinate with both collaborative and competing organizations. *Zodiac* frames the work of the inspectors as a convergence of well and ill-defined because the nature of their strategic inquiry shifts between alternating steps of regression and progression as they work to understand the nature of the killer, the composition of the letter, and the implications of both.

What is clear is that the path to task completion is never socially realized, and as the Zodiac purportedly assaults a woman and baby, and as three more Zodiac letters arrive in four months, the inspectors' task becomes further compounded when the Zodiac begins taking credit for crimes he didn't commit. The film illustrates this idea of ill-defined or ill-structured work environments by dramatizing how a torrent of false leads and phony confessions hamper Toschi and Armstrong's efforts to focus on Allen (John Carroll Lynch). Additionally, the prolonged nature of their tasks takes its toll on the inspectors, and as Armstrong transfers out of homicide and as Toschi is accused of composing a Zodiac letter, Graysmith doggedly picks up when official police investigations stall or die. Thematically, *Zodiac* illustrates why these organizations failed to close this case.

These sequences bring us to the Zodiac. As Fincher portrays him, we see the serialist execute his plans in four succinct movements.[15] In each attack, we understand Zodiac's strategy is to control his task environments. In every instance, he has the advantage because he initiates his actions and understands how surprising his victims gives him a strategic advantage. Given his repeated offenses, the Zodiac's main objectives are to kill his victims and escape his task environment to meet his goal to remain free to harm again. To be successful, he has to control as many variables as he can, so choosing isolated victims, surprising them by making the first move, masking his identity, and leaving undetected are objectives that help him meet his goal.

The Zodiac's criminal actions create an ill-structured domain full of cognitive load problems for his victims and his pursuers. For instance, when the Zodiac attacks, we see a perceptual haze grip his victims as they work to figure out what is happening; then, this phase is followed by some initial disbelief that leads to complying with the killer's requests for the Lake Berryessa couple, for example. Thereafter, after the Zodiac escalates the problem by trying to kill his victims, as far as we can tell, few are capable of fighting back. When the Zodiac tricks Kathleen Johns (Ione Skye) into his car, and when we encounter her and her baby on the side of the road afterward, we get the sense that he spares her life. This scene marks the end of his serial offenses. For Fincher, the Zodiac's attacks illustrate how convergent task environments become a competing plane of divergent interests because the Zodiac works to kill his victims while they are tasked to survive his attacks. In this dynamic intersection, the well-structured attacks of the killer converge with the ill-structured defenses of his victims, but despite the Zodiac having more advantages than his victims, he leaves three of the five victims alive because he exits the crime scenes without confirming their deaths. Though the Zodiac fails in some of these tasks, no one was arrested for these crimes, so he still succeeds in managing the Serial Killer's Dilemma.

Near the end of the film when Graysmith visits Avery to discuss writing a book, we see a version of Pong on Avery's television. This explicit gaming reference is not meant just to illustrate Avery's idleness, isolation and dependency; rather, it works to reinforce the film's primary theme of how people organize and express their agency within the varied kinds of task environments. Clearly, Pong represents a well-structured task environment where the roles of the players and the rules and boundaries are explicit—though the game in this scene remains idle. For Fincher, the thematic purpose is to reinforce an understanding of the strategic interaction between decision-makers—even when agents decide to retreat (Avery) or are removed (Toschi) from the tasks. This scene makes thematic references to other kinds of media, including the 1932 film version of Richard Connell's *The Most Dangerous Game* (1924). After his visit with Avery, we follow Graysmith going to different police departments and key sources to track down leads to build his case for his book. What this sequencing suggests is that Rick Marshall and Bob Vaughn possess knowledge of the letters while Arthur Leigh Allen is connected to the killings.

NEGATIVE AND POSITIVE SUM GAMES: THE SERIAL KILLER'S DILEMMA: THE *MENS REA* AND *ACTUS REA* OF THE SERIAL KILLER'S DILEMMA

In strategic studies, understanding the relational differences between a goal, objectives, tactics and strategy are essential, particularly for game theorists. From a gaming perspective, the goals of the GSK and Zodiac are deductively clear: (1) maintain freedom in order to (2) repeatedly commit murder. These two goals compose the *Serial Killer's Dilemma* of a guilty mind (*mens rea*) plotting and carrying out guilty acts (*actus rea*). When contemplating this process, we understand what constitutes the dilemma: the goals of remaining free to repeatedly kill are inherently contradictory. By routinely committing acts of violence, serial killers regularly jeopardize their freedom because of a largely effective social structure that pursues, captures, and punishes serial killers.

In this sense, I posit that both GSK and Zodiac understood that no matter how much the criminal justice system appears to operate on a Zero Sum Game approach to justice (e.g., when the courts mediate between criminals and their victims, or when legislators work to balance the investigative purview of the police and the civil liberties of individuals), these serial killers acknowledge that crime is a mixture of negative and positive sum games based on a few kinds of logical constraints. Here is how the logic could work: GSK and Zodiac could have worked within (as well as reliably prove) two syllogistic structures. First, the major premise would be: *all crimes are not solved*.[16] Because all crimes are not (and will not be) solved, their crimes have a degree of probability of remaining unsolved. This probability goes up if they remain tactically evasive. In this syllogistic sequence, the specific criminal choices

GSK and Zodiac were making worked in their own self-interest. After all, if the major premise (all crimes are unsolved) is valid, then the minor premise that follows (the Zodiac's offenses are crimes) will lead to the conclusion: the Zodiac's crimes will not be solved. This logic did work for GSK until a new methodology of data analysis was used to capture him. However, to the best of our knowledge, the Zodiac did not leave useful DNA evidence at his crime scenes, and the saliva left under a stamp was "incomplete" in its forensic value—though complete enough to rule out Arthur Leigh Allen.

This broader logical structure plays out in more narrower kinds of syllogisms. For example, unlike the syllogism related to most crimes *in totem*, applying a narrow structure for serial crimes makes more sense. Although most reported serial murder cases are statistically cleared,[17] the Zodiac's cases remained unsolved. Even if the Zodiac was captured for other (perhaps lesser) crimes, he has not confessed to law enforcement regarding the crimes attributed to him. Confessing his crimes by cooperating with the police would only undermine this goal, so both the GSK and Zodiac were noncooperative as they engaged in a highly radicalized set of criminal behaviors where they understood the social rules and consciously comprehended their disruptive actions violated these rules. That's why they never stuck around to be captured and punished. They left their task environments mercurially and even antagonized law enforcement with their messages afterward.

In their cases, it is plausible to argue that the *mens rea* of both killers understood the importance and impact of *now* and could predict the consequences of the *future*, so they could work to solve the very problems they created to enact their mutual goals: commit crimes and stay free to offend again. This sort of strategic thinking requires planning and executing tasks while improvise the openings their victims gave them. Here, they probably understood the GT principle of *think forward, reason backward*.[18] Now, if we accept that their goals were to remain free to commit more crimes, we must deduce the most obvious objectives that help these operators meet their goals.

Below is a focused list:

- Objective #1: stay anonymous, for anonymity decreases the chances of being observed and recognized;
- Objective #2: find ordinary and easy victims; and . . .
- Objective #3: locate these victims in areas where ingress and egress have few barriers for the killers; and in these areas with potential victims, ensure that the potential for . . .
- Objective #4: few or no witnesses to observe these crimes.[19]

Understanding these four main objectives helps us see how both criminals worked to meet their goals. In *Zodiac*, Fincher illustrates these objectives by allowing us "to see" the Zodiac and his actions but never really permitting us to grasp his identity. We see him moving in the darkness and in the daylight and observe his victims right before and as they are attacked; and we see him create and exit most of his crime scenes. In *Zodiac*, with the exception of the murder of Paul Stine, we do get sympathetic scenes of the victims conversing and relating to one another; however, the film is about their criminal victimization, so the film focuses more on the Zodiac engaging his crimes. In GSK's case, his objective of finding vulnerable victims meant employing a strategy of trapping them in their homes where he could be alone with them for hours, often breaking in and tying up witnesses (usually the husbands) to rape the women. One reason why GSK purposely left witnesses in his stint in northern California was because (like the Zodiac) he masked his identity. There are, of course, other tactics to consider, but these well-defined variables point to the *mens rea* of setting objectives and goals and composing a strategy that upholds the primary goal of staying free to offend again.

Despite their attention to detail, the Zodiac and GSK left witnesses and evidence of their tactics, and their gendered-based identities. However, though this evidence was enough to lead to GSK's eventual capture, Zodiac's identity remains unknown. In this context, the Zodiac has negotiated the *Serial Killer's Dilemma* of staying free to serially offend by selfishly managing his criminal plans, a point Fincher suggests with the closing of *Zodiac* when the film implies Arthur Leigh Allen's guilt and his death as a legally free man boxed in by suspicion and a record of prior offenses.

CONCLUSION

Though the closure rates for serial killings in the American criminal justice system hover at 60 percent, a 40 percent evasion rate for killers is too high. For this reason, the criminal justice system must revise its methodology to improve its closure rates and the speed by which those rates are closed. This growth in methodological analysis means changing organizational culture to broaden partnerships, multiply resources, and enhance research methods. One key point that Fincher and Vanderbilt emphasize is the need for criminal justice organizations to engage interdisciplinary partnerships in order to responsibly share information, techniques, and knowledge. No doubt, since the period of the Zodiac, the criminal justice system has broadened its data collection and sharing methods as well as its methodologies related to analyzing data.

But what *Zodiac* also suggests is that these organizations broaden their investigative skill set by engaging with game theory while its investigators become more agile in their *ludostrategic* abilities. This approach requires an intentional engagement with aspects of game theory and the more practical applications of game playing, particularly as a way to think about and categorize the data related to empirical and forensic evidence, criminal choices in relation to deterrent and compellent tactics, and the varied task environments in which crime occurs.

What the film suggests in the Zodiac's case is that law enforcement and the media's abilities to process information exceeded their separate efforts to locate useful schemas to effectively engage the super wicked problems the Zodiac case presented. The argument for cooperative acts of gamesmanship is that when an agent's vocabulary expands, and the vocabulary connects to terminology and taxonomies of various practices, then the schemas or the mental models that agents carry with them grow and can be synthesized with others and applied in a variety of task environments, as Graysmith seems to manage while more skilled practitioners of investigative journalism and detective work, such as Avery and Toschi, fall off the trail. As a character, Graysmith becomes more cognitively capable of recognizing key indicators and mapping their relational importance to the Zodiac only when he departs from the organizational confines of his work and the immediate needs of his family. His success at tracking down clues is often attributed to his obsessive behaviors, but what is often overlooked is that the film portrays his success because he doggedly works within a conflictive context of competition that views crime as a negative sum game. From Avery and Toschi to Graysmith, pursuing justice leads to some linear progression, but it also leads to personal loss, so Graysmith adopts the ethos of a punisher who takes personal risks to catch the serial transgressor.

Though the film ends with Graysmith successfully publishing his book and seemingly profiting from his critical labor, *Zodiac* concludes by offering some insight into how storytelling helps with processing and resolving wicked problems. In the film's final scene, we see Graysmith's book populate airport bookstands and Detective Bawart's briefcase as the Vallejo detective interviews an older Mike Mageau. The scene can be interpreted a few ways, but it primarily suggests that the success of the book and Graysmith's belief in Allen's involvement has influenced Bawart (James Le Gros) in some professional capacity. The scene also leaves open the possibility that Mageau has read the book, and as the men come together in schema-building mode, they negotiate their uncertainty by engaging in a discourse that concludes with Allen's probable involvement in the crimes against Darlene Ferrin and Mageau. This scene is interesting because it argues that paperback narratives can actively alter the way we not only remember and interpret information but change the way we engage ill-structured or wicked problem-solving challenges—particularly those problems created by storytelling (or cryptographic letters) itself, the kind that introduces facts and data while also obfuscating or undermining the veracity of such facts and data. Fincher and Vanderbilt suggest that as people sift through data, they adopt and shift information to their frame of reference, and this schema-building helps people better recontextualize ill-structured problems into more solvable ones.

As *Zodiac* argues, when a story synthesizes fact and fiction, or when useful forensic data is embedded within fictive constructs, audiences must interpret this narrative by actively sharing their insights. This shared inquiry not only improves the deliberative process, but it also enhances the problem-solving discourse that is so necessary to shrink the closure rates for serial offenses. Knowledge sharing means not only crossing disciplinary boundaries but also engaging with emergent kinds of processes and technologies that permit researchers to take data and reframe and refilter them in different ways. Because working with commercialized biogenetic data is an emergent field of transnational inquiry, this data collection process has included using covert methods that works with and potentially skirts the service and user agreements of individual companies and their customers. This *ludostrategic* agility is how the Golden State Killer was finally apprehended (St. John 2020). In order for researchers and investigators to better engage this area of inquiry, organizational leaders must not only adopt a set of general practices that responsibly uses emergent and biogenetic technologies to help researchers manage data smartly, ethically, and legally, but they must also provide a series of incentives to close cases that promotes a professional self-interest to share information, coordinate investigations, cooperate in interpreting data, and collaborate in apprehending suspects.

NOTES

1. This chapter provides a preliminary context for criminology as well as amateur, independent, and organizationally affiliated criminologists, criminal justice planners, and law enforcement to better understand aspects of GT that could prove useful to their already game-oriented work. The criminal justice system already labors to understand the complex and complicated interplay of law enforcement, criminals, victims, and the public in the areas of risk assessment, community preservation, and criminal justice.

2. This ad hoc era begins with the Manson-Zodiac killings in 1969 and ends with the last known crime committed by the East Area Rapist/Golden State Killer in 1986.

3. Not to be confused with the Green River Killer Gary Ridgeway. He was convicted of forty-nine murders in Washington during the 1980s and 1990s and is suspected of killing many more.

4. David Fincher's *Mindhunter* (Netflix, 2017) perceptively covers some of this ground.

5. International and domestic workers from China to Oregon came to California only to work and leave the region, never intending to settle (331). Others, including ex-servicemen from the Mexican-American War, came to California to seek fortune and excitement in the new "El Dorado" (332). Doris Marion Wright. *California Historical Society Quarterly* Vol. 19, No. 4 (Dec., 1940), pp. 323–343.

6. The *New York Times* reports that mental patients in state facilities in California in 1959 numbered at 37,500 "but fell to 22,000 when Ronald Reagan attained that office in 1967" (Lyons, 1984).

7. Inspection games focus on understanding the interdependent action of agents with nonaligned interests by auditing, detecting, and correcting the agency of misbehavior and deviation.

8. This approach has precedents, including Tsebelis 1990.

9. For more on intermedial analysis, see Bruhn 2016.

10. Though the Zodiac haunts our literary imaginations as our rendering of Jack the Ripper, GSK escaped popular notice much like the overwhelming majority of serial killers (Hitchcock 279).

11. My effort is interstitial. It is meant to work congruently with other more richly sedimented inquiries—perhaps compliment them in some way.

12. As a field and discourse, criminal justice certainly involves strategic decision-making, and as the criminal justice system evolves into a technologically centered series of interconnected organizations, criminal justice practitioners and advocates would find GT a good companion to engage crime solving, training, and planning (as have businesses and other organizations) for culture-forming and structure-building.

13. Successful organizations make clear distinctions between structure and culture, and as criminal justice systems build and expand their structures, they must also create a culture that promotes a more agile, interdisciplinary approach to deep learning as a basis for problem-solving. As law enforcement organizations work to include more emergent technology in its efforts, GT can help human agents better understand the workings of machine learning and artificial intelligence as bots, drones, and robots become more integrated in criminal justice efforts.

14. Ill-structured does not necessarily mean unsolvable. Unsolvable problems are often identified as wicked problems.

15. The first two actions are played by the same actor as he attacks two different couples; however, the third and fourth attacks, on Stine and Johns separately, are played by two different actors.

16. In 1965, 90 percent of homicides in the United States went uncleared. By 2015, 62 percent of U.S. homicides were cleared, according to the Pew Research Center. By 2017, California's clearance rate for murders was 62 percent, according to the Murder Accountability Project.

17. Other information on serial killers can be searched online at Radford University's Serial Killer Information Center.

18. The computer scientist and philosopher David Gelernter makes distinctions between reasoning and logic. For Gelernter, "rational thought also means picking out the right techniques and the right shortcuts—the right heuristics. Following timelines

is a crucial heuristic" (143). In this sense, Zodiac and GSK could game plan rationally and probably improvise and solve heuristics extemporaneously.

19. For a case study understanding how one serial killer composed his goals, objectives, strategies and tactics, examine the audio tapes of sadist and serial offender Mike DeBardeleben.

REFERENCES

Bonn, Scott. 2014. "5 Myths about Serial Killers and Why They Persist." [Excerpt] *Scientific American,* October 24. Accessed April 5, 2019, https://www.scientificamerican.com/article/5-myths-about-serial-killers-and-why-they-persist-excerpt/.

Breton, Marcos. 2016. "East Area Rapist Still Haunts Sacramento." *The Sacramento Bee.* Accessed May 7, 2019, http://www.sacbee.com/news/local/news-columns-blogs/marcos-breton/article85174522.html#storylink=cpy.

Brown, Valerie A., John A. Harris and Jacqueline Y. Russell. 2010. *Tackling Wicked Problems through the Transdisciplinary Imagination.* London, UK: Earthscan.

Bruhn, Jergen. 2016. *The Intermediality of Narrative Literature: Medialities Matter.* London, UK: Palgrave Macmillan.

CBS News. 2018. "After Golden State Killer Case, Could DNA be Used to Find the Zodiac Killer?" May 3. Accessed August 13, 2019, https://www.cbsnews.com/video/after-golden-state-killer-case-could-dna-be-used-to-find-the-zodiac-killer/.

Dixit, Avinash and Barry J. Nalebuff. 2008. *The Art of Strategy: A Game Theorist's Guide to Success in Business and Life.* New York, NY: W.W. Norton and Company.

Dowd, Katie. 2019. "Will DNA submitted to genealogy sites also finally catch the Zodiac Killer?" *SFGate.com,* July, 22. Accessed July 25, 2019, https://www.sfgate.com/bayarea/article/zodiac-killer-dna-profile-evidence-genealogy-12878262.php.

Epstein, Edward Jay. 2012. *The Annals of Unsolved Crime.* London, UK: Melville House.

Federal Bureau of Investigation. 2016. "Cold Case Killer: Help Us Catch the East Area Rapist." *FBI.gov,* June 15. Accessed July 1, 2019, https://www.fbi.gov/news/stories/help-us-catch-the-east-area-rapist.

Gelernter, David. 2016. *The Tides of Minds.* New York, NY: Liveright Publishing Corporation.

Hickey, Eric W. 2013. *Serial Murderers and Their Victims.* Boston, MA: Cengage Learning.

Hitchcock, James. 1994. "Murder as One of the Liberal Arts." *American Scholar* 63 (2) Spring: 277–285.

Murder Accountability Project. 2019. "America's Declining Homicide Clearance Rates: 1965–2015." Accessed May 2, 2019, http://www.murderdata.org/p/blog-page.html.

Lyons, Richard. 1984. "How Release of Mental Patients Began." *The New York Times,* October 30. Accessed April 1, 2019, https://www.nytimes.com/1984/10/30/science/how-release-of-mental-patients-began.html.

Oswell, Douglas Evander. 2007. *The Unabomber and the Zodiac.* Self-published.

St. John, Paige. 2020. "The Untold Story of How the Golden State Killer was Found: A Covert Operation and Private DNA." *Los Angeles Times,* December 8, 2020. Accessed February 16, 2021, https://www.latimes.com/california/story/2020-12-08/man-in-the-window.

Tsebelis, George. 1990. "Penalty has no Impact on Crime: A Game-Theoretic Analysis." *Rationality and Society* 2 (3): 255–286.

Chapter 12

The Killers Speak

The Sound of Violence in David Fincher's Zodiac *and* Mindhunter *(2017–2019)*

Deborah L. Jaramillo

Zodiac and *Mindhunter* (Netflix, 2017–2019), released ten years apart, brandish the name David Fincher and benefit from accumulated knowledge about the style attributed to his work. Understood as an exacting filmmaker who imbues his narratives, images, and sounds with a dark sensibility, Fincher has a history in television via his early work in music video and his executive producer credit for *House of Cards* (Netflix, 2013–2017). Fincher's name and stylistic connotations may form connective tissue between *Zodiac* and *Mindhunter*, but I am less interested in ascribing a coherent vision to the person and more interested in studying how the works' thematic similarities announce themselves in stylistically divergent ways via different media. Depictions of violence and, more specifically, violence against women are among the ties that bind the film and the TV series to each other. A key contrast emerges in the actual scenes of violent expression. In a few potent vignettes, *Zodiac* embraces both deliberate and frantic action replete with furious eruptions of blood and music. *Mindhunter* operates in the opposite way, amplifying the power of voice and stillness in communicating violence.[1]

This chapter will use *Zodiac* and *Mindhunter* not only to explore their contrasting expressions of violence, but to draw attention to the latter's use of dialogue as a vehicle for horrific detail. Spoken words and the captions that convey them for deaf and hard-of-hearing viewers may seem to offer a more sanitized way to deliver graphic scenes of violence. Accordingly, *Mindhunter*, associated with the visual excess of Fincher, may appear more restrained than *Zodiac*. However, *Mindhunter* entangles restraint and excess with the bare minimum of bloodshed. The visual restraint of *Mindhunter*, almost shocking given the painful representations of violence that have emerged on broadcast, cable, and streaming television, allows excessive language to blossom, forcing an historicization of such a balancing act. We have seen, or rather, heard something similar before. Instead of relying only on Fincher's filmmaking to provide a frame of reference for *Mindhunter*, we would benefit from looking to early radio's stylistic innovations in horror, thriller, and mystery programming.

SOUND, RADIO, AND POSSIBILITIES FOR VIOLENCE

The study of screen violence tends to be sequestered within media effects research; with good reason social scientists ask how representations of violence might influence human behavior. Increasingly, screen violence is registering as a topic for aesthetic or stylistic analysis. As Xavier Aldana Reyes (2013) notes, "scopophilia," or the pleasure in looking, has been catered to by "horror's post-9/11 interest in scenes of cruelty and torture" (146). In her "continuum" of mediated violence, Gwyn Symonds (2008) has advanced one way to gauge the encoding of violent representations (2). At one extreme of Symonds's continuum is "indexical" violence and at the other is "stylized" violence (2). Of course, indexicality is not devoid of style; it is a construction propped up by a style that carries and exploits markers of realism. Symonds argues that her category of indexical violence represents the transformation of the "lived experience of violence" into a "text" and maintains a strong link to the event that happened (5). The strength of that link bears on where a particular representation of violence would fall on the continuum that moves between "visceral indexicality" and a "fantastical imagining in the frivolities of the spectacular" (5).

Symonds's continuum is useful for thinking through the relative weight of violent images within specific genres. Dialogue presents an interesting problem for this model because it signifies much differently than images do, and because its history of signification differs according to the medium in which it is used. In *Overhearing Film Dialogue* (2000) Sarah Kozloff issues a pioneering analysis of film dialogue to stimulate a broader consideration of which sounds should be studied and what purposes those sounds serve. Kozloff's larger goal is to dislodge film scholars from their bias in favor of the moving image. So-called anti-dialogue critics have overlooked the value of the spoken word as one of the "varied means" cinema has "at its disposal for affecting its audience" (62–63). To that end, Kozloff elaborates on the functions of film dialogue. Dialogue works by situating the storyworld and its inhabitants; explaining why things happen and what will happen; existing as narrative events, themselves; giving dimension to characters; sustaining "the code of realism"; and regulating viewers' responses to events (33).

Furthermore, dialogue can harness the "resources of language" in the service of poetry, comedy, or irony; it can insert "authorial commentary" relevant to the film's theme; and it can offer a platform for "stars with unique histrionic talents" (34, 56, 60).

Kozloff decries the theoretical tradition that valorizes the film image at the expense of sound and especially dialogue. The study of radio, exempt from the celebration of the image, clearly privileges sound but has had to negotiate a lack of early recordings. Consequently, scholars of radio have tended to focus on the "cultural dimensions" of early radio *listening*, as Shawn VanCour (2015) explicates (8, 9, 19). The existence of later examples of early radio, however, made possible the study of sonic strategies within genres as varied as soap opera and horror. For example, Matthew Killmeier's (2013) analysis of *Dark Fantasy* expounds upon the expressive abilities of sound in the mystery-thriller genre. For Killmeier, radio was the only possible home for the more horrific mystery-thrillers because if the events were "expressed visually [they] would be absurd" or "would appear fake relative to what we could imaginatively conjure from an audio treatment" (5). He also cites the "intimacy" created by voice that essentially puts the audience to work in the "co-creation of the play" (5). For Susan Douglas (2004), the participation required of the radio listener was atavistic; it "carried people back into the realms of preliteracy, into orality, to a mode of communication reliant on storytelling, listening, and group memory" (29). Killmeier (2012) detects this atavism in the ways early radio returned to the Gothic as it constructed horror with sound, "contravening the visual with its aural expressionism and exercising the emotions and imagination" (76). *Mindhunter*'s reliance upon vocal performance is similarly atavistic; by relying on spoken violence, this series on a streaming platform ostensibly free of censorship recalls the creative strategies of early radio. This is not to say *Mindhunter* entirely foregoes striking visual images for striking moments of dialogue. Rather, the representations of violence rarely transpire as *dramatized acts*. The abundance of violent language that displaces those acts brings to mind the power of voice in radio genres intended to scare or disturb listeners.

Radio scholars have engaged with the voice as a device with genre-specific implications. In assessing the effective construction of monsters in early horror radio, Katherine Barnes Echols (2018) notes how sound effects and "dialogue as description" manufactured "a sense of realism" (58). The use of first-person narration, as well, forged an "intimate" relationship with the audience (58). Neil Verma (2012) elaborates on the category of 1940s radio called the "transmission drama," which was composed of "pathological talkers and compulsive listeners" (125). In these dramas, persistent, persuasive voices bombarded and/or terrorized characters "highly vulnerable to external suggestion" (125). Verma points out that these dramas feature not institutional transmitters but individual ones that "are often the ones that bombard, dupe, and infantilize, most often by dint of personal charisma or 'will' alone" (128). As I will show, the minimal visual style of *Mindhunter*'s violent scenes allows the spoken word to flourish in ways indebted to the aural strategies of mystery-thrillers, horror, and transmission dramas.

In her work on the "elision of listening" in television histories, Kate Lacey (2016) asserts that because radio and the practice of listening were so embedded in everyday life, and because early TV's technology was so primitive, early discourses about television positioned the image as "a supplementary embellishment of the real stuff of broadcasting—words and music" (53). In Lacey's analysis, "sound came first in television," but just as radio's creative workers forged paths away from theatrical antecedents, so did television's producers attempt to carve out a medium-specific identity and style (53). VanCour (2017) explores the transitional moment in which this carving out involved not a wholesale disposal or disruption of radio conventions in favor of the visual, but an adoption and modification of those sonic strategies that had proven successful and that would thrive on TV (164). VanCour notes that although first-person narration did not disappear from TV, producers looked to "visually oriented alternatives" to the voice-heavy techniques of radio (170). He argues that we should not regard television's audiovisual regime as a definitive break from radio's; rather, radio's influence on "television's evolving sonic repertoire" was "formative" (174). The voice, whether it narrated events or chronicled interior thoughts, helped to set the tone in radio and would continue to do so on television. As exemplified by the hosts of such horror/thriller radio programs as *Suspense* (CBS Radio, 1940–62), *Appointment with Fear* (BBC Radio, 1943–55), and *Inner Sanctum Mysteries* (NBC/CBS Radio, 1941–52), the carefully crafted voice, be it "sardonically humorous" or tinged with fear, "fram[ed] the plays with a certain mood" to amplify their affective force (Hand 2014, 100). One need only look to *Thriller*, a horror anthology TV series on NBC hosted by Boris Karloff, to see the coalescence of the voice and the visuals in the service of the genre.

Experimentation with sound in 1920s radio built the foundation for sonic techniques in both television and early sound cinema (VanCour 2018, 98). Of course, both sound cinema and television's use of visuals stirred panic, especially with regard to violence and sex. Radio elicited similar panic, to be sure, but moving pictures made visible what was previously confined to the imagination. The taste-based elevation of print and even audio media above visual media is perhaps one reason why images of violence assault cultural sensibilities more than spoken violence does. For instance, Alison Young (2010) classifies *Zodiac*'s murder scenes as "ultraviolence," a category signifying the use of multiple aural and visual modes in the recreation of actual incidents of horrific trauma (157). Operating without *Zodiac*'s visual flair,

Mindhunter might not fall into that category even though its dialogue offers scenes of violence far fouler than *Zodiac*'s scenes. Before we approach the series' strategies, though, let us first sort through *Zodiac*'s audiovisual treatment of serial killings.

ZODIAC AND THE AUDIOVISUAL ALLURE OF VIOLENCE

Zodiac's engagement with the true crime genre echoes but does not precisely match the morbid fascination of the genre as it exists on television. Broadcast TV's emphasis on the cadaver and its dissection in dramatic series and reality programs, alike, speaks to a standards-driven avoidance of the *act* but embrace of the *aftermath*. *Zodiac* ignores the cadavers visually, attending to them instead via descriptions offered by police and journalists. But before the living, breathing people become dead bodies, the film fixes on their tragedies, creating stylistically alluring exits (or near-exits) for the victims of our mystery killer.

Darlene Ferrin and Mike Mageau, July 4, 1969, Vallejo, CA

From the firing of the first bullet to the fade to black, the interplay of music, diegetic sound, and pace in *Zodiac*'s first murder scene creates an extraordinarily hectic forty seconds, which is unexpected given that the two victims are seated in a stationary car. *Zodiac* opens in Vallejo, California, and we quickly follow Darlene and Mike as they make their way first to a diner and then to a lovers' lane. Menace presents itself first in the form of a surprise burst of firecrackers that startles the pair and then in the form of headlights—a car slowly pulling into the now-deserted lovers' lane and promptly exiting. Darlene's worried face betrays her familiarity with the driver. Not one minute later the squeal of tires precedes the return of the headlights, and the car reenters the lovers' lane. Making no attempt to flee, the two steady themselves to face a policeman since the driver exits his car and wields a flashlight. "Man, you really creeped us out," says Mike, who is the first to be shot.

Donovan's "Hurdy Gurdy Man" plays on the soundtrack, first as diegetic music and then as scene-enveloping, nondiegetic music once the Zodiac fires the first bullet. The music gradually crescendos as eleven slow-motion shots take us through the attack. The initial bullet passes through Mike's neck, spraying thick, deep-red blood, and a cut reveals Darlene with the spatter on her upper arm and face. The recurring shot of the silenced gun firing is intercut with shots of Darlene reeling from the impact. A shot of the car radio clashes with the sound of the music, whose quality signals its source cannot possibly emanate from 1960s-era car speakers. The Zodiac lowers his gun, and Darlene slumps against the interior of the car door. The film returns to regular speed as the Zodiac returns to his car. But the scene does not end, as he sees movement in the car and returns to finish off Mike. Shot from a high angle, the Zodiac fires into the car as Mike jumps into the backseat. A fade to black matches the diminishing volume of the song.

Bryan Hartnell and Cecelia Shepard, September 29, 1969, Napa Valley

Both the Vallejo and Napa attacks transpire against a peaceful, natural soundscape. In Vallejo, the empty lovers' lane is pitch black and noiseless. In Napa, the bank of Lake Berryessa is similarly quiet, though the stabbing of the pair occurs in broad daylight. As Bryan and Cecelia relax by the water, the hulking figure in black walking behind a tree and then toward the couple contrasts sharply with the brightness of the Napa day. The natural soundscape, undisturbed by music, continues throughout the scene. No slow-motion cinematography or stylized blood spatter carry us through the assault. Instead, long shots of the encounter transition into more subjective camerawork once the Zodiac has the two on the ground, hogtying them. On their stomachs, Bryan and Cecelia look directly into the camera (at each other) as they process their situation. Once the stabbing begins, Bryan remains face down as the camera lingers on a close-up of his face that fills the screen. A shot of Bryan on screen left and Cecelia on screen right, facing Bryan, shows both screaming. While the Zodiac begins stabbing Cecelia we see the same tight shot of Bryan's face. The intimacy of the close-ups shifts as the stabbing continues; suddenly the camera is on the left side of Cecelia. She struggles as the Zodiac stabs her and writhes so that the knife penetrates her side and stomach. A cut reveals a long shot of the lake, and the sound of screaming diminishes as the screen fades to black.

Although it lacks an impactful piece of music and does not extend and dwell on painful details, the Napa stabbing scene, which lasts all of fourteen seconds, crafts a real-time experience that leans toward the "indexical" end of Symonds's continuum. Overall, though, the two *Zodiac* scenes discussed thus far present opportunities to think of the blending of various points on the continuum. The intimacy of the point-of-view close-ups carry stylistic flourish *and* realistically mimic the panic the two must have felt. The sounds of stabbing contribute to a soundscape that, by this point in the scene, is dominated by screams and no additional sonic artifice. Linda Williams (1991) refers to the screams in horror films as aural "excess," but in Symond's formulation the scene's indexicality diffuses the excess of the screams, while the liberal use of close-ups challenges the realism (4). The commingling of real time, sourced sounds, and subjective camera work creates a starkly different representation of violence—and one with greater character identification—than was present in Vallejo.

Paul Stine, October 11, 1969, San Francisco

With the murder of Paul Stine, the film returns to the type of visual and sonic devices employed in the Vallejo shooting. The scene begins with a honking car horn that bleeds from the previous scene's discussion of *The Most Dangerous Game* (Ernest B. Schoedsack and Irving Pichel, 1932). Disembodied voices and music stitch together the first shots. Aerial views of San Francisco couple with the sounds of a call-in radio show. A crane shot of a city street descends to street level and focuses on one taxi cab. The volume of "Bang Bang" by Vanilla Fudge rises with the callers still in the sonic foreground, and a bird's eye view shot follows the taxi as it navigates the streets. Two dissolves bring us closer to the taxi. A cut to the side of the cab as it makes its final stop provides a view of both Stine and his passenger. The passenger in the back seat pulls out a gun, grabs Stine by the right shoulder/neck area and fires. A quick cut to a head-on shot of Stine, with the passenger visible in the backseat, shows in slow-motion both the burst of light created from the firing of the gun and the thick blood spewing from the driver's neck. A street lamp lights only Stine, shrouding the rest of the car and screen in the dark. The blood remains visible, however, as it moves from the dark space of the entry wound to his lit face. The movements of the victim resemble those of Darlene's in Vallejo. Stine's body, propelled by the energy of the bullet, shifts and moves fluidly as the song's guitar slows and engulfs the soundtrack. Stine's head turns from right to left—his right cheek visible to the camera—and then tilts back so it faces the roof of the car. He falls back onto the passenger seat. Here the violence ends, but the scene wraps up with the sound of an operator and a child witness on the 911 call and the eerie nursery rhyme ("Ring around the Rosie") from "Bang Bang" as the crane rises to a high-angle shot of the cab.

Slow motion prolongs the shooting and dying so that probably two seconds of action stretch into seven. Unlike the Vallejo and Napa murders, this one lacks any engagement with the victim. His face becomes visible just before the Zodiac shoots him, and he does not speak. Moreover, the Zodiac does not speak to him (that we can see). The impersonal construction of the scene does not rob the Stine character of his moment, though, which commences when the bullet meets his neck and his body involuntarily dances to the psychedelic guitar of "Bang Bang." With one edit, the suddenness of the act—the quick touch of the shoulder and raising of the gun—slows and invites an examination of its traumatic effects. A single gunshot passes too quickly for a spectator to appreciate the extent of its damage. The Vallejo and San Francisco shooting scenes are invitations to ruminate on trauma while binding that trauma to their historical moments, signified through song. The Napa stabbing is its own animal, a prolonged affair—stabbings requiring both time and energy—that affords the victims the time to express pain while we look them in the eye.

SPEAKING ABOUT VIOLENCE AND SPEAKING VIOLENCE

Audiences are versed in the sounds of the types of violence perpetrated in mainstream film and television. Similarly, police procedurals have normalized the way viewers hear *about* violence. When the police arrive at the Stine crime scene, for instance, the two detectives at the center of the Zodiac case—Dave Toschi and William Armstrong—break down the events as they imagined them.

Armstrong: He stops, puts it in park, boom.
Toschi: I shoot him on the right side, he slumps right?
Armstrong: Maybe you've got your hand on his collar when you shoot.
Toschi: Alright, so either way I just dumped a quart of blood in the front seat.

Using another cop as a stand-in for Stine, Toschi matter-of-factly runs down the incident that viewers just saw choreographed on screen. The retelling of the violence unfolds without emotion.

The dialogue in the three *Zodiac* murder scenes accomplishes multiple goals. In Vallejo, Darlene and Mike speak playfully and then fearfully as their evening on lovers' lane turns fatal. In their brief time on screen, their words and performance hint that Darlene may know their assailant—a key piece of information that emerges later in the film. The complete absence of dialogue in San Francisco emphasizes the apparent randomness of Stine's murder. In Napa, Cecelia and Bryan fruitlessly attempt to negotiate with the Zodiac and insert some rationality into this terrifying moment. Crucially, in Napa, the viewer gets to hear the Zodiac speak in person. In other scenes the voice of the Zodiac emerges only on the phone. In calls to the police following his murders, he reports his deeds coldly and somewhat mockingly. Over a static shot of a wounded Mike lying against Darlene's car, we hear this call: "I want to report a double murder. If you go one mile east on Columbus Parkway, a public park, you'll find kids in a brown car." Over a different shot of the interior of the car, he says, "They were shot with a 9 millimeter Luger." The camera moves as a policeman walks around the car, and the Zodiac continues, "I also killed those kids last year." His tone shifts from direct and commanding to playful and sinister as he concludes the call by almost singing "Goooood byyyye."

Assuming the viewer believes the same man tried to kill Kathleen Johns on the highway, then the viewer does get to hear the Zodiac speak in person a second time. His most chilling line does not describe what he has done, as in his other vocal performances, but what he *will* do. Without looking at Kathleen, he intones, "Before I kill you, I'm gonna throw your baby out the window." The Zodiac Killer's sparse, eerie dialogue contrasts with the rich portrayals of his murders. Brief but spectacular, *Zodiac*'s scenes of violence privilege both visuals and sounds in ways that align with our expectations of Fincher's work. *Mindhunter*, a television series created by Joe Penhall and executive produced by Fincher, moves in a different direction altogether, creating distance between its violence and any expectation of graphic images. Fincher's body of work and his reputation circulate around the film and TV series as important paratexts, but, like Kozloff (2000), I am concerned with the "finished [television program], which takes on a life of its own" (33). So, the extent to which Fincher developed the series, ran the writers' room, rewrote Penhall's original scripts, refashioned Penhall's bible, and directed episodes is not at issue here (Chitwood 2017). The focus of this analysis is the dialogue of violence: the words that signify gruesome acts that *Mindhunter* does not show.

MINDHUNTER AND THE VIOLENCE OF WORDS

In its infancy, TV drew from radio's refinement of sound-based entertainment; more recently, we have seen television series that emphasize visuals over sound celebrated as "cinematic," a buzzword associated with a high level of quality. Series that embrace graphic violence and sex on cable channels like HBO and FX are likewise celebrated for bringing mature sensibilities to television storytelling. What does it mean, then, that *Mindhunter*, a streaming television series branded with the Fincher name, would wrap its violence inside dialogue?

Home base for *Mindhunter* is the FBI Academy at Quantico, Virginia, where gunfire is frequently audible in the background. Two of the main characters—Holden Ford (Jonathan Groff) and Bill Tench (Holt McCallany)—travel around the country educating local police forces about the behavioral psychology of criminals. This set-up branches into two distinct but thematically connected streams. The trips become opportunities for local cops to enlist Holden and Bill on their more difficult cases, resulting in side cases for the two agents. Once they launch their project to interview and document the stories of what we now call "serial killers," their journeys veer toward maximum security prisons. Many episodes begin by following a suspicious, unnamed man in Park City, Kansas—the BTK Killer (Sonny Valicenti)—whose murders Tench investigates in season two. Season two tends to reproduce the same dynamic as season one, with the pair spending a considerable amount of time in Atlanta investigating the disappearance of multiple children.

Although I focus on how *Mindhunter* deploys dialogue to convey violence, the series does begin with a violent act. In the cold open of episode one, Holden negotiates with a hostage taker who thinks he is invisible. Without warning, the man blows his head off with a shotgun. The camera stays on him as he draws the shotgun to his neck and pulls the trigger. A large chunk of red tissue pops off his head as his hostage looks on in horror. An exploding head is a striking way to begin the series, but it deceives us. We are not in store for more of what the cold open offers. The remainder of the violent images in season one primarily take the form of crime scene photographs and, in the final episode, hand drawings of murders we have not seen take place. In season two, the series maintains its emphasis on crime scene photos, but we see more physical traces: a chalk outline of a crucified child on a basement floor and four Black victims in Atlanta—two boys who are decomposed and unrecognizable, one boy who is pulled from a river at a distance with the on-screen text obscuring identifying details, and a man who is nude and face down in the river. The accumulation of bodies makes the urgency of the hunt in Atlanta palpable, but the steps taken *not* to show the fresh and decomposing corpses in excessive detail (even the shots of decomposition are illuminated too brightly by flashlight, rendering the image difficult to discern) demonstrate that the series is repeating what broadcast TV historically has relied on: the aftermath and not the act.

Amanda Greer (2017) writes that *Mindhunter* (and crime media, generally) converts women's bodies into evidence—"a site of information, of knowledge" that absolves the audience from complicity because they do not need to conjure the images themselves (158). Certainly, with one exception in season one, that evidence is primarily photographic. However, one recurring home for violent images is the opening title sequence, which contains sudden flashes of decaying body parts. These startling moments are not the focus but rather the jarring interruption. The title sequence concerns itself mostly with close-ups of a reel-to-reel tape recorder. So, while the cold open signals that graphic violence lies ahead, the title sequence indicates that viewers will hear it and not see it. Most of all, the sequence features the *preparation* of a tape recorder. A shot of a disembodied hand positioning a microphone on a table points to the premium placed on the speaker.

What They See and Say on the Job

As with *Zodiac*, standard police-speak about crimes and bodies is common. The spoken descriptions of gruesome acts clue viewers in early to the type of violence the series features. For example, the first side case that Holden and Bill are consulted on, the murder of Ada Jeffries and her son in Iowa, perplexes the local detective, but he remains composed. He describes the crime without emotion: "She was found cuffed and lashed to the bed. A broomstick perforated her rectum. Whoever it was made the boy watch, then did the same thing to him." Crime scene photos—in color—match the detective's words, and as Holden and Bill scan them, we see a bloody mess that spares no detail. The broomstick, the rectal bleeding, and a blank, staring eye are all present as evidence of a monstrous perpetrator. In episode two, Sacramento police seek guidance from Holden and Bill on a case involving a woman, beaten with an inch of her life, and her dog, whose throat was cut. Photos capture a bruised and swollen woman and a dog lying in a pool of blood. Episode three continues the story of this killer when a second victim is discovered; her dog was "slit from ear to ear." The line "the dog's fucking lasagna" precedes out-of-focus photographs of both the dog and the woman.

The Beverly Jean Shaw case that spans episodes four, five, and six leans heavily on description with a few black-and-white photographs to underscore the more heinous aspects of the murder. The body, found without its breasts in a garbage dump, had been mutilated in other ways. A policeman, clearly shaken, describes the disposition of the corpse to Bill and Holden: "He blacked both her eyes, broke her jaw, multiple stab wounds. You see he kind of frogged her legs out there. And there was—sorry. We don't get this kind of thing. It's hard to—there was an incision. From her vagina to her, um, anus." The shaken officer's description resembles that of a detective in season two who must handle the crucified child's case in Bill's town. The emotion evident in both cases deviates from the typically cold delivery of homicide details. The photos of the body with the missing breasts resurface in episode five—an episode that features a vivid recounting of the events leading up to Beverly Jean's death. One suspect, Rose, confesses and paints a picture of frenzied violence in a bathroom, but no flashbacks take us there. Only dialogue puts us in the room. The suspect summons the scene: "I saw Benji. He—he had his head in his hands. He was crying. There was blood everywhere. Splashing. And then I see Beverly Jean in the bathtub." Bill asks if she was alive. Rose replies, "Dead. She had her top on but no panties." These extra bits of information give us backstory for the body in the dump, but in episode six our focus is pushed back onto the remains.

In their interview with another suspect, Benji, Bill uses the condition of the body to force a response. He asks, "Why would you do that to Beverly Jean?

Fractured jaw. Two black eyes. Why? Fourteen stab wounds in the torso with a kitchen knife. Blow to the head. Blunt force trauma. Her breasts were amputated. I need to know this. Why would you do that to your girlfriend?" He follows up soon after by asking, "Why would a man, any man, do that to a woman's breasts? And who would take a hunting knife to a woman's reproductive organs?" His final question centers on the one area of the body only addressed once so far: "How does stabbing someone in the asshole make you feel better?" Significantly, Benji does not detail this mutilation. The details come from the mouths of FBI agents, so the words, though graphic, include judgment and confusion. Rose's words, grabbing at painful memories, indicate regret. The violence voiced in this collection of examples animates the crime scene photographs, which are used sparingly. The camera is stingy with the evidence and allows only fleeting glimpses of the victims. The work of satisfying the taste for violence in a series about a particularly heinous brand of killer is left to dialogue, but the lines do not deal a consistent blow. The speaker matters.

Intimacy, Bonding, and Ed Kemper

In episode one, *Mindhunter* aligns viewers with the law and with an openness to understanding psychology and motive. In episode two, the series extends an invitation to hear from a killer. While in Santa Cruz, California, a local policeman in Holden's class advises him to meet Ed Kemper, "The Co-ed Killer," who is imprisoned in Vacaville. The dialogue mixes vernacular with clinical detachment and demonstrates Holden's morbid curiosity.

Cop: [Kemper] killed a bunch of co-eds right here in Santa Cruz. Six teenage girls, chops their heads off, has sexual intercourse with the corpses. Kills his mom with a claw hammer, has sexual intercourse with her head.
Holden: Bullshit.
Cop: In her mouth.
Holden: NO.
Cop: Yeah.

Holden is now enthralled, and a subsequent conversation at a bar solidifies his resolve to meet Kemper. One cop recounts that, while driving Kemper back to California to face his charges, Kemper "wouldn't stop yakking. Going into forensic detail." The irony of Kemper's first interview is that he practically begins by declaring, "I don't fucking talk, period." In this introductory interview, conducted without Bill, Holden and Kemper size each other up. The physical contrast between the two is conspicuous. Kemper is six foot five and heavy set; Holden is thin and significantly shorter. Wearing glasses

The Killers Speak 241

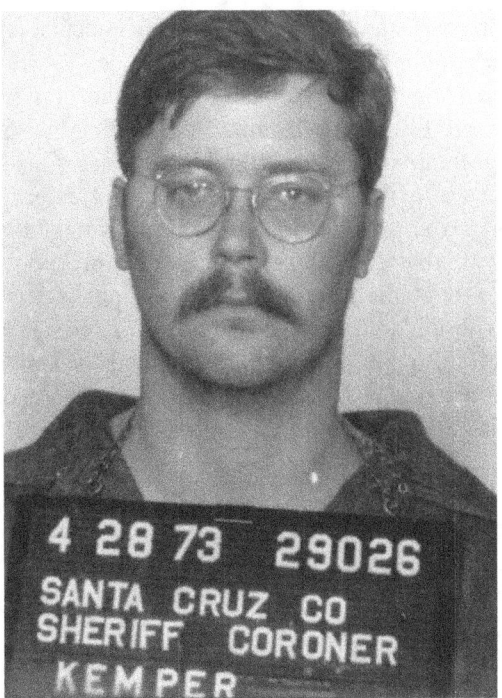

Figure 12.1 Mug shot of Edmund Kemper, April 28, 1973, Santa Cruz County Sheriff (portrayed by Cameron Britton in *Mindhunter*).

and sporting a moustache, Kemper has the look of a mild-mannered man. His deliberate elocution, delivered in moderately deep tones, softens him to the extent that he could be described as a gentle giant. But the over-enunciated words pouring from his mouth contradict the softness. When he declares, "Butchering people is hard work," the violent sentiment from the soft-spoken vessel creates a sense of dissonance. He is no Hannibal Lecter; there is no relish or deviousness in the voice. His killing, or his "hunt" as he puts it, is his labor, so he explains his job as anyone would. Kemper's performance is compelling enough that Holden works to convince Bill that he is a viable subject:

Holden: "He's not some frenzied thriller killer, Bill. I think we need to face that."
Bill: "He chopped off women's heads and had sex with the corpses."

Bill's skepticism means that he is not immediately persuaded to accompany Holden to Vacaville, so Holden returns on his own.

During this visit the full force of Kemper's sonic violence begins to emerge. The stark, muted, industrial setting of the prison interview room is the stage for Kemper's stardom. His presence is undeniably weighty. When he walks, his chains clink slowly. When he sits down, we hear his heft on the chair. Holden's conversation with Kemper begins crassly as Holden tries to coax Kemper into discussing his crimes. Asserting his sexual prowess to create a common frame of reference, Holden discusses his current relationship. Kemper then asks if he performs anal sex on his girlfriend. Holden's face betrays his inexperience, and Kemper exploits this to build a bridge to his own aberrant sexual experience. Anal sex is great, he claims, because the anus is "literally a hole that sucks." He continues, "But when you fuck somebody in the neck it's different. It's nothing *but* resistance. It's really difficult. Let me." At this point, Kemper puts his hands on Holden's neck. "You feel this? Feel it. It's all muscle." Kemper feels Holden's neck, while Holden stares straight ahead at Kemper's torso. Kemper continues, "Cartilagenous." Holden coughs, and Kemper silently reassures him, gently placing his hand on top of Holden's hand. Kemper's instructional tone guides Holden to contemplate the challenges of penetrating a corpse's neck with his penis as though this were routine. The partial demonstration Kemper offers complements his graphic description and makes apparent that this type of behavior is not necessarily isolated to Kemper and his mother.

Kozloff (2000) writes that one function of dialogue is to *be* an event. According to speech-act theory, speech is "doing something" like threatening, questioning, or apologizing (41). When Kemper speaks about the neck's resistance, he doubtless scares Holden, but he also reaches him. The violent speech-acts access something within Holden that is susceptible to them. Dialogue exposes character, as Kozloff writes, and little by little the interviews reveal more about Holden than his subjects (44). Dialogue potentially exposes the audience, as well. In her article on the true crime podcast, *My Favorite Murder* and disembodied female voices, Greer argues that when the hosts recount violent acts in excruciating detail, they render the imaginative audience complicit (156). Left to their own mental imagery, listeners perform individual "re-construction[s]" of the murders, much as *Mindhunter* viewers might do when listening to Kemper (156). Placing the burden of reconstruction onto its viewers, the series embraces dialogue and performance. Liberated from scenes of violent acts, the series also solves a practical problem. Recall Killmeier's contention that early radio horror could not feasibly transition to visual horror without looking "absurd" (2013, 5). The quantity of body horror in television series since the 2010s indicates that the TV landscape has integrated without much controversy the sort of violence Kemper describes, but Killmeier's argument instills doubt that an act of neck violation might achieve the same effect that Kemper's scene with Holden does.

Bill finally accompanies Holden to Vacaville at the end of episode two, and at this point Kemper discloses more backstory. In the same calm manner we have now become accustomed to, he recounts how his behavior escalated from "mutilating" "inanimate objects" to "strangling" dogs and cats and "burying them in the backyard." Twice Holden holds up his hand, asking Kemper to pause because he is without recording equipment and must transcribe the interview by hand. These humorous interruptions impede the rapt attention a scene like this typically demands; the story's intensity stutters, and the impact of such a harrowing background loses a bit of its punch. When he gets to the murder of his mom, Kemper distills what could have been a frightful on-camera dramatization into a few sentences: "I knew a week before she died I was gonna kill her. [. . .] She said, 'for seven years,' she said, 'I haven't had sex with a man because of you, my murderous son. So I got a clawhammer, and I beat her to death. Then I cut her head off. And I humiliated her. And I said, 'there, now you've had sex.' " He finishes this sentence with greater volume and assertiveness. A final reaction shot of Bill concludes this violent scene-within-a-scene. A long shot of the three of them—Bill and Holden facing Kemper, who stares straight ahead in the direction of the camera—allows Kemper some concluding remarks that elicit a wary look from Holden.

Three things are worth noting here. First, Kemper, having illustrated the difficulty of raping through cartilage, spares detail this time around and opts to offer an explanation instead: humiliation. Second, speaking the violence rather than showing the murder and defilement creates distance but also allows Kemper to be introspective. Finally, Kemper's speech lacks passion; it actually plays as a joke with a set-up and a punch line. For Kozloff, humorous dialogue lightens the mood, but Kemper's gallows humor, delivered as aggressively as Kemper's mildness allows, enhances his menace (53).

The intermixture of menace, camaraderie, and humor springs up at unexpected points. In episode three the following interaction concludes a difficult exchange about Kemper and his mother:

Bill: Is it true that you put part of her into the garbage disposal?
Kemper: Her vocal chords.
Holden: Why?
Kemper: Because I couldn't shut her up. She wanted to destroy me with words, literally, so I shut her up for good. And now everyone knows it was because of what she did to me.

The camera slowly dollies closer to Kemper as he responds to Holden, heightening the drama of his answer. A pause then fills the room. Reaction shots of Bill and Holden show the pair struck speechless. Suddenly the jingling of keys breaks the silence. Kemper turns to see a prison guard enter the room with a pizza box. He turns back to Bill and Holden and exclaims, "Pizza!

You guys!" Bill issues a wry smile. A jump cut shows the trio working their way through the pizza and discussing Kemper's murders as though they were swapping tales of adolescent shenanigans. We hear the midpoint of a story: "So I'm home, walking up the stairs to our apartment with a freshly severed head draining about a pint of blood into a duffel bag." With awe written on his face, Holden leans in and asks, "You just got it under your arm? Just like that?" The prison interview has transitioned fully into a line of questioning brimming with morbid curiosity mixed with admiration for Kemper's audacity. Significantly, in season two, curious neighbors and colleagues ask Bill to share these anecdotes at a backyard barbecue (of Kemper Bill remarks, "He killed 'em then carved 'em up like a Christmas turkey"), an appointment with a social worker, and at FBI events. The words emerge from Kemper as violent rage and gallows humor, and they live on as verbal party favors in professional and social circles.

Kemper earns this attentive audience by manufacturing a series of colorful and grotesque vignettes. The violence he speaks is reframed as a story and as a bonding exercise; a dramatization would have walled off these multiple functions. The violent punchlines he adds reinforce the bond and bring the scenes to oddly comedic conclusions. In one case, Kemper recounts his mother's relief that he had never been on a date, to which Holden replies, "That bitch." Kemper explains, "This is when I started burying the heads in the backyard." Kemper lays out the gore as is and underscores its depravity with his own mischievous brand of humor. He continues, "Right underneath Mom's bedroom window. Their faces looking right up at her window while she was at home. Right under her nose, man. I couldn't help myself." At this point, he pauses while Holden quietly asks, "What the fuck?" Kemper's pause is preparation for the one-liner he seems to have kept in his back pocket: "I know it's silly, but mom always liked people to look up to her." His grin and hand gestures beg for a rimshot, but he has to settle for shocked laughter from Bill and Holden.

The introduction of the tape recorder in episode three triggers some ambivalence on Kemper's part. As the reel-to-reel sits in the foreground, Kemper stares at it from the background. When Holden moves the microphone toward Kemper, he gets up and walks away. Nevertheless, he talks. Speaking about his "inability to communicate socially, sexually," Kemper explains that he began targeting women by picking them up and taking them to isolated spots. Without a gun, though, he went no further.

Bill: So you picked up women but didn't kill them?
Kemper [as if ignoring Bill's question]: But then, a gun is in the car, and this craving, this awful raging, eating feeling is inside me. I would've loved to have just raped them. But not having any experience at all, I could feel it consuming my insides, this fantastic passion.

We can imagine Kemper as a psychotic killer in a radio drama, giving the audience his inner monologue. He acknowledges his own ability to spin a yarn.

Holden: Fantastic passion?
Kemper: It's a good phrase, no?

A few more questions and answers lead to a primer on cutting throats. The blocking is reminiscent of the second interview when Kemper handled Holden's neck.

Kemper: [Kemper walks up to Holden and puts his hand on his neck] Look, when you slit a person's throat you need to cut it from ear to ear in order to sever the windpipe and the jugular so that they bleed and suffocate at the same time. Otherwise they'll just be in a great deal of pain. That's how I learnt the term "ear to ear." Literally what that meant. People think it's just an expression. It's not. It's an instruction. You don't want to. You have to.

Kemper commands the scene, dominating the speaking time, but also dominating Holden physically when he pokes at his windpipe and subsequently places a reassuring hand on Holden's shoulder. He once again demonstrates Holden's complete vulnerability, even with a guard present. The violence Kemper speaks would lend itself to a quick cutaway of a throat actually being slit, but instead he walks Holden and Bill through the mechanics of it, including the bleeding and the pain. Kemper's speech is active; it asserts expertise and dominance but also works to bond Kemper to Holden. Before Kemper launches into his lecture, Holden remarks that eventually Kemper had "begun to enjoy the thrill." Kemper emphasizes the care and planning that go into slicing open a neck, rationalizing the act and tempering Holden's expectation of exuberance. Kemper's words also bring him closer to Holden physically. Kemper can easily model the act on his own neck, but he chooses to push the limits with Holden again, knowing how much he holds sway and knowing that Holden will not object.

In her article "Sonic Horror," Isabella Van Elferen (2016) describes sound as the "sinister" presence lurking behind us (267). Sound suits the horror genre because of this inherent "dorsality" (267). *Mindhunter*'s reliance on the sounds of chilling voices like Kemper's, Richard Speck's, and Charles Manson's, coupled with the premise, itself, which forces face-to-face interactions with serial rapists and murderers, asks viewers to confront repeatedly the monsters whose sonic traces would normally lurk behind our protagonists. *Mindhunter*'s brand of audio-forward, dialogue-heavy storytelling adopts the sonic strategies of early radio horror, which relies on the power of sound's dorsality, but embraces the uneasiness generated by proximity to the screen and intimacy with the source of the sound.

Lies, Admissions, and Remorse: Rissell, Brudos, Speck, Hance, and Watson

The spectacle manufactured by Kemper creates the expectation that all subsequent interviews will veer toward the elaborately eccentric and profane, but that standard is not reached consistently. Monte Rissell tells his story with the sort of animation and emotion he might use to describe any Saturday night misadventure. Like Kemper, he attempts to add humor to cap off the repulsive narrative. But the colorfulness of Kemper's dialogue renders Rissell's words dull and inadequate. They do not live up to the violence they signify. Jerome Brudos, a sequence killer introduced by Dr. Wendy Carr, Bill and Holden's partner in their project, rivals Kemper's ferocity. Dr. Carr's description of his crimes sets the stage: "He also amputated the breasts of his first and third victims. [. . .] He plaster cast the breasts and made them into bronze paperweights. [. . .] He amputated a foot, which he stored in his freezer." Accompanying Dr. Carr's description are photos of a woman lying face down with bare legs splayed, the plaster cast breasts, and an amputated foot upright in a high-heeled shoe. We learn that at least some of these are Brudos's own photographs. After getting Brudos to open up by accommodating his shoe fetish and by conducting the interview as a series of hypothetical questions about the "real" killer's motives and deeds, Holden crafts the conditions for a calm and intimate exchange. Missing from the interview is the level of detail present in Kemper's accounts. The closest we get to graphic dialogue is when Brudos speculates that the killer must have fantasized about "choking them, chopping them up, all the stuff they said I did." The rest of the conversation uses language that skirts the deeds and focuses on the motivations. Brudos says, "It might not have been about watching them die. [. . .] It might just have been about having them quiet." The "it" is the choking and dismemberment, but as with Kemper's sex act on his mother's neck, the crimes have been identified already. Repeating them would be gratuitous in a program already practicing visual restraint.

Holden and Bill's interview with Richard Speck, who raped and killed eight nurses one night in 1966, carries a sustained tone of suspicion and hostility. Imprisoned in Joliet Correctional Center, Speck is thin and weathered with a southern drawl and is not nearly as chatty or introspective as Kemper. After Bill fails to get a response from Speck by asking him direct questions about the mass murder, Holden tries to penetrate Speck's armor by speaking his presumed language, asking "What gave you the right to take eight ripe cunts out of the world?" and "How the hell did you even fuck eight women in the same night?" Speck clarifies, "I only fucked one of them" but assures Holden he "could have fucked all of them." Holden's use of the word "fuck" rather than "rape" siphons the violence from the dialogue. Aggression becomes virility.

Unlike Kemper, Speck refuses to elaborate on a night that must have been a sonic and visual nightmare. On the topic of the one girl who "spit" at Speck, the conversation is clipped and to the point.

Holden: Why'd you kill her?
Speck: Cause I wanted to.
Holden: How'd you do her?
Speck: Choked her. Took forever.
Holden: Is that why you stabbed the others? It was faster?
Speck: That's right.

Holden quickly learns that Speck will offer no further insight, but, crucially, Speck pinpoints what the dialogue-as-violence has brought out of Holden. After Holden describes Speck's victims as "cunts," Speck, taken aback, responds while laughing, "You're crazy. That's a fine line that separates you and me." Later, after hearing the tape with the infamous "cunt" line, Holden's boss offers a similar reading of Holden: "I never again want to listen to a tape where I can't tell the difference between my agent and some incarcerated lowlife."

Holden attempts to forge relationships with the subjects based certainly on scientific curiosity but also on something else entirely. We see glimpses of this in his interactions with Kemper, and we see it when he woos Brudos with a woman's shoe and fawns over Speck's tattoo—even going so far as to roll up Speck's sleeve at Speck's invitation. We see it again when Holden, during an interview with a suspected pedophile, unsettles the room by faking (?) an interest in young girls who appear more mature than they are. He gets his man, but for most people in the room, he ventures into territory that is disturbing and obscene. Weeks of interviews with misogynistic sequence killers have burrowed into his brain. Whereas dialogue has disgusted Holden's colleagues as well as the audience, it has bonded Holden to his subjects. Consequences of this bond ensue at the end of season one, but Holden's fawning behavior with Charles Manson in season two—he stands when Manson approaches the interview room, and he happily gives up his sunglasses when Manson asks for them—shows a return to previous, disconcerting behavior.

Season two sees Holden, Dr. Carr, and Bill frequently part ways, each conducting interviews with killers of varying degrees of infamy and even with one victim of BTK. In Atlanta, while partnered with Agent Barney, Holden interviews William Pierce Jr., who denies committing the murders Holden briefly describes. They also sit with William Henry Hance, whose simple and calm description of his crimes starkly contrasts with Kemper's introspective and elaborate narrativization. Speaking about one his victims, he says, "I beat her so you can't recognize her." Speaking about a second victim, he offers more detail: "Beat her, too. Her head come off. So's you can't tell who it is." Absent the performative storytelling style of Kemper or Speck, Hance strips down the violence in a matter-of-fact way that removes all spectacle or lore, leaving viewers just with faceless, headless bodies. At the opposite end is Tex Watson, who murdered on behalf of Manson. Where Hance delivers his story calmly and without remorse, Tex sounds pained as he remembers the Tate-La Bianca murders. His recollections are most gruesome when they position the acts as labor. "I remember the knife going up and down like, um, a hammer in an engine block until my fist disappeared in the mess," he says, after Holden reminds him that he stabbed one victim twenty-eight times and another fifty-one times. On the subject of the murder of Sharon Tate, who was pregnant at the time, Tex remarks, "It's hard stabbin' people, Agent Ford. Sometimes you hit bone. My hands are aching." Off-screen, elsewhere in the prison, a woman screams and cries, giving a sense of what the series refuses to show.

CONCLUSION

This chapter has shown that dialogue is a dynamic space for representations of violence. The visualization of violence in *Zodiac* is arresting, but the retelling of violence—the dialogue, itself—brings the Zodiac down from the world of stylistic embellishment to the everyday territory of cops and journalists. *Mindhunter* relies almost solely on dialogue to transmit its violence, jealously guarding even the least explicit evidence of bloodshed. A consideration of radio and radio studies historicizes the role of dialogue in the series that, to borrow from Douglas and Killmeier, is gleefully atavistic. The self-conscious fixation on sound recording is just one way the series opens our ears. The violence that rolls off the tongues of cops and criminals, alike, recalls the threat that radio posed to would-be censors: the uncontrollable imagination of listeners. The threat posed to Holden as he continues to listen to the violence of his subjects speaks to the power of dialogue that Kozloff explicates—a power Verma also explores in his discussion of the transmission drama on radio. With an eye to industry or modes of storytelling, *Zodiac* and *Mindhunter* may dwell in different circles. With an ear to sonic expressions of violence, they remain in each other's orbit.

NOTE

1. Discussions of film and television style typically privilege an imagined audience that is able to hear and see. A more comprehensive analysis would include the ways in which audio description narrates images for blind audiences and captions show dialogue and sound effects for deaf and hard-of-hearing viewers, as well as others who rely on captions for different reasons. See Kleege (2019) and Zdenek (2015).

REFERENCES

Aldana Reyes, Xavier. 2013. "Violence and Mediation: The Ethics of Spectatorship in the Twenty-First Century Horror Film." In *Violence and the Limits of Representation*, edited by Graham Matthews and Sam Goodman, 145–160. London, UK: Palgrave Macmillan.

Chitwood, Adam. 2017. "Just how involved was David Fincher in *Mindhunter?*" *Collider*, October 16. Accessed August 20, 2018, http://collider.com/mindhunter-david-fincher-showrunner/#joe-penhaal.

Douglas, Susan J. 2004. *Listening in: Radio and the American imagination.* Minneapolis, MN: University of Minnesota Press.

Echols, Katherine Barnes. 2018. "The Monster's transformation on American radio (1930s-50s)." *University of Toronto Quarterly* 87 (1): 42–61.

Hand, Richard J. 2014. *Listen in Terror: British horror radio from the advent of broadcasting to the digital age.* Manchester, UK: Manchester University Press.

Killmeier, Matthew. 2012. "Aural Atavism: The Witch's Tale and Gothic Horror Radio." *Journal of Radio & Audio Media* 19 (1): 61–82.

———. 2013. "More than Monsters: *Dark Fantasy*, the Mystery-Thriller and Horror's Heterogeneous History." *Journal of Radio & Audio Media* 20 (1): 165–180.

Kleege, Georgina. 2017. *More than Meets the Eye: What Blindness Brings to Art.* New York, NY: Oxford University Press.

Kozloff, Sarah. 2000. *Overhearing Film Dialogue.* Berkeley, CA: University of California Press.

Lacey, Kate. 2016. "From Radio Listening to Television Viewing in the 1950s: Reflections on a Blindspot in Media History." In *Broadcasting in the UK and US in the 1950s: Historical Perspectives,* edited by Jamie Medhurst, Siân Nicholas, and Tom O'Malley, 49–70. Newcastle upon Tyne, UK: Cambridge Scholars.

Symonds, Gwyn. 2008. *The Aesthetics of Violence in Contemporary Media.* New York, NY and London, UK: Continuum.

VanCour, Shawn. 2015. "Early Radio Listening as Modernist Practice: Ambient Radio and the Aesthetic of Distraction." *Modern Cultures* 10 (1): 6–25.

———. 2017. "From Radio to Television: Sound Style and Audio Technique in Early TV Anthology Dramas." In *The Routledge Companion to Screen Music and Sound* edited by Miguel Mera, Ronald Sadoff, and Ben Winters, 163–175. New York and London: Routledge.

———. 2018. *Making Radio: Early Radio Production and the Rise of Modern Sound Culture*. New York, NY: Oxford University Press.

Van Elferen, Isabella. 2016. "Sonic Horror." *Horror Studies* 7 (2): 165–172.

Verma, Neil. 2012. *Theater of the Mind: Imagination, Aesthetics, and American Radio Drama*. Chicago, IL: University of Chicago Press. ProQuest Ebook Central.

Williams, Linda. 1991. "Film Bodies: Gender, Genre, and Excess." *Film Quarterly* 44 (4): 2–13.

Young, Allison. 2013. *The Scene of Violence: Cinema, Crime, Affect*. London, UK: Routledge.

Zdenek, Sean. 2015. *Closed-Captioned Media and Popular Culture*. Chicago, IL: University of Chicago Press.

Index

absolute music, 176
Academy Awards, 3
Act of Violence (Fred Zinneman, 1948), xii
adult cinema (pornography), 32, 34, 39–41, 48n4, 49n5
Alfred Hitchcock Presents: "Museum Piece" (NBC, 1961), 33
Alien³ (David Fincher, 1992), 3
Allen, Arthur Leigh, 4, 7, 28, 31, 76, 82, 119, 127–29, 152, 165, 205, 213, 216, 221–23
All the President's Men (Alan J. Pakula, 1976), 3, 70, 203, 205
amateur detective, 89
American Genre Film Archive (AGFA), 55, 57
anti-ethos, 104, 105
art-horror, 9, 171, 173, 177–79, 181–83
Avery, Paul, 53, 58–59

basements, 143
Bauhaus, 125, 134, 136, 137
BBC's "The 100 Greatest Films of the 21st Century," 9
The Beast from 20,000 Fathoms (Eugène Lourié, 1953), 161, 163, 204
Beckett, Samuel, xiv
Belli, Melvin, 4, 37, 76, 194

Benjamin, Walter, 192
Berardi, Bifo, 195–96, 206
Bianchi, Kenneth, 210
The Black Cat (Edgar G. Ulmer, 1934), 8, 16, 121–25, 127, 128, 131, 132, 134, 138, 139, 143, 147
Bordwell, David, 191
The Boston Strangler (Richard Fleischer, 1968), 18, 19, 26, 36, 48
Bridle, James, 191, 197, 200–203
Brokeback Mountain (Ang Lee, 2005), 4
Brudos, Jerome, 247
BTK Killer, 238
Bullitt (Peter Yates, 1968), 4, 41, 42, 151, 153, 157, 159, 204
Bundy, Ted, 210
Buono, Angelo, 210

Capital Gazette shooting, 205
Chaplin (Richard Attenborough, 1992), 4
Chinatown (Roman Polanski, 1974), 39, 62, 94, 99, 203
Chomsky, Noam, 191
Cicero's three offices of an orator, 112
cipher, 6, 33, 43, 72, 74, 75, 81, 85, 88, 89, 91, 102, 107–10, 112, 116–18, 134, 159, 183, 190, 193, 194, 199, 200, 215, 219

classical rhetorical theory/rhetorical theory, 101
"code/space," 201, 203
Collier's, 6
Connell, Richard, 6, 33, 121, 156, 183, 221
Corman, Roger, 22
Cox, Brian, 76
Craig, Daniel, 80
crime/police thriller, 31, 41–43, 49n6
criminalist, 90
criminal justice system, 98, 210, 211, 215, 221, 223, 225, 226
Cross of Iron (Sam Peckinpah, 1977), xii

Dante, 9, 151
Dawn of the Dead (George A. Romero, 1978), 27
DeAngelo, Joseph James, 209
DeBardeleben, Mike, 227
Deleuze, Gilles, 143
Diabolique (Henri-Georges Clouzot, 1955), 16
dialogue, 3, 5, 6, 9, 38, 53, 55, 59, 97, 102, 192, 193, 198, 204, 229–31, 233, 236–38, 240, 242, 245–48
Dickson, Sam, 191–92, 197, 200
Dirty Harry (Don Siegel, 1971), 2, 7, 18, 19, 23, 31–32, 34, 39–46, 48, 48n3, 49n7, 49n8, 53, 63, 151, 158–59, 204–5
Dixit, Avinash K., 214, 217
Dog Day Afternoon (Sidney Lumet, 1975), 3
Donnie Darko (Richard Kelly, 2001), 4
doppelganger, 157
Dostoyevsky, Fyodor, 159
Double Indemnity (Billy Wilder, 1944), 27
Douthat, Russ, 6
Downey Jr., Robert, 4, 5, 38, 53, 59, 73, 78, 86, 106, 129, 151, 193, 219
Dracula (Tod Browning, 1931), 15, 16
Dr. Seuss, 160

East Area Rapist. *See* Golden State Killer
Eastwood, Clint, 34, 41, 44, 49n8, 53, 63
Edwards, Anthony, 4, 87, 127, 155, 189, 219
eristic, 114
ethos, 101–8, 110–12, 114, 118–19
evaluative theory of emotion, 171
The Exorcist III (William Peter Blatty, 1990), 48, 173, 181
exploitation film, 32, 34–36, 39
expressionism, 3, 122, 126, 129, 231
Eyes Without a Face (Georges Franju, 1960), 16

Facebook, 198, 205
failure, 85–87, 92–98; and capitalism, 92
Falkenau Nazi concentration camp, Czechoslovakia, 22
Faust, 206
Fight Club (David Fincher, 1999), 3, 130, 135, 206n1
film noir, 2, 16, 19–21, 25, 27, 32, 39–40, 87, 89
Film Noir and Spaces of Modernity (Edward Dimendberg, 2004), 20
Film Threat, xi
Frankenstein (James Whale, 1931), 15, 16
Freaks (Tod Browning, 1932), 15
Freccero, John, 155
Freeman, Morgan, 80
Fuller, Sam, 7, 8, 19, 22, 28

game theory, 211–23; cognitive strategies, 217–21; deterrent moves, 216–17; *ludostrategy*, 211, 215, 223; negative and positive sum games, 221–23; think forward, reason backward, 222; well-structured, ill-structured tasks, 217–21, 224, 226
Gawker, 205
Gein, Ed, xii

Index

Gelernter, David, 226–27
Gewirtz, Russell, 3
Girard, René, 151–52, 159, 162, 165n12
The Girl with the Dragon Tattoo (David Fincher, 2011), 69, 80
Golden State Killer (aka East Area Rapist), 209–23, 225–26
gothic, 192, 197, 200, 202; criminology, 200, 202; literature, 202; ontological, 200
Gramsci, Antonio, 190
Greek, Cecil, 16, 200, 202
Groff, Jonathan, 76
Gyllenhaal, Jake, 4–6, 9, 47, 51, 53, 73–75, 85, 106, 121, 151, 174, 192, 216

Halloween (John Carpenter, 1978), 198
handwriting analysis, 118
Hanson, Tom, 8, 32, 34–39, 53–66
hegemony (definition), 9, 190, 194
Hegesius, the death orator, 110
Hellraiser III: Hell on Earth (Anthony Hickox, 1992), xiii
Henry: Portrait of a Serial Killer (1986, released 1990), 17–19
Herman, Edward, 191
Herrmann, Bernard, 201
heuristics, 115
Hitchcock, Alfred, 16, 17, 22, 23, 33, 37, 151, 156–57, 159, 160, 164, 166
Holmes, John, 63
homophobia, 38
homosexuality, 43, 45, 95, 99, 165
Humbert, David, 151, 160, 162–63
"Hurdy Gurdy Man" (Donovan), 104–6, 233
hyperrealism, 3

Illegal (Lewis Allen, 1955), 141, 164, 204
inartistic proofs, 111
Inside Man (Spike Lee, 2006), 3
investigative journalism, 5, 224
I Shot Jesse James (Samuel Fuller, 1949), 22

The Island of Lost Souls (Erle C. Kenton, 1932), 15

Jameson, Fredric, xiv
Jones, Bob, 54, 65
Judgment at Nuremberg (Stanley Kramer, 1961), xii

Kaczynski, Ted, 63
Kelleher, Michael D., 1
Kemper, Ed, 240–46
Kiss Me Deadly (Robert Aldrich, 1955), xii, 21
Kiss of Death (Henry Hathaway, 1947), 23
Klein, Melanie, 138–39
Koteas, Elias, 4, 127, 200

Lake, Leonard, 210
Larsson, Stieg, 69
The Last Picture Show (Peter Bogdanovich, 1971), 22
Ledger, Heath, 4
Lee, Spike, 3
Leitch, Thomas, 2, 5, 18, 87–89, 94, 95, 99
logos, 102, 104, 154
Lou Grant: "Samaritan" (CBS, 1979), 8, 32, 45–48
Lynch, John Carroll, 4, 7, 28, 31, 76, 91, 127, 128, 165, 213, 216, 220

M (Fritz Lang, 1931), 17
macabre-interest, 172
Manson, Charles, xii, 209, 211, 247, 248
Manufacturing Consent: The Political Economy of Mass Media, 191
The Man Who Shot Liberty Valance (John Ford, 1962), xi
Marathon Man (John Schlesinger, 1976), 3
masculinity, 85, 94, 98; critique of, 93, 99; hegemonic masculinity, 88, 93; and heroism, 90, 93, 95; tough masculinity, 88, 93, 98

The Matrix (Lana and Lilly Wachowski), 153
Mayfield, Laray, 4
McCallany, Holt, 77
McQueen, Steve, 204
Michael Clayton (Tony Gilroy, 2007), 3
mimetic desire, 151, 155, 157, 160, 162–63, 165n6
Mindhunter (Netflix, 2017–19), 9, 70, 76–79, 81, 195, 206, 229–33, 237–38, 240–42, 245, 248
The Most Dangerous Game (Irving Pichel and Ernest B. Schoedsack, 1932), 6, 8, 33, 119, 121, 122, 138, 141–43, 156, 197, 204, 206, 221, 235
Motion Picture Association of American (MPAA), 17
The Mouthpiece (James Flood and Elliott Nugent, 1932), 141
Muller, Eddie, 7
Murders in the Rue Morgue (Robert Florey, 1932), 15
mystery-thriller, 231, 232

Nalebuff, Barry J., 214, 217
Naremore, James, 3
Netflix, 70, 76, 229
Neuman, Alfred E., 109
Ng, Charles, 210
Nightcrawler (Dan Gilroy, 2014), 9
Night Moves (Arthur Penn, 1975), 3
No Country for Old Men (Joel and Ethan Coen, 2007), 3
nondisclosure agreement, 3

other/otherness, 95, 99

Pakula, Alan J., 70
Panic Room (David Fincher, 2002), 1, 3
paradox of the heart, 171
Park Row (Samuel Fuller, 1952), 22
Peeping Tom (Michael Powell, 1960), 16
Penhall, Joe, 9, 77, 237
Picart, Caroline Joan "Kay" S., 16, 200, 202

Pickup on South Street (Samuel Fuller, 1953), 22
Pitt, Brad, 80
Platt, Polly, 7, 19
The Pledge (Sean Penn, 2001), 97
Poe, Edgar Allan, 15
police film, 87, 98
police procedurals, 236
Pong, 196, 220, 221
post-traumatic stress disorder (PTSD), 44
private-eye film, 86, 94, 98
Production Code, 17
program music, 176
proto-noir, 25
Psycho (Alfred Hitchcock, 1960), 16, 24, 26, 36, 38, 173, 195

Race with the Devil (Jack Starrett, 1975), 19
radio horror, 245
Rambo: First Blood Part II (George P. Cosmatos, 1985), xiii
Ramirez, Richard, 210
Rancho Cordova, 209
realism, 3
Rear Window (Alfred Hitchcock, 1954), 23
Reed, Hal, 54, 56, 65–66
Repo Man (Alex Cox, 1984), 27
Return of the Living Dead III (Brian Yuzna, 1993), 27
Ridgeway, Gary, 225
Robinson, Andrew, 63
Robin Wood, xi, 17, 19, 20, 27
role of audience, 113, 118
Rooney, Mara, 80
Ruffalo, Mark, 4, 5, 31, 53, 73, 85, 127, 151, 189, 219

Sam Dobbs Meets the Zodiac (a.k.a. *The Zodiac Rapist*, John Lamb, 1971), 8, 32, 34, 39–41, 48, 48n4, 63
San Francisco Chronicle, 4–6, 31, 33, 38, 45, 47, 53, 58, 72, 105–11, 115, 167, 170, 189, 190, 194, 219

San Francisco Examiner, 1, 6, 33, 42, 49, 72, 107, 169, 183, 190
Savides, Harris, 5
Schreiber, Michele, 153, 191
Se7en (David Fincher, 1995), xiii, 3, 6, 18, 27, 69, 80–82, 93, 94, 99, 130, 151, 153, 159, 164, 165
Sedgwick, Eve Kosofsky, 139
semiocapitalism, 196
Serial Killer's Dilemma, 212, 217, 220–23
Sevigny, Chloë, 4, 74, 90, 132, 160, 199
Sharrett, Christopher, 20
Siegel, Don, 2, 7, 31, 41–44, 49, 53
The Silence of the Lambs (Jonathan Demme, 1991), xiii
simulation, 153
Sly and the Family Stone, 189, 198
The Sniper (Edward Dymytrk, 1952), 17, 21, 25, 27
Sobchack, Vivian, 16
The Social Network (David Fincher, 2010), 205
Something Weird Video, 55–57
Sorrento, Matthew, 166n14
Spacey, Kevin, 80, 81
spatial film theory, 19
Speck, Richard, 245–47
spree killer, 16, 20, 22, 24–27; definition of, 18–19
Starkweather, Charles, xii
The Steel Helmet (Samuel Fuller, 1951), 22
Stefano, Joseph, 16
Stewart, Garrett, 200
The Strangler (Burt Topper, 1964), 36, 37, 48n3
style (prose), 117
stylistic proof, 119
success, 21, 39, 87, 92, 96, 99
Suspense (CBS, 1942–63), 232

Tarantino, Quentin, 3
Targets (Peter Bogdanovich, 1968), 8, 16, 18–27

Taubin, Amy, 153
television, 31–33, 40, 42, 45–48, 48n2, 49n10
terrible house (Robin Wood), 27
The Terror (Roger Corman, 1963), 22, 26
They Shoot Horses, Don't They? (Sydney Pollack, 1969), 21
Thiel, Peter, 205
The Third Man (Carol Reed, 1949), 7
Thompson, Kristin, 191
Thriller (NBC, 1960–1962), 232
thriller, 31, 33–37, 43–44, 49n6
Torv, Anna, 77
Toschi, David, 31, 32, 40, 42, 47, 49n11, 53
Towne, Robert, 62
transmission drama, 231, 232, 248
true crime, 233, 242

Ulmer, Edgar G., 16, 121–25, 138
Unruh, Howard, 27

Vallejo Times-Herald, 6, 33, 107, 108, 169, 183, 190
Vanderbilt, James, 1, 2, 5, 6, 8, 9, 70, 133, 197, 212–16, 223, 225
Van Nuys, David, 1
vice figure, 131
Vietnam, 35, 42, 44
vigilante film, 35, 42
violence, xii, 9, 18, 19, 24, 26, 33, 37, 41, 80, 90, 91, 94, 95, 151, 152, 155, 161–63, 165, 166, 175, 195, 202, 206, 221, 229–33, 235–48

Wall, Angus, 5
war trauma, 44, 138
Watergate, xi
Watson, Tex, 248
Weaver, Doodles, 62
Western hero/cowboy, 88, 95
White Heat (Raoul Walsh, 1947), 23, 27
Whitman, Charles, 8, 22, 23, 27, 44, 49
wicked problems, 215, 224
Winters, Andrew, 85

wristwatch, 43, 129, 130
The Wrong Man (Alfred Hitchcock, 1956), 162–64, 166n14, 203

Ziemba, Joseph A., 57
Zinoman, Jason, 22
The Zodiac Killer (Tom Hanson, 1971), 32, 34–40, 48, 48n3, 53–66
Zodiac Rapist. See Sam Dobbs Meets the Zodiac
zodiacsploitation, 31, 41
Zuckerberg, Mark, 205

About the Contributors

Jeremy Carr teaches film studies at Arizona State University and has written for *Film International, Cineaste, Senses of Cinema*, and *MUBI/Notebook*. He is the author of *Roman Polanski's* Repulsion (Auteur Publishing, 2021), and he is a contributor to the collections *ReFocus: The Films of Elaine May* (Edinburgh University Press, 2019), and the forthcoming *Hard to Get: The Women and Films of Howard Hawks* (McFarland).

Daniel R. Fredrick is an associate professor in the English Department at the American University of Sharjah, United Arab Emirates. He has written and presented on numerous topics related to the field of rhetoric, from Gorgias to the Gospels.

Deborah L. Jaramillo is an associate professor of Film & Television Studies at Boston University. Her research interests include television history, broadcast regulation, and television news. She is the author of *Ugly War, Pretty Package: How CNN and Fox News Made the Invasion of Iraq High Concept* (Indiana University Press, 2009) and *The Television Code: Regulating the Screen to Safeguard the Industry* (University of Texas Press, 2018).

Martin Kevorkian is the author of *Color Monitors: The Black Face of Technology in America* (Cornell University Press, 2006) and *Writing beyond Prophecy: Emerson, Hawthorne, and Melville* (LSU Press, 2013), as well as articles on Alfred Hitchcock, Tim Burton, John Ashbery, Samuel Beckett, Toni Morrison, William Faulkner, and Jean Toomer. He is a professor and chair of English at the University of Texas at Austin.

Rod Lott runs the genre film website FlickAttack.com from Oklahoma City. A former professional journalist whose film criticism and features were named his state's best for four years, he has appeared in the books *More Mirth of a Nation: The Best Contemporary Humor*, *May Contain Nuts: A Very Loose Canon of American Humor*, *101 Damnations: The Humorists' Tour of Personal Hells* and, due in 2021, *Flick Attack Movie Arsenal: Book One*.

Theresa Rodewald, MA, studied Cinema Studies at Stockholm University in Sweden and Cultural Studies in Germany and Ireland. She writes for a number of independent film magazines, including *L-MAG*, *Berliner Filmfestivals*, and *Film International*, and has written about critiques of capitalism in current gangster films, masculinity in *Scarface* (1932), and the representation of queer women in mainstream cinema.

Jake Rutkowski holds an MA in English from Rutgers University-Camden, where he studied genre semantics and the African-American hero in Western films of the 1970s. He contributes reviews and interviews at *Film International* and blogs at *Cutting to Continuity*. He currently works as a writing program administrator at the University of Pennsylvania.

David Ryan is an academic director and faculty chair of the Master of Arts of Professional Communication program at the University of San Francisco where he teaches courses in strategic and technical communication, reputation management, and rhetoric studies. His essays have appeared in *Rhetoric Review*, *Film International*, and many journals and books, including Wiley-Blackwell's *A Companion to the War Film* (June 2016).

Christopher Sharrett is a professor emeritus of Film Studies at Seton Hall University. He is a contributing editor for *Film International*. His book on the television series *Breaking Bad* was recently published by Wayne State University Press.

Matthew Sorrento teaches film studies at Rutgers University-Camden. He is co-editor of the journal *Film International* and editor-in-chief of *Retreats from Oblivion: the Journal of NoirCon*. The coauthor, with Dean Goldberg, of a forthcoming study of film noir and the Hollywood blacklist, Sorrento has contributed to *Senses of Cinema*, *Film & History*, *Critical Studies in Television*, and *Journal of the Fantastic in the Arts*.

George Toles is a distinguished professor of Literature and Film at the University of Manitoba and the author of *A House Made of Light* (Wayne

State University Press), *Paul Thomas Anderson* (University of Illinois Press), and the recently published *Curtains of Light: Theatrical Space in Film* (SUNY Press). He has also authored or coauthored the screenplays of numerous Guy Maddin films, including *My Winnipeg, Careful, Archangel,* and *The Saddest Music in the World.*

Christopher Weedman is an assistant professor of Film Studies in the Department of English at Middle Tennessee State University. His scholarship has appeared in *Film International, Jewish Film & New Media,* and *Journal of Cinema and Media Studies.* He is currently completing his monograph *Anne Heywood: Beauty, Sex, and the Controversial Film* (University Press of Mississippi) and a coedited collection *Adult Themes: British Cinema and the "X" Rating, 1958–1972* (Bloomsbury).

Andrew M. Winters teaches philosophy and religious studies at Yavapai College in Prescott, Arizona, USA.

www.ingramcontent.com/pod-product-compliance
Lightning Source LLC
Chambersburg PA
CBHW061709300426
44115CB00014B/2610